the Complete
Whole Grains
Cookbook

the Complete Whole Grains Cookbook

150 Recipes for Healthy Living

Judith Finlayson

Robert
ROSE

For complete cataloguing information, see page 276.

Disclaimers
The recipes in this book have been carefully tested by our kitchen and our tasters. To the best of our knowledge, they are safe and nutritious for ordinary use and users. For those people with food or other allergies, or who have special food requirements or health issues, please read the suggested contents of each recipe carefully and determine whether or not they may create a problem for you. All recipes are used at the risk of the consumer.

We cannot be responsible for any hazards, loss or damage that may occur as a result of any recipe use.

For those with special needs, allergies, requirements or health problems, in the event of any doubt, please contact your medical adviser prior to the use of any recipe.

Editor: Carol Sherman
Recipe Editor: Jennifer MacKenzie
Copy Editor: Sheila Wawanash
Proofreader: Karen Campbell-Sheviak
Design and Production: PageWave Graphics Inc.
Photography: Colin Erricson
Food Styling: Kate Bush and Kathryn Robertson
Prop Styling: Charlene Erricson

Cover photo: Tailgaters' Favorite Stew (page 162)
Page 2 photo: Pork Pozole (page 184)
Page 6 photo: Zuni Stew (page 216)

We acknowledge the financial support of the Government of Canada through the Book Publishing Industry Development Program (BPIDP) for our publishing activities.

Published by Robert Rose Inc.
120 Eglinton Avenue East, Suite 800, Toronto, Ontario, Canada M4P 1E2
Tel: (416) 322-6552 Fax: (416) 322-6936

Printed in Canada

1 2 3 4 5 6 7 8 9 TCP 16 15 14 13 12 11 10 09 08

Contents

Acknowledgments

As they say, "it takes a village." This is true of many endeavors, none more so than producing a cookbook. Once the author has completed the manuscript, it passes to others who take the words and numbers and transform them into that magical entity, a book.

Thanks to the group at PageWave Graphics — Andrew Smith, Joseph Gisini, Kevin Cockburn and Daniella Zanchetta — who are responsible for much of the visual impact of this book. They design the pages and art direct the photographs while overseeing all the niggling details associated with production and keeping things on schedule. Then there are food stylists *par excellence* Kate Bush and Kathryn Robertson, who make my recipes look mouthwatering, and prop stylist Charlene Erricson, who works closely with them to create the stage upon which they perform. And, of course, Colin Erricson, whose breathtaking photographs are simply wonderful to behold.

Before my work reaches the design and photography stage, a number of people have contributed to its quality. Jennifer MacKenzie and Audrey King test recipes and, when required, offer helpful suggestions for improvement. My editor, Carol Sherman, cheerfully protects me from the worst aspects of myself and keeps me on a path of continuous improvement. Eagle-eyed copy editor Sheila Wawanash catches things the rest of us don't see.

I also need to thank Bob Dees and Marian Jarkovich at Robert Rose, who work very hard at supporting all my books once they're in the marketplace.

Nutrient Analysis

The nutrient analyses for all the whole grains and the recipes were prepared by Info Access (1988) Inc., Don Mills, Ontario. This also includes the evaluation of recipe servings as sources of nutrients and the servings of whole grain per $\frac{1}{2}$ cup (125 mL) of cooked grains.

The nutrient analyses were based on:

- Imperial measures and weights (except for food typically packaged and used in metric).
- The larger number of servings when there was a range. The smaller amount of ingredients when there was a range.
- The first ingredient listed when there was a choice. The exclusion of "optional" ingredients.
- The exclusion of ingredients with "non-specified" or "to taste" amounts.

The evaluation of recipe servings as sources of nutrients combined U.S. and Canadian regulations. Bearing in mind that the two countries have different reporting standards, the highest standard was always used. As a result, some recipes that would have been identified as an excellent source of a particular nutrient in one country may only be identified as a source of that nutrient because the standard is so much higher in the other country.

Introduction

As someone who strongly believes that eating is one of life's great pleasures, I've spent significant parts of my adult life searching out memorable experiences revolving around food. I'll eat just about anything so long as it's delicious — "delicious" being the operative word. But I'm also committed to eating food that is nutritious and have become more and more concerned about the nutrient content of what I eat. That's why, spurred on by burgeoning information on the healthful properties of whole grains, I set out to expand my consumption of these wholesome foods.

Naturally, I was committed to eating only those that tasted good and, fortunately, I soon discovered that didn't limit my horizons. I'd long been a fan of common grains, such as barley, which I added to soups or turned into "risotto," and steel-cut oats, which I made for weekend breakfasts, but it didn't take long to develop a passion for more "exotic" offerings, such as quinoa, bulgur and wheat berries. As for rice, I've always enjoyed the crunchy texture and slightly nutty flavor of brown rice. Little did I know how quickly I'd also fall in love with the panoply of red and black varieties that are popping up in stores all over the place. With hindsight, I have trouble imagining why nutritionally deficient and basically bland white rice reigned supreme for so long.

One reason is that my generation, which also grew up eating bleached white flour, rather than whole wheat, became accustomed to the dull taste of refined foods. Another is that whole grains traditionally have been plagued by an image problem. While there is much to admire about the back-to-the-earth, whole-food movement of the 1960s, which first brought the nutritional virtues of whole grains to public consciousness, it is not identified with culinary excellence. In the minds of many people, whole grains are inextricably linked with macrobiotic diets, brown rice gruels, leaden muffins and a righteous attitude: eat it because it's good for you, but don't expect it to taste good.

Now, after testing and tasting hundreds of recipes built around these fabulous foods, I'm prepared to dismiss that bad rap. Quite simply, whole grains are delicious. Their flavors vary from earthy and slightly grassy to nutty and sweet. All are appetizing on their own, marry well with a wide variety of seasonings and add taste and texture to any dish. They are also extraordinarily healthful. Nowadays it's difficult to pick up a publication containing nutrition-related information without coming across an article on these wholesome foods. So not surprisingly, when the U.S. Dietary Guidelines were updated in 2005, they recommended that adults consume at least three servings of whole grains every day. When Canada's Food Guide was updated in 2007, it recommended that adults eat 3 to 4 servings of a variety of whole grains each day.

Whole grains contain a wide range of health-promoting nutrients, some of which scientists are just beginning to identify. The good news is they have been linked with a variety of health benefits, from reduced risk of chronic illnesses, such as cardiovascular disease, diabetes and obesity, to lower death rates from certain kinds of cancer. The bad news is most North Americans aren't eating enough of these beneficial foods.

While most of us know we should be increasing our consumption of whole grains, it hasn't always been easy to do so. Over the course of decades, these wholesome foods, which were pantry staples in our grandparents' time, lost their prominence in grocery stores. They were gradually replaced by refined and enriched products, processed foods with inferior nutritive value, but superior shelf life. It's only recently that whole grains have gone relatively mainstream and can be found in many supermarkets. In the past they were available almost exclusively in natural foods stores.

Another problem is that whole grains can be difficult to identify. For instance, when a label lists "wheat flour" as an ingredient, it's reasonable to assume it means whole wheat flour. However, "wheat flour" is likely refined white flour — if it were the whole grain product, it would be specifically labeled as such. And if that's not confusing enough, misconceptions about what actually constitutes a whole grain are likely to muddy the waters even more. For instance, bran cereals and wheat germ, which have healthful properties, are not whole grains since each contains only one part of the grain. Pearled barley, the most widely available form of the grain, is not a whole grain because the germ and most of the bran have been removed in refining. And in Canada, consumers were dismayed to discover that much of flour sold as "whole wheat" may actually contain only 30% of the wheat germ, due to mind-boggling reasoning on the part of Health Canada, the country's nutritional watchdog.

The good news is that despite these problems, consumer interest in whole grains is growing by leaps and bounds and steps are being taken to ensure that whole grains are more easily identifiable (see page 12). Moreover, because savvy marketers have recognized that health-conscious consumers are making the effort to include more whole grains in their diets, they are becoming increasingly available. Even my neighborhood supermarket, a small satellite store, has a commendable collection of whole grains and related products. I can walk down to the corner and choose from several varieties of brown, red and wild rice, wheat berries, bulgur and quinoa. If I'm looking for pasta, I can choose from Kamut, spelt or whole wheat. If I want couscous, my options are whole wheat or spelt. Moreover, the store stocks a wide selection of appetizing whole-grain breads, supplied by an excellent local bakery.

Just thinking of these options makes me hungry, but I've been cooking with whole grains for years and I know how delicious they can be. Their wholesome goodness makes me nostalgic for bygone days: a steaming bowl of mushroom barley soup, nutty oatmeal cookies and whole wheat bread warm from the oven, or grandma's Sunday morning special, buckwheat pancakes swimming in maple syrup. That kind of old-fashioned flavor depends upon natural whole foods.

Once you begin to enjoy whole grains, I strongly believe you'll realize that whole grains taste better than the processed versions we once accepted as the norm. In addition to their superior nutrient value, they have flavor, texture and a kind of life that is completely lacking in refined products. If your palate, like many, has been seduced by processing, you may need to be eased into the stronger taste and more robust texture of whole grains. If that's the case, experiment to find a few you like — quinoa and millet are particularly mild with a very pleasing, almost sprightly texture — and build upon expanding your repertoire over time.

I decided to write this book because I wanted to share how delicious whole grains can be and to reinforce the message that good taste and excellent nutrition are not mutually exclusive. In fact, I strongly believe they go hand in hand. By introducing more whole grains into your diet, you will be better nourished and will enjoy the experience of eating more. I hope you'll use the recipes in this book to expand the varieties of whole grains you consume and, like me, will soon make them a regular part of your everyday life. Happy healthy cooking.

— *Judith Finlayson*

A Whole Grains Primer

What are Whole Grains?

Whole grains are the seeds of certain plants. The inedible outermost layer (husk) of the grain is removed, leaving the resulting "berry" or "groat." They differ from grains that are not whole (refined) because they contain all three parts of the grain: bran, germ and endosperm.

Currently, most of the grains typically consumed in North America — for instance, white wheat flour, white rice, pearled barley and steel-ground cornmeal — are highly refined. During the milling process, the bran and the germ, which contain valuable nutrients, are removed, leaving the endosperm. While the endosperm is the largest part of the grain, it also has the fewest vitamins and minerals. Although refined grains are subsequently "enriched" with the addition of some nutrients, such as riboflavin, thiamin and iron (see chart below), they are far less nutritious than whole grains. Not only do they lack the full range of vitamins, minerals, healthy fats, antioxidants and phytonutrients found in whole grains, refined grains provide far less fiber. They also lack the synergistic benefits of whole foods, which scientists are just beginning to explore. For instance, recent research suggests the phytonutrients found in plant foods fight disease more effectively when they work together, rather than as supplements on their own.

Why Should I Eat More Whole Grains?

Not only do whole grains taste good, they contain a wide range of nutrients. Although the nutrient content of individual grains varies, in general terms, most whole grains will provide at least small amounts of B vitamins (niacin, riboflavin, thiamine and folate), vitamin E, manganese, magnesium, potassium, iron, copper and selenium. They also contain fiber, beneficial fatty acids, antioxidants and phytonutrients. All these substances work together to fight disease and keep you healthy.

As we understand more about the relationship between diet and health, it's becoming increasingly clear that eating nutritious food can help to reduce

NUTRIENTS IN WHEAT FLOUR: Refined, Whole and Enriched

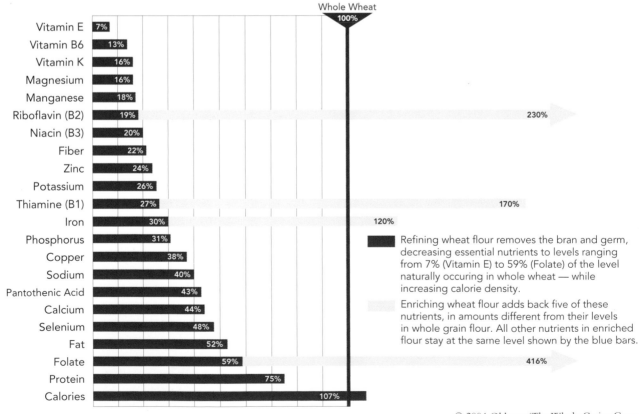

Refining wheat flour removes the bran and germ, decreasing essential nutrients to levels ranging from 7% (Vitamin E) to 59% (Folate) of the level naturally occuring in whole wheat — while increasing calorie density.

Enriching wheat flour adds back five of these nutrients, in amounts different from their levels in whole grain flour. All other nutrients in enriched flour stay at the same level shown by the blue bars.

© 2004 Oldways/The Whole Grains Council

the risk of illness and disease. Today our nutritional focus is shifting, from limiting how much we eat toward understanding that eating certain foods can actually be beneficial to our health.

Research has linked eating whole grains with a wide range of health benefits. Studies show that regular consumption of whole grains:

- reduces the possibility you will develop Type-2 diabetes
- makes it less likely you will have a heart attack
- helps to keep your blood pressure under control
- lowers your risk for certain types of cancer
- assists with keeping your weight under control and helps to ensure that you have a healthier waist-to-hip ratio
- fights gum disease
- promotes regularity

And, if that isn't enough, scientists are actively engaged in studying substances contained in whole grains, such as lignans and oligosaccharides, which function as prebiotics. Prebiotics are ingredients that stimulate the growth of healthy bacteria, such as lactobacilli and bifidobacteria (which are known as probiotics). By promoting the growth of beneficial intestinal flora, prebiotics help to keep your gut in tiptop health. In addition, prebiotics appear to have a wide range of other health benefits, from preventing hair loss to reducing menopausal symptoms.

What about Fiber?

When scientists started noticing that the consumption of whole grains was linked with certain health benefits, they initially attributed these positive results to their high fiber content. We now know that fiber is just one of many healthful substances found in whole grains. By keeping you regular, a fiber supplement may help to keep you well, but it won't help your body to ward off disease.

There are two kinds of fiber — insoluble and soluble. The substance we traditionally associate with fiber is insoluble fiber, which doesn't dissolve in water. (It's what my mother called "roughage.") Insoluble fiber absorbs water in your digestive track and moves waste through your system, preventing constipation. The other kind of fiber, soluble fiber, does dissolve in water, forming a gel-like substance.

It helps to lower blood cholesterol levels and to control blood sugar levels.

Despite its many benefits, most people in North America do not consume enough fiber. Adult women should consume 21 to 25 grams a day, while men should eat 30 to 38 grams a day. Some health professionals recommend that children should consume, on a daily basis, an amount equal to or greater than their age plus 5 grams. A diet high in whole grains will help you to meet these goals.

The fiber in whole grains is concentrated in the bran, which explains why whole grains (which also include the endosperm and the germ) may contain less fiber per comparable weight than some refined cereals, such as bran. However, the whole grain does contain the entire package of nutrients, which may create synergy in the health-promoting effects.

FIBER FIGHTS FAT

Did you know that fiber helps to keep your weight under control? Because foods that are high in fiber take longer to chew, your body has time to recognize its appetite has been satisfied, reducing the possibility you'll overeat.

Whole Grains Help to Control Blood Sugar and Weight

You may have heard of the Glycemic Index (GI), a method for assessing aspects of the dietary value of high-carbohydrate foods by measuring the speed at which they are converted to blood sugar. High GI foods (bad) release glucose quickly, prompting a strong insulin response and providing short-lived bursts of energy. Those that are low on the GI (good) release glucose more slowly, providing sustained energy. The lower a food is on the scale, the longer it takes to raise blood sugar, which is good for everyone but is particularly important for people with diabetes. Moreover, a study published in the *Archives of Internal Medicine* showed that moderate reductions in glycemic load appeared to increase the rate at which the body lost fat. Whole grains tend to be low on the Glycemic Index.

Whole Grains and Antioxidants

In 2004, Dr. Rui Hai Liu and his colleagues at Cornell University discovered a previously unknown benefit to eating whole grains: They contain potent antioxidants. Although scientists have been aware of the antioxidant power of fruits and vegetables for many years, the ones in whole grains were overlooked because they appeared in a different form and there was no known way of identifying their presence. These qualities help to explain why diets high in whole grains appear to be protective against diseases, such as diabetes and heart disease, as well as colon, breast and prostate cancers. Over 80% of these protective substances are found in the bran and the germ, which are removed when the grain is refined.

WHOLE GRAINS AND HEART HEALTH

A study published in *Nutrition, Metabolism and Cardiovascular Disease* concluded that eating whole grains benefits cardiovascular health. People who consumed on average 2.5 daily servings of whole grains reduced their risk of heart disease and stroke by 21%, compared with those who consumed only 0.2 servings.

Whole Grains and Cancer

Whole grains contain a number of substances that appear to have cancer-fighting properties. These include antioxidants and phytochemicals, such as lignans, saponins and phytoestrogens. They also contain fiber, the consumption of which has been linked with reduced cancer risk. When the American Institute for Cancer Research combined data from 40 studies, they concluded that people who consumed large amounts of whole grains reduced their cancer risk by 34% when compared with those who ate small quantities.

How Much Should I Eat?

When the U.S. Dietary Guidelines were updated in 2005, they recommended that adults consume at least three servings of whole grains every day. Canada's Food Guide recommends 6 to 8 servings of grains daily (3 to 4 for children), half of which should be whole grains. The USDA defines a serving

WHAT'S A SERVING?

- 1 slice of whole-grain bread
- 1 ounce/28 grams (¾ to 1 cup/ 175 to 250 mL) ready-to-eat whole-grain cereal
- ½ cup (125 mL) cooked whole wheat pasta
- 3 cups (750 mL) popped popcorn

of whole grains as any food containing 16 grams of whole grain or an "ounce equivalent" (28 grams) of bread or cereal. Sixteen grams is just a little more than half an ounce — so three servings (48 grams) of whole grains are just under two ounces.

Recognizing Whole Grains

Increasing your intake of whole grains may be challenging because it's not always clear from labels whether grains are whole or refined or, in the case of food products, if they actually contain whole grains. In general terms, you'll know you're eating whole grains when the modifier "whole," appears in front of the variety of grain. When buying prepared foods, such as cereals and breads, read the ingredient list on food labels and look for the word "whole" preceding the name of the grain. The whole grain should be the first ingredient listed on the label.

You can also look for the whole-grain health claim on food product labels. It reads: "Diets rich in whole grain foods and other plant foods and low in total fat, saturated fat and cholesterol, may help reduce the risk of heart disease and certain cancers." A food bearing this label must contain 51% or more whole grains by weight. Canadians will see these labels on imported whole-grain products.

The Whole Grains Council, an industry association in the United States, has developed an eye-catching stamp, a sheaf of grain on a golden-yellow background, with a black border. It has two variations: 100% whole grain or whole grain. You'll know you've eaten three servings of whole grains when you eat three foods with the 100% stamp or six foods with the whole-grain stamp. If there is no stamp on the product, the labeling should say "100% WHOLE Grain Excellent Source."

Many Whole Grains Cook Quickly

Many people overlook whole grains because they believe they take too long to cook. While this is true of some, many whole grains are actually quick cooking. The following cook in 25 minutes or less: amaranth, buckwheat, bulgur, quinoa, millet and teff; whole wheat, spelt and barley couscous; and Bhutanese red and brown Kalijira rice.

Liquid and Timing are Approximate

When cooking whole grains, be aware that the amount of liquid specified as well as the cooking times I've provided are approximate. As natural foods, whole grains are affected by many variables. These include how much of the bran has been lost in hulling, the size of the grain (it can vary quite a bit), and how long it's been stored, among other things. The best test is taste — when cooked it will be tender to the bite and somewhat chewy, depending upon the grain. How you want it cooked also depends upon how you'll be using the grain — firmer for salads and quite soft if you're serving it for breakfast.

Cooking Methods

Whole grains cook nicely on the stovetop in a heavy pot with a tight-fitting lid, and unless your stove has a true simmer, most benefit from having a heat diffuser placed under the pot. (Some grains, such as bulgur and couscous, don't even need to be cooked — they just need to be soaked or steamed.) However, some do just as well cooked by more convenient methods, such as in a microwave oven, rice cooker or slow cooker. I've provided stovetop instructions for all the grains and, where appropriate, alternative cooking methods. In general terms, I've found that longer-cooking grains do not do well in a microwave, but respond favorably to pressure cookers and slow cookers. My rice cooker, which uses fuzzy logic technology to sense grain and liquid ratios and adjust its cycle accordingly, does a fabulous job of cooking most whole grains, but because it incorporates soaking and steaming time, it takes longer to complete its cycle than do conventional rice cookers. I don't recommend using a rice cooker for very tiny grains, such as amaranth and teff, as they will plug the steam vent.

To Soak or Not to Soak

There are differences of opinion on the subject of soaking long-cooking grains prior to cooking. Many people feel it cuts down on the cooking time and others think it helps the grains to cook more evenly. In my experience, I have not found that presoaking affects either the cooking time or the results, with a few exceptions. (It does seem to improve the consistency of risotto.) However, you may beg to differ, in which case, presoak your grains.

Cooked Grains Soak Up Liquid

When left to sit or refrigerated, cooked whole grains soak up liquid like a sponge. When reheating most dishes, be prepared to add liquid — either additional water or some of the stock in which the dish was cooked.

Gluten and Gluten-Free Grains

Gluten is a useful ingredient in grains as it supports leavening. On the other hand, some people have varying degrees of intolerance for gluten, and those with celiac disease can't stomach it at all. Here is the gluten/gluten-free breakdown of the grains in this book.

GRAINS WITH GLUTEN

- Barley
- Rye
- Wheat, including varieties such as spelt, Kamut and farro, and forms such as bulgur and couscous

GLUTEN-FREE GRAINS

- Amaranth
- Buckwheat
- Corn
- Millet
- Oats (see below)
- Quinoa
- Rice
- Sorghum
- Teff
- Wild Rice

Gluten-Free Oats

While oats do not appear to contain gluten, until recently it was thought they were unsuitable for people with celiac disease. Recent research indicates that the problem is not with oats per se but rather because the grain is contaminated with gluten from neighboring crops or during processing. Now, organizations, including the American Dietetic Association, agree that most people with celiac disease may consume small amounts of oats from a source that guarantees it has taken the appropriate steps to eliminate cross-contamination. For further information, consult your physician or a reputable celiac organization.

Just the Grains

Amaranth

The name "amaranth" comes from the Greek word meaning "unfading." Amaranth is a bushy plant related to spinach and the leaves, which taste like spinach, are used in various cuisines around the world. For instance, in Asia they are steamed or added to stir-fries and in the Caribbean they add depth to the regional stew, callaloo. The seeds are used as a grain.

Amaranth played an important role in Aztec culture. The emperor Montezuma collected the grain as a tax and it figured prominently in religious rituals. The Aztecs made amaranth cakes, which symbolized the flesh and blood of their gods and were shared like Christian communion, a practice that so horrified the Spanish they banned cultivation of the plant. As a result, it almost disappeared, surviving in only a few remote areas of Mexico and the Andes.

Like quinoa, amaranth grows in adverse conditions and is heat and drought resistant. In India and Mexico, the seeds are popped and made into a candy, and in Peru, they are used to make beer. Amaranth has been grown in the U.S. since the mid-1970s, mainly in Colorado, Wyoming, Nebraska and California.

WHOLE GRAIN FORMS OF AMARANTH

AMARANTH SEEDS, a tiny beige seed resembling a small mustard seed.

AMARANTH FLOUR, which is ground from the seeds.

AMARANTH FLAKES, an ingredient in some commercially prepared breakfast cereals.

amaranth seeds

Culinary Profile

Amaranth is a bit of an acquired taste because it has a strong earthy flavor and almost gummy texture. In my opinion, it usually works best in dishes with an abundance of zest to provide balance. You can mellow its effect somewhat by toasting the seeds before cooking.

I enjoy amaranth as a breakfast cereal, combined with millet (see Hot Millet Amaranth Cereal, page 52), or as a nutritional boost in quick bread (see Amaranth Banana Walnut Bread, page 44), but it can also be served as a side dish. In that case, I'd cook it like polenta and flavor it with assertive ingredients, such as chiles and tomatoes, which share its native habitat. Just be aware that once it is cooked, amaranth should be served promptly because it releases a starch and becomes glutinous on standing. Although it doesn't fluff up when cooked, it becomes soft while retaining a slight pleasant crunch.

Amaranth flour may be substituted for about one-quarter of the all-purpose flour in recipes that

---

Nutritional Profile

Amaranth is a highly digestible gluten-free grain. It is a source of complete and high-quality vegetable protein and provides valuable nutrients, such as magnesium, iron, copper and zinc.

Nutrients per ½ cup (125 mL) cooked amaranth	
Calories	73
Protein	2.8 g
Carbohydrates	12.9 g
Fat (Total)	1.3 g
Saturated Fat	0.3 g
Monounsaturated Fat	0.3 g
Polyunsaturated Fat	0.6 g
Dietary Fiber	3.0 g
Sodium	6 mg
Cholesterol	0 mg

- **GOOD SOURCE OF** magnesium and manganese
- **SOURCE OF** phosphorus, iron, zinc and copper
- **CONTAINS** a moderate amount of dietary fiber

How much whole grain am I eating? Based on the USDA definition of a serving of whole grains, ½ cup (125 mL) cooked amaranth provides 1.2 servings of whole grains.

don't require much leavening, such as cookies and quick breads, or it can be used on its own to make flatbreads and pastas.

Worth Knowing
Amaranth contains a relatively high proportion of the amino acid lysine, which makes it one of the best sources of vegetable protein.

Buying and Storing
Compared to some other whole grains, amaranth is relatively high in polyunsaturated fats, so unless you're using it immediately, store both the seeds and the flour in the refrigerator or freezer to prevent rancidity. It will keep in the refrigerator for up to 6 months or in the freezer for up to 1 year.

Cooking
Many people prefer the taste of amaranth if it is toasted before being cooked. To toast amaranth, cook in a dry nonstick skillet over medium heat, stirring often, until fragrant, about 4 minutes.

GENERAL COOKING INSTRUCTIONS (APPROX.)

Grain Quantity	Liquid Quantity	Cooking Time	Yield (approx.)
1 cup (250 mL)	2½ cups (625 mL)	20 minutes	2½ cups (625 mL)

Stovetop
Bring water to a boil and add the grain in a steady stream, stirring well. Return to a boil. Reduce heat to low. Cover and simmer, stirring occasionally, until tender and thickened, about 20 minutes.

Storing Cooked Amaranth
Cover tightly and refrigerate for up to 2 days. Amaranth does not freeze well.

Barley

Barley, one of our most ancient grains, has been cultivated for more than 4,000 years. It is also one of the most popular grains in terms of cultivation, ranking fourth after wheat, rice and corn. Over the centuries, barley has been an important food for humans and animals. It has also been recognized for its medicinal and strength-giving qualities. For instance, recent research analyzing the bones of more than 70 Roman gladiators concluded they were vegetarians who existed on a diet of barley and beans, which explains why gladiators were often called *hordearii* or "barley men."

Today, barley is a staple in Eastern Europe and the Middle East. Much is used to make malt, which is turned into malt syrup, a sweetener, or fermented to make beer. It can also be distilled into whiskey. Single malt whiskey, made exclusively from barley, is considered by most connoisseurs to be the best in the world.

Culinary Profile
Barley has a mild, slightly nutty flavor and a pleasingly complex texture, being simultaneously

Nutritional Profile
Although it does contain gluten, barley is low in that protein, so some people with wheat sensitivity may be able to enjoy the grain. Barley contains a high amount of dietary fiber and is especially high in soluble fiber. In fact, the U.S. Food and Drug Administration has authorized a health claim for the beta-glucan soluble fiber in barley — it can reduce the risk of coronary heart disease by helping to keep cholesterol under control. A half-cup (125 mL) serving of barley is also a good source of selenium, a mineral that acts as an antioxidant. Selenium appears to boost the immune system and may have anticarcinogenic properties.

Nutrients per ½ cup (125 mL) cooked barley	
Calories	93
Protein	3.3 g
Carbohydrates	19.3 g
Fat (Total)	0.6 g
Saturated Fat	0.1 g
Monounsaturated Fat	0.1 g
Polyunsaturated Fat	0.3 g
Dietary Fiber	4.5 g
Sodium	5 mg
Cholesterol	0 mg

- **EXCELLENT SOURCE OF** manganese
- **GOOD SOURCE OF** selenium
- **SOURCE OF** thiamine, niacin, phosphorous, iron, zinc and copper
- **CONTAINS** a high amount of dietary fiber

How much whole grain am I eating? Based on the USDA definition of a serving of whole grains, ½ cup (125 mL) cooked whole grain barley provides 1.6 servings of whole grain.

WHOLE GRAIN FORMS OF BARLEY

The nomenclature for whole-grain barley is a bit confusing. In some places it is called "whole" barley, in others "hulled" barley. Although it isn't quite a whole grain "pot" barley undergoes a minimal amount of refining that leaves some of the bran and germ intact. Pot barley is fairly widely available and makes a preferable alternative to the pearled variety, from which most if not all of the bran and germ layers have been removed. In any case, you can differentiate whole-grain barley from pearled barley by its darker color and more substantial size. There is also a hull-less version, which is a whole grain heirloom variety.

WHOLE (HULLED) BARLEY is the whole grain. Only the outer indigestible hull is removed, leaving the bran, germ and endosperm in tact.

HULL-LESS BARLEY is an heirloom variety, which is not widely available. It is slightly more pointed than regular whole barley and supposedly even more nutritious. In my experience, it soaks up more water during cooking (about 4 cups/1 L per cup/250 mL of grain) and takes quite a bit longer to cook. When cooked it is brownish in color and has a chewier texture than other varieties.

BARLEY GRITS, which are bits of sliced whole-grain barley, are sometimes available in natural foods stores. Their one advantage is that they cook in about half the time it takes to prepare whole-grain barley.

BARLEY FLOUR can be substituted for some of the wheat flour in recipes that don't require a high amount of gluten, such as muffins, quick breads, cookies and pancakes. One advantage to using barley flour is that it's finely ground and not as robustly flavored as its whole wheat counterpart. It adds whole-grain goodness to baked goods, while enabling them to sustain a light texture traditionally associated with refined flour. Since most barley flour is made from pearled barley, read the label carefully to ensure your flour has been ground from whole barley or ask your supplier. You can also make your own barley flour by grinding hulled barley in a flour mill. Tightly wrapped, it will keep in the freezer for up to 4 months.

BARLEY COUSCOUS (also known as barley grits couscous) is a specialty of Morocco's Berber people. It is grainier and has a slightly nuttier flavor than couscous made from semolina. It is particularly useful for people with sensitivity to wheat (but not people suffering from celiac disease), or those who wish to expand the range of whole grains in their diets, as it can be substituted for regular couscous in any recipe since the cooking instructions are the same. Look for it in well-stocked natural foods stores or at specialty purveyors.

whole (hulled) barley

slightly crackly and a bit glutinous. It is an excellent addition to soups, stews and casseroles, and holds its own in salads. Like wheat berries, the grain it most resembles in appearance, whole-grain barley takes a long time to cook — depending upon the variety, from 1 to 1¾ hours.

Worth Knowing

Barley contains virtually twice as much beta-glucan soluble fiber as whole oats, the only other whole grain containing a significant amount of this substance. (Per 100 g serving; barley contains 4.3 to 5.5 g of beta-glucan soluble fiber compared to 2.2 to 6.6 g for oats, depending upon the variety.) The FDA health claim that the soluble fiber in barley may reduce the risk of heart disease when consumed as part of a diet low in saturated fat and cholesterol is based on eating 3 grams of beta-glucan soluble fiber daily.

Buying and Storing

It is best to buy hulled barley from a purveyor with high turnover. Half the fat in whole-grain barley is polyunsaturated, which is beneficial to your health, but highly perishable. For best results, store barley in an airtight container in a cool dry place or, if you live in a hot, humid climate, the refrigerator or freezer. It will keep for up to 1 year.

Cooking

GENERAL COOKING INSTRUCTIONS (APPROX.)

Grain Quantity	Liquid Quantity	Cooking Time	Yield (approx.)
1 cup (250 mL)	2½ cups (625 mL)	50 to 105 minutes	3 cups (750 mL)

Stovetop

When cooking barley on the stove, in my opinion, it is preferable to immerse it in boiling liquid, which helps the grains to remain separate. I like to rinse barley thoroughly under cold running water before cooking, but this isn't necessary.

In a heavy saucepan, bring 2½ cups (625 mL) water or stock to a rapid boil. Add 1 cup (250 mL) rinsed and drained whole (hulled) barley. Return to a rapid boil. Reduce heat to low. Cover and place a heat diffuser under the pot, if necessary. Cook until barley is tender, from 50 minutes to 1 hour and 45 minutes, depending upon the variety. You can also combine the barley with cold water or stock and bring to a boil, but it will clump together more using this method.

Rice Cooker

In rice cooker bowl, combine 1 cup (250 mL) whole (hulled) barley and 2½ cups (625 mL) water. Stir to combine. (If you don't have a fuzzy logic rice cooker and have time, let soak for 1 hour before starting the machine.) Cook on Regular or Brown Rice setting until completed, about 1 hour. Let rest on Warm cycle for at least 15 minutes. Fluff with a fork before using.

Slow Cooker

For best results, add boiling water to the slow cooker stoneware, then stir in barley.

If you're only cooking 1 cup (250 mL) barley, use a small (3½ quart) slow cooker. Combine 1 cup (250 mL) rinsed and drained whole (hulled) barley and 2½ cups (625 mL) boiling water or stock. Stir well. Cover and cook on Low for 4 hours or on High for 2½ to 3 hours, until barley is tender. Fluff with a fork before using. If you're cooking larger quantities of barley, use a large (minimum 5 quart) slow cooker.

In my experience, barley will be tender after about 3 hours on Low if you add it to boiling water, but will hold quite nicely for up to 8 hours at that temperature.

Pressure Cooker

Before using your pressure cooker, consult the manufacturer's instructions to ensure you are not over- or underfilling the appliance. Whole grains generate a great deal of foam, so the cooker shouldn't be more than half full. Combine 2 cups (500 mL) whole (hulled) barley with 5 cups (1.25 L) water. Cook on High pressure for 35 minutes. Drain off water.

Storing Cooked Barley

Because it takes so long to cook, when cooking barley it's a good idea to make more than you need. You can refrigerate the extra, tightly covered, for up to 3 days. It can also be frozen for up to 3 months. Before freezing, cool thoroughly and, for convenience, add to resealable plastic bag(s) in 1-, 2- or 3-cup (250, 500 or 750 mL) increments. Defrost overnight in the refrigerator, or remove from the plastic bag and microwave. You can also defrost frozen barley on the stovetop in a heavy pot. Add 1 tbsp (15 mL) or so of water or stock, cover and steam over low heat.

Buckwheat

While buckwheat is technically not a grain — it is the seed of a plant related to rhubarb that is native to northern Europe and Asia — it is classified as a grain because it has many of the characteristics of wheat. Buckwheat, too, grows better in cooler climates, such as Canada, Russia and northern Japan. In that country, the seeds are ground into flour where they form the basis of soba noodles, which, depending upon the quantity of buckwheat they contain, may be the world's most nutritious noodles. Buckwheat flour is also the essential ingredient in blinis, the tiny pancakes traditionally served with the world's best caviar. In North America, many consumers are familiar with buckwheat through its association with honey. The flowers of the buckwheat plant are particularly attractive to bees and buckwheat honey is a robustly flavored variety produced in regions where the grain is cultivated. Buckwheat is also malted to produce beer suitable for people who can't tolerate gluten.

Culinary Profile

Buckwheat has a unique intense flavor, which may take a bit of getting used to. However, once you have learned to appreciate it, buckwheat can become something of a delicacy. The grains, known as groats, are usually toasted before using or can be

WHOLE GRAIN FORMS OF BUCKWHEAT

BUCKWHEAT GROATS (or kasha) is whole-grain buckwheat. Groats are the kernel from which the inedible outer hull has been removed. You can buy buckwheat groats either unroasted or roasted, in which case they will be called kasha. For the mildest taste, buy the unroasted version and toast them yourself (see Cooking, page 18).

BUCKWHEAT FLOUR is ground groats. It is used to make noodles, pancakes and baked goods, such as quick breads. You can buy buckwheat flour in natural foods stores or well-stocked supermarkets or you can grind your own, using a flour mill or blender.

buckwheat groats

kasha

purchased already toasted under the name "kasha." Buckwheat is a quick-cooking grain, ready in about 15 minutes. It is also very versatile. Use buckwheat in salads and pilafs, as a substitute for some of the ground meat in meat loaves, or, in its flour form, to make quick breads, noodles or that North American classic, buckwheat pancakes. If you find its taste overpowering, but still want to add it to your diet, try stirring a portion of cooked buckwheat into cooked rice and enjoy it as a side dish.

Worth Knowing

In a placebo-controlled study, Canadian researchers found that buckwheat may be particularly beneficial in managing diabetes. Buckwheat extracts lowered blood glucose levels of rats from 12 to 19%. They believe the compound d-chiro-inositol, which is found in relatively high amounts in buckwheat but not commonly found in other foods, may be responsible for this positive effect and further research is underway.

Buying and Storing

Buy buckwheat from a purveyor with rapid turnover. Store, tightly sealed, in a cool dark place for up to 6 months. If you live in a warm climate, keep it in the refrigerator. Buckwheat flour should be stored in the refrigerator, where it will keep for up to 2 months, or the freezer for up to 6 months.

Cooking

If you're using buckwheat groats rather than kasha, which has already been toasted, toast the groats in a dry skillet over medium-high heat, stirring constantly, until fragrant, about 4 minutes. Then cook as follows.

Nutritional Profile

Buckwheat is gluten-free, making it an ideal grain for people who are sensitive to gluten or those with celiac disease. It is also a source of high-quality vegetable protein as it contains all the essential amino acids. A half cup (125 mL) serving of cooked buckwheat provides a range of valuable nutrients. such as magnesium, folate, pantothenic acid, phosphorus, iron, zinc, copper and selenium. Buckwheat is also rich in phytochemicals. For instance, it is the major food source of the bioflavonoid rutin, a powerful antioxidant, which researchers are studying for its medicinal properties.

Nutrients per ½ cup (125 mL) cooked buckwheat groats

Calories	113
Protein	4.2 g
Carbohydrates	24.6 g
Fat (Total)	0.8 g
Saturated Fat	0.2 g
Monounsaturated Fat	0.2 g
Polyunsaturated Fat	0.2 g
Dietary Fiber	3.3 g
Sodium	5 mg
Cholesterol	0 mg

- **EXCELLENT SOURCE OF** manganese
- **GOOD SOURCE OF** magnesium
- **SOURCE OF** niacin, folate, pantothenic acid and phosphorus, iron, zinc copper and selenium
- **CONTAINS** a moderate amount of dietary fiber

How much whole grain am I eating? According to the USDA definition of a serving of whole grain, ½ cup (125 mL) cooked buckwheat groats provides 2.1 servings of whole grains.

GENERAL COOKING INSTRUCTIONS (APPROX.)

Grain Quantity	Liquid Quantity	Cooking Time	Yield (approx.)
1 cup (250 mL)	2 cups (500 mL)	10 minutes	2½ cups (625 mL)

Stovetop

Toasted groats or kasha: In a saucepan over medium-high heat, bring 2 cups (500 mL) water to a boil. Add salt to taste, if using. Add 1 cup (250 mL) of the grain in a steady stream, stirring constantly. Reduce heat to low. Cover and simmer until all the liquid is absorbed, about 10 minutes. Remove from heat and let stand, covered, for 5 minutes. Fluff with a fork.

Rice cooker

In rice cooker bowl, combine 1 cup (250 mL) toasted groats or kasha and 2 cups (500 mL) water. Add salt to taste, if using. Stir to combine. Cook on Regular or Brown Rice setting until completed, about 25 minutes on Regular setting. Let rest on Warm cycle for about 15 minutes. Fluff with a fork.

Storing Cooked Buckwheat Groats

Let cool, then cover and refrigerate for up to 2 days. Cooked buckwheat does not freeze well.

Corn

Corn is one of the most popular foods in North America, so not surprisingly it is eaten in a variety of forms. The sweet corn we enjoy fresh from the field in summer has a high sugar content and, in nutritional and culinary terms, is considered a vegetable. Field corn, which is starchier, is different. Although some is eaten fresh, most is allowed to dry on the stalk. During this process, the sugar is converted into starch. A significant amount of field corn is used as animal feed, but some is ground into grits, cornmeal or flour, which may or may not be whole-grain products. Popcorn, which was first cultivated by the Incas for snacking, is a whole-grain food. Corn is traditionally used to make "moonshine" and is the basis for bourbon, a whiskey originating in Kentucky, which is aged in charred oak casks.

stone-ground cornmeal

white corn grits

hominy

WHOLE GRAIN FORMS OF CORN

HOMINY (also known as pozole): Whole dried kernels of corn cooked in a solution of lye or slaked lime to loosen the hull, which is discarded. In the course of being washed, the remaining kernels swell and are subsequently dried. When hominy is partially ground, the result is hominy grits. Hominy flour is used to make masa harina, the basis for Mexican tortillas. Hominy is widely available already cooked and canned and can be found in its dried form in Latin American food stores.

HOMINY GRITS: Broken grains of hominy.

STONE-GROUND CORNMEAL: Dried ground corn, which is crushed between millstones and ground the old-fashioned way with the power of water. It has a coarse texture and, because it is very perishable, should be freshly ground. Italian versions of cornmeal are often known as polenta. Although most polenta sold in North America is made from refined dried corn that has been hulled and degermed, some artisanal producers, both in North America and Italy, are producing whole-grain polenta. Check the label to ensure the product is whole grain. Cornmeal comes in white, yellow and blue varieties, depending upon the corn. All are equally nutritious so long as the product is stone-ground. Stone-ground cornmeal is available in well-stocked supermarkets and natural foods stores.

STONE-GROUND GRITS: The coarsest grind of whole corn. For the best flavor and nutrition, look for coarse texture and dark flecks of germ and bran scattered throughout. The best grits are available online or by mail order from artisanal producers in the U.S., such as Anson Mills or Hoppin' John's, who make their product from heirloom varieties of corn.

POPCORN: A variety of corn that pops when heated. It is a whole grain and, so long as it isn't slathered with butter, a nutritious, low-cal snack.

CORN FLOUR: Finely ground cornmeal. Check the label to make sure it is whole grain.

MASA HARINA: Flour made from hominy.

Culinary Profile

Whole-grain corn is dried kernels of corn sold whole (hominy) or ground (cornmeal or grits). Because it is processed the old-fashioned way, with water-powered millstones, stone-ground cornmeal has more texture and flavor than refined versions. Hominy is a great addition to soups and stews, and grits make a sumptuous soft porridge that is a staple of Southern cooking in dishes like shrimp and grits. Cornmeal is the basis for polenta, which can be topped with a wide variety of sauces. It is also delicious made into cornbread and muffins or as pie-like crusts for chilies and stews or as a coating for fried foods. When cornmeal is finely ground, it becomes corn flour, which, depending upon the type of cornmeal used, may or may not be a whole-grain product. Corn flour shouldn't be confused with cornstarch, which is a highly refined product used for thickening sauces.

Worth Knowing

A recent study shows that corn has the highest level of antioxidants of any grain or vegetable — almost twice the antioxidant activity of apples.

Buying and Storing

Because the germ is loaded with healthful unsaturated oils, whole-grain corn is very perishable. Buy it from a source with high turnover. Store it in an airtight container, in the refrigerator, for up to 2 months. You can also store it airtight in the freezer for up to 6 months.

Cooking

(See also Basic Polenta and Grits, page 242)

GENERAL COOKING INSTRUCTIONS (APPROX.)

Grain Quantity	Liquid Quantity	Cooking Time	Yield (approx.)
1 cup (250 mL)	4½ cups (1.125 mL)	20 minutes to 2 hours	3½ cups (825 mL)

Stovetop

Bring 4½ cups (1.125 L) water or stock to a rapid boil. Season to taste with salt and freshly ground black pepper. Add 1 cup (250 mL) stone-ground cornmeal or grits in a steady stream, stirring constantly and ensuring the water maintains a rapid boil. Reduce heat to low. Cook, stirring frequently, until thickened, about 20 minutes for finely ground cornmeal and up to 2 hours for coarse-ground grits. Stir in butter to taste, if desired.

Microwave

In an 8-cup (2 L) baking dish, combine 1 cup (250 mL) stone-ground cornmeal or grits with 4 cups (1 L) water or stock. Season to taste with salt and freshly ground black pepper. Cook, uncovered, on High for 10 minutes. Stir well. Return to oven and cook for 8 minutes. Stir in butter to taste, if desired. Serve warm or cool and cut into squares.

Rice Cooker

Using 4 cups (1 L) water produces polenta with a creamy consistency. If you prefer a slightly firmer

---

Nutritional Profile

Corn is a gluten-free grain. Most of the cornmeal sold in supermarkets is ground with steel rollers, which removes the bran and the germ and, in the process of refining, strips away most of the B vitamins, fiber, iron and healthful phytochemicals, although iron may subsequently be returned through fortification. Whole-grain yellow cornmeal contains more than twice as much magnesium, phosphorus and zinc and significantly more potassium and selenium than the de-germed variety. Corn also contains many powerful phytonutrients. For instance, whole-grain yellow cornmeal contains the carotenoids, beta-carotene, lutein and zeaxanthin. Carotenoids have been linked with a variety of health benefits.

Nutrients per ½ cup (125 mL) cooked stone-ground yellow cornmeal

Calories	63
Protein	1.2 g
Carbohydrates	13.4 g
Fat (Total)	0.7 g
Saturated Fat	0.1 g
Monounsaturated Fat	0.2 g
Polyunsaturated Fat	0.3 g
Dietary Fiber	2.3 g
Sodium	4 mg
Cholesterol	0 mg

- **SOURCE OF** magnesium
- **CONTAINS** a moderate amount of dietary fiber

How much whole grain am I eating? According to the USDA definition of a serving of whole grains, ½ cup (125 mL) cooked stone-ground yellow cornmeal provides 1.1 servings of whole grain.

consistency, reduce the quantity of water to 3¾ cups (925 mL). In rice cooker bowl, combine 1 cup (250 mL) stone-ground cornmeal or grits and 4 cups (1 L) water. Add salt to taste. Stir to combine. (If you don't have a fuzzy logic rice cooker and have the time, allow to soak for 1 hour.) Cook on Regular or Brown Rice setting until completed, about 30 minutes. Let rest on Warm cycle for at least 15 minutes.

Storing Cooked Cornmeal or Grits
Cooling cooked cornmeal causes it to solidify. Spread any excess in a lightly greased baking dish in a 1-inch (2.5 cm) thin layer. Smooth, cover with plastic wrap and chill until firm, about 2 hours or for up to 3 days. To use, turn out, cut into squares and top with your favorite sauce. Or, if you prefer, heat a small amount of oil in a heavy skillet and sauté the squares until golden, about 1 minute per side.

Job's Tears (hato mugi)

A tropical plant, native to Asia, Job's tears is not commonly available in North America. It is used mainly in China, Japan, Vietnam and Korea. Its presence in the West has been associated with macrobiotic diets, although its popularity is slowly growing. Refined versions of the grain look like a cross between white oatmeal and pearled barley with a brown stripe down the center and can be found in well-stocked Asian markets. The whole-grain version (premium hato mugi) is available by mail order. In China and Korea, hato mugi is often made into a tea-like beverage or distilled into liquor. The name "Job's tears" comes from its hard seed casings, which resemble tear-shaped beads. As a result, the grain is often used to make prayer beads and jewelry.

Culinary Profile
Job's tears is chewy and has a distinctive nutty taste. It can be combined with brown rice (1 part Job's tears to 3 parts rice) to make a wonderful side dish. Add it to soups or stews along with other long-cooking whole grains.

Worth Knowing
Job's tears is commonly used as a medicinal food in Asia, where it is used to treat joint conditions such as arthritis.

WHOLE GRAIN FORMS OF JOB'S TEARS
Whole-grain Job's tears is very difficult to find. The grain is ivory colored and looks like a cross between oatmeal and pearled barley with a brown line running down the center. When cooked, it looks a bit like pumped-up barley. It swells and becomes uniquely curvy. It can be purchased online.

Nutritional Profile
Job's tears is gluten-free. It is reputed to be particularly nutritious. At the time of this writing, nutrient data for the whole-grain version was not available to allow for further nutritional analysis.

Buying and Storing
Store Job's tears in an airtight container in the refrigerator for up to 3 months or in the freezer for up to 6 months.

Cooking

GENERAL COOKING INSTRUCTIONS (APPROX.)

Grain Quantity	Liquid Quantity	Cooking Time	Yield (approx.)
1 cup (250 mL)	2 cups (500 mL)	60 minutes	2½ cups (625 mL)

Stove Top
Some suggest toasting the grains before cooking, although I haven't found this to be necessary. To toast Job's tears, place in a dry skillet over medium heat and cook, stirring, until fragrant, about 5 minutes. Meanwhile, bring 2 cups (500 mL) water or stock to a boil. Add 1 cup (250 mL) Job's tears. Return to a boil. Reduce heat to low and simmer until grains

Job's tears

swell and become tender, about 1 hour. Remove from heat and let stand, covered, for 10 minutes.

Rice Cooker

In rice cooker bowl, combine 1 cup (250 mL) Job's tears and 2½ cups (625 mL) water. Stir to combine. (If you don't have a fuzzy logic rice cooker and you have time, allow to soak for 1 hour before starting the machine.) Cook on Regular or Brown Rice setting until completed, about 45 minutes. Let rest on Warm cycle for at least 15 minutes.

Storing Cooked Job's Tears

Because Job's tears is a long-cooking grain, it's a good idea to make more than you need. You can refrigerate the extra, tightly covered, for up to 3 days. It can also be frozen for up to 3 months. Before freezing, cool thoroughly and, for convenience, add to resealable plastic bag(s) in 1-cup (250 mL) increments. Defrost overnight in the refrigerator, or remove from the plastic bag and microwave. You can also defrost frozen Job's tears on the stovetop in a heavy pot. Add 1 tbsp (15 mL) or so of liquid, cover and steam over low heat.

Millet

An ancient grain that is still a major form of sustenance in much of the world, including northern China, Africa and India, millet is possibly the world's oldest crop, predating wheat and rice as a cultivated grain. Herodotus described it growing in the hanging gardens of Babylon and it covered the base of the Colossus in Rhodes. Before corn was grown in Italy, it was the original ingredient used to make polenta. Teff, which is prominent in Ethiopian cuisine and is now grown in the United

---

VARIETIES OF WHOLE-GRAIN MILLET

MILLET GRAINS, a small round grain, usually yellow, with a mild flavor.

MILLET FLOUR can be used as a substitute for up to 25% of the wheat flour in baked goods that don't require much leavening.

TEFF GRAINS, a very tiny grain, darker in color with a more intense flavor than millet.

TEFF FLOUR can be used as a substitute for up to 25% of the wheat flour in baked goods that don't require much leavening.

Nutritional Profile

As a grain, millet has two big advantages: it is gluten-free and particularly easy to digest. A half-cup (125 mL) serving of millet is a good source of magnesium, which helps to keep bones strong and supports the nervous system. It also contains a moderate amount of dietary fiber. Millet also provides manganese and small amounts of the minerals phosphorous, zinc and copper, as well as an assortment of beneficial phytochemicals.

Nutrients per ½ cup (125 mL) cooked millet

Calories	108
Protein	3.2 g
Carbohydrates	21.4 g
Fat (Total)	0.9 g
Saturated Fat	0.2 g
Monounsaturated Fat	0.2 g
Polyunsaturated Fat	0.5 g
Dietary Fiber	2.7 g
Sodium	2 mg
Cholesterol	0 mg

- **GOOD SOURCE OF** magnesium
- **SOURCE OF** thiamine, niacin, folate, phosphorus, manganese, zinc and copper
- **CONTAINS** a moderate amount of dietary fiber

How much whole grain am I eating? Based on the USDA definition of a serving of whole grains, ½ cup (125 mL) cooked millet provides 1.8 servings of whole grains.

States, is a variety of millet. It is notable for its very tiny seeds and perhaps best known as the major ingredient in *injera*, the Ethiopian flatbread, upon which various cooked dishes are served.

Culinary Profile

Light gold in color, millet resembles mustard seeds in appearance. It cooks quickly, has a mild nutty flavor and is easy to digest. A quick toasting prior to cooking brings out its full flavor. Millet can be eaten as a breakfast cereal or as a substitute for other grains, such as rice, couscous or quinoa. It makes a tasty pilaf. Millet flour can be used in some baked goods, such as flatbreads, and to thicken soups and stews. Teff is usually brown in color with a sweet molasses–like flavor. It has a much more intense flavor than millet and is used as a breakfast cereal or in polenta–style dishes.

Worth Knowing

A report in the *Archives of Internal Medicine* found a link between the intake of dietary fiber and magnesium and a reduced rate of diabetes. People who consumed the most cereal fiber and magnesium had a much lower risk of developing diabetes than those who consumed the least amount of those nutrients.

Buying and Storing

Compared to some other whole grains, millet is relatively high in polyunsaturated fats and, therefore, is more perishable. As a result, it is particularly important to buy it from a source with high turnover. Millet will keep in a cool dry place for up to 2 months, in the refrigerator for up to 4 months, or tightly wrapped in the freezer for up to 6 months.

Cooking

For best results, before cooking toast millet in a dry skillet over medium heat, stirring constantly, until fragrant, about 5 minutes.

GENERAL COOKING INSTRUCTIONS (APPROX.)			
Grain Quantity	Liquid Quantity	Cooking Time	Yield (approx.)
1 cup (250 mL)	2½ cups (625 mL)	25 minutes	3½ cups (875 mL)

Stovetop

In a saucepan, bring 2½ cups (625 mL) water or stock to a rapid boil. Add toasted millet in a steady stream and season with salt and freshly ground black pepper to taste. Return to a rapid boil. Reduce heat to low. Cover tightly and simmer until liquid is absorbed, about 25 minutes. Remove from heat and let stand, covered, for 5 minutes. Fluff with a fork before serving.

millet grain

teff grain

Note: if you're eating millet as a cereal, increase the quantity of cooking water (use about 4 cups/1 L per cup/250 mL of millet) and stir occasionally while cooking to produce a porridge consistency. Cooking millet by this method produces a creamy texture. The result could also be used like polenta.

Rice Cooker

In rice cooker bowl, combine 1 cup (250 mL) toasted millet and 2 cups (500 mL) water or stock. If using water, add salt to taste. Cook on Regular or Brown Rice setting until completed, about 35 minutes. Let rest on Warm cycle for at least 15 minutes.

Storing Cooked Millet

Cooked millet can be refrigerated for up to 2 days. Millet doesn't freeze well.

Oats

Although oats have earned their place in history — for instance as the only food Alexander the Great would feed to his legendary horse, Bucephalus — they also have the distinction of being the most popular whole grain in North America. To some extent, this is due to the fact that oats are easy to grow in parts of the continent because they thrive in cooler climates, but probably the most significant reason is that most oat products are not refined. Unlike other grains, oats contain a natural chemical that acts as a preservative. This means it isn't necessary to refine the grain to extend its shelf life. Normal processing for oats consists of roasting and hulling, which leaves the bran and germ layers intact.

In North America, most oats are consumed at breakfast in the form of cereal or used in baking. In Scotland, oats are an integral ingredient in the national dish, haggis, a sausage-like mélange of seasoned sheep's heart, liver and lungs, also mixed with suet and onions and boiled in a casing of sheep's stomach. I've tried it and wasn't impressed, but I do know native Scots who find it a great delicacy.

WHOLE GRAIN FORMS OF OATS

OAT GROATS: The whole oat kernel, which has not been cut or flattened in any way. They are good for breakfast or can be used in grain salads, like barley and wheat berries.

STEEL-CUT OATS (also known as Irish or Scottish oatmeal), these are whole oat groats cut into smaller pieces. Flavorful and nicely chewy, they are the ultimate breakfast cereal.

ROLLED OATS: Less toothsome than steel-cut oats, these are groats that have been softened by steaming, then rolled. The form of oats usually used in baking, they also make a great cooked breakfast cereal or an ingredient in muesli or granola.

OAT FLOUR: A flour made from ground whole oats, used in baking, often in combination with flours containing gluten. You can easily grind your own in a food processor.

Culinary Profile

Unlike other grains, after being harvested and cleaned, oats are roasted, which gives them their unique flavor. Because they are high in soluble fiber, they easily become smooth and creamy when cooked with liquid, making them an ideal thickener for soups and puddings. They have a natural sweetness, which makes them appealing for baked goods, such as cookies. They are often used as extenders for dishes, such as meat loaf or stuffing.

Worth Knowing

Oats contain avenanthramides, a powerful antioxidant that has been linked with a reduced risk of heart disease. The compound prevents LDL (bad cholesterol) from becoming oxidized. Interestingly, when vitamin C was consumed along with oats, the combination created synergy, significantly extending the positive effect of the phytonutrient. So enjoy a glass of orange juice with your oatmeal every morning, and give your heart a hug.

rolled oats

Nutritional Profile

One half-cup (125 mL) cooked oatmeal is a good source of the antioxidant manganese, which slows down the aging process. They also contain beta-glucan, a type of fiber that is particularly beneficial in controlling cholesterol levels and may reduce the risk of heart disease. A recent University of Ottawa study showed the consumption of oat bran, which is high in beta-glucan, stabilized blood sugar, which may also make it beneficial to people with Type-2 diabetes.

Nutrients per ½ cup (125 mL) cooked rolled oats	
Calories	45
Protein	1.8 g
Carbohydrates	7.9 g
Fat (Total)	0.8 g
Saturated Fat	0.2 g
Monounsaturated Fat	0.2 g
Polyunsaturated Fat	0.3 g
Dietary Fiber	1.0 g
Sodium	4 mg
Cholesterol	0 mg

- **GOOD SOURCE OF** manganese
- **SOURCE OF** phosphorus and magnesium

How much whole grain am I eating? Based on the USDA definition of a serving of whole grains, ½ cup (125 mL) cooked rolled oats provides 0.7 servings of whole grain.

Buying and Storing

Because oats, unlike most whole grains, are not highly perishable, acceptable products are widely available. Oats will keep so long as you use them up within a reasonable amount of time.

Cooking

GENERAL COOKING INSTRUCTIONS (APPROX.)

Grain Quantity	Liquid Quantity	Cooking Time	Yield (approx.)
1 cup (250 mL)	2 to 4 cups (500 mL to 1 L)	10 to 50 minutes	3 to 4 cups (750 mL to 1 L)

Stovetop

Oat Groats: In a saucepan, brings 4 cups (1 L) water to a boil. Add salt to taste and stir in 1 cup (250 mL)

steel-cut oats

oat groats

oat groats. Reduce heat to low and simmer, stirring occasionally to prevent sticking, until liquid is absorbed and oats are tender, about 50 minutes.

Steel-Cut Oats: In a saucepan, bring 3 cups (750 mL) water to a boil. Add salt to taste and stir in 1 cup (250 mL) steel-cut oats. Reduce heat to low and simmer, stirring occasionally to prevent sticking, until liquid is absorbed and oats are tender, about 30 minutes.

Rolled Oats: In a saucepan, bring 2 cups (500 mL) water to a boil. Add salt to taste and stir in 1 cup (250 mL) rolled oats. Reduce heat to low and simmer, stirring occasionally to prevent sticking, until liquid is absorbed and oats are tender, about 10 minutes.

Microwave

Steel-Cut Oats: In an 8-cup (2 L) baking dish, combine 1 cup (250 mL) steel-cut oats with 4 cups (1 L) water and a pinch of salt. Cover and cook on High for 8 minutes. Stir well. Return to oven and cook, uncovered, for 8 minutes. Cover and let stand for 5 minutes.

Rolled Oats: In an 8-cup (2 L) baking dish, combine 1 cup (250 mL) rolled oats, 2⅓ cups (575 mL) water and a pinch of salt. Cook, uncovered, for 4 minutes on High and stir well. Return to oven and cook for 4 minutes. Let stand for 1 minute.

Slow Cooker

Use a small (3½ quart) slow cooker. If you're using a large (minimum 5 quart) slow cooker, double or triple the quantity.

Oat Groats or Steel-Cut Oats: In lightly greased stoneware, combine 1 cup (250 mL) steel-cut oats

and 4 cups (1 L) water. Add salt to taste. Cover and cook on Low for 8 hours. Stir well.

Rolled Oats: In lightly greased stoneware, combine 1¼ cups (300 mL) rolled oats, ½ tsp (2 mL) salt and 4 cups (1 L) water. Cover and cook on Low for 8 hours. Stir well.

Storing Cooked Oatmeal
Cover and refrigerate for up to 3 days. Oatmeal does not freeze well.

Quinoa

Although it is considered a grain, quinoa is actually the seed of a leafy plant related to spinach. Originally grown in the Andes, quinoa, which the Incas called "the mother of all grains," was known for keeping their armies strong. It made its way to North America in the 1980s and has been rediscovered as a good-for-you "ancient grain." The plant thrives in circumstances that mimic its origins in the Andes. It loves drought, poor alkaline soil and altitude, conditions under which few grains would even survive.

Culinary Profile
Quinoa is commonly sold in yellow or red varieties, although black quinoa, which is much less common, is also available in some locations. Subtly flavored, quinoa has a mild nutty taste that is very pleasing. It cooks quite quickly (in about 15 minutes) and you can tell when it's cooked because the germ unfolds like a little white tail. When cooked, it fluffs up but maintains an appealing, slightly crunchy texture. It can be substituted for rice, pasta, couscous or potatoes at most meals. Quinoa grains are naturally

WHOLE GRAIN FORMS OF QUINOA
QUINOA SEEDS: Quinoa seeds are commonly sold in yellow and red. These varieties are fundamentally the same, although the red version is less common, has a firmer texture and a more striking color.

QUINOA FLOUR: Higher in healthy fats than wheat flour, quinoa flour can be used to replace some of the flour in many recipes.

coated with saponin, a natural detergent found in many plants that has an unpleasant bitter taste. By the time you purchase it, most has been washed off, but a thorough rinsing before use is always a good idea.

yellow quinoa

red quinoa

Worth Knowing

Copper is a nutrient that plays important roles in the body, from helping wounds to heal and boosting your energy, to keeping bones strong. In 2006, researchers at the USDA found that copper helped prevent the calcium loss from bones associated with dieting.

Buying and Storing

Compared to other whole grains, quinoa is relatively high in polyunsaturated fats, so buy it from a source that has a high turnover. It should be stored in an airtight container in the refrigerator, where it will keep for up to 6 months. Quinoa flour should be stored in the freezer.

Cooking

It's always a good idea to rinse quinoa before using to remove any bitter saponin residue. Fill a bowl with warm water and swish the kernels around, then transfer to a sieve and rinse thoroughly under cold running water. If desired, toast the rinsed drained quinoa in a dry skillet over medium heat, stirring constantly, until it darkens, about 4 minutes.

Nutritional Profile

Quinoa is gluten-free and is known as a "supergrain" not only because it is relatively high in protein, but also because it is one of the few vegetable sources of complete protein, including lysine. A half-cup (125 mL) serving of cooked quinoa is a good source of iron and magnesium, among other nutrients, and, like all whole grains, provides beneficial phytochemicals.

Nutrients per ½ cup (125 mL) cooked quinoa	
Calories	106
Protein	3.7 g
Carbohydrates	19.5 g
Fat (Total)	1.6 g
Saturated Fat	0.2 g
Monounsaturated Fat	0.4 g
Polyunsaturated Fat	0.7 g
Dietary Fiber	2.0 g
Sodium	8 mg
Cholesterol	0 mg

- **EXCELLENT SOURCE OF** manganese
- **GOOD SOURCE OF** iron and magnesium
- **SOURCE OF** phosphorus, zinc, copper, riboflavin, niacin and folate
- **CONTAINS** a moderate amount of dietary fiber

How much whole grain am I eating? Based on the USDA definition of a serving of whole grains, ½ cup (125 mL) cooked quinoa provides 1.8 servings of whole grain.

GENERAL COOKING INSTRUCTIONS (APPROX.)

Grain Quantity	Liquid Quantity	Cooking Time	Yield (approx.)
1 cup (250 mL)	2 cups (500 mL)	15 minutes	3 cups (750 mL)

Stovetop

In a pot, bring 2 cups (500 mL) water to a boil. Add quinoa in a steady stream, stirring to prevent lumps from forming, and return to a boil. Reduce heat to low. Cover and simmer until tender, about 15 minutes. Look for a white line around the seeds — it's the germ, and when it bursts out, the grain is cooked. If water still remains in the bottom of the pot, remove the lid and stir occasionally until all the liquid evaporates, being careful not to overcook. You want the quinoa to maintain a bit of pleasant pop. Remove from heat and let stand, covered, for 5 minutes. Fluff with a fork before using.

Rice Cooker

In rice cooker bowl, combine 1 cup (250 mL) quinoa and 2 cups (500 mL) water or stock. If using water, add salt to taste. Cook on Regular or Brown

Rice setting until completed, about 35 minutes. Let rest on Warm cycle for at least 15 minutes.

Microwave

In a microwaveable bowl, combine 1 cup (250 mL) quinoa and 2 cups (500 mL) water. Add salt to taste, if desired. Microwave on High for 10 minutes. Stir well. Microwave on High for 7 minutes. Remove from oven. Cover and let stand for 5 minutes.

Storing Cooked Quinoa

Refrigerate for up to 3 days in a tightly sealed container. Quinoa doesn't freeze well.

Rice

Rice is the dietary staple for almost half the world's population. In countries such as China, Japan, India and Thailand, it plays a major role in the national diet. First cultivated in China, rice made its way to ancient Greece via Arab traders. It still plays a significant role in Mediterranean cuisine, as evidenced by signature dishes, such as Italian risotto and Spanish paella. The United States has been a significant producer of rice since the late-17th century, when it was first planted in South Carolina. Today, rice is grown in a number of southern states, notably Arkansas, California and Louisiana, as well as in other locations around the world.

Most whole-grain rice is brown, although specialty varieties, such as black and red rice are rapidly becoming widely available. Whole-grain rice is husked, but not milled or polished, leaving the outer layers in tact. Milling, which removes the bran and much of the germ, produces white rice, which is no longer a whole grain. Most white rice is polished, which strips away further nutrients from the grain. Interestingly, parboiled (or converted) brown rice that has been steamed under pressure and dried is more nutritious than white rice because technically it is still a whole grain. The rice is left in its hull and boiled, usually under pressure, which forces nutrients into the endosperm. It cooks more quickly than regular brown rice and produces a fluffier result.

Culinary Profile

Simple steamed rice is the perfect side dish and, in its refined white form, has long been the most common substitute for potatoes in the traditional North American diet. Now, more and more people are finding they actually prefer brown rice and to satisfy consumer demand chefs are adapting by preparing dishes, such as sushi, made with short-grain brown rice or offering a brown rice option with Chinese food. The main types of rice, Indica, Japonica and Javanica, are generally classified according to their length: long, medium or short grain. Rice can also be sticky or glutinous. Whatever kind you use, whole-grain rice is much chewier than its refined counterpart and has a sweet nutty flavor that lends itself to a wide array of dishes, from breakfast to dessert. Most also make a great side, simply cooked. Unless it is a glutinous variety (such as black sticky rice or short-grain brown rice), whole-grain rice generally cooks up to be relatively fluffy. Most varieties take a relatively long time to cook (about 55 minutes), although some, such as brown Kalijira rice from Bangladesh and Bhutanese red rice, both heirloom varieties, cook in less than 30 minutes.

Worth Knowing

The bran layer of rice, which is lost to polishing in the production of white rice, contains the compound

short-grain brown rice   long-grain brown rice

gamma oryzanol, which appears to have antioxidant properties. Preliminary studies suggest that this compound may help to keep cholesterol under control.

VARIETIES OF WHOLE-GRAIN RICE

LONG-GRAIN BROWN RICE: The grains of long-grain brown rice are long and narrow. When cooked, it is quite fluffy, with individual grains that remain separate.

SHORT-GRAIN BROWN RICE: Short-grain rice has short, stubby grains that tend to stick together when cooked. From a culinary perspective, this means you can easily produce risotto-like dishes with relatively little stirring.

SPECIALTY VARIETIES OF WHOLE-GRAIN RICE: Nowadays, many varieties of specialty rice are quite widely available, either in Asian markets, specialty stores or well-stocked supermarkets, including black, red and brown rice. Other varieties, such as Brown Pecan or popcorn rice from the southern U.S., are available in specialty stores. All these varieties have unique qualities and it's wise to consult the purveyor who sold you the product, or the package it came in for specific instructions.

Black rice includes Chinese black rice, Thai black sticky rice, Italian Black Venere rice, and Black Japonica rice.

Red rice: Several kinds are available, such as Bhutanese red rice, an heirloom variety grown in the Himalayas, Thai red rice, Italian wild red rice, Colusari red rice, red rice from the Camargue region of France, and Wehani rice. Most varieties of red rice can be used interchangeably in recipes, although the cooking times may vary.

Brown Kalijira is a tiny-grained rice, often described as baby basmati, which is destined to become popular because it cooks in less than 30 minutes. It makes an excellent substitute for plain white rice and a side dish or accompaniment for Asian dishes, such as stir-fries or curries.

BROWN RICE FLOUR: Although it has a nutty flavor, the texture is very smooth, so this flour can easily be substituted for some of the all-purpose flour in many recipes. However, it won't work in yeast breads because it is gluten-free. It is available in natural foods stores. Because it contains volatile oils, it is quite perishable. Store brown rice flour in the refrigerator for up to 5 months or in the freezer for up to 1 year.

BROWN RICE PASTA: A wide variety of conventional pasta forms, such as spaghetti, fettuccini, spirals, elbows and lasagna noodles, are made from brown rice. This is a boon to people with celiac disease as they are gluten-free. When cooked, brown rice pasta is softer than that made from wheat, but it has a mild, very pleasant taste.

Buying and Storing

Because the germ layer contains healthful oils, brown (and red and black) rice, like most whole grains, turns rancid if not properly stored. As a result, it's important to buy from a source with high turnover. If possible, smell before buying — you'll know immediately if it's past its peak. Before I knew better, I often bought packaged brown rice in the supermarket and was frequently disappointed with the result. Once I opened it at home, one whiff told me I'd made a mistake. Rice should have a fresh nutty aroma with no hint of bitterness. Store whole-grain rice in a cool dry place and use within 1 month of purchase.

Nutritional Profile

Rice is a gluten-free grain. Although many of the world's population consume white rice, brown rice is far more nutritious. Rich in complex carbohydrates, it contains much more fiber than white rice (1/2 cup/ 125 mL of white rice contains 0.3 grams of dietary fiber, while you'll get 1.5 grams from the same quantity of brown). A half-cup (125 mL) serving of brown rice is also an excellent source of manganese, a mineral that helps your body utilize key nutrients and keep your bones healthy. Rice also supplies varying degrees of minerals, such as magnesium, selenium, phosphorus, zinc, copper, thiamine and niacin, as well as valuable phytonutrients. Recent research suggests that brown rice is rich in beneficial antioxidants, particularly phenolic compounds (found in many fruits and vegetables), which have been shown to protect against cardiovascular disease.

Nutrients per 1/2 cup (125 mL) cooked long-grain brown rice

Calories	114
Protein	2.6 g
Carbohydrates	23.6 g
Fat (Total)	0.9 g
Saturated Fat	0.2 g
Monounsaturated Fat	0.3 g
Polyunsaturated Fat	0.3 g
Dietary Fiber	1.5 g
Sodium	5 mg
Cholesterol	0 mg

- **EXCELLENT SOURCE OF** manganese
- **GOOD SOURCE OF** magnesium and selenium
- **SOURCE OF** phosphorus, zinc, copper, thiamine and niacin

How much whole grain am I eating? Based on the USDA definition of a serving of whole grains, 1/2 cup (125 mL) cooked long-grain brown rice provides 1.9 servings of whole grain.

Italian black rice

Thai black sticky rice

Camargue red rice

Bhutanese red rice

Or cover tightly and refrigerate for up to 3 months, my favorite method.

Cooking

These are general instructions that work for all varieties of rice. You may prefer slightly firmer rice, in which case use a bit less water. If you're cooking a type of specialty rice, consult the package instructions. If there are none, follow these general instructions and subsequently adjust the quantity of water or cooking time to suit your preference.

GENERAL COOKING INSTRUCTIONS (APPROX.)

Grain Quantity	Liquid Quantity	Cooking Time	Yield (approx.)
1 cup (250 mL)	2½ cups (625 mL)	50 minutes	3 cups (750 mL)

Stovetop

Rinse under cold running water and drain. For 1 cup (250 mL) short- or long-grain brown rice bring approximately 2½ cups (625 mL) water to a boil in a heavy pot with a tight-fitting lid (for specialty varieties of rice, follow package instructions). Stir in rinsed rice and return to a rapid boil over high heat. Reduce heat to low. Cover tightly and simmer until rice is tender and all the water is absorbed, about 50 minutes. Remove from heat and let stand, covered, for 5 minutes. If using long-grain rice, fluff with a fork.

Rice Cooker

Combine 1 cup (250 mL) rice and 2¼ cups (550 mL) water in rice cooker bowl. If you don't have a fuzzy logic rice cooker and have time, allow to soak for 1 hour before starting the machine. Cook on Regular or Brown Rice cycle until done, about 40 minutes. Let rest on Warm cycle for 15 minutes.

Tip: If you're cooking whole grains, such as barley, wheat berries or brown rice, in a fuzzy logic rice cooker, expect them to take longer to cook than the times I have suggested because the machines allow time for soaking the raw grain and steaming it after it is cooked. This produces more evenly cooked grains, but the cycle takes longer. However, you do not need to allow for a resting period after the cycle is completed, as with conventional rice cookers. I find long-cooking grains can take almost 2 hours in my machine, but the results are terrific.

brown Kalijira rice

Oven

Preheat oven to 350°F (180°C). In a baking dish, combine 2½ cups (625 mL) boiling water and 1 cup (250 mL) long-grain brown rice. Cover and bake in preheated oven until liquid is absorbed, about 45 minutes.

Tip: Rice is cooked when the top looks like a crater.

Pressure Cooker

Before using your pressure cooker, consult the manufacturer's instructions to ensure you are not over- or underfilling the appliance. We used a 7.4-quart (7 L) pressure cooker. Combine 2 cups (500 mL) brown rice, 4 cups (1 L) water and, if desired, salt to taste. Cook under high pressure for 15 minutes. Release pressure and let stand, covered, for 5 minutes. Drain off water.

Storing Cooked Rice

To store cooked rice, place in a shallow container and let cool slightly (the steaming should have subsided) and then refrigerate for no more than 2 days. A toxin often present in rice, called *Bacillus cereus*, can multiply quickly on cooked rice that isn't cooled quickly enough and then stored. Brief reheating (such as stir-frying) isn't enough to destroy the toxin and it can cause food-borne illness.

To freeze, cool rice completely, then transfer to a resealable plastic bag in 2- or 3-cup (500 to 750 mL) quantities. Frozen rice will keep for up to 3 months. Defrost overnight in the refrigerator or remove from plastic bag and defrost in a microwave oven.

Rye

This nutritious grain was brought to North America by settlers from northern parts of France and Germany and was planted in French Canada as early as the 17th century. It is particularly hardy. Rye ferments easily, so perhaps not surprisingly, most of the rye grown in North America is used to make rye whiskey.

Culinary Profile

Most people are familiar with rye as a slightly acidic bread that makes a wonderful companion to robustly flavored foods, such as smoked salmon or egg salad. Surprisingly, rye berries, from which the flour is milled, are slightly sweet. (The pungent flavor of rye bread is created during bread making when fermentation takes place.) When cooked, they have a

---

VARIETIES OF WHOLE-GRAIN RYE

RYE BERRIES: Similar in appearance to wheat berries but more slender and browner in color. Use like wheat berries in salads, soups and stews.

RYE FLAKES: Steamed and rolled rye berries. They are often cooked like oatmeal for breakfast.

RYE FLOUR: Ground from rye berries, it has less gluten than wheat, but makes dark robust breads that are particularly nourishing.

---

pleasantly chewy texture, much like wheat berries. They can be substituted for wheat, spelt or Kamut berries in recipes containing foods with pluck, such as fennel, beets and cruciferous vegetables.

Worth Knowing

A Finnish study that followed almost 22,000 male smokers for 6.1 years found a reduced risk of death from coronary heart disease associated with the intake of rye.

Cooking

GENERAL COOKING INSTRUCTIONS (APPROX.)

Grain Quantity	Liquid Quantity	Cooking Time	Yield (approx.)
1 cup (250 mL)	2 cups (500 mL)	60 minutes	2⅓ cups (575 mL)

Stovetop

Bring 2 cups (500 mL) water to a boil. Add 1 cup (250 mL) rye berries and return to a boil. Reduce heat to low. Cover and simmer until berries are tender, about 1 hour. Remove from heat and let stand, covered, for 10 minutes.

Oven

Preheat oven to 350°F (180°C). Bring 2 cups (500 mL) water to a boil over high heat. Add 1 cup (250 mL) rye berries and return to a boil. Transfer to an 8-cup (2 L) baking dish. Cover and bake in preheated oven until berries are tender and water is absorbed, about 55 minutes.

Rice Cooker

Combine 1 cup (250 mL) rye berries and 2½ cups (625 mL) water in rice cooker bowl. (If you don't have a fuzzy logic rice cooker and have time, allow to

rye berries

Nutritional Profile

Aficionados believe that rye, not wheat, is truly the staff of life, a magic strength-giving, disease-fighting elixir. While they may be assigning supernatural powers to a mere food, there is little doubt that rye is extremely nutritious and deserves a place in the whole-grain pantry. Interestingly, the fiber in rye is also found in the endosperm, not just the bran, which is usually the case. This means that rye products are usually lower on the Glycemic Index than those made from wheat.

Nutrients per ½ cup (125 mL) cooked rye berries

Calories	113
Protein	5.0 g
Carbohydrates	23.6 g
Fat (Total)	0.8 g
Saturated Fat	0.1 g
Monounsaturated Fat	0.1 g
Polyunsaturated Fat	0.4 g
Dietary Fiber	4.6 g
Sodium	4 mg
Cholesterol	0 mg

- **EXCELLENT SOURCE OF** manganese
- **GOOD SOURCE OF** magnesium and selenium
- **SOURCE OF** thiamine, riboflavin, niacin, folate, pantothenic acid, phosphorus, iron, zinc and copper
- **CONTAINS** a high amount of dietary fiber

How much whole grain am I eating? According to the USDA definition of a serving of whole grains, ½ cup (125 mL) cooked rye berries provides 2.1 servings of whole grains.

soak for 1 hour before starting the machine.) Cook on Regular or Brown Rice cycle until done, about 1 hour. Let rest on Warm for at least 15 minutes.

Slow Cooker

Lightly grease the slow cooker stoneware and combine 1 cup (250 mL) rinsed rye berries and 2½ cups (625 mL) water in a small (3½ quart) slow cooker. If you're using a large (minimum 5 quart) slow cooker, double or triple the quantity. Cover and cook on Low for 6 hours or on High for 3 hours, until berries are softened and water is absorbed.

Pressure Cooker

Combine 2 cups (500 mL) rye berries, 4 cups (1 L) water and ½ tsp (2 mL) salt. Cook under high pressure for 30 minutes. Drain off water.

Storing Cooked Rye Berries

Because they take so long to cook, when cooking rye berries it's a good idea to make more than you need. You can refrigerate the extra, tightly covered, for up to 3 days. Rye berries can also be frozen for up to 3 months. Before freezing, cool thoroughly and, for convenience, add to resealable plastic bag(s) in 1-cup (250 mL) increments. Defrost overnight in the refrigerator, or remove from the plastic bag and microwave. You can also defrost frozen rye berries on the stovetop in a heavy pot. Add 1 tbsp (15 mL) or so of water or stock, cover and steam over low heat.

Sorghum

Sorghum, also known as milo, is a tropical plant originating in Northeast Africa. It is a round grain, yellowy-beige in color and looks most like millet, although it is lighter in color and significantly larger. (One friend described it as millet on steroids.) It's an ancient grain that can withstand a reasonable amount of drought, making it a particularly valuable food in areas of the world that tend to be arid. Perhaps not surprisingly, it is one of the principal cereal grains grown in Africa and India, where sorghum flour is used to make bhakri, an unleavened bread that is a staple in many parts of the country. In China, it is distilled into beverages, such as maotai, a liquor that achieved international fame when it won a gold medal at the 1915 Panama-Pacific Exposition in San Francisco. In the United States, sorghum has been used to make gluten-free beer. Sorghum syrup, which is made from the juice extracted from the stalks of a non-grain variety known as sugar sorghum, is considered a great delicacy and is used in Southern U.S. cooking.

Culinary Profile

Most of the sorghum grown in the U.S. is used as animal feed, although it is reasonable to assume that the grain will grow in popularity because it is gluten-free. The actual grain, which is difficult to obtain in North America, is eaten instead of rice in some parts of Asia and ground and made into porridge in Africa. It has a mild, pleasant taste, which is accented by toasting. Sorghum grain makes a tasty pilaf or, cooked simply in stock or water, a good substitute for barley or wheat berries. Add it to soups

sorghum grain

or stews, along with or instead of other long-cooking grains. Sorghum flour, which tastes more like wheat than any of the other gluten-free flours, is readily available in natural foods stores. It adds a slightly nutty flavor to baked goods.

WHOLE GRAIN FORMS OF SORGHUM

SORGHUM GRAIN: Small beige seeds with a tiny brown dot. It has a chewy texture and earthy taste. It is available by mail order from gluten-free markets.

SORGHUM FLOUR: According to gluten-free experts Donna Washburn and Heather Butt, sorghum flour is the best general-purpose gluten-free flour, as it most resembles wheat flour. Most is stone-ground.

Worth Knowing

A study reported in the *Journal of Food Science* found that some varieties of sorghum are extremely high in antioxidants and also contain compounds (policosanols) that may be heart-healthy.

Buying and Storing

Because it contains a relatively high amount of polyunsaturated fat, sorghum should be stored in the refrigerator or freezer. Sorghum will keep, frozen, for up to 6 months.

Cooking

For best results, before cooking, toast sorghum in a dry skillet over medium heat, stirring constantly, until fragrant, about 5 minutes.

Nutritional Profile

Compared to other whole grains, sorghum is relatively high in polyunsaturated fats, which means it should be stored in the refrigerator or freezer. A half-cup (125 mL) serving also provides phosphorus, iron, thiamine, niacin and dietary fiber, among other nutrients.

Nutrients per ½ cup (125 mL) cooked sorghum grain	
Calories	130
Protein	4.3 g
Carbohydrates	28.7 g
Fat (Total)	1.3 g
Saturated Fat	0.2 g
Monounsaturated Fat	0.4 g
Polyunsaturated Fat	0.5 g
Dietary Fiber	2.4 g
Sodium	4 mg
Cholesterol	0 mg

- **GOOD SOURCE OF** phosphorus
- **SOURCE OF** iron, thiamine, niacin and phosphorus
- **CONTAINS** a moderate amount of dietary fiber

How much whole grain am I eating? Based on the USDA definition of a serving of whole grains, ½ cup (125 mL) cooked sorghum grain provides 2.4 servings of whole grain.

GENERAL COOKING INSTRUCTIONS (APPROX.)

Grain Quantity	Liquid Quantity	Cooking Time	Yield (approx.)
1 cup (250 mL)	2 cups (500 mL)	50 minutes	2½ cups (625 mL)

Stovetop

Bring 2 cups (500 mL) water to a boil. Add sorghum. Reduce heat to low, cover and cook until grains are tender and uniform in color, about 50 minutes.

Storing Cooked Sorghum

Cooked sorghum can be refrigerated in an airtight container for up to 2 days. Cooked sorghum doesn't freeze well.

Wheat

Wheat is the most commonly used grain in North America and one of the most versatile. It has been around since antiquity and appears to have originated in southwestern Asia. It was introduced to North America by Christopher Columbus, but wasn't broadly cultivated until toward the end of the 19th century, when Russian immigrants imported a particularly hardy variety known as Turkish red, which flourished in the Midwest. Today, about 100 varieties of wheat are grown in North America, and in recent years, ancient varieties of the grain have been revived. These include spelt, an ancient red wheat, which remained popular in some parts of Europe; Kamut, an ancient durum wheat; and farro, also known as emmer.

Culinary Profile

When people think about wheat, flour is usually the first product that comes to mind. In culinary terms, there are two main kinds of wheat: durum wheat,

WHOLE GRAIN FORMS OF WHEAT

BULGUR is steamed hulled wheat berries that are dried and cracked. Bulgur ranges in color from light to dark and in grinds from fine to coarse. The darker and coarser varieties are more strongly flavored and require more cooking. The finer, lighter kinds need only to be soaked in cold water. Bulgur should smell fresh and slightly nutty when purchased and, because it contains wheat germ, should be stored in an airtight container in the refrigerator or freezer.

COUSCOUS is North African in origin. It is granules of flour that have been rolled, dried and steamed. Most couscous is made from semolina flour, which is made from durum wheat. (Barley, millet and corn couscous exist but are specialty items.) Whole wheat couscous is tastier and far more nutritious than its refined counterpart and equally quick and easy to prepare. At the time of this writing, three kinds are widely available: couscous made from whole durum wheat, spelt or Kamut.

EMMER, which is known as farro or grano farro in Italy, is an ancient strain of wheat that is staging a comeback. It is often confused with spelt and is not yet widely available in North America. Whether farro needs to be soaked before cooking is a hotly discussed topic. However, much of the farro sold in North America has been at least partially pearled, in which case it will cook in about 30 minutes with no presoaking necessary. That means it is particularly important to check the package instructions and nomenclature when using this grain. Pearled farro, from which the bran has been removed, doesn't qualify as a whole grain. It will be labeled perlato. Partially pearled contains much of the bran and will be labeled semi-perlato. Farro has a pleasant nutty flavor and a chewy texture and can often be tolerated by people with sensitivities to wheat. Specialty stores often stock farro pasta, which is particularly tasty.

KAMUT, which is related to durum wheat, but is generally lower in gluten, is widely available as berries, pasta (including couscous) and flour. Because it is not as high in gluten as regular wheat flour, it should replace a maximum of one-third the quantity of flour called for in any bread recipe.

SPELT is another ancient form of wheat. It is widely available as berries, flour, pasta and couscous and apparently offers a wider spectrum of nutrients than most varieties of wheat, which have been inbred.

TRITICALE is a hybrid of wheat and rye, developed in Scotland in 1875. It is available as berries, flour or in flakes but is not easy to find. It tastes like wheat with a more pronounced rye flavor and is noted for its high protein content. Most of the world's crop is grown in Europe, although farmers in other jurisdictions, such as South Africa, Canada and the U.S., are expanding their production of this nutritious grain.

WHEAT BERRIES are the whole kernels of the wheat plant (just as spelt and Kamut berries are the kernels of those plants). The berries are usually ground into flour and, depending on the variety, used to make bread, baked goods, pasta or couscous. When crushed, wheat berries become cracked wheat. Cooked on their own, they make delicious salads and are a wonderful addition to soups and stews. There are many types of wheat berries — for instance, my neighborhood natural foods store sells both hard red and soft. While the distinctions are important when grinding the kernels into flour, they make little difference to the result when wheat berries are used in recipes. They are widely available in bulk and natural foods stores.

WHOLE WHEAT PASTA is now widely available and tastes better than ever before. In addition to excellent texture and taste (depending on the brand), it is much more nutritious than enriched white pasta. Ounce for ounce it contains slightly fewer calories, a bit more protein and significantly more magnesium and fiber (a 2-ounce/60 gram serving of whole wheat pasta has 4.7 grams of fiber compared to 1.4 grams in enriched white pasta). Most whole wheat pastas are made from regular wheat, but specialty products, such as those made from farro, spelt and Kamut, are becoming increasingly available.

bulgur

wheat berries

which is used for making pasta, including couscous; and bread wheat, which is used in baked goods.

Wheat flour is the prominent ingredient in most baked goods sold in North America, because the grain is particularly high in the protein gluten, a key ingredient in getting baked goods to rise. Most often, wheat products, such as pasta and bread, are made from refined white flour, although more and more whole-grain products are being produced in response to consumer demands. Whole-grain wheat is also available as wheat berries and bulgur and as ancient grains, such as spelt, Kamut and farro. These heirloom varieties are reputed to be more nutritious than regular wheat and can often be tolerated by people who are sensitive to wheat, although not by those suffering from celiac disease. They can be substituted in the same form for wheat berries or other wheat products, such as pasta and couscous.

Buying and Storing

Like all whole grains, wheat berries are perishable and should be purchased from a source with high turnover. I like to keep mine in the refrigerator, where they will keep for at least a month. If you're not using them within that time frame, transfer to a resealable plastic bag and freeze for up to 6 months.

Worth Knowing

Whole wheat contains plant lignans, which may protect against heart disease and breast cancer. Research from Kansas State University is showing that the orthophenols in wheat contain powerful antioxidants.

Cooking

These general instructions work for all wheat berries, including Kamut, spelt and farro, although the quantity of liquid required, cooking times and yields may vary slightly.

Nutritional Profile

Like most whole grains, whole wheat contains a smattering of nutrients, many of which appear in quantities too minute to be identified in terms of daily values, but all of which work together, likely in synergy, to promote health. A half-cup (125 mL) serving of cooked wheat berries is an excellent source of manganese and selenium and a good source of phosphorus and magnesium. It also contains iron, zinc and copper and provides a high amount of dietary fiber.

Nutrients per ½ cup (125 mL) cooked wheat berries

Calories	111
Protein	3.5 g
Carbohydrates	24.9 g
Fat (Total)	0.5 g
Saturated Fat	0.1 g
Monounsaturated Fat	0.1 g
Polyunsaturated Fat	0.2 g
Dietary Fiber	4.3 g
Sodium	3 mg
Cholesterol	0 mg

- **EXCELLENT SOURCE OF** manganese and selenium
- **GOOD SOURCE OF** phosphorus and magnesium
- **SOURCE OF** iron, zinc, copper, thiamine, niacin and folate
- **CONTAINS** a high amount of dietary fiber

How much whole grain am I eating? Based on the USDA definition of a serving of whole grains, ½ cup (125 mL) cooked wheat berries provides 2.1 servings of whole grain.

GENERAL COOKING INSTRUCTIONS (APPROX.)

Grain Quantity	Liquid Quantity	Cooking Time	Yield (approx.)
1 cup (250 mL)	2½ cups (625 mL)	45 minutes to 1 hour	2½ cups (625 mL)

spelt

Kamut

Tip: The length of time you cook wheat berries should vary according to how you intend to use them. For salads, they should be a bit *al dente*, about 45 minutes on the stovetop. If you want them to be softer, cook for longer.

Stovetop

Rinse berries under cold running water and drain. For 1 cup (250 mL) wheat berries, bring 2½ cups (625 mL) water to a boil in a heavy pot with a tight-fitting lid. Stir in rinsed berries and return to a rapid boil over high heat. Reduce heat to low. Cover tightly and simmer until the berries are tender, but still a bit chewy, 45 minutes to 1 hour. Remove from heat and let stand, covered, for 5 minutes. Drain off any excess water.

Rice Cooker

Combine 1 cup (250 mL) rinsed wheat berries and 2½ cups (625 mL) water in rice cooker bowl. (If you don't have a fuzzy logic rice cooker and have time, let soak for 1 hour before starting the machine.) Cook on Regular or Brown Rice cycle until done, about 1 hour. Let rest on Warm cycle for at least 15 minutes.

Slow Cooker

Lightly grease the slow cooker stoneware and combine 1 cup (250 mL) rinsed wheat berries and 2¼ cups (550 mL) water in a small (3½ quart) slow cooker. If you're using a large (minimum 5 quart) slow cooker, double or triple the quantity. Cover and cook on Low for 6 to 8 hours or on High for 3 to 4 hours, stirring once or twice, if possible, until desired texture is achieved.

Pressure Cooker

Wheat berries cooked in a pressure cooker have a particularly nice texture. The downside is that in order to ensure even cooking you need to use extra water, which must be drained off. Before using your pressure cooker, consult the manufacturer's instructions to ensure you are not over- or underfilling the appliance. Whole grains generate a great deal of foam, so the cooker shouldn't be more than half full. We used a 7.4-quart (7 L) pressure cooker. Combine 2 cups (500 mL) wheat berries, 5 cups (1.25 L) water and, if desired, 1 tsp (5 mL) salt. Cook under high pressure for 35 minutes. Drain off water.

Storing Cooked Wheat Berries

Store cooked wheat berries, tightly covered, in the refrigerator for up to 3 days. To freeze, cool completely, then transfer to a resealable plastic bag in 1-, 2- or 3-cup (250, 500 or 750 mL) quantities. Frozen wheat berries will keep for up to 3 months. Defrost overnight in the refrigerator or remove from plastic bag and defrost in a microwave oven.

Wild Rice

Not a rice or technically even a grain, wild rice is actually the seed of an aquatic grass. However, it is categorized as a grain because it is cooked like one and has a similar nutritional profile. Wild rice is native to North American wetlands and has been harvested for centuries by Native people of the northern Midwest (Manitoba, Saskatchewan and Minnesota), where it is known as manomin, "a gift from the Creator." Harvesting has a religious and cultural significance for the Ojibwa people, who

WHOLE GRAIN FORMS OF WILD RICE

All wild rice is whole grain. It is not made into flour or any other forms.

gather the crop in canoes, with the use of "knockers," specially designed wooden sticks, which are used to bend the stalks so the grains fall into the canoe. However, today most wild rice is commercially grown, although it can be difficult to ascertain this fact from labeling. Since the best wild rice is foraged, look for the word "organic" and some indication that the product is hand-harvested, although even this is no guarantee that you are purchasing the real thing. Wild rice is traditionally cured after harvesting, which results in a mildly fermented product. It is then dried.

Culinary Profile

Wild rice has a soft chewy texture and a delicious nutty flavor. The naturally grown, hand-harvested varieties are considered to have the most delicate and complex flavors, and although they are the most expensive, connoisseurs believe they are worth the extra cost. In general terms, the longer the grain, the more it costs — premium grains are about 1 inch (2.5 cm) long, while the least expensive are broken grains, which are often added to mixes. In fact, wild rice is most often consumed in a blend with other types of rice or grains because its robust flavor dominates the mix. Its presence can be felt with a ratio of as little as 2 tbsp (25 mL) to 1 cup (250 mL) brown or white rice. It pairs well with foods that are equally assertive, such as smoked turkey, dark mushrooms, dried fruits and nuts, or those that grow in its natural habitat, such as blueberries and cranberries.

Worth Knowing

A 100-gram serving of wild rice contains 26 grams of folate, a B vitamin that helps to keep homocysteine levels under control and assists in the formation of red blood cells. (A comparable quantity of brown rice has 4 grams of this nutrient.) A vital nutrient for pregnant women, folate prevents neural tube defects, such as spina bifida.

Buying and Storing

Because it has undergone a mild process of fermentation and drying, wild rice has a longer shelf life than most whole grains. It will keep covered in a cool, dark place for up to 1 year.

Cooking

GENERAL COOKING INSTRUCTIONS (APPROX.)

Grain Quantity	Liquid Quantity	Cooking Time	Yield (approx.)
1 cup (250 mL)	2 to 3 cups (500 to 625 mL)	45 to 65 minutes	3½ cups (875 mL)

Wild rice should be rinsed thoroughly and drained before cooking. Because the grains can range so wildly in size, it is difficult to be specific about cooking times and the quantity of water required. As a rule of thumb, the longer the grain, the more water it needs. When cooking 1 cup (250 mL) wild rice, count on about 3 cups (750 mL) water for longer grains and as little as 2 cups (500 mL) for the shortest. The safest strategy is to use a bit more water than you think you will need and drain off the excess, although it's wise to be judicious in the quantity of water you add because any that is discarded will carry away nutrients. You will know when the wild rice is done if about half the grains have burst.

wild rice

Stovetop

Bring 2 to 3 cups (500 to 750 mL) water or stock to a boil. Add 1 cup (250 mL) rinsed drained wild rice and return to a boil. Reduce heat to low. Cover and simmer until the kernels begin to burst, 45 to 65 minutes. Remove from heat and let stand, covered, for 10 minutes. Fluff with a fork.

Rice Cooker

Combine 1 cup (250 mL) rinsed drained wild rice and 2½ cups (625 mL) water in rice cooker bowl. Stir well. (If you don't have a fuzzy logic rice cooker and have time, allow to soak for 1 hour before starting the machine.) Cook on Regular or Brown Rice cycle until done, about 1 hour. Let rest on Warm cycle for 15 minutes.

Slow Cooker

In a small (3½ quart) slow cooker, combine 1 cup (250 mL) rinsed drained wild rice and 2½ cups (625 mL) water. Stir well. Cover and cook on High for 2½ hours, until water is absorbed and rice is tender. If you're using a large (minimum 5 quart) slow cooker, double or triple the quantity. Cover and cook on Low for 6 to 8 hours or on High for 3 to 4 hours, stirring once or twice, if possible, until desired texture is achieved.

Pressure Cooker

Before using your pressure cooker, consult the manufacturer's instructions to ensure you are not over- or underfilling the appliance. Whole grains generate a great deal of foam, so the cooker shouldn't be more than half full. Combine 1 cup (250 mL) wild rice, 2½ cups (625 mL) water and, if desired, 1 tsp (5 mL) salt. Cook under high pressure for 25 minutes. Drain off water.

Tip: If you're using packaged wild rice, I recommend using the instructions provided by the producer, who knows their product. The most effective way to ensure good results is to cook wild rice and most other whole grains in an overabundance of water, then drain off the excess. However, I usually prefer not to do this, as nutrients disappear down the drain.

Storing Cooked Wild Rice

Store cooked wild rice, covered, in the refrigerator for up to 5 days. Freeze for up to 3 months in resealable plastic bags in 1-cup (250 mL) quantities. Defrost in the refrigerator or remove from plastic bag and defrost in a microwave.

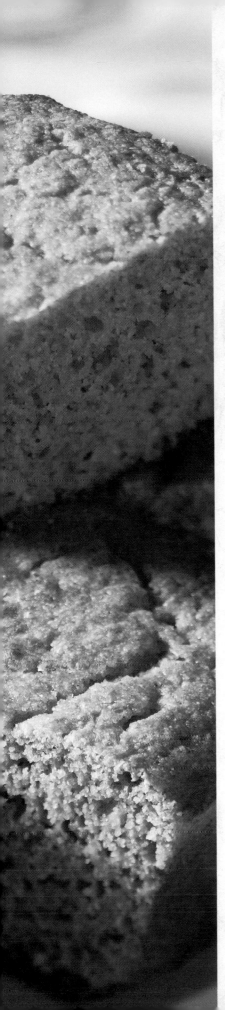

Bread and Breakfasts

Old-Fashioned Cornbread

Old-Fashioned Cornbread

This traditional favorite is the perfect accompaniment to soups, stews and chilies that have a down-home feel. Use leftovers to make cornbread stuffing, or for a great snack, enjoy with a bit of salsa.

Makes 8 servings

TIP

As with other quick breads, when making cornbread, one key to success is not to overmix the batter.

- **Preheat oven to 400°F (200°C)**
- **8-inch (2 L) square baking pan, lightly greased**

1 cup	stone-ground yellow cornmeal	250 mL
1 cup	whole barley flour	250 mL
2 tbsp	granulated sugar	25 mL
4 tsp	baking powder	20 mL
½ tsp	salt	2 mL
2	eggs	2
1¼ cups	milk	300 mL
2 tbsp	melted butter	25 mL

1. In a bowl, combine cornmeal, barley flour, sugar, baking powder and salt. Whisk to blend and make a well in the center.

2. In a separate bowl, beat eggs. Add milk and butter and beat well. Pour into well and mix with dry ingredients just until blended. Spread in prepared pan and bake in preheated oven until top is golden and springs back, about 30 minutes. Let cool in pan on wire rack for 5 minutes. Serve warm.

Nutrients per serving

Calories	197
Protein	5.8 g
Carbohydrates	31.3 g
Fat (Total)	5.7 g
Saturated Fat	2.8 g
Monounsaturated Fat	1.7 g
Polyunsaturated Fat	0.7 g
Dietary Fiber	3.9 g
Sodium	348 mg
Cholesterol	57 mg

EXCELLENT SOURCE OF selenium.

GOOD SOURCE OF phosphorus and magnesium.

SOURCE OF vitamins A and E (alpha-tocopherol), thiamine, riboflavin, niacin, folate, pantothenic acid, calcium, iron, manganese, zinc and copper.

CONTAINS a moderate amount of dietary fiber.

Cheesy Jalapeño Cornbread

Slightly spicy, intriguingly savory and deliciously comforting. What more could you want? Serve this cornbread as an accompaniment to dinner or just enjoy it on its own.

Makes 8 servings

TIP

Not only does pulsing blend the dry ingredients, it also aerates them slightly, contributing to a lighter result.

- **Preheat oven to 400°F (200°C)**
- **8-inch (2 L) square baking pan, lightly greased**

1 cup	stone-ground yellow cornmeal	250 mL
¾ cup	whole wheat flour	175 mL
1 tbsp	granulated sugar	15 mL
2 tsp	baking powder	10 mL
½ tsp	baking soda	2 mL
½ tsp	salt	2 mL
¼ cup	cold butter, cubed	50 mL
1¼ cups	buttermilk	300 mL
2	eggs, separated	2
¼ tsp	baking soda, dissolved in 1 tbsp (15 mL) water	1 mL
1	jalapeño pepper, seeded and minced	1
1 cup	shredded Cheddar cheese, preferably old	250 mL

1. In a food processor, combine cornmeal, flour, sugar, baking powder, baking soda and salt. Pulse to blend. Add butter and pulse until mixture resembles coarse crumbs. In a measuring cup, combine buttermilk, egg yolks and jalapeño pepper and beat well. Pour over cornmeal mixture and pulse just until blended.

2. In a mixer on high speed, beat egg whites until stiff peaks form. Fold in cheese. Fold in cornmeal mixture and spoon into prepared pan. Bake in preheated oven until top is golden and springs back, about 25 minutes. Let cool in pan on a wire rack for 5 minutes. Serve warm.

Variation

Cheesy Chipotle Cornbread: Substitute 1 minced chipotle pepper in adobo sauce for the jalapeño.

Nutrients per serving

Calories	249
Protein	9.3 g
Carbohydrates	24.2 g
Fat (Total)	13.2 g
Saturated Fat	7.6 g
Monounsaturated Fat	3.8 g
Polyunsaturated Fat	0.9 g
Dietary Fiber	3.5 g
Sodium	515 mg
Cholesterol	80 mg

EXCELLENT SOURCE OF manganese and selenium.

GOOD SOURCE OF calcium, phosphorus and magnesium.

SOURCE OF vitamins A and E (alpha-tocopherol), thiamine, riboflavin, niacin, folate, pantothenic acid, iron, zinc and copper.

CONTAINS a moderate amount of dietary fiber.

Buttermilk Buckwheat Pancakes

This is one of my favorite Sunday breakfasts. I add a slice or two of bacon for a treat and a good portion of maple syrup. I savor every bite.

Makes 12 to 14 pancakes or 6 servings

2½ cups	buttermilk	625 mL
2 tsp	baking powder	10 mL
1 tsp	baking soda	5 mL
½ tsp	salt	2 mL
1 tbsp	light (fancy) molasses	15 mL
1	egg	1
2 cups	buckwheat flour (see Tips, left)	500 mL

TIPS

Buckwheat flour is available in natural foods stores. If you don't have it, you can make your own by processing kasha or toasted buckwheat groats in a food processor until finely ground.

You can make this batter ahead and keep, covered, in the refrigerator for up to 2 days. The batter will thicken a bit, so you may need to add a little buttermilk to thin it out. Your pancakes will not be as airy as those made immediately after mixing, but they will still be delicious.

1. In a food processor, combine buttermilk, baking powder, baking soda and salt. Pulse to blend. Add molasses and egg and pulse to blend. Add buckwheat flour and pulse just until combined. Set aside for 5 minutes. Mixture should be of a pourable consistency. If necessary, add more flour or buttermilk and pulse until blended.

2. Heat a lightly greased nonstick skillet over medium heat until water dropped on the surface bounces before evaporating. Add about ¼ cup (50 mL) batter at a time and cook until bubbles appear all over the top surface, then flip and cook until bottom side is browned, about 1 minute per side. Keep warm. Continue with remaining batter.

Nutrients per serving

Calories	92
Protein	4.4 g
Carbohydrates	15. 8 g
Fat (Total)	1.8 g
Saturated Fat	0.8 g
Monounsaturated Fat	0.6 g
Polyunsaturated Fat	0.2 g
Dietary Fiber	1.2 g
Sodium	260 mg
Cholesterol	17 mg

GOOD SOURCE OF magnesium and manganese.

SOURCE OF thiamine, riboflavin, niacin, folate, phosphorus, calcium, iron, zinc, copper and selenium.

Blueberry Wild Rice Pancakes

The combination of flavors in these delicious pancakes is quintessentially North American, especially when finished with real maple syrup. They make a great Sunday breakfast any place, any time, but I find them particularly enjoyable at a lakeside cottage. They are a great way to use up leftover wild rice and are not only gluten-free, but also, a friend tells me, diet friendly at only 1 Weight Watchers® point apiece.

Makes 4 servings

TIP

When measuring flour for this or any other recipe, always use a dry measuring cup so the flour can be leveled off with the back of a knife and be sure not to pack it down.

1 cup	rice milk or milk	250 mL
½ cup	cooked wild rice (see cooking instructions, page 36)	125 mL
1 tbsp	granulated sugar	15 mL
1	egg, separated	1
1 tsp	vanilla extract	5 mL
1 cup	brown rice flour	250 mL
1 tsp	baking powder	5 mL
½ tsp	salt	2 mL
1 cup	fresh or frozen blueberries	250 mL
	Maple syrup or blueberry jam	

1. In a saucepan over medium heat, combine milk, wild rice and sugar. Heat, stirring, until sugar dissolves and bubbles appear around the edge. Remove from heat. Stir in egg yolk and vanilla. Set aside.

2. In a bowl, combine rice flour, baking powder and salt. Add to milk mixture, stirring just until blended. Fold in blueberries. Beat egg white until stiff and gently fold into batter.

3. Heat a lightly greased nonstick skillet over medium heat until water dropped on the surface bounces before evaporating. Scoop out ¼ cup (50 mL) of batter per pancake and cook until bubbles appear all over the top surface, then flip and cook until bottom side is lightly browned, about 1 minute per side. Keep warm. Continue with remaining batter. Serve with maple syrup or blueberry jam.

Nutrients per serving

Calories	249
Protein	5.7 g
Carbohydrates	50.1 g
Fat (Total)	3.0 g
Saturated Fat	0.6 g
Monounsaturated Fat	1.3 g
Polyunsaturated Fat	0.7 g
Dietary Fiber	3.9 g
Sodium	404 mg
Cholesterol	47 mg

EXCELLENT SOURCE OF manganese.

GOOD SOURCE OF niacin, phosphorus and magnesium.

SOURCE OF vitamin C, thiamine, riboflavin, folate, pantothenic acid, calcium, iron, copper and selenium.

CONTAINS a moderate amount of dietary fiber.

Amaranth Banana Walnut Bread

This rich, dense, wholesome quick bread is delicious for breakfast and makes a wonderful snack any time of the day. It's also a great way to use up any leftover Hot Amaranth Millet Cereal (see Variation, below).

**Makes 1 loaf
or 16 servings**

TIP
Be sure not to overmix the batter once you combine the wet and dry ingredients.

- **Preheat oven to 350°F (180°C)**
- **9-by 5-inch (2 L) loaf pan, lightly greased**

1 cup	cooked amaranth grain, cooled (see cooking instructions, page 15)	250 mL
2 cups	whole wheat pastry flour	500 mL
2 tsp	baking powder	10 mL
½ cup	chopped walnuts	125 mL
1 cup	mashed ripe bananas (about 3)	250 mL
½ cup	liquid honey	125 mL
2	eggs	2
3 tbsp	melted butter or olive oil	45 mL
1 tsp	vanilla extract	5 mL

1. In a bowl, combine flour, baking powder and walnuts. Mix well.

2. In a separate bowl, beat bananas, honey, eggs, butter and vanilla until blended. Add amaranth and mix well. Pour mixture over dry ingredients and mix just until combined. Pour into prepared pan. Bake in preheated oven until a tester inserted in the center comes out clean, about 1 hour. Let cool in pan on a wire rack for 10 minutes. Remove from pan and let cool completely on rack.

Variations

Amaranth Millet Banana Walnut Bread: Substitute 1 cup (250 mL) leftover Hot Millet Amaranth Cereal (see recipe, page 52) for the amaranth.

Amaranth Banana Walnut Bread with Dates: Substitute ½ cup (125 mL) finely chopped soft dates, such as Medjool, for half of the bananas.

Nutrients per serving

Calories	158
Protein	3.9 g
Carbohydrates	25.2 g
Fat (Total)	5.6 g
Saturated Fat	1.9 g
Monounsaturated Fat	1.2 g
Polyunsaturated Fat	2.1 g
Dietary Fiber	2.7 g
Sodium	63 mg
Cholesterol	29 mg

EXCELLENT SOURCE OF manganese.

GOOD SOURCE OF magnesium and selenium.

SOURCE OF thiamine, riboflavin, niacin, folate, phosphorus, iron, zinc and copper.

CONTAINS a moderate amount of dietary fiber.

Zucchini Lemon Loaf with Cranberries

When I have some of this loaf at home, I find it very difficult to resist the urge to nibble. It's so tasty and nutritious that I just enjoy it with the thought that it's adding welcome nutrients to my diet. The combination of barley with wheat flour, and the quantity of zucchini, means that it doesn't rise as much as a more traditional loaf, but trust me, you'll enjoy it every bit as much.

Makes 1 loaf or 18 servings

TIP

Bake this loaf as soon as you have mixed it to ensure the leavening has maximum strength.

- **Preheat oven to 350°F (180°C)**
- **9-by 5-inch loaf pan, lightly greased**

1 cup	whole barley flour	250 mL
1 cup	whole wheat pastry flour	250 mL
1 cup	granulated sugar	250 mL
1 tbsp	baking powder	15 mL
½ tsp	baking soda	2 mL
½ tsp	salt	2 mL
1½ cups	grated unpeeled zucchini	375 mL
½ cup	chopped walnuts	125 mL
3	eggs	3
¼ cup	vegetable oil	50 mL
1 tbsp	finely grated lemon zest	15 mL
¼ cup	freshly squeezed lemon juice	50 mL
½ cup	chopped fresh or frozen cranberries	125 mL

1. In a large bowl, combine whole barley and wheat flours, sugar, baking powder, baking soda and salt. Add zucchini and walnuts and mix well. Make a well in the center.

2. In a separate bowl, beat eggs, oil and lemon zest and juice. Pour into well and mix with dry ingredients just until combined. Fold in cranberries. Spoon into prepared pan. Bake in preheated oven until a tester inserted in the center comes out clean, about 70 minutes. Let cool in pan on a wire rack for 10 minutes. Remove from pan and let cool completely on rack.

Nutrients per serving

Calories	159
Protein	3.4 g
Carbohydrates	23.8 g
Fat (Total)	6.2 g
Saturated Fat	0.7 g
Monounsaturated Fat	2.5 g
Polyunsaturated Fat	2.7 g
Dietary Fiber	2.2 g
Sodium	160 mg
Cholesterol	31 mg

GOOD SOURCE OF manganese and selenium.

SOURCE OF vitamin E (alpha-tocopherol), thiamine, niacin, folate, phosphorus, iron, magnesium, zinc and copper.

CONTAINS a moderate amount of dietary fiber.

Cranberry-Orange Pecan Muffins

These muffins are so delicious it's hard to believe they are also nutritious and convenient to boot. You can make the batter ahead of time and refrigerate overnight (see Tips, left). Put them in the oven before you shower, and by the time you're finished, your muffins will be ready to eat.

Makes 12 muffins

TIPS

If you're making the batter ahead of time, don't add the cranberries until you're ready to bake. You can chop them, cover and refrigerate overnight. The batter will keep for two nights, so if you're baking half, chop half the cranberries and do the remainder the following night.

Use fresh or frozen cranberries, as you prefer. If using frozen, partially thaw them and blot in paper towel before adding to the batter.

- **Preheat oven to 375°F (190°C)**
- **12-cup muffin tin, lightly greased**

1 cup	whole wheat flour	250 mL
½ cup	whole barley flour	125 mL
½ cup	unbleached all-purpose flour	125 mL
¾ cup	granulated sugar	175 mL
¾ cup	chopped pecans	175 mL
2 tsp	baking powder	10 mL
½ tsp	salt	2 mL
¼ tsp	baking soda	1 mL
1	egg	1
½ cup	sour cream	125 mL
2 tsp	finely grated orange zest	10 mL
½ cup	freshly squeezed orange juice	125 mL
¼ cup	vegetable oil	50 mL
1½ cups	cranberries, coarsely chopped (see Tips, left)	375 mL

1. In a large bowl, combine whole wheat, barley and all–purpose flours, sugar, pecans, baking powder, salt and baking soda. Mix well and make a well in the center.

2. In a separate bowl, beat egg. Add sour cream, orange zest, orange juice and oil and beat well. Pour into the well and mix with dry ingredients just until blended. Fold in cranberries. Divide batter evenly among prepared muffin cups. Bake in preheated oven until the top springs back when lightly touched, about 25 minutes. Let cool on a wire rack for 5 minutes before removing from pan.

Nutrients per serving

Calories	242
Protein	4.1 g
Carbohydrates	32.6 g
Fat (Total)	11.6 g
Saturated Fat	1.8 g
Monounsaturated Fat	6.1 g
Polyunsaturated Fat	3.1 g
Dietary Fiber	3.3 g
Sodium	183 mg
Cholesterol	19 mg

EXCELLENT SOURCE OF manganese.

GOOD SOURCE OF selenium.

SOURCE OF vitamins C and E (alpha-tocopherol), thiamine, riboflavin, niacin, folate, phosphorus, iron, magnesium, zinc and copper.

CONTAINS a moderate amount of dietary fiber.

Blueberry Lemon Muffins

It's hard to beat the flavor combination of blueberries and lemon. Throw in some buttermilk to mellow the mixture and the result is divine.

Makes 12 muffins

TIPS

If you use large frozen blueberries, you may need to cook these muffins for as long as 25 minutes.

When making muffins and quick breads, you can use a wooden spoon or an electric mixer to blend ingredients. Use whatever method suits you best.

- **Preheat oven to 400°F (200°C)**
- **12-cup muffin tin, lightly greased**

1½ cups	whole barley flour	375 mL
1 cup	whole wheat flour	250 mL
¾ cup	granulated sugar	175 mL
2 tsp	baking powder	10 mL
2 tsp	finely grated lemon zest	10 mL
½ tsp	baking soda	2 mL
½ tsp	salt	2 mL
2	eggs	2
1¼ cups	buttermilk	300 mL
¼ cup	butter, melted	50 mL
1 tsp	vanilla extract	5 mL
1½ cups	fresh or frozen blueberries (see Tips, left)	375 mL

1. In a large bowl, combine barley and whole wheat flours, sugar, baking powder, lemon zest, baking soda and salt. Mix well and make a well in the center.

2. In a separate bowl, beat eggs. Add buttermilk, butter and vanilla and beat well. Pour into the well and mix with dry ingredients just until blended. Fold in blueberries. Divide batter evenly among muffin cups. Bake in preheated oven until tops are golden and spring back when lightly touched, about 16 minutes. Let cool on a wire rack for 10 minutes before removing from pan.

Nutrients per serving

Calories	218
Protein	5.5 g
Carbohydrates	37.8 g
Fat (Total)	5.7 g
Saturated Fat	3.1 g
Monounsaturated Fat	1.6 g
Polyunsaturated Fat	0.5 g
Dietary Fiber	3.6 g
Sodium	260 mg
Cholesterol	43 mg

EXCELLENT SOURCE OF manganese and selenium.

SOURCE OF vitamins A and E (alpha-tocopherol), thiamine, riboflavin, niacin, folate, magnesium, calcium, phosphorus, iron, zinc and copper.

CONTAINS a moderate amount of dietary fiber.

Rhubarb Orange Muffins

Thanks to gluten-free experts Donna Washburn and Heather Butt for allowing me to use their recipe for these delicious muffins, which appears in the Complete Gluten-Free Cookbook. *The walnuts add healthy omega-3 fats. What a great way to enjoy rhubarb, which is one of my favorite springtime treats.*

Makes 12 muffins

TIPS

When using frozen rhubarb, it is easier to chop while still partially frozen. The rhubarb must be finely chopped; otherwise, the finished muffin will be crumbly.

Xanthan gum, which is made from corn syrup, is used as a thickener. It is available in natural foods stores.

If you're making these muffins for anyone who can't tolerate gluten, check your baking powder, as some brands contain wheat starch. You may need to purchase a gluten-free variety.

- 12-cup muffin tin, lightly greased

1¾ cups	finely chopped rhubarb (see Tips, left)	425 mL
⅓ cup	granulated sugar	75 mL
1⅓ cups	sorghum flour	325 mL
⅓ cup	quinoa flour	75 mL
⅓ cup	potato starch	75 mL
1½ tsp	xanthan gum (see Tips, left)	7 mL
1 tbsp	baking powder (see Tips, left)	15 mL
1 tsp	baking soda	5 mL
½ tsp	salt	2 mL
1	egg	1
2 tbsp	finely grated orange zest	25 mL
⅔ cup	freshly squeezed orange juice	150 mL
3 tbsp	vegetable oil	45 mL
1 tsp	vanilla extract	5 mL
½ cup	chopped walnuts	125 mL

1. In a bowl, combine rhubarb and sugar. Mix well and set aside for 10 minutes.
2. In a large bowl, combine sorghum and quinoa flours, potato starch, xanthan gum, baking powder, baking soda and salt.
3. In a separate bowl, using an electric mixer, beat egg, orange zest, orange juice, oil and vanilla until combined. Stir in rhubarb, then dry ingredients just until combined. Stir in walnuts.
4. Divide batter evenly among prepared muffin cups. Let stand for 30 minutes. Meanwhile, preheat oven to 350°F (180°C). Bake in preheated oven until firm to the touch, 18 to 20 minutes. Remove from pan immediately and let cool completely on a wire rack.

Variations

Rhubarb Orange Bread: Spoon batter into a lightly greased 9- by 5-inch (2 L) loaf pan and bake in preheated oven until a tester inserted in the center comes out clean, 55 to 65 minutes.

Substitute pecans or ¼ cup (50 mL) green pumpkin seeds for the walnuts.

Nutrients per serving

Calories	172
Protein	2.9 g
Carbohydrates	24.4 g
Fat (Total)	7.6 g
Saturated Fat	0.7 g
Monounsaturated Fat	2.7 g
Polyunsaturated Fat	3.5 g
Dietary Fiber	1.9 g
Sodium	292 mg
Cholesterol	16 mg

SOURCE OF vitamins C and E (alpha-tocopherol), folate, calcium, phosphorus, iron, magnesium, manganese and copper.

Lemon Poppy Seed Blueberry Scones

Try these scones. They are so unbelievably light it's hard to imagine they were made with whole-grain flour. Enjoy them for a breakfast on the run or a pleasant afternoon tea.

Makes about 18 scones

TIPS

If you prefer, mix the dough in a food processor. Use cold butter and process until mixture resembles coarse crumbs. Transfer to a bowl and stir in blueberries, poppy seeds, lemon zest and yogurt. Continue with recipe.

The high heat helps the scones to rise. If the tops are browning too quickly, cover the pan with foil.

- **Preheat oven to 425°F (220°C)**
- **Baking sheet, ungreased**
- **2-inch (5 cm) round biscuit cutter**

1 cup	whole wheat pastry flour	250 mL
1 cup	whole barley flour	250 mL
2 tbsp	granulated sugar	25 mL
1 tbsp	baking powder	15 mL
½ tsp	baking soda	2 mL
½ tsp	salt	2 mL
½ cup	butter, cubed	125 mL
½ cup	fresh or frozen blueberries	125 mL
1 tbsp	poppy seeds	15 mL
2 tsp	finely grated lemon zest	10 mL
½ cup	plain yogurt (minimum 4% M.F.)	125 mL
GLAZE, OPTIONAL		
1 tbsp	milk or cream	15 mL
1 tbsp	raw or granulated sugar	15 mL

1. In a bowl, combine whole wheat and barley flours, sugar, baking powder, baking soda and salt. Using a pastry blender, two knives or your fingers, cut in butter until mixture resembles coarse crumbs. Mix in blueberries, poppy seeds and lemon zest and, using a fork, stir in yogurt.

2. Turn out onto a floured work surface and, using your hands, knead to form a smooth dough. Pat into a circle about ¾ inch (2 cm) thick. Using a biscuit cutter, cut into rounds. Repeat with scraps of dough to make additional scones. Place 2 inches (5 cm) apart on baking sheet.

3. *Glaze (optional):* Brush tops with milk and sprinkle with sugar.

4. Bake in preheated oven until tops are lightly browned, about 12 minutes. Let cool in pan on a wire rack for 10 minutes. Serve warm or at room temperature.

Variation

Currant-Studded Scones: Substitute ½ cup (125 mL) currants for the poppy seeds and blueberries.

Nutrients per serving

Calories	110
Protein	2.1 g
Carbohydrates	13.6 g
Fat (Total)	5.7 g
Saturated Fat	3.4 g
Monounsaturated Fat	1.4 g
Polyunsaturated Fat	0.5 g
Dietary Fiber	1.8 g
Sodium	188 mg
Cholesterol	14 mg

GOOD SOURCE OF manganese and selenium.

SOURCE OF vitamin A, thiamine, niacin, phosphorus, magnesium and zinc.

Chapati

Chapatis are a traditional Indian bread made from whole wheat flour that has been very finely milled. Here, I have added barley flour for lightness. They make an excellent accompaniment to curries and stews, as they are great for soaking up the sauce.

Makes 8 chapatis

TIP

If you have access to chapati flour, a very finely milled whole wheat flour that is available in Indian grocery stores, substitute it for the whole wheat pastry flour called for in this recipe.

1 cup	whole wheat pastry flour (approx.)	250 mL
½ cup	whole barley flour	125 mL
½ tsp	salt	2 mL
3 tbsp	melted butter or olive oil, divided (approx.)	45 mL
⅓ to ½ cup	lukewarm water	75 to 125 mL

1. In a bowl, combine whole wheat and barley flours and salt. Add 1 tbsp (15 mL) melted butter and mix well. Make a well in the center and gradually, in a stream, add water, stirring gently to incorporate the flour, until the mixture is crumbly. Knead until the dough is smooth and leaves the sides of the bowl, adding a bit more water if necessary. (Kneading makes the dough lighter, so the more the better.) Cover with a damp cloth and let rest for 1 hour to ensure moisture is evenly distributed.

2. Divide dough into 8 equal portions and form each into a ball. Return balls to the bowl and keep covered with the damp cloth. One at a time, on a floured surface, roll each ball out to about 6 inches (15 cm) in diameter.

3. Heat a nonstick skillet over medium-high heat until almost smoking. Add approximately ¼ tsp (1 mL) of the butter to the pan and disperse over the surface. Add one chapati and cook until bubbles rise and brown spots appear on the underside, about 40 seconds. Turn over and cook until brown spots appear on the underside, about 30 seconds. Transfer to a plate and brush lightly with melted butter. Keep warm. Repeat until all dough is used up, adding fresh butter to pan with each chapati and adjusting heat as necessary to prevent burning.

Nutrients per serving

Calories	121
Protein	3.1 g
Carbohydrates	17.8 g
Fat (Total)	4.7 g
Saturated Fat	2.8 g
Monounsaturated Fat	1.2 g
Polyunsaturated Fat	0.4 g
Dietary Fiber	2.8 g
Sodium	175 mg
Cholesterol	11 mg

EXCELLENT SOURCE OF manganese and selenium.

SOURCE OF thiamine, niacin, phosphorus, iron, magnesium, zinc and copper.

CONTAINS a moderate amount of dietary fiber.

Hot Millet Amaranth Cereal

Here's a great way to start your day and add variety to your diet. Both millet and amaranth are relatively quick and easy to cook — so long as you keep the temperature low, they don't need to be stirred. Use a sweetener of your choice and add dried fruit and nuts as you please.

Makes 6 servings

TIP

For best results, toast the millet and amaranth before cooking. Stir the grains in a dry skillet over medium heat until they crackle and release their aroma, about 5 minutes.

2½ cups	water	625 mL
½ cup	millet, toasted (see Tip, left)	125 mL
½ cup	amaranth	125 mL
	Honey, maple syrup or raw cane sugar	
	Milk or non-dairy alternative	
	Dried cranberries, cherries or raisins, optional	
	Toasted chopped nuts, optional	

1. In a saucepan over medium heat, bring water to a boil. Add millet and amaranth in a steady stream, stirring constantly. Return to a boil. Reduce heat to low (see Tip, page 54). Cover and simmer until grains are tender and liquid is absorbed, about 25 minutes. Serve hot, sweetened to taste and with milk or non-dairy alternative. Sprinkle with cranberries and nuts, if using.

Slow Cooker Method

Use a small (3½ quart) lightly greased slow cooker. Combine ingredients in stoneware, adding ½ cup (125 mL) additional water to mixture. Place a clean tea towel, folded in half (so you will have two layers), over top of the stoneware to absorb moisture. Cover and cook on Low for 8 hours or overnight, or on High for 4 hours.

Nutrients per serving

Calories	124
Protein	4.2 g
Carbohydrates	23.3 g
Fat (Total)	1.6 g
Saturated Fat	0.4 g
Monounsaturated Fat	0.3 g
Polyunsaturated Fat	0.7 g
Dietary Fiber	4.0
Sodium	6 mg
Cholesterol	0 mg

EXCELLENT SOURCE OF manganese.
GOOD SOURCE OF magnesium.
SOURCE OF thiamine, niacin, folate, phosphorus, iron, zinc and copper.
CONTAINS a high amount of dietary fiber.

Breakfast Rice

I've enjoyed rice for breakfast since I was a child. It always seemed there were leftovers when we ate it for dinner and it was a simple matter to warm it up in the morning and enjoy a bowl with brown sugar and milk. Nowadays, I make this in a slow cooker overnight. When I wake up the house is fragrant and I enjoy the sense of well-being that hot cereal and a nutritious breakfast provide.

Makes 6 servings

TIP

Unless you have a stove with a true simmer, after reducing the heat to low I recommend placing a heat diffuser under the pot to prevent the mixture from boiling. This device also helps to ensure the grains will cook evenly and prevents hot spots, which might cause scorching, from forming. Heat diffusers are available at kitchen supply and hardware stores and are made to work on gas or electric stoves.

4 cups	vanilla-flavored enriched rice milk	1 L
1 cup	long- or short-grain brown rice, rinsed and drained	250 mL
½ cup	dried cherries, cranberries or blueberries	125 mL
	Raw cane sugar, honey or maple syrup, optional	
	Chopped toasted nuts, optional	

1. In a large saucepan over medium heat, bring rice milk to a boil. Gradually stir in rice and cherries. Return to a boil. Reduce heat to low (see Tip, left). Cover and simmer until rice is tender, about 50 minutes. Stir well and serve with your favorite sweetener, if desired.

Variation

Use half rice and half wheat, spelt or Kamut berries or whole barley. Increase the cooking time to about 1 hour, until the grain is tender.

Slow Cooker Method

Use a small (3½ quart) lightly greased slow cooker. Combine ingredients in stoneware, adding ½ cup (125 mL) water or additional rice milk to mixture. (With the quantity of liquid recommended above, it will be a bit crunchy around the edges.) Place a clean tea towel, folded in half (so you will have two layers), over top of the stoneware to absorb moisture. Cover and cook on Low for up to 8 hours or overnight, or on High for 4 hours.

Nutrients per serving

Calories	242
Protein	3.8 g
Carbohydrates	51.5 g
Fat (Total)	2.5 g
Saturated Fat	0.2 g
Monounsaturated Fat	1.5 g
Polyunsaturated Fat	0.7 g
Dietary Fiber	4.3 g
Sodium	62 mg
Cholesterol	0 mg

EXCELLENT SOURCE OF manganese.

GOOD SOURCE OF calcium, phosphorus, magnesium and selenium.

SOURCE OF vitamin A, thiamine, niacin, iron, zinc and copper.

CONTAINS a high amount of dietary fiber.

Irish Oatmeal

Although rolled oats are very tasty, my favorite oat cereal is steel-cut oats, which are often sold under the name "Irish Oatmeal." They have more flavor than rolled oats and an appealingly crunchy texture.

Makes 6 servings

TIP

Although it's a bit of work to prepare long-cooking whole-grain cereals, such as steel-cut oats, they can actually be quite convenient. Make a big batch on Sunday, cover and refrigerate leftovers. You can enjoy them throughout much of the week. When you're ready to serve, add a little water and cover. Reheat on the stovetop or in a microwave oven.

4 cups	water	1 L
½ tsp	salt	2 mL
1 cup	steel-cut oats	250 mL
	Raisins, chopped bananas or pitted dates, optional	
	Maple syrup, honey, raw cane sugar, optional	
	Toasted nuts and seeds, optional	
	Milk or non-dairy alternative, optional	

1. In a large saucepan over medium heat, bring water and salt to a boil. Gradually stir in oats and return to a boil. Reduce heat to low (see Tip, page 54). Cover and simmer, stirring occasionally, until oats are tender, about 40 minutes. Serve with raisins, maple syrup, nuts and milk or non-dairy alternative, if using.

Slow Cooker Method

Use a small (3½ quart) lightly greased slow cooker. Combine ingredients in stoneware. Cover and cook on Low for 8 hours or overnight, or on High for 4 hours.

Nutrients per serving

Calories	60
Protein	2.4 g
Carbohydrates	10.5 g
Fat (Total)	1.0 g
Saturated Fat	0.3 g
Monounsaturated Fat	0.3 g
Polyunsaturated Fat	0.4 g
Dietary Fiber	1.4 g
Sodium	196 mg
Cholesterol	0 mg

EXCELLENT SOURCE OF manganese.

SOURCE OF thiamine, phosphorus, iron, magnesium and zinc.

Multigrain Cereal with Fruit

A steaming bowl of this tasty cereal gets you off to a good start in the morning and will help to keep you energized and productive throughout the day.

Makes 8 servings

TIP

For best results, toast the millet before cooking. Stir the grains in a dry skillet over medium heat until the millet crackles and releases its aroma, about 5 minutes.

4 cups	water	1 L
¼ tsp	salt, optional	1 mL
½ cup	long- or short-grain brown rice, rinsed and drained	125 mL
½ cup	millet (see Tip, left)	125 mL
½ cup	wheat berries	125 mL
½ tsp	vanilla extract	2 mL
2	all-purpose apples, peeled, cored and thinly sliced	2
½ cup	chopped pitted soft dates, such as Medjool	125 mL
	Milk or non-dairy alternative	
	Maple syrup	
	Chopped toasted nuts, optional	

1. In a large saucepan over medium heat, bring water and salt, if using, to a boil. Gradually stir in rice, millet, wheat berries, vanilla and apples and return to a boil. Reduce heat to low. Cover and simmer, placing a heat diffuser under the pot, if necessary, until wheat berries are tender, about 1 hour. Stir in dates. Serve with milk or non-dairy alternative and maple syrup. Sprinkle with nuts, if using.

Slow Cooker Method

Use a small (3½ quart) lightly greased slow cooker. Combine ingredients, except dates, in stoneware, adding ½ cup (125 mL) additional water to mixture. Place a clean tea towel, folded in half (so you will have two layers), over top of the stoneware to absorb moisture. Cover and cook on Low for 8 hours or overnight, or on High for 4 hours. Stir in dates.

Nutrients per serving

Calories	171
Protein	3.8 g
Carbohydrates	38.5 g
Fat (Total)	1.0 g
Saturated Fat	0.2 g
Monounsaturated Fat	0.2 g
Polyunsaturated Fat	0.4 g
Dietary Fiber	4.2 g
Sodium	5 mg
Cholesterol	0 mg

EXCELLENT SOURCE OF manganese.

GOOD SOURCE OF selenium and magnesium.

SOURCE OF thiamine, niacin, folate, pantothenic acid, phosphorus, iron, zinc and copper.

CONTAINS a high amount of dietary fiber.

Cranberry Quinoa Porridge

If you're not organized enough to make hot cereal ahead of time, here's one you can enjoy in less than half an hour, start to finish, and that doesn't require any attention while it's cooking.

Makes 6 servings

TIP

Unless you have a stove with a true simmer, after reducing the heat to low I recommend placing a heat diffuser under the pot to prevent the mixture from boiling. This device also helps to ensure the grains will cook evenly and prevents hot spots, which might cause scorching, from forming. Heat diffusers are available at kitchen supply and hardware stores and are made to work on gas or electric stoves.

3 cups	water	750 mL
1 cup	quinoa, rinsed and drained	250 mL
½ cup	dried cranberries	125 mL
	Maple syrup or honey	
	Milk or non-diary alternative, optional	

1. In a saucepan over medium heat, bring water to a boil. Stir in quinoa and cranberries and return to a boil. Reduce heat to low. Cover and simmer until quinoa is cooked (look for a white line around the seeds), about 15 minutes. Remove from heat and let stand, covered, about 5 minutes. Serve with maple syrup and milk or non-dairy alternative, if using.

Variations

Substitute dried cherries or blueberries or raisins for the cranberries.

Use red quinoa for a change.

Nutrients per serving

Calories	137
Protein	3.7 g
Carbohydrates	27.8 g
Fat (Total)	1.8 g
Saturated Fat	0.2 g
Monounsaturated Fat	0.5 g
Polyunsaturated Fat	0.7 g
Dietary Fiber	2.5 g
Sodium	8 mg
Cholesterol	0 mg

EXCELLENT SOURCE OF manganese.

GOOD SOURCE OF iron and magnesium.

SOURCE OF riboflavin, niacin, folate, pantothenic acid, phosphorus, zinc and copper.

CONTAINS a moderate amount of dietary fiber.

Orange-Flavored Breakfast Barley with Cranberries and Pecans

Whole barley takes a long time to cook, so I often make this in a slow cooker because I can cook it overnight and wake up to a delicious, nutritious breakfast.

Makes 4 servings

TIP

Unless you have a stove with a true simmer, after reducing the heat to low I recommend placing a heat diffuser under the pot to prevent the mixture from boiling. This device also helps to ensure the grains will cook evenly and prevents hot spots, which might cause scorching, from forming. Heat diffusers are available at kitchen supply and hardware stores and are made to work on gas or electric stoves.

2½ cups	water	625 mL
1 tbsp	finely grated orange zest	15 mL
Pinch	salt	Pinch
½ cup	whole (hulled) barley, rinsed and drained	125 mL
½ cup	dried cranberries	125 mL
¼ cup	toasted chopped pecans	50 mL
	Milk or non-dairy alternative, optional	
	Raw cane sugar, honey or maple syrup, optional	

1. In a saucepan over medium heat, bring water, orange zest and salt to a boil. Stir in barley and cranberries. Return to a boil. Reduce heat to low. Cover and simmer until barley is tender, about 1 hour. Ladle into bowls and garnish with pecans. Serve with milk or non-dairy alternative and/or sugar, if using.

Slow Cooker Method

Use a small (3½ quart) lightly greased slow cooker. Combine all ingredients except pecans in stoneware, adding ½ cup (125 mL) additional water to mixture. Place a clean tea towel, folded in half (so you will have two layers), over top of the stoneware to absorb moisture. Cover and cook on Low for 8 hours or overnight, or on High for 4 hours. Garnish with pecans.

Nutrients per serving

Calories	176
Protein	3.5 g
Carbohydrates	30.6 g
Fat (Total)	5.6 g
Saturated Fat	0.5 g
Monounsaturated Fat	2.9 g
Polyunsaturated Fat	1.8 g
Dietary Fiber	5.6 g
Sodium	6 mg
Cholesterol	0 mg

EXCELLENT SOURCE OF
manganese.

SOURCE OF thiamine, niacin, phosphorus, iron, zinc, copper and selenium.

CONTAINS a high amount of dietary fiber.

Almond-Flavored Millet with Cherries

Since millet is particularly easy to digest, it's an excellent way to get your day off to a great start. Although it's an extra step, I recommend toasting millet before cooking, as it really brings out its pleasing nutty flavor. Once the pot is on the stove, it simmers away on its own requiring no attention from you.

Makes 6 servings

TIPS

Almond milk is available in natural foods stores.

I like to add the dried cherries along with the liquid, as they rehydrate while cooking, becoming almost plump.

Unless you have a stove with a true simmer, after reducing the heat to low I recommend placing a heat diffuser under the pot to prevent the mixture from boiling. This device also helps to ensure the grains will cook evenly and prevents hot spots, which might cause scorching, from forming. Heat diffusers are available at kitchen supply and hardware stores and are made to work on gas or electric stoves.

1 cup	millet	250 mL
4 cups	vanilla-flavored almond milk	1 L
½ cup	dried cherries	125 mL
	Maple syrup or honey	
	Toasted sliced almonds, optional	

1. In a saucepan over medium heat, toast millet, stirring, until it crackles and releases its aroma, about 5 minutes. Transfer to a bowl and set aside. Add almond milk to saucepan and bring to a boil. Gradually stir in millet and cherries and return to a boil. Reduce heat to low (see Tips, left). Cover and simmer until liquid is absorbed, about 30 minutes. Remove from heat and let stand, covered, about 5 minutes. Serve with maple syrup and sprinkle with almonds, if using.

Nutrients per serving

Calories	227
Protein	4.9 g
Carbohydrates	45.5 g
Fat (Total)	3.0 g
Saturated Fat	0.3 g
Monounsaturated Fat	0.3 g
Polyunsaturated Fat	0.6 g
Dietary Fiber	4.6 g
Sodium	105 mg
Cholesterol	0 mg

GOOD SOURCE OF magnesium and manganese.
SOURCE OF thiamine, riboflavin, niacin, folate, phosphorus, iron, zinc and copper.
CONTAINS a high amount of dietary fiber.

Soups

Wheat Berry Minestrone with Leafy Greens

Wheat Berry Minestrone with Leafy Greens

Here's a hearty meal-in-a-bowl that makes a delicious lunch or light supper any time of the year. Wheat berries combined with legumes and leafy greens, such as kale or Swiss chard, make a soup that is equally delicious and nutritious, containing a very high amount of dietary fiber, among other nutrients. I like to serve this soup for supper, accompanied by whole-grain bread and a simple green salad. Leftovers make an excellent second meal, a great snack or a superb welcome home for hungry travelers.

Makes 6 main-course servings

TIPS

For this quantity of beans, soak and cook 1 cup (250 mL) dried beans.

For enhanced flavor, if you have a boot of Parmesan, the tough rind that is left over from a whole piece, add it to the soup along with the tomatoes.

To make crostini: Brush 8 to 10 baguette slices with olive oil on both sides. Toast under preheated broiler, turning once, until golden, about 2 minutes per side.

When using leafy greens, such as kale or Swiss chard, be sure to remove the tough stems before chopping. Also, since they can be quite gritty, pay extra attention when washing. I always swish the leaves around in a basin of lukewarm water to remove any grit, then rinse thoroughly under cold running water before using.

Unless you have a stove with a true simmer, after reducing the heat to low I recommend placing a heat diffuser under the pot to prevent the mixture from boiling. This device also helps to ensure the grains will cook evenly and prevents hot spots, which might cause scorching, from forming. Heat diffusers are available at kitchen supply and hardware stores and are made to work on gas or electric stoves.

2 cups	cooked white kidney beans or 1 can (14 to 19 oz/398 to 540 mL) beans, drained and rinsed (see Tips, left)	500 mL
4 cups	Homemade Vegetable Stock (see recipe, page 75) or reduced-sodium chicken stock, divided	1 L
1 tbsp	olive oil	15 mL
2	onions, chopped	2
4	stalks celery, diced	4
4	cloves garlic, minced	4
2 tsp	dried Italian seasoning	10 mL
¼ tsp	cayenne pepper	1 mL
1 cup	wheat, spelt or Kamut berries, rinsed and drained	250 mL
1	can (14 oz/398 mL) no-salt-added diced tomatoes with juice	1
2 cups	water	500 mL
8 cups	coarsely chopped, trimmed kale or Swiss chard (see Tips, left)	2 L
	Salt and freshly ground black pepper	
	Crostini, optional (see Tips, left)	
	Freshly grated Parmesan cheese, optional	
	Extra virgin olive oil	

1. In a food processor, combine beans with 1 cup (250 mL) of the stock and purée until smooth. Set aside.

2. In a large saucepan or a Dutch oven, heat oil over medium heat for 30 seconds. Add onions and celery and cook, stirring, until celery is softened, about 5 minutes. Add garlic, Italian seasoning and cayenne and cook, stirring, for 1 minute. Add wheat berries, tomatoes with juice, water, reserved bean mixture and remaining 3 cups (750 mL) of the stock and bring to a boil.

3. Reduce heat to low. Cover and simmer until wheat berries are almost tender, about 1 hour. Stir in kale. Cover and cook until kale and wheat berries are tender, about 15 minutes. Season to taste with salt and black pepper.

4. When ready to serve, ladle soup into bowls. Float 1 or 2 crostini in each bowl, if using. Sprinkle liberally with Parmesan, if using, and drizzle with olive oil.

Variation

Substitute an equal quantity of rye berries or farro for the wheat berries. If using farro, check the package to make sure it's a whole-grain version, as well as for cooking times and whether presoaking is required.

Slow Cooker Method

Complete Steps 1 and 2, reducing the quantity of water to 1 cup (250 mL). Transfer mixture to slow cooker stoneware. Cover and cook on Low for 8 hours or on High for 4 hours, until wheat berries are tender. Stir in kale. Cover and cook on High until tender, about 20 minutes. Complete Step 4.

KALE

The kale in this soup is deemed by many researchers to be a "superfood." That's because kale is a member of the Brassica family, a group of vegetables that includes broccoli, cabbage and collard greens, all of which are known to be rich in cancer-protective compounds, among other benefits. Kale is a particularly good source of the phytonutrient sulforaphane, which is formed when the vegetable is chopped or chewed. This substance encourages the liver to produce enzymes that detoxify carcinogenic chemicals and has also been shown (in animal studies) to inhibit the growth of breast cancer. More recent research conducted at Rutgers University found that sulforaphane may inhibit the growth of colon cancer in people who are genetically predisposed to the disease. Over the years, several studies have linked the consumption of cruciferous vegetables, such as kale, with lower rates of prostate, colon and lung cancers. Kale also contains the antioxidant lutein, which may help to keep your eyes healthy, among other benefits.

Nutrient Tip

One serving of this soup will provide a typical woman with about half the recommended daily intake of dietary fiber.

Nutrients per serving

Calories	278
Protein	12.8 g
Carbohydrates	53.9 g
Fat (Total)	3.9 g
Saturated Fat	0.6 g
Monounsaturated Fat	1.8 g
Polyunsaturated Fat	0.8 g
Dietary Fiber	12.0 g
Sodium	85 mg
Cholesterol	0 mg

EXCELLENT SOURCE OF vitamins A and C, thiamine, folate, phosphorus, iron, magnesium, manganese, copper and selenium.

GOOD SOURCE OF vitamin E (alpha-tocopherol), niacin, riboflavin, calcium and zinc.

SOURCE OF pantothenic acid.

CONTAINS a very high amount dietary fiber.

Traditional Cockaleekie Soup

This chicken, leek and barley soup is an old Scottish favorite. The prunes, which deepen the flavor and add a pleasant note of sweetness, are traditional. Although they may seem unconventional, they do enhance the soup, but if you're averse to this image-challenged fruit, they may be omitted and the end result will be something along the lines of a classic chicken soup with barley.

Makes 8 main-course servings

TIPS

Be aware that the cooking times for different varieties of whole barley vary dramatically. Some can take as long as 1¾ hours to cook.

To clean leeks: Fill sink full of lukewarm water. Split leeks in half lengthwise and submerge in water, swishing them around to remove all traces of dirt. Transfer to a colander and rinse under cold water.

10	pitted prunes, finely chopped (about ½ cup/ 125 mL whole pitted prunes), optional	10
3 cups	water, divided	750 mL
1 tbsp	olive oil	15 mL
4	large leeks, white part with just a bit of green, cleaned and thinly sliced (see Tips, left)	4
4	stalks celery, diced	4
4	carrots, peeled and diced	4
1 tsp	dried thyme leaves, crumbled	5 mL
½ tsp	cracked black peppercorns	2 mL
4	whole cloves	4
1	piece cinnamon, about 1 inch (2.5 cm) long	1
1¼ cups	whole (hulled) barley, rinsed and drained	300 mL
2 lbs	skinless boneless chicken thighs, coarsely chopped	1 kg
4 cups	reduced-sodium chicken stock	1 L
½ cup	finely chopped parsley	125 mL

1. In a small bowl, combine prunes and 1 cup (250 mL) of the water. Stir well. Cover and set aside.

2. In a large saucepan, stockpot or Dutch oven, heat oil over medium heat for 30 seconds. Add leeks, celery and carrots and cook, stirring, until softened, about 7 minutes. Add thyme, peppercorns, cloves and cinnamon stick and cook, stirring, for 1 minute. Add barley and toss until well coated with mixture. Add chicken, stock and 2 cups (500 mL) of water and bring to a boil.

3. Reduce heat to low. Cover and simmer until chicken is falling apart and barley is tender, about 1 hour. Discard cloves and cinnamon stick.

4. Add prunes and soaking water, if using. Stir well. Cover and cook to allow flavors to meld, about 15 minutes. Ladle into bowls and garnish with parsley.

Nutrients per serving

Calories	335
Protein	28.0 g
Carbohydrates	38.0 g
Fat (Total)	8.5 g
Saturated Fat	1.9 g
Monounsaturated Fat	3.2 g
Polyunsaturated Fat	2.1 g
Dietary Fiber	7.9 g
Sodium	453 mg
Cholesterol	95 mg

EXCELLENT SOURCE OF vitamin A, niacin, phosphorus, iron, manganese, zinc and selenium.

GOOD SOURCE OF thiamine, riboflavin, folate, pantothenic acid, magnesium and copper.

SOURCE OF vitamins C and E (alpha-tocopherol) and calcium.

CONTAINS a very high amount of dietary fiber.

Slow Cooker Method

Complete Steps 1 and 2, reducing the quantity of water in Step 2 to 1 cup (250 mL). Transfer to slow cooker stoneware. Cover and cook on Low for 8 hours or on High for 4 hours, until barley is tender. Add prunes and soaking water, if using. Cover and cook on High for 15 minutes, until heated through.

Old-Fashioned Scotch Broth

This hearty meal-in-a-bowl is the perfect dish for cold winter weekends. Serve steaming mugs after a brisk walk or a day on the slopes. To enhance the experience, make it in your slow cooker so it's ready and waiting when you come through the door, desperate for some heat-infusing sustenance. Add a tossed salad and whole-grain bread for a great light meal.

Makes 8 main-course servings

Nutrient Tip
Parsnips don't usually spring to mind when thinking about vegetables, but they have a pleasantly sweet taste and provide fiber, folate, potassium and vitamin C, among other nutrients.

Nutrients per serving

Calories	293
Protein	19.5 g
Carbohydrates	39.5 g
Fat (Total)	7.1 g
Saturated Fat	2.0 g
Monounsaturated Fat	3.1 g
Polyunsaturated Fat	1.0 g
Dietary Fiber	9.6 g
Sodium	749 mg
Cholesterol	40 mg

EXCELLENT SOURCE OF vitamin A, thiamine, niacin, iron, manganese, zinc and selenium.

GOOD SOURCE OF vitamin C, folate, riboflavin, phosphorus, magnesium and copper.

SOURCE OF vitamin E (alpha-tocopherol), pantothenic acid and calcium.

CONTAINS a very high amount of dietary fiber.

1 to 2 tbsp	olive oil	15 to 25 mL
1 lb	boneless lamb shoulder or stewing beef, trimmed of fat and diced	500 g
3	leeks, white and light green parts only, cleaned and thinly sliced (see Tips, page 64)	3
4	stalks celery, diced	4
4	carrots, peeled and diced	4
2	parsnips, peeled and diced	2
2 tsp	dried thyme leaves, crumbled	10 mL
½ tsp	cracked black peppercorns	2 mL
1	bay leaf	1
1¼ cups	whole (hulled) barley, rinsed and drained	300 mL
8 cups	reduced-sodium beef stock	2 L
2 cups	water	500 mL
1½ cups	green peas, thawed if frozen	375 mL
½ cup	finely chopped parsley	125 mL

1. In a large saucepan, stockpot or Dutch oven, heat 1 tbsp (15 mL) oil over medium–high heat for 30 seconds. Add lamb, in batches, and cook, stirring, until browned, about 1 minute per batch. Transfer to a plate as completed.

2. Reduce heat to medium. Add more oil to pot, if necessary. Add leeks, celery, carrots and parsnips and cook, stirring, until vegetables are softened, about 7 minutes. Add thyme, peppercorns and bay leaf and cook, stirring, for 1 minute. Add barley and toss until well coated with mixture. Add stock, water and reserved lamb and bring to a boil.

3. Reduce heat to low. Cover and simmer until barley is tender, about 1 hour. Add green peas and cook until tender, about 5 minutes. Discard bay leaf. Serve hot, liberally garnished with parsley.

Slow Cooker Method
Complete Steps 1 and 2, reducing the quantity of water to 1 cup (250 mL), and transfer mixture to slow cooker stoneware. Cover and cook on Low for 8 hours or on High for 4 hours, until barley is tender. Add green peas. Cover and cook on High for 10 minutes, until tender. Garnish with parsley.

Mushroom-Scented Quinoa Congee with Zucchini

It took me a long time to appreciate congee, the bland rice porridge traditionally served for breakfast in Asia. It wasn't until a Chinese friend took me to his favorite restaurant in Vancouver and introduced me to a delicious version made with scallops and a delicate fish broth that I understood the appeal. Although the ingredients and flavors are very different, this thick creamy soup has the same comforting texture and subtle flavoring. I like to serve this for Sunday lunch, but it also makes a great snack any time of the day.

Makes 6 main-course servings

TIPS

I like to use dried portobello, porcini or mixed wild mushrooms in this soup.

White mushrooms work well in this soup, but if you prefer a stronger mushroom taste, use cremini or portobello mushrooms.

Nutrients per serving

Calories	143
Protein	4.4 g
Carbohydrates	24.9 g
Fat (Total)	3.7 g
Saturated Fat	0.5 g
Monounsaturated Fat	2.0 g
Polyunsaturated Fat	0.8 g
Dietary Fiber	3.9 g
Sodium	201 mg
Cholesterol	0 mg

EXCELLENT SOURCE OF copper and manganese.

GOOD SOURCE OF niacin, folate, pantothenic acid, magnesium, phosphorus and iron.

SOURCE OF vitamins A, C and E (alpha-tocopherol), thiamine, riboflavin, zinc and selenium.

CONTAINS a moderate amount of dietary fiber.

1	package (½ oz/14 g) dried mushrooms (see Tips, left)	1
1 cup	hot water	250 mL
1 tbsp	olive oil	15 mL
2	onions, chopped	2
2	cloves garlic, minced	2
1 tsp	dried oregano leaves, crumbled	5 mL
½ tsp	salt	2 mL
½ tsp	freshly ground black pepper	2 mL
8 oz	fresh mushrooms, chopped (see Tips, left)	250 g
¾ cup	quinoa, rinsed and drained	175 mL
4 cups	cubed (½-inch/1 cm) zucchini	1 L
6 cups	Homemade Vegetable Stock (see recipe, page 75) or reduced-sodium chicken stock	1.5 L

1. In a heatproof bowl, soak mushrooms in hot water for 30 minutes. Strain through a coffee filter or a sieve lined with a damp paper towel, reserving liquid. Pat mushrooms dry and chop finely. Set mushrooms and liquid aside separately.

2. In a stockpot or large saucepan, heat oil over medium heat for 30 seconds. Add onions and cook, stirring, until softened, about 3 minutes. Add garlic, oregano, salt, pepper and reserved dried mushrooms and cook, stirring, for 1 minute. Add fresh mushrooms and cook, stirring, until well coated with mixture. Add quinoa and cook, stirring until coated. Add zucchini, stock and reserved mushroom soaking liquid and bring to a boil.

3. Reduce heat to low. Cover loosely and simmer until zucchini is tender and quinoa is cooked, about 15 minutes. Remove from heat. Using an immersion blender, purée soup. (You can also do this, in batches, in a food processor.) Serve immediately.

Variation

Mushroom-Scented Millet Congee with Zucchini: Substitute an equal quantity of toasted millet for the quinoa. Cook a bit longer, about 25 minutes.

Luscious Avgolemono Soup with Wheat Berries

This classic Greek soup, usually made with orzo or white rice, takes on a whole new spin when made with nutrient-packed wheat berries. I love their heft and slightly crunchy texture, which transforms this tasty concoction into a light main course. If you prefer an even more substantial soup, add cooked chicken. In either case, follow with a tossed green salad for a complete meal.

2½ cups	cooked wheat, spelt or Kamut berries (see cooking instructions, page 34)	625 mL
1 tbsp	olive oil	15 mL
3	leeks, white and light green parts only, cleaned and sliced (see Tips, page 64)	3
1 tsp	paprika	5 mL
8 cups	reduced-sodium chicken or vegetable stock	2 L
½ cup	chopped fresh dill	125 mL
⅓ to ½ cup	freshly squeezed lemon juice (see Tips, left)	75 to 125 mL
4	egg yolks	4
	Shredded cooked chicken, optional	
	Salt and freshly ground black pepper	

Makes 6 main-course servings

TIPS

Vary the quantity of lemon juice to suit your taste. The smaller quantity produces a nicely lemony soup. If you really enjoy a strong lemon flavor, choose the larger amount.

Once you've added the egg mixture to the soup, watch carefully to be sure it doesn't boil. Otherwise, you'll have curdled eggs in your soup.

1. In a large saucepan or stockpot, heat oil over medium heat for 30 seconds. Add leeks and cook, stirring, until softened, about 5 minutes. Add paprika and cook, stirring, for 1 minute. Add cooked wheat berries and stock and bring to a boil. Reduce heat and simmer for 10 minutes to blend flavors.

2. Stir in dill. Remove from heat. Using an immersion blender, purée soup. (You can also do this, in batches, in a food processor.) Return to low heat. Add chicken, if using, and heat until warm.

3. In a small bowl, whisk lemon juice and egg yolks. Gradually beat in 1 cup (250 mL) of the hot stock, whisking constantly. Return to pot and cook, stirring, for 1 minute. Remove from heat (see Tips, left). Season to taste with salt and pepper.

Nutrients per serving

Calories	197
Protein	9.2 g
Carbohydrates	27.7 g
Fat (Total)	6.6 g
Saturated Fat	1.5 g
Monounsaturated Fat	3.4 g
Polyunsaturated Fat	1.0 g
Dietary Fiber	4.4 g
Sodium	817 mg
Cholesterol	137 mg

EXCELLENT SOURCE OF manganese and selenium.

GOOD SOURCE OF folate, phosphorus, iron and magnesium.

SOURCE OF vitamins A, C and E (alpha-tocopherol), thiamine, riboflavin, niacin, pantothenic acid, calcium, zinc and copper.

CONTAINS a high amount of dietary fiber.

Slow Cooker Method

Rinse the wheat berries, but do not precook them. Complete Step 1, reducing the quantity of stock to 7 cups (1.75 mL). Transfer to slow cooker stoneware. Cover and cook on Low for 8 hours or on High for 4 hours, until wheat berries are tender. Continue with Step 2. If adding chicken, heat on High until heated through, about 15 minutes. Ensure temperature is set to High and complete Step 3.

Gingery Chicken and Wild Rice Soup

The addition of a flavorful whole grain, leeks and a hint of ginger is a particularly delicious spin on classic chicken and rice soup. I like to make the stock a day ahead so it can be refrigerated, which makes easy work of skimming off the fat (see Tip, below). This makes a great light dinner accompanied by whole-grain rolls and a tossed salad.

Makes 6 main-course servings

TIP

For best results, make the stock and cook the chicken the day before you plan to serve the soup. Cover and refrigerate stock and chicken separately. The fat will rise to the surface of the stock and can be easily removed. It will be easy to remove the skin and chop the cold chicken. Save the excess chicken to make sandwiches or a salad such as Chicken and Wheat Berry Salad with Avocado (see recipe, page 87).

Nutrients per serving	
Calories	269
Protein	21.8 g
Carbohydrates	27.0 g
Fat (Total)	8.3 g
Saturated Fat	1.9 g
Monounsaturated Fat	3.9 g
Polyunsaturated Fat	1.7 g
Dietary Fiber	2.4 g
Sodium	276 mg
Cholesterol	79 mg

EXCELLENT SOURCE OF niacin, phosphorus and manganese.
GOOD SOURCE OF thiamine, folate, pantothenic acid, magnesium, zinc and selenium.
SOURCE OF vitamin E (alpha-tocopherol), riboflavin, iron and copper.
CONTAINS a moderate amount dietary fiber.

1	whole chicken (about 3 lbs/1.5 kg), cut into pieces	1
1	onion, coarsely chopped	1
2	carrots, peeled and diced	2
2	stalks celery, diced	2
4	sprigs parsley	4
1	clove garlic	1
1	bay leaf	1
½ tsp	salt	2 mL
½ tsp	cracked black peppercorns	2 mL
12 cups	water	3 L
1 tbsp	olive oil	15 mL
2	large leeks, white part only, cleaned and sliced (see Tip, page 64)	2
2	cloves garlic, minced	2
2 tbsp	minced gingerroot	25 mL
1 cup	brown and wild rice mixture, rinsed and drained (see Tips, page 89)	250 mL

1. In a stockpot, combine chicken, onion, carrots, celery, parsley, whole garlic, bay leaf, salt, peppercorns and water. Bring to a boil over high heat. Using a slotted spoon, skim off foam. Reduce heat to medium–low and simmer, uncovered, until chicken is falling off the bone, about 1½ hours. Drain, reserving chicken and liquid separately. Let cool. Cut the chicken into bite-size pieces, discarding skin and bones. Skim off fat from the stock (see Tip, left).

2. Measure 2 cups (500 mL) of chicken and set aside in the refrigerator. (Refrigerate remainder for other uses, see Tip, left.) In a large saucepan or stockpot, heat oil over medium heat for 30 seconds. Add leeks and cook, stirring, until softened, about 5 minutes. Add minced garlic and ginger and cook, stirring, for 1 minute. Add rice and toss to coat. Add reserved stock and bring to a boil. Reduce heat and simmer, uncovered, until rice is quite tender, about 1 hour. Add reserved chicken. Cover and simmer until chicken is heated through, about 15 minutes.

Variation

Substitute an equal quantity of rinsed wild rice for the mixture. You may need to increase the cooking time, depending upon the size of the grains.

Creamy Cabbage Borscht with Bulgur and Dill

This is a lighter version of traditional borscht, made lusciously creamy with the addition of fontina cheese. Make sure your stock is flavorful. If necessary, make an enhanced stock (see Tip, below). I like to serve this as the centerpiece of a soup and salad dinner, accompanied by rye bread and a sliced tomato or grated carrot salad.

Makes 6 main-course servings

TIP

To enhance this quantity of stock, place in a large saucepan with 2 peeled and coarsely chopped carrots, 1 tsp (5 mL) celery seeds, 1 tsp (5 mL) cracked black peppercorns, ½ tsp (2 mL) dried thyme, 4 parsley sprigs, 1 bay leaf and 1 cup (250 mL) dry white wine. Bring to a boil and simmer, covered, for 30 minutes. Strain.

Nutrients per serving

Calories	305
Protein	17.4 g
Carbohydrates	28.5 g
Fat (Total)	14.9 g
Saturated Fat	7.7 g
Monounsaturated Fat	5.1 g
Polyunsaturated Fat	1.2 g
Dietary Fiber	5.2 g
Sodium	1170 mg
Cholesterol	47 mg

EXCELLENT SOURCE OF manganese.
GOOD SOURCE OF vitamin A, calcium, phosphorus, magnesium, zinc and selenium.
SOURCE OF vitamins C and E (alpha-tocopherol), niacin, thiamine, riboflavin, folate, pantothenic acid, iron and copper.
CONTAINS a high amount of dietary fiber.

1 tbsp	olive oil	15 mL
2	onions, finely chopped	2
4	cloves garlic, minced	4
1 tbsp	caraway seeds	15 mL
2 tsp	sweet paprika	10 mL
	Freshly ground black pepper	
2 tbsp	tomato paste	25 mL
8 cups	reduced-sodium beef, mushroom or vegetable stock (see Tip, left)	2 L
1 cup	bulgur	250 mL
6 cups	shredded cabbage	1.5 L
½ cup	finely chopped dill	125 mL
2 cups	shredded fontina cheese	500 mL

1. In a large saucepan, stockpot or Dutch oven, heat oil over medium heat for 30 seconds. Add onions and cook, stirring, until softened, about 3 minutes. Add garlic, caraway seeds, paprika and pepper to taste and cook, stirring, for 1 minute. Stir in tomato paste. Add stock and bring to a boil. Gradually stir in bulgur. Add cabbage and bring to a boil. Reduce heat to low. Cover and simmer until cabbage is tender, about 30 minutes.

2. Stir in dill. Add cheese, stirring until melted. Serve immediately.

Variation

Cabbage Borscht: Omit fontina cheese. Top each serving with a dollop of sour cream.

Fennel-Scented Tomato and Wild Rice Soup

If, like me, you get cravings for tomatoes, this soup is for you. It's especially welcome in the winter when delicious fresh tomatoes are hard to find. When made with fire-roasted tomatoes (see Tips, left), it provides a real tomato hit. The fennel brings intriguing licorice flavor, which complements the tomatoes, and the wild rice adds texture and nutrients such as dietary fiber to make this soup particularly enjoyable.

Makes 8 servings

TIPS

Toasting fennel seeds intensifies their flavor. To toast fennel seeds, stir them in a dry skillet over medium heat until fragrant, about 3 minutes. Transfer to a mortar or spice grinder and grind.

For a slightly more intense tomato flavor, substitute 2 cans (each 14 oz/398 mL) fire-roasted tomatoes with juice for the crushed tomatoes.

Cooking times for wild rice vary. Expect your grains to be cooked anywhere between 50 minutes to more than 1 hour.

Nutrients per serving

Calories	123
Protein	4.5 g
Carbohydrates	23.9 g
Fat (Total)	2.3 g
Saturated Fat	0.3 g
Monounsaturated Fat	1.3 g
Polyunsaturated Fat	0.4 g
Dietary Fiber	4.3 g
Sodium	50 mg
Cholesterol	0 mg

EXCELLENT SOURCE OF manganese.

GOOD SOURCE OF folate, iron, magnesium and copper.

SOURCE OF vitamins A, C and E (alpha-tocopherol), thiamine, riboflavin, niacin, pantothenic acid, calcium, phosphorus and zinc.

CONTAINS a high amount of dietary fiber.

1 tbsp	olive oil	15 mL
2	leeks, white part only with just a hint of green, cleaned and sliced (see Tips, page 74)	2
1	bulb fennel, base and leafy stems discarded, bulb thinly sliced on the vertical	1
3	cloves garlic, sliced	3
1 tsp	fennel seeds, toasted and ground (see Tips, left)	5 mL
½ tsp	salt, optional	2 mL
½ tsp	freshly ground black pepper	2 mL
5 cups	Homemade Vegetable Stock (see recipe, page 75) or reduced-sodium chicken stock, divided	1.25 L
1	can (28 oz/796 mL) crushed tomatoes (see Tips, left)	1
¾ cup	wild rice, rinsed and drained	175 mL
	Whipping (35%) cream, optional	
	Finely chopped parsley	

1. In a large saucepan or stockpot, heat oil over medium heat for 30 seconds. Add leeks and fennel and cook, stirring, until vegetables are softened, about 7 minutes. Add garlic, fennel seeds, salt, if using, and pepper and cook, stirring, for 1 minute. Stir in 2 cups (500 mL) of the stock and tomatoes. Remove from heat. Using an immersion blender, purée soup. (You can also do this, in batches, in a food processor, and return to the pot.) Return to medium heat. Add remaining stock and wild rice and bring to a boil.

2. Reduce heat to low. Cover and cook until rice is tender and grains have begun to split, about 1 hour. Ladle into bowls, drizzle with cream, if using, and garnish with parsley.

Slow Cooker Method

Complete Step 1, reducing the quantity of stock to 4 cups (1 L). Transfer contents of saucepan to slow cooker stoneware. Cover and cook on Low for 8 hours or on High for 4 hours, until rice is tender.

Fragrant Beef and Barley Soup with Chinese Mushrooms

Here's an updated version of a classic soup — beef, barley and mushrooms. The Chinese accents add intriguing flavors and give it a global spin without detracting from its traditional appeal. It's still a great cold weather pick-me-up — I can't imagine anything more perfect for après ski than a steaming bowl of this hearty brew.

Makes 6 main-course servings

TIPS

Chinese 5-spice powder is available in the spice section of well-stocked supermarkets or in Asian markets.

If desired, use 1 box (1 quart/ 900 mL) ready-to-use reduced-sodium beef stock for this quantity.

If you prefer a milder mushroom flavor, substitute 1 package (½ oz/14 g) dried wood ear mushrooms for the dried shiitakes.

Unless you have a stove with a true simmer, after reducing the heat to low I recommend placing a heat diffuser under the pot to prevent the mixture from boiling. This device also helps to ensure the grains will cook evenly and prevents hot spots, which might cause scorching, from forming. Heat diffusers are available at kitchen supply and hardware stores and are made to work on gas or electric stoves.

8	dried shiitake mushrooms	8
4 cups	hot water	1 L
1 tbsp	vegetable oil	15 mL
8 oz	stewing beef, trimmed and cut into bite-size pieces	250 g
2	onions, finely chopped	2
4	stalks celery, diced	4
8 oz	fresh shiitake mushrooms, stems removed and caps sliced	250 g
1 tbsp	minced garlic	15 mL
1 tbsp	minced gingerroot	15 mL
½ tsp	freshly ground black pepper	2 mL
½ tsp	Chinese 5-spice powder (see Tips, left)	2 mL
⅔ cup	whole (hulled) barley, rinsed and drained	150 mL
4 cups	reduced-sodium beef stock (see Tips, left)	1 L
¼ cup	reduced-sodium soy sauce	50 mL
	Finely chopped green onions, optional	

1. In a bowl, combine dried shiitake mushrooms with hot water. Let stand for 30 minutes. Strain through a coffee filter or a sieve lined with a damp paper towel, reserving liquid. Remove stems. Pat mushrooms dry and chop finely. Set mushrooms and liquid aside separately.

2. In a stockpot or Dutch oven, heat oil over medium heat for 30 seconds. Add beef, onions, celery, fresh mushrooms and reserved dry mushrooms and cook, stirring, for 1 minute. Reduce heat to low. Cover and cook until vegetables are softened, about 8 minutes. Add garlic, ginger, pepper and 5-spice powder and cook, stirring, for 1 minute. Add barley and toss until well coated with mixture. Add stock and reserved mushroom soaking water and bring to a boil over high heat.

3. Reduce heat, loosely cover and simmer gently until barley is tender, about 1 hour. Stir in soy sauce. Ladle into bowls and garnish with green onions, if using.

Vegetarian Alternative

Barley Soup with Chinese Mushrooms: Substitute 8 oz (250 g) stemmed, gilled, chopped portobello mushrooms for the stewing beef and an equal quantity of vegetable or mushroom stock for the beef stock. If using mushroom stock, you may want to substitute dried wood ear mushrooms for the dried shiitakes (see Tips, left) to ensure the soup doesn't have too strong a mushroom taste.

Slow Cooker Method

Complete Steps 1 and 2, reducing the quantity of hot water to 3 cups (750 mL). Transfer contents of stockpot to slow cooker stoneware. Cover and cook on Low for 8 hours or on High for 4 hours, until barley is tender. Stir in soy sauce and continue with Step 3.

SHIITAKE MUSHROOMS

I love the shiitake mushrooms in this soup, not only for the deep rich flavor they add to the broth, but also for their superb nutritional profile. Shiitake mushrooms, which have been used in Chinese medicine for thousands of years, are thought to promote longevity, and once you understand the nutrients they contain, it's easy to see why. When the USDA updated its nutrient data on mushrooms in 2006, they found that all varieties were a significant source of copper and potassium, while providing smaller amounts of key nutrients, such as folate and niacin. And, thanks to new analytical tools, researchers at Pennsylvania State University recently discovered that mushrooms are the richest food source of ergothioneine, a powerful antioxidant. Depending upon the variety, mushrooms contain up to 40 times more ergothioneine than wheat germ, which was previously thought to be the richest food source. Shiitake mushrooms also contain lentinan, a compound that appears to strengthen the immune system and may have cancer-fighting properties.

Nutrients per serving	
Calories	211
Protein	15.2 g
Carbohydrates	26.7 g
Fat (Total)	5.7 g
Saturated Fat	1.3 g
Monounsaturated Fat	2.4 g
Polyunsaturated Fat	1.1 g
Dietary Fiber	5.9 g
Sodium	840 mg
Cholesterol	20 mg

EXCELLENT SOURCE OF manganese and zinc.

GOOD SOURCE OF thiamine, niacin, riboflavin, pantothenic acid, selenium, phosphorus and iron.

SOURCE OF vitamins C and E (alpha-tocopherol), folate, copper and magnesium.

CONTAINS a high amount of dietary fiber.

Turkish-Style Wheat Berry Soup

The flavors in this soup are classic Middle Eastern and it's hard to believe such a simple recipe can taste so delicious. The slightly crunchy wheat berries add great depth of flavor as well as texture. The yogurt and lemon juice finish adds creaminess, as well as a pleasant hint of tartness.

Makes 6 servings

TIPS

Unless you have a stove with a true simmer, after reducing the heat to low I recommend placing a heat diffuser under the pot to prevent the mixture from boiling. This device also helps to ensure the grains will cook evenly and prevents hot spots, which might cause scorching, from forming. Heat diffusers are available at kitchen supply and hardware stores and are made to work on gas or electric stoves.

To clean leeks: Fill sink full of lukewarm water. Split leeks in half lengthwise and submerge in water, swishing them around to remove all traces of dirt. Transfer to a colander and rinse under cold water.

1 tbsp	cumin seeds	15 mL
1 tbsp	olive oil	15 mL
2	leeks, white part only with just a hint of green, cleaned and thinly sliced (see Tips, left)	2
4	cloves garlic, minced	4
2 tsp	freshly grated lemon zest	10 mL
	Salt and freshly ground black pepper	
8 cups	Homemade Vegetable Stock with no-salt-added or reduced-sodium vegetable or chicken stock (see recipe, right)	2 L
¼ tsp	crumbled saffron threads, dissolved in 2 tbsp (25 mL) boiling water	1 mL
1 cup	wheat, spelt or Kamut berries, rinsed and drained	250 mL
⅓ cup	freshly squeezed lemon juice	75 mL
½ cup	finely chopped parsley	125 mL
	Plain yogurt	

1. In a dry stockpot or Dutch oven, toast cumin seeds over medium heat, stirring constantly, until fragrant, about 3 minutes. Transfer to a mortar or spice grinder and grind. Set aside.

2. Add oil to pot and heat over medium heat for 30 seconds. Add leeks and cook, stirring, until softened, about 5 minutes. Add garlic, lemon zest, salt and pepper to taste and reserved cumin and cook, stirring, for 1 minute. Add stock, saffron liquid and wheat berries and bring to a boil.

3. Reduce heat to low. Cover and simmer until wheat berries are tender, about 1½ hours. Stir in lemon juice and parsley and adjust seasoning, if necessary. Cover and simmer to blend flavors, for 5 minutes. To serve, ladle soup into bowls and top with a dollop of yogurt.

Variation

Turkish-Style Barley Soup: Substitute an equal quantity of barley for the wheat berries.

Slow Cooker Method

Complete Steps 1 and 2, reducing the quantity of stock to 7 cups (1.75 mL). Transfer to slow cooker stoneware. Cover and cook on Low for 8 hours or on High for 4 hours, until wheat berries are tender. Stir in lemon juice and parsley and continue with Step 3.

HOMEMADE VEGETABLE STOCK

You can dramatically reduce your sodium intake by making your own vegetable stock with no salt added. Use your favorite recipe or make this simple version. In a stockpot, combine 12 cups (3 L) water, 6 sprigs parsley, 3 bay leaves, 10 black peppercorns and 1 tsp (5 mL) dried thyme leaves with 3 onions and 3 cloves garlic, coarsely chopped. Add 8 carrots and 6 stalks celery, scrubbed and coarsely chopped. Bring to a boil over high heat. Reduce heat to low. Cover and simmer for 2 hours. Strain and discard solids. Cover and refrigerate for up to 5 days or freeze in an airtight container. If you prefer, make the stock in your slow cooker. Cover and cook on Low for 8 hours or on High for 4 hours.

Nutrients per serving	
Calories	158
Protein	3.8 g
Carbohydrates	26.9 g
Fat (Total)	5.3 g
Saturated Fat	0.7 g
Monounsaturated Fat	3.5 g
Polyunsaturated Fat	0.7 g
Dietary Fiber	4.5 g
Sodium	10 mg
Cholesterol	0 mg

EXCELLENT SOURCE OF
manganese and selenium.

GOOD SOURCE OF phosphorus, iron and magnesium.

SOURCE OF vitamins C and E (alpha-tocopherol), thiamine, niacin, folate, zinc and copper.

CONTAINS a high amount of dietary fiber.

Curried Sweet Potato and Millet Soup

This soup is a lovely combination of flavors and texture. It has a mild curry taste, enhanced with the addition of orange and a hint of sweetness from the maple syrup. The toasted walnuts add taste and an appealing bit of crunch, while the optional yogurt provides a creamy finish. Although this is a great cold weather soup, it's light enough to be enjoyed any time of the year — perhaps even for dinner with the addition of salad and some whole-grain bread.

Makes 6 servings

TIPS

To get this quantity of puréed sweet potato, bake, peel and mash 2 medium sweet potatoes, each about 6 oz (175 g). You can also use a can (14 oz/398 mL) sweet potato purée.

While it's not necessary to toast millet, toasting does bring out its pleasantly nutty flavor. To toast millet, heat in a dry skillet over medium heat, stirring constantly, until it crackles and releases its aroma, about 5 minutes.

Nutrients per serving

Calories	240
Protein	4.8 g
Carbohydrates	48.8 g
Fat (Total)	3.5 g
Saturated Fat	0.4 g
Monounsaturated Fat	1.6 g
Polyunsaturated Fat	1.2 g
Dietary Fiber	5.5 g
Sodium	46 mg
Cholesterol	0 mg

EXCELLENT SOURCE OF vitamin A and manganese.

GOOD SOURCE OF vitamin C, thiamine, folate, magnesium and zinc.

SOURCE OF vitamin E (alpha-tocopherol), riboflavin, niacin, pantothenic acid, calcium, phosphorus, iron and copper.

CONTAINS a high amount of dietary fiber.

1 tbsp	vegetable oil	15 mL
2	onions, finely chopped	2
2	carrots, peeled and diced	2
2	stalks celery, diced	2
2	cloves garlic, minced	2
2 tsp	minced gingerroot	10 mL
2 tsp	curry powder	10 mL
1 tsp	freshly grated orange zest	5 mL
2 cups	sweet potato purée (see Tips, left)	500 mL
6 cups	Homemade Vegetable Stock (see recipe, page 75) or reduced-sodium chicken stock	1.5 L
¾ cup	millet, toasted (see Tips, left)	175 mL
1 cup	freshly squeezed orange juice	250 mL
¼ cup	pure maple syrup	50 mL
	Salt and freshly ground black pepper	
	Toasted chopped walnuts or sliced almonds	
	Plain yogurt, optional	

1. In a large saucepan or stockpot, heat oil over medium heat for 30 seconds. Add onions, carrots and celery and cook, stirring, until carrots have softened, about 7 minutes.

2. Add garlic, ginger, curry powder and orange zest and cook, stirring, for 1 minute. Add sweet potato and stock and stir well. Bring to a boil. Stir in millet. Reduce heat to low. Cover and simmer until millet is tender and flavors have blended, about 30 minutes.

3. Add orange juice and maple syrup and heat through. Season to taste with salt and pepper. Ladle into bowls and garnish with toasted walnuts and a drizzle of yogurt, if using.

Variation

Curried Sweet Potato and Quinoa Soup: Substitute an equal quantity of quinoa for the millet. Do not toast it, but rinse thoroughly before adding to the soup.

Southwestern Turkey Chowder

This soup is so good I can't wait to finish the celebratory turkey and get it started. I think it's the best way to use up leftover turkey and any leftover bits of long-cooking whole grains. If you're planning to eat lightly following a holiday, it makes a perfect dinner with the addition of salad.

TIPS

For the best flavor, toast and grind whole cumin seeds rather than buying ground cumin. Simply stir seeds in a dry skillet over medium heat until fragrant, about 3 minutes. Immediately transfer to a spice grinder or mortar and grind.

Use any combination of long-cooking whole grains in this soup, such as barley, wheat berries or brown, red or wild rice. All will be delicious.

10 cups	turkey stock (see recipe, right)	2.5 L
1 tbsp	olive oil	15 mL
3	onions, diced	3
4	stalks celery, diced	4
1 tbsp	ground cumin (see Tips, left)	15 mL
2 tsp	dried oregano leaves	10 mL
4	cloves garlic, minced	4
½ tsp	cracked black peppercorns	2 mL
1½ cups	long-cooking whole grains, rinsed and drained (see Tips, left)	375 mL
1	can (28 oz/796 mL) no-salt-added diced tomatoes with juice	1
2 to 3	ancho, guajillo or mild New Mexico dried chiles	2 to 3
1 cup	loosely packed fresh cilantro leaves	250 mL
2 cups	diced cooked turkey	500 mL
2 cups	corn kernels	500 mL

1. In a stockpot, heat oil over medium heat for 30 seconds. Add onions and celery and cook, stirring, until vegetables are softened, about 5 minutes. Add cumin, oregano, garlic and peppercorns and cook, stirring, for 1 minute. Add whole grains and toss until coated. Add tomatoes with juice and stock and bring to a boil.

2. Reduce heat to low. Cover and simmer until grains are tender, about 1 hour.

3. In a heatproof bowl, 30 minutes before grains have finished cooking, combine dried chiles and 2 cups (500 mL) boiling water. Set aside for 30 minutes, weighing chiles down with a cup to ensure they remain submerged. Drain, discarding soaking liquid and stems and chop coarsely. Transfer to a blender. Add cilantro and ½ cup (125 mL) of stock from the chowder. Purée. Add to stockpot along with the turkey and corn. Cover and cook until corn is tender and flavors meld, about 20 minutes.

Variation

Southwestern Chicken Chowder: Substitute chicken stock for the turkey stock and diced cooked chicken for the turkey.

Slow Cooker Method

Complete Step 1, reducing the quantity of turkey stock to 9 cups (2. 25 L), and transfer to slow cooker stoneware. Cover and cook on Low for 8 hours or High for 4 hours, until grains are tender. Complete Step 3. After adding the chile mixture, turkey and corn, cover and cook on High until corn is tender, about 20 minutes.

TURKEY STOCK

To make turkey stock, break the carcass into manageable pieces and place in a stockpot. Add 2 each carrots, celery stalks and onions, quartered, plus 8 whole peppercorns. Add water to cover. Bring to a boil over medium–high heat. Reduce heat to low. Cover and simmer for 3 hours. Strain, reserving liquid and discarding solids.

Nutrients per serving

Calories	320
Protein	21.4 g
Carbohydrates	48.0 g
Fat (Total)	6.6 g
Saturated Fat	1.5 g
Monounsaturated Fat	2.6 g
Polyunsaturated Fat	1.8 g
Dietary Fiber	8.3 g
Sodium	107 mg
Cholesterol	51 mg

EXCELLENT SOURCE OF niacin, phosphorus, iron, magnesium, manganese, zinc and selenium.

GOOD SOURCE OF vitamin A, folate, thiamine, riboflavin, pantothenic acid and copper.

SOURCE OF vitamins C and E (alpha-tocopherol) and calcium.

CONTAINS a very high amount of dietary fiber.

Miso-Spiked Vegetable Soup with Barley

Here's a hearty vegetable soup that's the perfect antidote to a blustery day. The addition of miso adds robustness and a hint of complexity, which is often lacking in simple vegetable soups. Serve this with your favorite sandwich for a delicious soup and sandwich meal.

Makes 6 main-course servings

TIPS

If you have fresh thyme, use 2 sprigs, stem and all. Remove and discard before serving.

I haven't added salt because the miso is quite salty. Taste and adjust seasoning when the soup is completed, if necessary.

Stir in freshly grated Parmesan for a hint of creaminess and additional flavor, if desired.

Nutrients per serving	
Calories	204
Protein	6.9 g
Carbohydrates	37.9 g
Fat (Total)	4.0 g
Saturated Fat	0.6 g
Monounsaturated Fat	1.9 g
Polyunsaturated Fat	1.1 g
Dietary Fiber	9.8 g
Sodium	477 mg
Cholesterol	0 mg

EXCELLENT SOURCE OF vitamin A and manganese.

GOOD SOURCE OF thiamine, niacin, folate, iron, zinc and selenium.

SOURCE OF vitamins C and E (alpha-tocopherol), riboflavin, pantothenic acid, calcium, phosphorus, magnesium and copper.

CONTAINS a very high amount of dietary fiber.

1 tbsp	olive oil	15 mL
2	onions, finely chopped	2
4	carrots, peeled and diced	4
4	stalks celery, diced	4
1 tsp	dried thyme (see Tips, left)	5 mL
	Freshly ground black pepper (see Tips, left)	
1 cup	whole (hulled) barley, rinsed and drained	250 mL
8 cups	Homemade Vegetable Stock (see recipe, page 75)	2 L
2 cups	sliced green beans	500 mL
¼ cup	dark miso	50 mL
½ cup	finely chopped parsley	125 mL
	Freshly grated Parmesan cheese, optional (see Tips, left)	

1. In a large saucepan or stockpot, heat oil over medium heat for 30 seconds. Add onions, carrots and celery and cook, stirring, until carrots are softened, about 7 minutes. Stir in thyme and season to taste with pepper. Add barley and toss until well coated with mixture. Add stock and bring to a boil.

2. Reduce heat to low. Cover and simmer until barley is tender, about 1 hour. Add green beans and miso. Cover and cook until beans are tender and flavors meld, about 15 minutes. Stir in parsley and serve. Garnish with Parmesan, if using.

Slow Cooker Method

Complete Step 1, reducing the quantity of stock to 7 cups (1.75 L), and transfer to slow cooker stoneware. Cover and cook on Low for 8 hours or on High for 4 hours, until barley is tender. Add green beans and miso. Cover and cook on High, until beans are tender, about 15 minutes. Continue with Step 2.

Minestrone Genovese

A specialty of Genoa, Italy, this robust soup is distinguished by the addition of basil pesto. The porcini mushrooms add earthiness and the brown rice, along with the traditional puréed beans, helps to thicken the soup. Served with whole-grain bread and a tossed salad, this makes a substantial and satisfying meal.

Makes 6 main-course servings

TIP

Unless you have a stove with a true simmer, after reducing the heat to low I recommend placing a heat diffuser under the pot to prevent the mixture from boiling. This device also helps to ensure the grains will cook evenly and prevents hot spots, which might cause scorching, from forming. Heat diffusers are available at kitchen supply and hardware stores and are made to work on gas or electric stoves.

Nutrients per serving

Calories	277
Protein	7.9 g
Carbohydrates	46.9 g
Fat (Total)	7.3 g
Saturated Fat	1.1 g
Monounsaturated Fat	3.1 g
Polyunsaturated Fat	2.3 g
Dietary Fiber	9.1 g
Sodium	305 mg
Cholesterol	1 mg

EXCELLENT SOURCE OF vitamin A, magnesium and manganese.

GOOD SOURCE OF folate, thiamine, niacin, pantothenic acid, phosphorus and copper.

SOURCE OF vitamins C and E (alpha-tocopherol), riboflavin, calcium, iron, zinc and selenium.

CONTAINS a very high amount of dietary fiber.

1	package (½ oz/14 g) dried porcini mushrooms	1
2 cups	hot water	500 mL
1	can (14 to 19 oz/398 to 540 mL) white kidney beans, drained and rinsed	1
6 cups	Homemade Vegetable Stock (see recipe, page 75) or reduced-sodium chicken stock, divided	1.5 L
2 tbsp	tomato paste	25 mL
1 tbsp	olive oil	15 mL
2	onions, finely chopped	2
2	carrots, peeled and diced	2
2	stalks celery, diced	2
4	cloves garlic, minced	4
1	dried red chile pepper, optional	1
	Salt and freshly ground black pepper	
1 cup	short-grain brown rice, rinsed and drained	250 mL
4 cups	shredded cabbage	1 L
1 cup	sliced green beans	250 mL
¼ cup	basil pesto	50 mL
	Freshly grated Parmesan cheese	

1. In a bowl, soak dried mushrooms in hot water for 30 minutes. Strain through a coffee filter or a sieve lined with a damp paper towel, reserving liquid. Pat mushrooms dry and chop finely. Set aside.

2. In a food processor, combine 1 cup (250 mL) of the beans, 1 cup (250 mL) of the stock and tomato paste and purée until smooth. Set aside.

3. In a large saucepan or stockpot, heat oil over medium heat for 30 seconds. Add onions, carrots and celery and cook, stirring, until carrots are softened, about 7 minutes. Add garlic, reserved chopped mushrooms, chile pepper, if using, and salt and pepper to taste. Cook, stirring, for 1 minute. Add rice and toss until well coated with mixture. Add whole and puréed beans, remaining stock and mushroom soaking liquid and bring to a boil.

4. Reduce heat to low. Cover and simmer for 45 minutes. Return to a boil. Stir in cabbage and green beans and cook until beans and rice are tender, about 8 minutes. Remove from heat and stir in pesto. Ladle into bowls and top with Parmesan.

Slow Cooker Method

Complete Steps 1, 2 and 3 but soak the mushrooms in only 1 cup (250 mL) of hot water. Cover and cook on Low for 8 hours on low or on High for 4 hours. Stir in cabbage and green beans. Cover and cook on High until beans and cabbage are tender, about 20 minutes.

Thai-Inspired Peanut and Wild Rice Soup

If your taste buds have grown tired of the same old thing, here's a delightfully different soup to wake them up. With basic flavors that are reminiscent of Thai peanut sauce and the addition of classic North American wild rice, this soup qualifies as fusion cooking. It makes a great lunch, or even a light dinner accompanied by a platter of stir-fried bok choy.

Makes 6 servings

Nutrient Tip

Although this soup is relatively high in fat, it is very low in saturated fat. Virtually all of the fat comes from the peanuts and most is the heart-healthy unsaturated kind. Moreover, peanuts have a very high antioxidant content.

Nutrients per serving	
Calories	365
Protein	15.8 g
Carbohydrates	30.5 g
Fat (Total)	22.9 g
Saturated Fat	3.2 g
Monounsaturated Fat	10.9 g
Polyunsaturated Fat	7.4 g
Dietary Fiber	4.0 g
Sodium	316 mg
Cholesterol	0 mg

EXCELLENT SOURCE OF niacin, folate, phosphorus, magnesium, manganese, zinc and copper.

GOOD SOURCE OF vitamins A and E (alpha-tocopherol), thiamine, riboflavin and iron.

SOURCE OF vitamin C, pantothenic acid, calcium and selenium.

CONTAINS a high amount of dietary fiber.

2 cups	cooked wild rice (see cooking instructions, page 36)	500 mL
2	stalks lemongrass, smashed and chopped	2
4	cloves garlic, minced	4
2 tbsp	minced gingerroot	25 mL
3	dried red chile peppers, crumbled	3
2 tbsp	tomato paste	25 mL
6 cups	Homemade Vegetable Stock (see recipe, page 75) or reduced-sodium chicken stock	1.5 L
2 cups	unsalted roasted peanuts	500 mL
3 tbsp	rice vinegar	45 mL
2 tbsp	soy sauce	25 mL
1 tbsp	liquid honey	15 mL
	Finely grated zest and juice of 1 lime	
	Finely chopped cilantro	
	Finely chopped fresh chile peppers, optional	

1. In a large saucepan or stockpot, combine lemongrass, garlic, ginger, dried chile peppers, tomato paste and stock. Bring to a boil over medium heat. Reduce heat to low. Cover and simmer for 30 minutes. Strain, discarding solids. Return liquid to pot.

2. In a food processor or blender, combine peanuts, rice vinegar, soy sauce, honey and lime zest. Process until mixture is the consistency of chunky peanut butter. Stir into liquid. Add wild rice and bring to a boil over medium heat. Reduce heat to low. Cover and simmer to allow flavors to meld, about 20 minutes. Stir in lime juice. Ladle into bowls and garnish with cilantro and chile peppers, if using.

Congee with Chinese Greens and Barbecued Pork

If you live near a Chinatown, where freshly cooked barbecued pork is readily available, this delicious soup is a snap to make. At our house, it's a favorite weekend lunch. I put the rice on in the morning and it's done by the time we're ready to eat. All I need to do is add the pork and Chinese greens and purée the soup.

Makes 6 servings

TIPS

Chinese broccoli, also known as gai lan, is available in Asian markets. If you can't find it, substitute an equal quantity of shredded bok choy.

Unless you have a stove with a true simmer, after reducing the heat to low I recommend placing a heat diffuser under the pot to prevent the mixture from boiling. This device also helps to ensure the grains will cook evenly and prevents hot spots, which might cause scorching, from forming. Heat diffusers are available at kitchen supply and hardware stores and are made to work on gas or electric stoves.

Nutrients per serving

Calories	150
Protein	8.9 g
Carbohydrates	23.1 g
Fat (Total)	2.6 g
Saturated Fat	0.8 g
Monounsaturated Fat	1.1 g
Polyunsaturated Fat	0.5 g
Dietary Fiber	3.1 g
Sodium	576 mg
Cholesterol	12 mg

EXCELLENT SOURCE OF manganese.

GOOD SOURCE OF vitamin C, thiamine and magnesium.

SOURCE OF vitamin A, niacin, pantothenic acid, phosphorus, iron, zinc and copper.

CONTAINS a moderate amount of dietary fiber.

4 cups	reduced-sodium chicken stock	1 L
4 cups	water	1 L
¾ cup	short-grain brown rice, rinsed and drained	175 mL
4 cups	shredded Chinese broccoli (see Tips, left)	1 L
4 oz	shredded boneless Chinese barbecued pork	125 g
¼ cup	thinly sliced green onions, white part with a bit of green	50 mL
	Chopped fresh chile pepper, optional	
	Soy sauce, optional	

1. In a saucepan, combine stock, water and rice. Bring to a boil over medium-high heat. Reduce heat to low and simmer until rice has almost dissolved and is creamy, about 2½ hours.
2. Add broccoli and cook, stirring, until greens are wilted, about 5 minutes. Remove from heat. Using an immersion blender, purée soup. (You can also do this, in batches, in a food processor.) Return to element, stir in pork and cook until heated through, about 5 minutes. Garnish with green onions and chile pepper, if using. Season to taste with soy sauce, if using.

Variation

Duck Congee: Substitute an equal quantity of Chinese barbecued duck for the pork.

Salads

Asian-Style Beef and Wheat Berry Salad with Arugula

Asian-Style Beef and Wheat Berry Salad with Arugula

When my friend Andrew Chase had his Toronto restaurant Youki Asian Bar and Bistro, I went there as often as I could just to eat his Asian beef salad, which was to die for. The memory of that fabulous dish dominates my mind every time I make my own simplified and nutritionally enhanced version, which includes fiber-rich wheat berries. It makes a great summer meal, and if you're organized, it's very convenient. Cook the wheat berries ahead of time. Grill the steak and assemble the salad just before serving.

Makes 4 servings

TIP

Use any Asian chili sauce, such as sambal oelek, but if you are heat averse, pay close attention to the quantity. You may want to start with ½ tsp (2 mL) and increase the amount if it suits your taste.

Nutrients per serving

Calories	318
Protein	20.1 g
Carbohydrates	27.2 g
Fat (Total)	15.5 g
Saturated Fat	3.2 g
Monounsaturated Fat	9.4 g
Polyunsaturated Fat	1.6 g
Dietary Fiber	5.4 g
Sodium	554 mg
Cholesterol	31 mg

EXCELLENT SOURCE OF niacin, folate, phosphorus, magnesium, manganese, selenium and zinc.

GOOD SOURCE OF vitamins A, C and E (alpha-tocopherol), thiamine and iron.

SOURCE OF riboflavin, pantothenic acid, calcium and copper.

CONTAINS a high amount of dietary fiber.

1½ cups	cooked wheat, spelt or Kamut berries, cooled (see cooking instructions, page 34)	375 mL
1 cup	cubed (½-inch/1 cm) peeled cucumber	250 mL
6	green onions, white part only, thinly sliced	6
2	tomatoes, seeded and diced	2
DRESSING		
2 tbsp	rice vinegar	25 mL
1 tbsp	reduced-sodium soy sauce	15 mL
1	Thai or long red chile pepper, seeded and minced, optional	1
3 tbsp	extra virgin olive oil	45 mL
DRIZZLE		
3 tbsp	freshly squeezed lime juice	45 mL
2 tbsp	fish sauce	25 mL
1 tsp	Asian chili sauce or to taste, optional (see Tip, left)	5 mL
4 cups	arugula leaves	1 L
12 oz	New York strip sirloin, grilled to desired degree of doneness and thinly sliced on the bias	375 g

1. In a bowl, combine wheat berries, cucumber, green onions and tomatoes.

2. *Dressing:* In a small bowl, combine rice vinegar, soy sauce and chile pepper, if using. Gradually whisk in olive oil. Add to wheat berry mixture and toss well.

3. *Drizzle:* In another small bowl, combine lime juice, fish sauce and chili sauce, if using. Set aside.

4. Line a serving bowl or deep platter with arugula. Spread wheat berry mixture evenly over top and lay beef strips evenly over mixture. Sprinkle with half of the drizzle. Pour remainder into a small serving bowl and pass at the table.

Variation

Asian-Style Beef and Rice Salad with Arugula: Substitute 2 cups (500 mL) cooked cooled long-grain brown rice for the wheat berries. To keep the grains of rice separate, rinse the hot cooked rice thoroughly under cold running water. Drain well and let cool.

Chicken and Wheat Berry Salad with Avocado

This is a simple main-course salad, yet very tasty and nutritious. It's also a great way to use up leftover chicken. It's enjoyable any time of the year, but is particularly pleasant on a hot summer evening, especially if you have cooked grains in the refrigerator. For a special treat, or if company is coming, use freshly grilled chicken breasts (see Variation, below) and garden-fresh arugula for the greens.

Makes 6 servings

TIPS

If you're in a hurry, substitute ½ cup (125 mL) bottled Italian dressing for the dressing.

Use leftover chicken or, for convenience, a cut-up rotisserie chicken.

Nutrient Tip

This recipe seems high in fat, but most comes from the olive oil, which is heart-healthy. The salad is also very high in fiber, which has many healthful benefits.

Nutrients per serving	
Calories	351
Protein	17.5 g
Carbohydrates	22.5 g
Fat (Total)	22.4 g
Saturated Fat	3.6 g
Monounsaturated Fat	14.5 g
Polyunsaturated Fat	3.0 g
Dietary Fiber	6.3 g
Sodium	258 mg
Cholesterol	42 mg

EXCELLENT SOURCE OF niacin, folate, manganese and selenium.

GOOD SOURCE OF vitamins A and E (alpha-tocopherol), pantothenic acid, magnesium, phosphorus, iron and zinc.

SOURCE OF vitamin C, thiamine, riboflavin, calcium and copper.

CONTAINS a very high amount of dietary fiber.

2 cups	cooked wheat, spelt or Kamut berries, cooled (see cooking instructions, page 34)	500 mL

DRESSING (SEE TIPS, LEFT)

2 tbsp	red wine vinegar	25 mL
½ tsp	salt	2 mL
¼ tsp	freshly ground black pepper	1 mL
6 tbsp	extra virgin olive oil	90 mL
2½ cups	diced cooked chicken (see Tips, left)	625 mL
2	stalks celery, diced	2
4	green onions, white part only, thinly sliced	4
1	tomato, peeled, seeded and diced	1
1	avocado, cubed	1
5 cups	torn salad greens	1.25 L
¼ cup	finely chopped parsley or dill, optional	50 mL

1. *Dressing:* In a small bowl, combine vinegar, salt and pepper, stirring until salt dissolves. Gradually whisk in olive oil.

2. In a bowl, combine wheat berries, chicken, celery, green onions, tomato and avocado. Add dressing and toss well.

3. Line a serving bowl with salad greens. Cover with wheat berry mixture. Garnish with parsley, if using.

Variation

Grilled Chicken and Wheat Berry Salad with Avocado: To dress this salad up, substitute the cooked chicken with about 2 lbs (1 kg) skin-on bone-in chicken breasts. Grill them using your favorite method. Let cool slightly, then slice the meat off the bone in thin strips and set aside, rather than combining with wheat berry mixture. Also set 1 tbsp (15 mL) of the dressing aside. Line a deep platter with salad greens, spread wheat berry mixture on top and arrange sliced grilled chicken over that. Drizzle reserved dressing over chicken. Garnish with parsley, if using.

Wild Rice and Smoked Turkey Salad with Dried Cherries

This is one of my daughter's favorite salads. When she was away at university, I'd try to have some on hand for those times she arrived home late at night in a famished state. The cherries add pleasing tartness and the almonds tasty crunch. Serve this over a bed of leaf lettuce for a light main course. It also makes a great buffet dish.

Makes 6 side servings

TIP

Rinsing cooked rice helps reduce stickiness, which is beneficial when making salads. Place cooked rice in a strainer and rinse under cold running water. Drain thoroughly before using.

Nutrients per serving

Calories	246
Protein	8.6 g
Carbohydrates	27.9 g
Fat (Total)	12.1 g
Saturated Fat	1.6 g
Monounsaturated Fat	8.3 g
Polyunsaturated Fat	1.8 g
Dietary Fiber	3.4 g
Sodium	559 mg
Cholesterol	9 mg

EXCELLENT SOURCE OF manganese.

GOOD SOURCE OF vitamin E (alpha-tocopherol), folate, phosphorus and magnesium.

SOURCE OF vitamins A and C, thiamine, riboflavin, niacin, calcium, iron, zinc, copper and selenium.

CONTAINS a moderate amount of dietary fiber.

2 cups	cooked brown and wild rice mixture, rinsed in cold water and drained (see Tip, left and page 89 and cooking instructions, page 36)	500 mL
DRESSING		
1 tbsp	red wine vinegar	15 mL
1 tbsp	Dijon mustard	15 mL
½ tsp	salt	2 mL
	Freshly ground black pepper	
¼ cup	extra virgin olive oil	50 mL
2 tbsp	finely chopped parsley	25 mL
1½ cups	diced smoked turkey (about 6 oz/175 g)	375 mL
2	stalks celery, diced	2
4	green onions, white part with a bit of green, thinly sliced	4
½ cup	dried cherries	125 mL
1	small head leaf lettuce	1
¼ cup	toasted sliced almonds	50 mL

1. *Dressing:* In a bowl, whisk together vinegar, mustard, salt and pepper to taste. Gradually whisk in olive oil. Whisk in parsley and set aside.
2. In a bowl, combine rice, turkey, celery, green onions and cherries. Add dressing and toss well.
3. Arrange lettuce in a shallow serving bowl or deep platter. Arrange rice mixture over top. Sprinkle with toasted almonds.

Variation

Wheat Berry and Smoked Turkey Salad with Dried Cherries: Substitute an equal quantity of cooked wheat, spelt or Kamut berries or farro for the rice.

Rice Salad Niçoise

This refreshing salad, with a mostly Mediterranean spin, is a perfect dinner solution for those summer days when it's too hot to cook and you can't bear the thought of a heavy meal. Just cook the rice in your rice cooker, rinse and drain. Complete Steps 1 and 2 and chill overnight. The salad is ready to eat whenever you are.

Makes 4 servings

TIPS

Lundberg makes a nice brown and wild rice mixture, which works very well in this salad. If you prefer, just combine equal quantities of plain brown and wild rice.

Rinsing cooked rice reduces stickiness. Place the cooked rice in a strainer and rinse under cold running water. Drain thoroughly before using.

Nutrient Tip

Virtually all of the fat in this salad comes from the olives, olive oil and the tuna, and is heart-healthy unsaturated fat.

Nutrients per serving	
Calories	345
Protein	13.5 g
Carbohydrates	26.9 g
Fat (Total)	21.3 g
Saturated Fat	3.1 g
Monounsaturated Fat	14.2 g
Polyunsaturated Fat	3.2 g
Dietary Fiber	3.9 g
Sodium	940 mg
Cholesterol	11 mg

EXCELLENT SOURCE OF vitamins C and E (alpha-tocopherol), niacin, manganese and selenium.

GOOD SOURCE OF vitamin A, magnesium and phosphorus.

SOURCE OF thiamine, riboflavin, folate, pantothenic acid, iron, zinc and copper.

CONTAINS a moderate amount of dietary fiber.

2 cups	cooked brown and wild rice mixture, rinsed in cold water and drained (see Tips, left and cooking instructions, page 36)	500 mL
1	can (6 oz/170 g) tuna, preferably Italian, packed in olive oil, drained	1
2	roasted red peppers, chopped	2
½ cup	chopped drained marinated artichoke hearts	125 mL
½ cup	pitted black olives, sliced	125 mL
½ cup	pitted green olives, sliced	125 mL
	Chopped hot pickled peppers, optional	

DRESSING

2 tbsp	red wine vinegar	25 mL
½ tsp	salt	2 mL
¼ tsp	freshly ground black pepper	1 mL
¼ cup	extra virgin olive oil	50 mL

Leafy lettuce, optional
Hard-cooked eggs, quartered, optional

1. In a serving bowl, combine rice, tuna, red peppers, artichoke hearts, black and green olives and hot pepper, if using.

2. *Dressing:* In a small bowl, combine vinegar, salt and black pepper, stirring until salt dissolves. Gradually whisk in olive oil. Add to rice mixture and toss well. Chill thoroughly.

3. Just before serving, spread over a bed of lettuce, if using. Garnish with eggs, if using.

Variations

Wheat Berry Salad Niçoise: Substitute an equal quantity of cooked wheat, spelt or Kamut berries for the rice.

Barley Salad Niçoise: Substitute an equal quantity of cooked barley for the rice.

Kasha and Beet Salad with Celery and Feta

I love the robust flavors of this hearty salad. Beets, parsley and feta are the perfect balance for assertive buckwheat. It's a great combination and a wonderful buffet dish, particularly if you're serving to guests who are sensitive to gluten, as buckwheat is gluten-free.

Makes 6 to 8 side servings

TIP

Buckwheat groats that are already toasted are known as kasha. If you prefer a milder buckwheat flavor, use groats rather than kasha in this dish. Just place them in a dry skillet over medium-high heat and cook, stirring constantly, until they are nicely fragrant, about 4 minutes. In the process they will darken from a light shade of sand to one with a hint of brown. Groats you toast yourself have a milder flavor than store-bought kasha.

Nutrients per serving

Calories	177
Protein	5.4 g
Carbohydrates	23.3 g
Fat (Total)	8.1 g
Saturated Fat	2.5 g
Monounsaturated Fat	4.4 g
Polyunsaturated Fat	0.8 g
Dietary Fiber	3.7 g
Sodium	571 mg
Cholesterol	10 mg

EXCELLENT SOURCE OF manganese.

GOOD SOURCE OF folate and magnesium.

SOURCE OF vitamins A, C and E (alpha-tocopherol), thiamine, riboflavin, niacin, pantothenic acid, calcium, phosphorus, iron, zinc, copper and selenium.

CONTAINS a moderate amount of dietary fiber.

2 cups	vegetable or chicken stock	500 mL
2	cloves garlic, minced	2
1 cup	kasha or buckwheat groats (see Tip, left)	250 mL
DRESSING		
1/4 cup	red wine vinegar	50 mL
1 tsp	Dijon mustard	5 mL
1/2 tsp	salt	2 mL
1/2 tsp	freshly ground black pepper	2 mL
3 tbsp	extra virgin olive oil	45 mL
2 cups	diced peeled cooked beets	500 mL
4	stalks celery, diced	4
6	green onions, white part only, thinly sliced	6
1/2 cup	finely chopped parsley	125 mL
3 oz	crumbled feta cheese	90 g

1. In a saucepan over medium–high heat, bring stock and garlic to a boil. Gradually add kasha, stirring constantly to prevent clumping. Reduce heat to low. Cover and simmer until all the liquid is absorbed and kasha is tender, about 10 minutes. Remove from heat. Fluff up with a fork and transfer to a serving bowl and let cool slightly.

2. *Dressing:* In a small bowl, combine vinegar, mustard, salt and pepper, stirring until salt dissolves. Gradually whisk in olive oil until blended. Add to kasha and toss well.

3. Add beets, celery and green onions to kasha and toss again. Chill until ready to serve. Just before serving, garnish with parsley and sprinkle feta over top.

Variation

Rice and Beet Salad with Celery and Feta: Substitute 3 cups (750 mL) cooked long-grain brown rice for the cooked kasha.

Cold Soba Noodles

This is one of my favorite summer dishes. I love to serve it when we're dining in the garden on a warm evening. In fact, it's a key component of one of my preferred al fresco dinners, served alongside grilled fish or chicken and a salad of cooled baby beets and sliced red onions tossed in a garlicky vinaigrette. Yum.

Makes 6 side servings

TIP

If you don't have a fresh chile pepper, substitute ¼ tsp (1 mL) or more (depending upon how much you like heat) of an Asian chili paste such as sambal oelek.

8 oz	dried soba noodles	250 g
1 tsp	sesame oil	5 mL
DRESSING		
3 tbsp	reduced-sodium soy sauce	45 mL
2 tbsp	rice wine vinegar	25 mL
½ tsp	salt	2 mL
1	long red chile pepper, seeded and finely chopped (see Tip, left)	1
1 tbsp	minced gingerroot	15 mL
2 tbsp	extra virgin olive oil	25 mL
1 tbsp	sesame oil	15 mL
½ cup	thinly sliced green onions, white part with a bit of green	125 mL
	Freshly ground black pepper	
2 tbsp	toasted sesame seeds	25 mL

1. In a large pot of boiling salted water, cook noodles until tender to the bite, about 7 minutes. Drain, rinse well in cold running water and drain again. Toss with sesame oil and chill until ready to serve.

2. *Dressing:* In a small bowl, combine soy sauce, vinegar, salt, chile pepper and ginger. Whisk in olive oil and sesame oil.

3. In a serving bowl, combine chilled noodles and green onions. Add dressing and toss well. Season to taste with black pepper. Sprinkle with sesame seeds.

Nutrients per serving

Calories	225
Protein	7.9 g
Carbohydrates	30.7 g
Fat (Total)	9.4 g
Saturated Fat	1.3 g
Monounsaturated Fat	5.2 g
Polyunsaturated Fat	2.5 g
Dietary Fiber	2.2 g
Sodium	701 mg
Cholesterol	0 mg

EXCELLENT SOURCE OF manganese.

GOOD SOURCE OF vitamin C.

SOURCE OF vitamins A and E (alpha-tocopherol), thiamine, niacin, folate, pantothenic acid, phosphorus, iron, magnesium, zinc and copper.

CONTAINS a moderate amount of dietary fiber.

Black Sticky Rice Salad

Serve this unusual and delicious salad as a side to grilled fish or meat. It is dense and very flavorful and acts almost as a condiment. You don't need much, but it makes a very pleasant accent to a simple meal. My fuzzy logic rice cooker does a fabulous job of cooking this rice on the Brown Rice setting. I just add the rice and soaking liquid, push the start button and it's ready in just under 2 hours.

Makes 8 side servings

TIP

Thai black sticky rice is available in Asian markets. Do not use Chinese black rice, which is not sticky. To cook this quantity of black sticky rice, use about ¾ cup (175 mL) raw rice and 1½ cups (375 mL) water. Soak the rice for at least 4 hours or overnight, then bring the rice and soaking liquid to a rapid boil in a heavy pot with a tight-fitting lid. Reduce heat to low and simmer until rice is tender, 30 to 45 minutes.

2 cups	cooked Thai black sticky rice, cooled (see Tip, left)	500 mL
1	red bell pepper, seeded and diced	1
1	long red or green chile pepper, seeded and diced	1
½ cup	finely chopped green onions, white part only	125 mL
DRESSING		
1 tbsp	seasoned rice vinegar	15 mL
½ tsp	salt	2 mL
3 tbsp	reduced-sodium soy sauce	45 mL
2 tbsp	sesame oil	25 mL

1. In a serving bowl, combine rice, bell pepper, chile pepper and green onion. Toss well.
2. *Dressing:* In a small bowl, combine vinegar and salt, stirring until salt dissolves. Add soy sauce and sesame oil and stir well. Pour over rice mixture and toss to blend. Chill thoroughly.

Nutrients per serving

Calories	107
Protein	2.0 g
Carbohydrates	16.6 g
Fat (Total)	3.8 g
Saturated Fat	0.5 g
Monounsaturated Fat	1.4 g
Polyunsaturated Fat	1.5 g
Dietary Fiber	0.6 g
Sodium	439 mg
Cholesterol	0 mg

EXCELLENT SOURCE OF vitamin C.
SOURCE OF vitamin A, thiamin, niacin, phosphorus and iron.

Asian-Style Quinoa Salad with Chili-Orange Dressing

Perhaps surprisingly, since quinoa is a "new world" grain, it takes very well to Asian ingredients such as water chestnuts. This is a nice light salad that is perfect for summer dining or a buffet. It's an ideal accompaniment to grilled meat or fish.

Makes 6 side servings

TIP
The chili sauce adds a pleasant bit of zest, but if you're heat averse you can omit it. Heat seekers can increase the quantity to taste.

3 cups	cooked quinoa, cooled (see cooking instructions, page 26)	750 mL

CHILI-ORANGE DRESSING

1 tsp	finely grated orange zest	5 mL
1/4 cup	freshly squeezed orange juice	50 mL
1 tbsp	reduced-sodium soy sauce	15 mL
1 tbsp	liquid honey	15 mL
2 tsp	sesame oil	10 mL
1/2 tsp	Asian chili sauce, such as sambal oelek (see Tip, left)	2 mL
	Freshly ground black pepper	
1	can (8 oz/227 g) water chestnuts, drained and chopped	1
1	red bell pepper, seeded and chopped	1
1 1/2 cups	chopped snow peas, cooked until tender-crisp and cooled	375 mL
4	green onions, white part with a bit of green, thinly sliced	4

1. *Chili-Orange Dressing:* In a small bowl, whisk together orange zest and juice, soy sauce, honey, sesame oil, chili sauce and pepper to taste. Set aside.

2. In a serving bowl, combine quinoa, water chestnuts, bell pepper, snow peas and green onions. Add dressing and toss until combined. Chill thoroughly.

Variation
Asian-Style Millet Salad with Chili-Orange Dressing: Substitute 3 cups (750 mL) cooked toasted millet (see cooking instructions, page 23) for the quinoa.

Nutrients per serving

Calories	166
Protein	5.3 g
Carbohydrates	30.0 g
Fat (Total)	3.3 g
Saturated Fat	0.4 g
Monounsaturated Fat	1.1 g
Polyunsaturated Fat	1.4 g
Dietary Fiber	3.7 g
Sodium	116 mg
Cholesterol	0 mg

EXCELLENT SOURCE OF vitamin C, iron and manganese.

GOOD SOURCE OF magnesium, and copper.

SOURCE OF vitamins A and E (alpha-tocopherol), folate, thiamine, riboflavin, niacin, pantothenic acid, phosphorus and zinc.

CONTAINS a moderate amount of dietary fiber.

Quinoa and Radish Salad with Avocado Dressing

Quinoa has a delicate texture and produces a salad that is refreshingly light. I love to make this salad in summer when tomatoes and radishes are abundant and at their peak. I put any leftovers in the fridge and enjoy them for snacks the following day.

Makes 6 side servings

TIPS

The bit of walnut oil adds appealing but subtle flavor along with beneficial omega-3 fats to this pleasantly mild vinaigrette, but if you don't have it, just use an extra tablespoon (15 mL) olive oil. When buying walnut oil, look for a cold-pressed version and, because it's highly perishable, be sure to keep it refrigerated and use it up quickly.

If field tomatoes aren't in season, halved or quartered cherry tomatoes also work well in this salad.

Nutrients per serving

Calories	239
Protein	5.1 g
Carbohydrates	26.4 g
Fat (Total)	13.5 g
Saturated Fat	1.7 g
Monounsaturated Fat	7.6 g
Polyunsaturated Fat	3.3 g
Dietary Fiber	5.5 g
Sodium	216 mg
Cholesterol	0 mg

EXCELLENT SOURCE OF
magnesium and manganese.
GOOD SOURCE OF vitamins C and E (alpha-tocopherol), folate, iron and copper.
SOURCE OF vitamin A, thiamine, riboflavin, niacin, pantothenic acid, phosphorous and zinc.
CONTAINS a high amount of dietary fiber.

3 cups	cooked quinoa, cooled (see cooking instructions, page 26)	750 mL

AVOCADO DRESSING

1	avocado, pitted and peeled	1
2 tbsp	extra virgin olive oil	25 mL
2 tbsp	white wine vinegar	25 mL
1 tbsp	walnut oil (see Tips, left)	15 mL
½ tsp	salt	2 mL
	Freshly ground black pepper	

2 cups	diced, cored tomatoes (see Tips, left)	500 mL
2 cups	thinly sliced radishes (see Variations, below)	500 mL

1. *Avocado Dressing:* In a food processor or blender, combine avocado, olive oil, vinegar, walnut oil, salt and pepper to taste. Process until smooth and blended.

2. In a serving bowl, combine tomatoes, radishes and quinoa. Add dressing and toss until combined. Chill until ready to serve.

Variations

Millet and Radish Salad with Avocado Dressing: Substitute 3 cups (750 mL) cooked toasted millet (see cooking instructions, page 23) for the quinoa.

If you don't have radishes, substitute ½ cup (125 mL) finely chopped red onion.

Barley Salad with Confetti of Carrot and Dill

Here's a refreshing salad with unusual but delicious flavors. The sweetness of the carrots and currants is nicely balanced by the tartness of the dill. The sunflower seeds add texture as well as taste and the sweet-and-sour theme is continued in the honey-Dijon dressing. It makes a great main course or side salad to accompany grilled chicken, fish or meat. The shredded carrots and dill, which resemble orange and green confetti, will add color to any buffet.

Makes 10 side servings

TIP

For an easy-to-make version of this dressing, combine 6 tbsp (90 mL) of your favorite Italian dressing with 2 tbsp (25 mL) honey-Dijon mustard.

3 cups	cooked whole (hulled) barley, cooled (see cooking instructions, page 16)	750 mL
DRESSING		
1 tbsp	white wine vinegar	15 mL
½ tsp	salt	2 mL
	Freshly ground black pepper	
1 tbsp	Dijon mustard	15 mL
1 tbsp	liquid honey	15 mL
¼ cup	extra virgin olive oil	50 mL
2 cups	shredded carrots	500 mL
½ cup	finely chopped dill	125 mL
¼ cup	currants	50 mL
¼ cup	sunflower seeds	50 mL
2 cups	shredded hearts of romaine, optional	500 mL

1. *Dressing:* In a small bowl, combine vinegar, salt and pepper to taste, stirring until salt dissolves. Whisk in mustard and honey until blended. Gradually whisk in olive oil until mixture is smooth and creamy. Set aside.

2. In a serving bowl, combine barley, carrots, dill, currants and sunflower seeds. Add dressing and toss well. Arrange shredded lettuce over top, if using. Cover and chill thoroughly. When ready to serve, toss well.

Variations

Substitute an equal quantity of cooked wheat, spelt, Kamut or rye berries or farro for the barley.

Nutrients per serving

Calories	161
Protein	3.6 g
Carbohydrates	20.9 g
Fat (Total)	7.8 g
Saturated Fat	1.0 g
Monounsaturated Fat	4.4 g
Polyunsaturated Fat	2.0 g
Dietary Fiber	4.4 g
Sodium	154 mg
Cholesterol	0 mg

EXCELLENT SOURCE OF vitamin A and manganese.

GOOD SOURCE OF vitamin E (alpha-tocopherol), thiamine and selenium.

SOURCE OF riboflavin, niacin, folate, pantothenic acid, phosphorus, iron, magnesium, zinc and copper.

CONTAINS a high amount of dietary fiber.

Sausage and Wheat Berry Salad with Shredded Hearts of Romaine

This is an absolutely delicious combination of ingredients. Serve it on a buffet table or bring it to a potluck and expect that it will quickly disappear. With additional lettuce and some whole-grain bread, it also makes a great lunch. Leave the shredded romaine on top and toss the salad just before you're ready to serve so the lettuce doesn't wilt.

Makes 8 side servings

TIPS

I like to use very hot pickled peppers, such as Tabasco, in this salad, but if you're heat averse, milder ones, such as banana peppers, taste good, too.

To shred lettuce, peel off the outer leaves of romaine and slice across the heart very thinly using a chef's knife.

Nutrients per serving

Calories	248
Protein	11.0 g
Carbohydrates	21.2 g
Fat (Total)	14.2 g
Saturated Fat	4.5 g
Monounsaturated Fat	7.2 g
Polyunsaturated Fat	1.8 g
Dietary Fiber	4.2 g
Sodium	569 mg
Cholesterol	13 mg

EXCELLENT SOURCE OF vitamin A, manganese and selenium.

GOOD SOURCE OF folate, phosphorus, magnesium and zinc.

SOURCE OF vitamins C and E (alpha-tocopherol), thiamine, riboflavin, niacin, pantothenic acid, calcium, iron and copper.

CONTAINS a high amount of dietary fiber.

3 cups	cooked wheat, spelt or Kamut berries, cooled (see cooking instructions, page 34)	750 mL
DRESSING		
2 tbsp	red wine vinegar	25 mL
2 tsp	Dijon mustard	10 mL
½ tsp	salt	2 mL
	Freshly ground black pepper	
1	clove garlic, finely grated or put through a press	1
¼ cup	extra virgin olive oil	50 mL
1 tbsp	finely diced drained pickled hot peppers (see Tips, left)	15 mL
8 oz	turkey kielbasa, diced	250 g
4 oz	Asiago cheese, diced	125 g
4	stalks celery, diced	4
1	small red onion, diced	1
6 cups	shredded hearts of romaine (see Tips, left)	1.5 L

1. *Dressing:* In a small bowl, combine vinegar, mustard, salt and black pepper to taste, stirring until salt dissolves. Stir in garlic. Gradually whisk in olive oil until blended. Stir in hot peppers and set aside.

2. In a serving bowl, combine wheat berries, kielbasa, Asiago, celery and red onion. Add dressing and toss well. Arrange shredded lettuce on top. Cover and chill thoroughly. When ready to serve, toss well.

Variation

Substitute 3 cups (750 ml) cooked cooled barley or farro for the wheat berries.

Southwestern Bean and Barley Salad with Roasted Peppers

Ingredients traditionally associated with the American Southwest, such as beans, corn and peppers, combine with hearty barley to produce this deliciously robust salad. Packed with nutrients, it is particularly high in dietary fiber. It makes a great addition to a buffet or potluck dinner. Keep leftovers in the fridge for a nutritious lunch or after-school snacks.

Makes 8 side servings

TIPS

For this quantity of beans, soak and cook 1 cup (250 mL) dried beans.

Poblano peppers are a mild chile pepper. If you are a heat seeker, you might want to add an extra one, or even a minced seeded jalapeño pepper for some real punch. The suggested quantity produces a mild result, which most people will enjoy. If you're heat averse, use bell peppers, instead.

Nutrients per serving

Calories	281
Protein	7.3 g
Carbohydrates	33.2 g
Fat (Total)	14.6 g
Saturated Fat	2.0 g
Monounsaturated Fat	10.3 g
Polyunsaturated Fat	1.8 g
Dietary Fiber	7.0 g
Sodium	197 mg
Cholesterol	0 mg

EXCELLENT SOURCE OF vitamin C, folate and manganese.

GOOD SOURCE OF vitamin E (alpha-tocopherol), thiamine, iron and magnesium.

SOURCE OF vitamin A, riboflavin, niacin, phosphorous, zinc, copper and selenium.

CONTAINS a very high amount of dietary fiber.

3 cups	cooked whole (hulled) barley, cooled (see cooking instructions, page 16)	750 mL
DRESSING		
3 tbsp	red wine vinegar	45 mL
½ tsp	salt	2 mL
	Freshly ground black pepper	
½	clove garlic, finely grated or put through a press	½
½ cup	extra virgin olive oil	125 mL
2 cups	cooked red kidney beans or 1 can (14 to 19 oz/398 to 540 mL) kidney beans, drained and rinsed (see Tips, left)	500 mL
2 cups	cooked corn kernels	500 mL
2	roasted poblano or roasted red bell peppers, peeled, seeded and diced (see Tips, left)	2
2	whole sun-dried tomatoes, packed in olive oil, finely chopped	2
1	small red onion, diced	1
¼ cup	finely chopped parsley	50 mL

1. *Dressing:* In a small bowl, combine vinegar, salt and pepper to taste, stirring until salt dissolves. Stir in garlic. Gradually whisk in olive oil. Set aside.

2. In a serving bowl, combine barley, kidney beans, corn, roasted peppers, sun-dried tomatoes and onion. Add dressing and toss well. Garnish with parsley. Chill until ready to serve.

Variations

Substitute an equal quantity of cooked wheat, spelt or Kamut berries or farro for the barley.

Lemon Lovers' Tabbouleh

I love the assertive lemon flavors in this tabbouleh, which is particularly refreshing on a hot summer day. This is a great dish for a buffet and even does double duty as an appetizer — just use the romaine as a dipper.

Makes 10 side servings

TIPS

If your tomatoes are particularly juicy, when seeding, save the seeds and juices and put them into a sieve. Push the juices through and discard the solids. Add to lemon juice before making the vinaigrette.

If you prefer, use an equal quantity of diced cherry tomatoes in this recipe.

1½ cups	medium or fine bulgur	375 mL
2 cups	ice water	500 mL
⅓ cup	freshly squeezed lemon juice	75 mL
1 tsp	ground cumin	5 mL
1 tsp	salt	5 mL
	Freshly ground black pepper	
⅓ cup	extra virgin olive oil	75 mL
2 cups	loosely packed parsley leaves, finely chopped	500 mL
2 cups	diced seedless cucumber	500 mL
2 cups	diced seeded peeled tomatoes (see Tips, left)	500 mL
½ cup	loosely packed mint leaves, finely chopped	125 mL
½ cup	chopped green onions, white part only	125 mL
	Hearts of romaine, optional	

1. In a bowl, combine bulgur and cold water. Stir well and set aside until liquid is absorbed, about 10 minutes.

2. Meanwhile, in a small bowl, combine lemon juice, cumin, salt and pepper to taste. Whisk in olive oil. Add to bulgur and set aside until liquid is absorbed, about 15 minutes.

3. Add parsley, cucumber, tomatoes, mint and green onions and toss well. Cover and chill thoroughly. If using the lettuce, line a serving bowl with hearts of romaine and add tabbouleh or serve romaine as a dipper to scoop the salad.

Variations

Quinoa Tabbouleh: Skip Step 1. Substitute 4 cups (1 L) cooked quinoa, cooled, for the bulgur.

Millet Tabbouleh: Skip Step 1. Substitute 4 cups (1 L) cooked toasted millet, cooled, for the bulgur.

Nutrients per serving

Calories	156
Protein	3.7 g
Carbohydrates	20.5 g
Fat (Total)	7.7 g
Saturated Fat	1.0 g
Monounsaturated Fat	5.4 g
Polyunsaturated Fat	0.9 g
Dietary Fiber	3.6 g
Sodium	247 mg
Cholesterol	0 mg

EXCELLENT SOURCE OF manganese.

GOOD SOURCE OF vitamins A and C, folate, iron and magnesium.

SOURCE OF vitamin E (alpha-tocopherol), thiamine, niacin, phosphorus, zinc and copper.

CONTAINS a moderate amount of dietary fiber.

VEGAN FRIENDLY

Cranberry Pecan Couscous Salad

This salad has a delectable combination of flavors and textures — the slightly tart cranberries and orange are beautifully balanced by the crunchy pecans and mildly nutty flavor of the couscous. It's exotic enough to liven up any buffet and makes a particularly delicious and delightfully different accompaniment to poultry.

Makes 8 side servings

TIP
Try other kinds of whole-grain couscous, such as barley or spelt, for a change.

1½ cups	water	375 mL
1 cup	whole wheat couscous	250 mL
	Salt, optional	
DRESSING		
¼ cup	freshly squeezed orange juice	50 mL
½ tsp	balsamic vinegar	2 mL
½ tsp	salt	2 mL
Pinch	freshly grated nutmeg	Pinch
	Freshly ground black pepper	
¼ cup	extra virgin olive oil	50 mL
1	red bell pepper, seeded and diced	1
½ cup	finely chopped parsley	125 mL
½ cup	dried cranberries	125 mL
½ cup	toasted chopped pecans	125 mL
2 tsp	finely grated orange zest	10 mL

1. In a saucepan with a tight-fitting lid, bring water to a boil. Gradually add couscous, stirring well. Season to taste with salt, if using. Remove from heat and let stand, covered, for at least 15 minutes. Fluff up with fork and break up any clumps, using your hands.

2. *Dressing:* In a small bowl, combine orange juice, vinegar and salt, stirring until salt dissolves. Add nutmeg and pepper to taste. Whisk in olive oil. Set aside.

3. In a serving bowl, combine bell pepper, parsley, cranberries, pecans and orange zest. Add fluffed couscous and toss. Add dressing and toss until combined. Chill thoroughly before serving.

Nutrients per serving

Calories	227
Protein	4.3 g
Carbohydrates	28.0 g
Fat (Total)	12.3 g
Saturated Fat	1.4 g
Monounsaturated Fat	7.8 g
Polyunsaturated Fat	2.2 g
Dietary Fiber	4.4 g
Sodium	147 mg
Cholesterol	0 mg

EXCELLENT SOURCE OF vitamin C.

GOOD SOURCE OF manganese.

SOURCE OF vitamins A and E (alpha-tocopherol), thiamine, magnesium, folate, iron and copper.

CONTAINS a high amount of dietary fiber.

Millet Salad with Lemony Chickpeas and Tomatoes

Although I enjoy this salad all year round, I especially like making it in winter when its light airy texture and Mediterranean flavors remind me that summer will come again. It makes a great addition to a buffet table, an interesting dish for a potluck and is an excellent side served with grilled fish or roast chicken. You can even use it as an appetizer — just put out hearts of romaine to use as dippers.

Makes 10 side servings

TIPS

If field tomatoes are in season, substitute an equal quantity of seeded diced tomatoes for the cherry tomatoes.

For this quantity of chickpeas, soak and cook 1 cup (250 mL) dried chickpeas.

1 cup	millet	250 mL
2 cups	water or vegetable stock	500 mL
DRESSING		
¼ cup	freshly squeezed lemon juice	50 mL
½ tsp	salt	2 mL
Pinch	cayenne pepper, optional	Pinch
	Freshly ground black pepper	
6 tbsp	extra virgin olive oil	90 mL
¼ cup	finely chopped parsley or dill	50 mL
2 cups	halved cherry tomatoes (see Tips, left)	500 mL
2 cups	cooked chickpeas or 1 can (14 to 19 oz/398 to 540 mL) chickpeas, drained and rinsed (see Tips, left)	500 mL
8	green onions, white part only, finely chopped	8
2 cups	thinly sliced radishes	500 mL
	Hearts of romaine, optional	

1. In a saucepan over medium heat, toast millet, stirring, until it crackles and releases its aroma, about 5 minutes. Transfer to a bowl. Add water to saucepan and bring to a boil. Stir in millet and return to a boil. Reduce heat to low. Cover and simmer until water is absorbed, about 25 minutes. Remove from heat and let stand, covered, for 10 minutes. Transfer to a serving bowl and fluff with a fork. Set aside and let cool.

2. *Dressing:* Meanwhile, in a small bowl, combine lemon juice, salt, cayenne, if using, and pepper to taste, stirring until salt dissolves. Whisk in olive oil. Add parsley. Set aside.

3. Add tomatoes, chickpeas, green onions and radishes to millet and toss. Add dressing and toss well. Cover and chill. If using lettuce, line a serving bowl with hearts of romaine and add salad. Or serve salad as an appetizer and use romaine as dippers.

Variations

To add variety to your grain consumption, use half quinoa and half millet. Rinse quinoa, but do not toast. Cook the grains together as per Step 1.

Quinoa Salad with Lemony Chickpeas and Tomatoes: Substitute quinoa for millet. Rinse quinoa thoroughly before using, but do not toast. Reduce the cooking time to 15 minutes.

Bulgur Salad with Lemony Chickpeas and Tomatoes: Skip Step 1. Combine 1 cup (250 mL) bulgur and 1¼ cups (300 mL) cold water. Stir well and set aside until liquid is absorbed, about 10 minutes. Continue with Step 2.

OLIVE OIL

I always use extra virgin olive oil when making salads because I love the flavor. I also love the fact that it is extremely good for you. Over the years, numerous studies have shown a link between the consumption of olive oil and a reduced rate of heart disease. Thus encouraged, the FDA allowed the following health claim in 2004: "Limited and not conclusive scientific evidence suggests that eating about 2 tablespoons (23 grams) of olive oil daily may reduce the risk of coronary heart disease due to the monounsaturated fat in olive oil. To achieve this possible benefit, olive oil is to replace a similar amount of saturated fat and not increase the total number of calories you eat in a day." But recent research suggests that olive oil does more than keep your heart healthy. Greek researchers have shown that it can help to keep your blood pressure under control and a study published in the *British Journal of Nutrition* linked the consumption of olive oil with improved bone health. Moreover, it's not just the monounsaturated fats that create health benefits. Olive oil is rich in oleic acid, which caused aggressive breast cancer cells to self-destruct in one laboratory study, and oleocanthal, a natural anti-inflammatory that acts like low-dose ibuprofen in the body. Researchers believe that keeping inflammation at bay may have multiple health benefits, such as reducing the risk of heart disease, stroke and certain types of cancer.

Nutrients per serving

Calories	217
Protein	5.8 g
Carbohydrates	27.5 g
Fat (Total)	9.7 g
Saturated Fat	1.3 g
Monounsaturated Fat	6.3 g
Polyunsaturated Fat	1.6 g
Dietary Fiber	4.3 g
Sodium	130 mg
Cholesterol	0 mg

EXCELLENT SOURCE OF folate and manganese.

GOOD SOURCE OF magnesium.

SOURCE OF vitamins A, C and E (alpha-tocopherol), thiamine, riboflavin, niacin, phosphorous, iron, zinc and copper.

CONTAINS a high amount of dietary fiber.

Everyday Tuna and Red Rice Salad

The use of Bhutanese red rice or more delicate brown Kalijira rice, both of which cook in less than 30 minutes, allows you to make this very tasty and nutritious rice salad for a weekday meal. This salad is very flexible. It is designed for convenience, which includes using ingredients you're likely to have on hand — that way, you can come home on a busy day when you haven't had time to shop and prepare a nutritious meal.

TIPS

Bhutanese red and Kalijira rice are available at specialty stores or Whole Foods. They are often sold under the Lotus Foods label.

Use a fine Microplane grater to grate garlic.

1½ cups	water	375 mL
¾ cup	Bhutanese red or Kalijira brown rice, rinsed and drained (see Tips, left)	175 mL
DRESSING		
1 tbsp	white wine vinegar or freshly squeezed lemon juice	15 mL
1 tsp	Dijon mustard	5 mL
½ tsp	salt	2 mL
	Freshly ground black pepper	
3 tbsp	extra virgin olive oil	45 mL
1	small shallot, minced, or 2 tbsp (25 mL) finely chopped green onion, white part only	1
½	clove garlic, finely grated or put through a press (see Tips, left)	½
1	can (6 oz/170 g) albacore tuna, drained	1
1 cup	cooked sliced green beans, cooled, optional	250 mL
½	red bell pepper, seeded and diced	½
¼ cup	sliced pitted black olives or 1 tbsp (15 mL) diced capers	50 mL
4	green onions, white part only, thinly sliced, or ¼ cup (50 mL) finely chopped red onion	4
1	sun-dried tomato, packed in olive oil, finely chopped, or ½ cup (125 mL) quartered cherry or grape tomatoes	1
2 tbsp	finely chopped parsley	25 mL
	Lettuce leaves or hearts of romaine, optional	

1. In a heavy saucepan with a tight-fitting lid, bring water to a rapid boil. Stir in rice and return to a boil. Reduce heat to low. Cover and simmer until liquid is absorbed and rice is tender, about 25 minutes. (If liquid remains, remove lid and return to element for a few minutes until it evaporates.) Fluff up with a fork.

2. *Dressing:* Meanwhile, in a small bowl, combine vinegar, mustard and salt, stirring until salt dissolves. Season to taste with pepper. Gradually whisk in olive oil. Stir in shallot and garlic.

3. In a bowl, combine tuna, green beans, if using, bell pepper, olives, green onions, sun-dried tomato and parsley. Toss until blended.

4. *To serve:* Spoon warm rice onto plates and top with tuna mixture. Or, if using lettuce and you want to increase your consumption of fiber, line a platter with leafy lettuce or hearts of romaine and spoon rice onto lettuce and top with tuna mixture.

Variations

If you aren't pressed for time (or have precooked rice on hand), by all means substitute another red rice that takes longer to cook, such as Camargue (about 40 minutes), Italian wild red (about 35 minutes), Thai (about 30 minutes) or Wehani (about 45 minutes). Long-grain brown rice also works well in this salad. Check the package instructions as the quantity of water required also varies among the different varieties.

TUNA

Tuna is one of the best sources of heart-healthy omega-3 fats, yet watchdogs such as the FDA have advised that tuna (along with other large fish, such as shark and swordfish) be consumed with caution because it is likely to contain high levels of mercury. The quantity of tuna in this salad easily falls within the guidelines for safe consumption, even for pregnant or nursing women (6 ounces/170 g per week), but if you're concerned, look for tins of tuna labeled "skipjack," rather than albacore. Albacore tuna have about three times more mercury than these smaller fish, which are a healthier alternative.

Nutrients per serving

Calories	296
Protein	12.1 g
Carbohydrates	29.8 g
Fat (Total)	14.8 g
Saturated Fat	2.1 g
Monounsaturated Fat	9.1 g
Polyunsaturated Fat	2.4 g
Dietary Fiber	3.1 g
Sodium	515 mg
Cholesterol	11 mg

EXCELLENT SOURCE OF vitamin C, niacin and selenium.

GOOD SOURCE OF vitamin E (alpha-tocoperol).

SOURCE OF vitamin A, folate, phosphorous, iron, magnesium and copper.

CONTAINS a moderate amount of dietary fiber.

Poultry

Roast Chicken with Fruited-Studded Wheat Berries

Roast Chicken with Fruit-Studded Wheat Berries

Here's a special-occasion dish that is both delicious and pretty to look at — perfect for Sunday dinner or if you're having guests. Serve this with steamed baby carrots seasoned with a dash of cumin to complement the flavors of the chicken.

Makes 4 servings

TIPS

With the addition of chicken stock, you'll have quite a bit of extra liquid, since the wheat berries should be submerged while baking to ensure they will be tender.

If your apricot jam is a bit chunky, chop the fruit finely or process the mixture in a mini-chopper until the jam is puréed and the mixture is blended.

To clean leeks: Fill sink full of lukewarm water. Split leeks in half lengthwise and submerge in water, swishing them around to remove all traces of dirt. Transfer to a colander and rinse under cold water.

- **Preheat oven to 350°F (180°C)**
- **Shallow 13-by 9-inch (3 L) baking dish, lightly greased**

½ cup	wheat berries	125 mL
1 cup	water	250 mL
1 cup	reduced-sodium chicken stock	250 mL
1 tbsp	olive oil	15 mL
2	large skin-on bone-in chicken breasts, each about 10 oz (300 g), cut in half, rinsed and patted dry	2
3	leeks, white part only, cleaned and thinly sliced (see Tips, left)	3
4	cloves garlic, minced	4
1 tbsp	minced gingerroot	15 mL
1 tbsp	ground cumin	15 mL
1	jalapeño pepper, seeded and minced	1
2 tsp	finely grated lemon zest	10 mL
½ cup	chopped dried apricots	125 mL
1 tbsp	melted butter	15 mL
	Freshly ground black pepper	

CHILI-APRICOT GLAZE

½ cup	apricot jam	125 mL
1 tbsp	freshly squeezed lemon juice	15 mL
1 tsp	Asian chili sauce, such as sambal oelek	5 mL

1. In a saucepan, combine wheat berries, water and stock. Bring to a boil over medium heat. Reduce heat to low. Cover and simmer for 30 minutes. Remove from heat and set aside. (Wheat berries will not be fully cooked and liquid won't be completely absorbed.)

2. Meanwhile, in a skillet, heat oil over medium–high heat for 30 seconds. Add chicken, in two batches, and brown, turning once, about 6 minutes per batch. Transfer to a plate and set aside.

3. Reduce heat to medium. Add leeks to pan and cook, stirring, until softened, about 3 minutes. Add garlic, ginger, cumin, jalapeño and lemon zest and cook, stirring, for 1 minute. Add apricots and wheat berries with liquid, stir well and bring to a boil. Transfer to prepared dish and spread evenly.

4. Brush skin side of the chicken with melted butter and season to taste with black pepper. Arrange evenly over wheat berry mixture, skin side up. Roast in preheated oven for 30 minutes.

5. *Chili-Apricot Glaze:* Meanwhile, in a bowl, combine apricot jam, lemon juice and chili sauce (see Tips, left). Pour half of the mixture into a small dish and set aside. Brush skin side of chicken with remainder and return to oven. Roast until no longer pink inside, about 15 minutes longer. To serve, pour reserved Chili-Apricot Glaze over the sizzling chicken.

Variation

Game Hens with Fruit-Studded Wheat Berries: Substitute 2 Rock Cornish hens, each 1 to 1½ lbs (500 to 750 g), cut in half down the breastbone, for the chicken breasts. Don't sear them (Step 2), but if you have time, brine them in a mixture of ½ cup (125 mL) kosher salt and 8 cups (2 L) water in the refrigerator for 1 to 2 hours prior to cooking. Rinse well and pat dry before cooking. Roast until an instant-read thermometer inserted into the thickest part of the thigh registers 165°F (75°C).

DRIED APRICOTS

Dried apricots are available year-round and make a colorful and flavorful addition to many savory dishes. They provide dietary fiber and vitamin A, among other nutrients. However, most dried apricots are treated with sulfates to preserve their bright color. A small number of people are allergic to these substances, so you may want to consider using organic dried apricots, which do not contain the preservative.

Nutrients per serving

Calories	505
Protein	27.9 g
Carbohydrates	62.4 g
Fat (Total)	18.1 g
Saturated Fat	5.3 g
Monounsaturated Fat	7.5 g
Polyunsaturated Fat	3.7 g
Dietary Fiber	5.5 g
Sodium	271 mg
Cholesterol	79 mg

EXCELLENT SOURCE OF niacin, phosphorus, iron, magnesium, manganese and selenium.

GOOD SOURCE OF vitamin E (alpha-tocopherol), folate, panthothenic acid, zinc and copper.

SOURCE OF vitamins A and C, thiamine, riboflavin and calcium.

CONTAINS a high amount of dietary fiber.

Arroz con Pollo

This Spanish approach to chicken and rice is a great one-dish meal, delicious enough to serve to guests. I love this version, which has quite a bit of liquid, because I enjoy spooning the luscious sauce over the chicken as I eat, and soaking it up with some rustic whole-grain bread. If you prefer a drier version, reduce the quantity of chicken stock by 1 cup (250 mL) and/or omit the wine. In addition to warm bread, a tossed green salad is all you need.

Makes 6 servings

TIP

If you don't have a Dutch oven, use a large ovenproof saucepan, or complete Steps 1 and 2 using a large skillet, then transfer the mixture to a covered baking dish.

Nutrient Tip

Most of the fat in this recipe comes from the chorizo and the chicken skin. If you're concerned about the quantity of fat, remove the skin from the chicken and reduce the quantity of sausage.

- **Preheat oven to 350°F (180°C)**

1 tbsp	olive oil	15 mL
4 oz	soft chorizo sausage, removed from casings	125 g
2 lbs	skin-on bone-in chicken pieces, cut into serving-size pieces, rinsed and patted dry	1 kg
2	onions, finely chopped	2
1	red bell pepper, seeded and diced	1
4	cloves garlic, minced	4
2 tsp	sweet paprika	10 mL
½ tsp	salt or to taste	2 mL
	Freshly ground black pepper	
1 cup	long-grain brown rice, rinsed and drained	250 mL
½ cup	dry white wine	125 mL
¼ tsp	crumbled saffron threads, dissolved in 2 tbsp (25 mL) boiling water	1 mL
2 cups	reduced-sodium chicken stock	500 mL
1	can (14 oz/398 mL) no-salt-added diced tomatoes with juice	1
1 cup	cooked green peas, optional	250 mL

1. In a Dutch oven or large ovenproof saucepan with a tight-fitting lid, heat oil over medium–high heat for 30 seconds. Add chorizo and cook, stirring and breaking up with a spoon, until cooked through, about 2 minutes. Using a slotted spoon, transfer cooked sausage to a plate. Add chicken, in batches, and cook, turning once, until nicely browned, about 5 minutes per batch. Set sausage and chicken aside. Drain off all but 1 tbsp (15 mL) fat from pan.

2. Reduce heat to medium. Add onions, bell pepper and garlic and cook, stirring, until vegetables are softened, about 5 minutes. Add paprika, salt and black pepper to taste and cook, stirring, for 1 minute. Add rice and cook, stirring, for 1 minute. Add white wine and saffron liquid and bring to a boil. Boil for 1 minute. Add stock and tomatoes with juice and bring to a boil. Boil for 2 minutes. Return sausage and chicken to pan.

3. Cover and cook in preheated oven until rice is tender and chicken is no longer pink inside, about 1 hour. Stir in green peas, if using, and cook until heated through.

Slow Cooker Method

If it's more convenient, use your slow cooker to make this dish. Use bone-in skinless chicken thighs and arrange them over the bottom of the stoneware without browning. Complete Steps 1 and 2, but do not include the bell pepper when softening the onions. Transfer mixture to slow cooker stoneware. Place a clean tea towel, folded in half (so you will have two layers), over top of stoneware. (Accumulated moisture affects the consistency of the rice. The tea towels will absorb the moisture generated during cooking.) Cover and cook on Low for 6 hours or on High for 3 hours, until juices run clear when chicken is pierced with a fork. Stir in bell pepper along with the green peas. Cover and cook on High until vegetables are tender, about 20 minutes.

SAFFRON

Saffron is the dried stigma of a particular kind of crocus. It has an intensely bitter but extremely appealing taste and a little goes a long way, which is fortunate since it is one of the costliest spices. In this recipe, it adds unmistakable flavor and color (a deep golden yellow) to the deep rich sauce.

Nutrients per serving

Calories	477
Protein	34.3 g
Carbohydrates	35.4 g
Fat (Total)	21.5 g
Saturated Fat	6.3 g
Monounsaturated Fat	9.9 g
Polyunsaturated Fat	3.7 g
Dietary Fiber	3.9 g
Sodium	715 mg
Cholesterol	93 mg

EXCELLENT SOURCE OF vitamin C, thiamine, niacin, phosphorus, magnesium, manganese and selenium.

GOOD SOURCE OF vitamin A, pantothenic acid, riboflavin, zinc, iron and copper.

SOURCE OF vitamin E (alpha-tocopherol), folate and calcium.

CONTAINS a moderate amount of dietary fiber.

Italian-Style Chicken and Rice

This mouthwatering combination of chicken and rice, accented with pancetta and hints of lemon and chile peppers, is comfort food, Italian-style. Finish this with a drizzle of your best extra virgin olive oil and, in season, add a tomato and bocconcini salad garnished with fresh basil.

TIP
Pancetta is a kind of Italian bacon, made from cured pork belly. It has a unique flavor, but if you can't find it, you can substitute an equal quantity of bacon.

Nutrient Tip
The nutrient analysis on this recipe was done using 2 oz (60 g) of bacon, which contributes 8.5 g of fat per serving. If you're concerned about your intake of fat, reduce the quantity of bacon or pancetta and remove the skin from the chicken, but be aware that the dish won't be nearly as tasty.

- **Preheat oven to 350°F (180°C)**
- **Covered 10-cup (2.5 L) baking dish**

1 cup	short-grain brown rice	250 mL
2½ cups	reduced-sodium chicken stock or water	625 mL
1 tbsp	olive oil	15 mL
2 lbs	skin-on bone-in chicken breasts, cut into serving-size pieces, rinsed and patted dry	1 kg
2 oz	chunk of pancetta, finely chopped (see Tip, left)	60 g
2	onions, thinly sliced on the vertical	2
4	cloves garlic, minced	4
2	dried red cayenne peppers	2
1 tbsp	finely grated lemon zest	15 mL
1½ tsp	dried Italian seasoning	7 mL
	Coarse sea salt	
	Freshly ground black pepper	
2 tbsp	freshly squeezed lemon juice	25 mL
	Extra virgin olive oil	

1. In a heavy saucepan with a tight-fitting lid, combine rice and stock. Bring to a rapid boil over high heat. Reduce heat to low. Cover and simmer for 15 minutes. Remove from heat and set aside.

2. Meanwhile, in a large skillet, heat oil over medium–high heat for 30 seconds. Add chicken, in batches, and cook, turning once, until nicely browned, about 5 minutes per batch. Transfer to a plate and set aside. Drain off all but 1 tbsp (15 mL) fat from pan.

3. Reduce heat to medium. Add pancetta and cook, stirring, for 2 minutes. Add onions and cook, stirring, until softened, about 3 minutes. Add garlic, dried peppers, lemon zest and Italian seasoning and cook, stirring, for 1 minute. Add reserved rice with liquid and bring to a boil.

4. Transfer to baking dish. Arrange chicken over top. Cover and bake in preheated oven until chicken is no longer pink inside and rice is tender, about 45 minutes. Remove and discard cayenne peppers.

5. Sprinkle chicken with sea salt and pepper to taste. Drizzle with lemon juice and olive oil.

Slow Cooker Method

If you prefer, make this recipe using your slow cooker. Skip Steps 1 and 2. Use an equal quantity of bone-in skinless chicken thighs and arrange them over the bottom of the slow cooker stoneware. Heat oil in pan and continue with Step 3. Add rice and stock, bring to a boil and boil rapidly for 2 minutes. Transfer to slow cooker stoneware. Place a clean tea towel, folded in half (so you will have two layers), over top of stoneware to absorb moisture. Cover and cook on Low for 6 hours or on High for 3 hours, until juices run clear when chicken is pierced with a fork. Finish as per Step 5.

Nutrients per serving

Calories	521
Protein	32.4 g
Carbohydrates	44.6 g
Fat (Total)	23.2 g
Saturated Fat	8.6 g
Monounsaturated Fat	12.6 g
Polyunsaturated Fat	4.8 g
Dietary Fiber	4.8 g
Sodium	486 mg
Cholesterol	89 mg

EXCELLENT SOURCE OF niacin, phosphorus, magnesium, manganese and selenium.

GOOD SOURCE OF pantothenic acid, thiamine, riboflavin, zinc and iron.

SOURCE OF vitamins A and C, folate and copper.

CONTAINS a high amount of dietary fiber.

Peppery Chicken Quinoa

Not only is this dish pretty to look at, it's very easy to make. Enjoy this when peppers are in season. It makes a great one-dish weeknight meal.

3 cups	reduced-sodium chicken stock, divided	750 mL
1 tbsp	harissa, optional (see Tip, left)	15 mL
1 cup	quinoa, rinsed and drained	250 mL
3 tbsp	extra virgin olive oil, divided	45 mL
½ tsp	cracked black peppercorns	2 mL
1 lb	skinless boneless chicken breasts, thinly sliced	500 g
4	cloves garlic, thinly sliced	4
3	red bell peppers, seeded and cut into thin strips	3
2 tbsp	sherry vinegar	25 mL
¼ cup	finely chopped parsley	50 mL

1. In a saucepan over medium heat, bring 2 cups (500 mL) of the stock to a boil. Stir in harissa, if using. Add quinoa in a steady steam, stirring constantly, and return to a boil. Reduce heat to low. Cover and simmer until tender, about 15 minutes. Remove from heat and let stand for 5 minutes. Fluff with a fork.

2. Meanwhile, in a large skillet or wok, heat 1 tbsp (15 mL) of the olive oil over medium–high heat. Add black peppercorns and stir well. Add chicken and cook, stirring, until it turns white and almost cooks through, about 5 minutes. Transfer to a plate.

3. Add remaining 2 tbsp (25 mL) of oil to pan. Add garlic and cook, stirring, just until it begins to turn golden, about 2 minutes. Add bell peppers and cook, stirring, until they begin to shimmer, about 2 minutes. Add remaining 1 cup (250 mL) of stock and sherry vinegar and cook until mixture is reduced by half, about 8 minutes. Return chicken to pan and toss until heated through. Remove from heat.

4. *To serve:* Spread cooked quinoa over a deep platter and scoop out an indentation in the middle. Fill with chicken mixture and garnish with parsley.

Variation

Instead of quinoa, serve this over couscous or brown or red rice. If using couscous, try spelt or barley couscous instead of whole wheat.

Coconut Chicken with Quinoa

This delightfully different chicken is a potpourri of mouthwatering flavors and beneficial nutrients. Add the chile if you like heat and keep the accompaniments simple. Steamed green beans make a nice finish.

2 tsp	cumin seeds (see Tip, left)	10 mL
1 tsp	whole allspice (see Tip, left)	5 mL
1 tbsp	olive oil	15 mL
1½ lbs	skin-on bone-in chicken breasts, rinsed and patted dry	750 g
1	onion, finely chopped	1
1	red bell pepper, seeded and diced	1
1	green bell pepper, seeded and diced	1
6	cloves garlic, minced	6
½ to 1	chile pepper, seeded and minced, optional	½ to 1
1 tsp	curry powder	5 mL
½ tsp	salt	2 mL
½ tsp	freshly ground black pepper	2 mL
¾ cup	quinoa, rinsed and drained	175 mL
1½ cups	reduced-sodium chicken stock	375 mL
½ cup	coconut milk	125 mL

1. In a dry large skillet over medium heat, combine cumin seeds and allspice. Toast, stirring constantly, until fragrant, about 4 minutes. Immediately transfer to a mortar or a spice grinder and grind. Set aside.

2. In same skillet, heat oil over medium heat for 30 seconds. Add chicken, in batches, skin side down, and brown well, about 4 minutes. Turn over, cover and cook for 10 minutes. Remove from pan and keep warm. Drain all but 1 tbsp (15 mL) fat from pan.

3. Add onion, bell peppers, garlic and chile pepper, if using, and cook, stirring, until vegetables are softened, about 5 minutes. Add curry powder, salt, black pepper, reserved ground spices and quinoa and cook, stirring, until quinoa is well integrated into mixture, about 1 minute. Add stock and coconut milk and bring to a boil. Lay chicken, skin side up, over mixture. Reduce heat to low. Cover and cook until chicken is no longer pink inside, about 30 minutes.

Chinese-Style Chicken Fried Rice

This flavorful stir-fry, rich in the appetizing flavors of soy sauce, ginger and shiitake mushrooms, is a great weeknight dinner that is relatively speedy to make so long as you have cooked the rice ahead of time. A plate of steamed or stir-fried bok choy makes a perfect finish.

Makes 4 servings

TIP
If you prefer, use leftover cooked chicken to make this recipe. Combine with the marinade and set aside for 15 minutes. Skip Steps 1 and 4. Drain off excess liquid and add to the pan along with the mushrooms.

2 cups	cooked brown rice (see cooking instructions, page 29)	500 mL
3 tbsp	reduced-sodium soy sauce, divided	45 mL
1 tbsp	Shaoxing wine, sake, dry vermouth or vodka	15 mL
1 tbsp	minced gingerroot	15 mL
2	cloves garlic, minced	2
	Freshly ground black pepper	
8 oz	skinless boneless chicken breast, thinly sliced (see Tip, left)	250 g
4	dried shiitake mushrooms	4
2 tbsp	reduced-sodium chicken stock	25 mL
1 tbsp	mushroom soaking liquid	15 mL
1 tbsp	oyster sauce	15 mL
1 tsp	sesame oil	5 mL
2 tbsp	olive oil, divided	25 mL
2	eggs, lightly beaten	2
6	green onions, white part with a bit of green, thinly sliced	6
1 cup	barely cooked green peas	250 mL

Nutrients per serving

Calories	379
Protein	23 g
Carbohydrates	45.3 g
Fat (Total)	12.5 g
Saturated Fat	2.3 g
Monounsaturated Fat	7.1 g
Polyunsaturated Fat	2.1 g
Dietary Fiber	5.6 g
Sodium	689 mg
Cholesterol	126 mg

EXCELLENT SOURCE OF riboflavin, niacin, pantothenic acid, magnesium, manganese, zinc, copper and selenium.

GOOD SOURCE OF folate, thiamine, phosphorus and iron.

SOURCE OF vitamins A, C and E (alpha-tocopherol) and calcium.

CONTAINS a high amount of dietary fiber.

1. In a bowl, combine 2 tbsp (25 mL) of the soy sauce, Shaoxing wine, ginger, garlic and pepper to taste. Add sliced chicken and toss to combine. Cover and set aside for 30 minutes.

2. Meanwhile, in a small bowl, combine dried mushrooms with hot water to cover. Ensuring they remain submerged, set aside until mushrooms are tender, about 30 minutes. Drain, reserving 1 tbsp (15 mL) of the mushroom soaking liquid. Remove stems, if necessary, and slice caps thinly. Set aside.

3. In another small bowl, combine stock, reserved mushroom soaking liquid, oyster sauce and sesame oil. Set aside.

4. In a wok or large skillet, heat 1 tbsp (15 mL) of the olive oil over medium high heat for 30 seconds. Add chicken with marinade and cook, stirring, until no longer pink, about 3 minutes. Transfer to a plate and set aside. Wipe pan clean.

5. Add remaining 1 tbsp (15 mL) oil to pan. Add eggs and cook until scrambled, about 30 seconds. Add mushrooms and green onions and cook, stirring, for 30 seconds. Add peas and toss well. Add reserved chicken and rice and toss well. Add reserved sauce and cook, stirring, until heated through, about 1 minute.

Chicken and Barley Bake

If you're tired of eating the same old thing, try this for a great weeknight dinner. The combination of sweet peppers, tomatoes, chicken and barley, finished with a cheeky lacing of dill, makes an unusual and nutritious one-dish meal, providing a wide range of nutrients.

Makes 6 servings		

TIPS

For added flavor, cook the barley in chicken stock rather than water.

Don't worry about the anchovies in this recipe even if you don't like their flavor. They dissolve into the sauce and add welcome richness rather than taste. If you prefer, substitute 1 tbsp (15 mL) anchovy paste for this quantity.

- **Preheat oven to 350°F (180°C)**
- **13-by 9-inch (3 L) baking pan or dish**

3 cups	cooked whole (hulled) barley (see cooking instructions, page 16)	750 mL
1 tbsp	olive oil	15 mL
2 lbs	skin-on bone-in chicken breasts, cut into serving-size pieces, rinsed and patted dry	1 kg
1 tsp	sweet, hot or smoked paprika	5 mL
2	onions, finely chopped	2
2	stalks celery, diced	2
1	red bell pepper, seeded and diced	1
1	green bell pepper, seeded and diced	1
4	cloves garlic, minced	4
3	anchovies, minced (see Tips, left)	3
2	bay leaves	2
½ tsp	salt	2 mL
	Freshly ground black pepper	
½ cup	dry red wine	125 mL
1	can (28 oz/796 mL) no-salt-added tomatoes with juice	1
½ cup	freshly chopped dill	125 mL

1. In a skillet, heat oil over medium heat for 30 seconds. Add chicken, in batches, skin side down, and cook until nicely browned, about 6 minutes. Turn skin side up and sprinkle with paprika. Arrange chicken in baking dish in one layer and set aside. Drain off all but 1 tbsp (15 mL) fat from skillet.

2. Add onions, celery, bell peppers and garlic to the skillet and stir well. Reduce heat to low. Cover and cook until vegetables are softened, about 10 minutes. Increase heat to medium-high. Add anchovies, bay leaves, salt and black pepper to taste and cook, stirring, for 1 minute. Add wine and bring to a boil. Cook, stirring, until most of the liquid evaporates, about 2 minutes. Add tomatoes with juice and cook, breaking up with a spoon, until mixture boils. Stir in cooked barley. Spoon over chicken.

3. Cover and bake in preheated oven until chicken is no longer pink, about 40 minutes. Remove and discard bay leaves. Sprinkle dill evenly over top.

Slow Cooker Method

Substitute 1 cup (250 mL) uncooked whole barley, rinsed, for the cooked, and skinless bone-in chicken thighs for the breasts. Skip Step 1. Arrange chicken over bottom of slow cooker stoneware. Complete Step 2, but set the peppers aside in the refrigerator rather than softening them with the onions and add 2 cups (500 mL) reduced-sodium chicken stock or water to the skillet along with the tomatoes. Cover and cook on Low for 5 hours or on High for 2½ hours, until juices run clear when chicken is pierced with a fork. Add peppers to stoneware and stir well. Cover and cook on High for 20 minutes, until peppers are tender. Remove and discard bay leaves. Garnish with dill and serve.

PAPRIKA

The paprika in this recipe adds beautiful color to the browned chicken and, depending upon the variety you use, lively flavor to the sauce. The influence of sweet paprika will be subtle, enhancing the flavor of the chicken and gently complementing the other ingredients in the sauce. If you prefer a bit of heat, use hot paprika. A teaspoon (5 mL) of smoked paprika will add pleasing smokiness reminiscent of bacon, but unless you're a real fan of the product, don't use more than that or the flavor will likely be too intense.

Nutrients per serving

Calories	414
Protein	32.0 g
Carbohydrates	40.5 g
Fat (Total)	14.4 g
Saturated Fat	3.6 g
Monounsaturated Fat	6.3 g
Polyunsaturated Fat	3.1 g
Dietary Fiber	9.4 g
Sodium	386 mg
Cholesterol	78 mg

EXCELLENT SOURCE OF vitamin C, thiamine, niacin, phosphorus, iron, manganese, copper and selenium.

GOOD SOURCE OF vitamins A and E (alpha-tocopherol), riboflavin, pantothenic acid, magnesium and zinc.

SOURCE OF folate and calcium.

CONTAINS a very high amount of dietary fiber.

Peppery Coconut Chicken with Wheat Berries

If your appetite is desperately seeking stimulation, this flavorful chicken with toothsome wheat berries may be just the thing. There's just a hint of coconut, but it's enough to add intriguing depth to what could be an uneventful tomato sauce. The wheat berries partially cook while you're doing prep work for the rest of the dish, making this a relatively time-efficient meal. Once it's in the oven, you can relax while it cooks. A green vegetable is the only addition you need.

Makes 6 servings

TIPS

If you have a favorite spice rub for chicken that complements the flavors in this recipe, by all means substitute it for the paprika. I've had excellent results using a prepared rub containing paprika and a variety of herbs.

If you prefer a more pronounced coconut flavor, substitute an equal amount of extra virgin coconut oil for the olive oil.

Nutrients per serving

Calories	462
Protein	23.9 g
Carbohydrates	33.6 g
Fat (Total)	27.2 g
Saturated Fat	9.7 g
Monounsaturated Fat	10.2 g
Polyunsaturated Fat	5.1 g
Dietary Fiber	6.6 g
Sodium	368 mg
Cholesterol	90 mg

EXCELLENT SOURCE OF niacin, iron, magnesium, manganese, zinc and selenium.

GOOD SOURCE OF vitamins A and C, thiamine, riboflavin, pantothenic acid, phosphorus and copper.

SOURCE OF vitamin E (alpha-tocopherol), folate and calcium.

CONTAINS a very high amount of dietary fiber.

- **Preheat oven to 350°F (180°C)**
- **13-by 9-inch (3 L) baking pan or dish**

2½ cups	reduced-sodium chicken stock	625 mL
1 cup	wheat berries, rinsed and drained	250 mL
2 lbs	skin-on bone-in chicken thighs, rinsed and patted dry	1 kg
1 tbsp	sweet paprika (see Tips, left)	15 mL
1 tbsp	olive oil (see Tips, left)	15 mL
2	onions, finely chopped	2
2	stalks celery, diced	2
1	bell pepper, any color, seeded and diced	1
4	cloves garlic, minced	4
½ tsp	cayenne pepper	2 mL
½ tsp	cracked black peppercorns	2 mL
	Salt	
1	can (14 oz/398 mL) no-salt-added diced tomatoes with juice	1
½ cup	coconut milk	125 mL

1. In a saucepan over medium–high heat, bring stock to a boil. Add wheat berries and return to a boil. Reduce heat to low. Cover and simmer for 30 minutes. Remove from heat and set aside. (Wheat berries will not be fully cooked and liquid won't be completely absorbed.)

2. Meanwhile, rub chicken all over with paprika. In a skillet, heat oil over medium–high heat for 30 seconds. Add chicken, in batches, and cook, turning once, until nicely browned, about 6 minutes per batch. Transfer to a plate. Drain off all but 1 tbsp (15 mL) fat from pan.

3. Reduce heat to medium. Add onions, celery and bell pepper and cook, stirring, until softened, about 5 minutes. Add garlic, cayenne, peppercorns and salt to taste and cook, stirring, for 1 minute. Add tomatoes with juice, coconut milk and partially cooked wheat berries with liquid and bring to a boil. Transfer to baking dish and lay chicken, skin side up, over top.

4. Bake in preheated oven until wheat berries are tender and juices run clear when chicken is pierced, about 45 minutes.

Variation

Substitute an equal quantity of spelt or Kamut berries for the wheat berries.

French-Style Red Rice with Chicken

I adapted this recipe from one that Paula Wolfert included in her book Mediterranean Grains and Greens. Camargue red rice, which is available in North America at stores specializing in products from France, has a delicate nutty flavor. If you can't find it, other varieties of red rice work well, but you'll need to adjust the cooking time. You want the rice to be tender to the bite, but not fully cooked, when it is placed in the oven.

Makes 6 servings

TIPS

If you're a heat seeker, you can use 2 chile peppers when making this recipe, or substitute hot paprika for some of the sweet version called for.

I've made this dish successfully using Wehani, which needs to cook for about 40 minutes before being added to the dish. If you're using Bhutanese red rice, it will be ready in about 15 minutes. If you can't find red rice, substitute a combination of brown and wild rice and cook it for about 40 minutes before adding to the oven.

Nutrients per serving

Calories	468
Protein	31.0 g
Carbohydrates	52.7 g
Fat (Total)	15.5 g
Saturated Fat	3.6 g
Monounsaturated Fat	6.9 g
Polyunsaturated Fat	2.8 g
Dietary Fiber	6.1 g
Sodium	817 mg
Cholesterol	77 mg

EXCELLENT SOURCE OF vitamins A and C, niacin, iron and selenium.

GOOD SOURCE OF vitamin E (alpha-tocopherol), pantothenic acid, phosphorus, magnesium and manganese.

SOURCE OF thiamine, riboflavin, folate, zinc, calcium and copper.

CONTAINS a very high amount of dietary fiber.

- **Preheat oven to 350°F (180°C)**
- **12-cup (3 L) baking dish**

1½ cups	Camargue or other red rice, rinsed and drained	375 mL
3 cups	reduced-sodium chicken stock	750 mL
1 tbsp	olive oil	15 mL
2 lbs	skin-on bone-in chicken breasts, cut into serving-size pieces, rinsed and patted dry	1 kg
2	onions, finely chopped	2
1	green bell pepper, seeded and diced	1
1	red bell pepper, seeded and diced	1
1	long red or green chile pepper, seeded and minced (see Tips, left)	1
4	cloves garlic, minced	4
1 tbsp	sweet paprika	15 mL
½ tsp	salt	2 mL
¼ tsp	cracked black peppercorns	1 mL
1	can (28 oz/796 mL) no-salt-added diced tomatoes with juice	1
½ cup	chopped pitted black olives	125 mL
2 tbsp	finely chopped parsley	25 mL

1. In a heavy saucepan with a tight-fitting lid, combine rice and stock. Bring to a rapid boil over high heat. Reduce heat to low. Cover and simmer until rice is tender to the bite, about 30 minutes. Remove from heat and set aside.

2. Meanwhile, in a skillet, heat oil over medium–high heat for 30 seconds. Add chicken, in batches, and cook, turning once, until nicely browned, about 5 minutes per batch. Transfer to a plate and set aside. Drain off all but 2 tbsp (25 mL) fat from pan.

3. Reduce heat to medium. Add onions, bell peppers, chile pepper and garlic and cook, stirring, until peppers have softened, about 5 minutes. Add paprika, salt and peppercorns and cook, stirring, for 1 minute. Add tomatoes with juice and bring to a boil. Cook, stirring, until mixture amalgamates and some of the liquid evaporates, about 2 minutes. Stir in rice with liquid and boil for 1 minute. Stir in olives and parsley. Transfer to baking dish and arrange chicken over top. Cover and bake in preheated oven until rice is tender and chicken is no longer pink, about 40 minutes.

Creole Chicken with Red Rice

I love the lively Cajun flavors of this dish. Served on a deep platter, surrounded by colorful rice and sprinkled with flecks of toasted sliced almonds, preferably with bits of skin for the visual effect, it's pretty enough to serve to guests.

TIP

I like to use red rice, such as Bhutanese, Thai, Camargue or Wehani, in this recipe for its visual effect, but the dish is equally delicious made with long-grain brown rice. Put the rice on to cook before you start the chicken and it will be ready when you are.

Nutrient Tip

One serving of this dish is relatively high in calories because it is a fairly large portion. Keep the sides to a minimum.

Nutrients per serving

Calories	454
Protein	29.9 g
Carbohydrates	42.7 g
Fat (Total)	18.5 g
Saturated Fat	3.9 g
Monounsaturated Fat	9.2 g
Polyunsaturated Fat	3.5 g
Dietary Fiber	5.5 g
Sodium	116 mg
Cholesterol	76 mg

EXCELLENT SOURCE OF manganese, selenium and niacin.

GOOD SOURCE OF vitamins C and E (alpha-tocopherol), pantothenic acid, phosporus, magnesium, iron, zinc and copper.

SOURCE OF vitamin A, calcium, thiamine, riboflavin and folate.

CONTAINS a high amount of dietary fiber.

3 cups	cooked red rice (see Tip, left)	750 mL
½ cup	whole wheat flour	125 mL
1 tsp	cayenne pepper	5 mL
1 tsp	cracked black peppercorns	5 mL
2 lbs	skin-on bone-in chicken breasts, cut into serving-size pieces, rinsed and patted dry	1 kg
2 tbsp	olive oil	25 mL
2	onions, chopped	2
2	stalks celery, diced	2
1	green bell pepper, seeded and diced	1
2	cloves garlic, minced	2
1	bay leaf	1
1	can (14 oz/398 mL) no-salt-added diced tomatoes with juice	1
1 cup	beer	250 mL
2 tsp	Worcestershire sauce	10 mL
	Salt	
¼ cup	toasted sliced almonds	50 mL

1. In a plastic bag, combine flour, cayenne and black peppercorns. Add chicken, in batches, tossing until well coated with mixture. Discard excess.

2. In a skillet, heat oil over medium–high heat. Add chicken, in batches, and brown, turning once, about 5 minutes per batch. Transfer to a plate and keep warm. Drain off all but 2 tbsp (25 mL) fat from pan.

3. Add onions, celery and bell pepper and cook, stirring, until softened, about 7 minutes. Add garlic and bay leaf and cook, stirring, for 1 minute. Add tomatoes with juice, beer and Worcestershire sauce and bring to a boil. Season to taste with salt. Return chicken to pan, skin side up. Cover and simmer, turning once or twice, until chicken is tender and no longer pink inside, about 45 minutes.

4. *To serve:* On a deep platter, arrange rice in a ring around the edge, leaving the center hollow. Arrange chicken in the hollow and garnish with almonds.

Barley Jambalaya

This is a great dish for a family dinner or a casual evening with friends. The robust flavors of the Italian sausage, peppers and Cajun seasonings are delicious any time of the year, but particularly appreciated on a chilly night. All you need to add is warm whole-grain rolls, a big salad and, if you're feeling festive, some robust red wine.

Makes 6 servings

TIPS

If you like heat, use hot Italian sausage and/or add a seeded diced chile pepper with the bell peppers. If you are cooking this in a slow cooker, add the chile pepper along with the roasted red pepper.

If you don't have Cajun seasoning, substitute 1 tsp (5 mL) of any variety of paprika — sweet, hot or smoked, depending on your taste.

3 cups	reduced-sodium chicken stock	750 mL
¾ cup	whole (hulled) barley, rinsed and drained	175 mL
1 tbsp	olive oil	15 mL
8 oz	Italian sausage, removed from casings	250 g
1 lb	skinless boneless chicken thighs, cut into bite-size pieces	500 g
2	onions, finely chopped	2
2	stalks celery, diced	2
2	bell peppers, such as 1 green and 1 red, seeded and diced	2
1	chile pepper, seeded and diced, optional (see Tips, left)	1
4	cloves garlic, minced	4
2 tsp	Cajun seasoning (see Tips, left)	10 mL
1 tsp	dried thyme leaves	5 mL
1	can (28 oz/796 mL) no-salt-added diced tomatoes with juice	1
8 oz	medium shrimp, cooked, peeled and deveined, optional	250 g

1. In a heavy saucepan with a tight-fitting lid, bring stock to a boil. Add barley and return to a boil. Reduce heat to low. Cover and simmer for 30 minutes. (Barley will not be fully cooked and liquid won't be completely absorbed.)

2. Meanwhile, in a Dutch oven, heat oil over medium heat for 30 seconds. Add sausage and cook, breaking up with a spoon, until no longer pink, about 4 minutes. Add chicken and cook, stirring, until very lightly browned, about 2 minutes. Transfer to a bowl. Drain off all but 1 tbsp (15 mL) fat from pan, if necessary.

3. Add onions, celery, bell peppers and chile pepper, if using, and cook, stirring, until softened, about 5 minutes. Add garlic, Cajun seasoning and thyme and cook, stirring, for 1 minute. Add tomatoes with juice and bring to a boil. Stir in partially cooked barley with liquid and return sausage and chicken to pot. Stir well.

4. Reduce heat to low. Cover and simmer until barley is tender and liquid is absorbed, about 30 minutes. Stir in shrimp, if using, and cook until heated through, about 10 minutes.

Slow Cooker Method

Skip Step 1. Complete Step 2 and transfer mixture to slow cooker stoneware. Proceed with Step 3, substituting 2 roasted red peppers for the bell peppers and adding them later, along with the shrimp. After the spices have been cooked, add uncooked barley and toss until thoroughly coated. Add stock along with the tomatoes and transfer mixture to slow cooker stoneware. Cover and cook on Low for 6 to 8 hours or on High for 3 to 4 hours. Add shrimp, if using, and roasted red pepper. Cover and cook on High until heated through.

BELL PEPPERS

I like to use one red and one green bell pepper in this jambalaya because I find the color combination particularly attractive, but you could use yellow, orange or even purple varieties, if you prefer. All taste relatively sweet (the purple has a hint of bitterness) and will add color and nutrients to the dish. A medium-size bell pepper has about 32 calories and is a rich source of powerful antioxidants, such as beta-carotene and vitamin C, which help to keep your immune system healthy, among other benefits. Vitamin C helps our bodies fight free radical damage and may help to prevent age-related aliments, such as heart disease and diabetes.

Nutrients per serving

Calories	351
Protein	27.6 g
Carbohydrates	35.5 g
Fat (Total)	12.1 g
Saturated Fat	3.5 g
Monounsaturated Fat	5.0 g
Polyunsaturated Fat	2.3 g
Dietary Fiber	8.1 g
Sodium	693 mg
Cholesterol	80 mg

EXCELLENT SOURCE OF vitamin C, thiamine, niacin, phosphorus, iron, manganese, zinc, selenium and copper.

GOOD SOURCE OF vitamin E (alpha-tocopherol), riboflavin, pantothenic acid and magnesium.

SOURCE OF vitamin A, folate and calcium.

CONTAINS a very high amount of dietary fiber.

Moroccan Chicken with Couscous and Cinnamon-Spiked Prunes

This is a wonderfully warming dish, a mélange of spirited flavors such as cinnamon, ginger, saffron and lemon. Remarkably, these combinations of sweet and savory work together to produce a deliciously different one-dish meal.

Makes 6 servings

Nutrient Tip
Although this recipe is a bit high in calories, it is also extremely high in fiber, which means one serving will really fill you up. You won't need much more than a few bites of a steamed vegetable in addition to feel completely sated.

1 cup	pitted prunes	250 mL
1 tsp	ground cinnamon	5 mL
1 tbsp	olive oil	15 mL
2 lbs	skin-on bone-in chicken breasts, cut into serving-size pieces, rinsed and patted dry	1 kg
3	onions, halved and thinly sliced on the vertical	3
2	cloves garlic, minced	2
2 tbsp	minced gingerroot	25 mL
1 tsp	ground cumin	5 mL
1 tsp	salt	5 mL
1 tsp	finely grated lemon zest	5 mL
¼ tsp	cayenne pepper	1 mL
	Freshly ground black pepper	
2 tbsp	freshly squeezed lemon juice	25 mL
3 cups	reduced-sodium chicken stock, divided	750 mL
¼ tsp	crumbled saffron threads, dissolved in 2 tbsp (25 mL) boiling water	1 mL
1 tbsp	liquid honey	15 mL
1 cup	whole wheat couscous	250 mL
	Toasted sliced almonds	

1. In a saucepan, combine prunes and cinnamon with cold water to cover. Bring to a boil over medium–high heat. Reduce heat and simmer until prunes are tender and water has been absorbed, about 30 minutes. Set aside.

2. In a skillet, heat oil over medium heat for 30 seconds. Add chicken, in batches, and cook, turning once, until nicely browned, about 6 minutes per batch. Transfer to a plate.

3. Add onions and cook, stirring, until they begin to brown, about 10 minutes. Add garlic, ginger, cumin, salt, lemon zest, cayenne and black pepper to taste and cook, stirring, for 1 minute. Add lemon juice, 1½ cups (375 mL) of the stock and saffron liquid and bring to a boil. Return chicken to pan, skin side up. Reduce heat to low. Cover and simmer until chicken is no longer pink inside, 25 to 40 minutes. Remove chicken from pan and keep warm.

4. Increase heat to medium and cook, stirring frequently, until mixture is reduced by one third, about 10 minutes. Add honey and stir well. Stir in reserved prunes and cook, stirring, until heated through. Return chicken to pan, cover and heat through.

5. Meanwhile, in a saucepan over medium heat, bring remaining 1½ cups (375 mL) of stock to a boil. Add couscous in a steady steam, stirring constantly. Remove from heat. Cover and let stand until tender and liquid is absorbed, about 15 minutes. Fluff with a fork and use your hands to break up any clumps.

6. *To serve:* On a deep platter, arrange couscous in a ring around the edge, leaving the center hollow. Arrange chicken mixture in hollow and garnish with almonds.

PRUNES

Prunes, which are a dried plum, are available year-round. Known for helping to keep you regular (due to the relatively high amount of dietary fiber they contain), they are also a source of powerful antioxidants, such as phenols and beta-carotene. They are rich in malic acid, a compound found in many fruits, which helps your body to convert nutrients to usable energy and are also low on the Glycemic Index, which is good news for people with diabetes.

Nutrients per serving

Calories	443
Protein	31.5 g
Carbohydrates	50.7 g
Fat (Total)	13.8 g
Saturated Fat	3.4 g
Monounsaturated Fat	6.2 g
Polyunsaturated Fat	2.6 g
Dietary Fiber	8.1 g
Sodium	749 mg
Cholesterol	77 mg

EXCELLENT SOURCE OF niacin and selenium.

GOOD SOURCE OF pantothenic acid, phosphorus, iron and magnesium.

SOURCE OF vitamins A and C, thiamine, riboflavin, folate, calcium, manganese, zinc and copper.

CONTAINS a very high amount of dietary fiber.

Chicken Chile Pie with Millet Crust

I have a real weakness for the flavors in this dish — chicken cooked with chipotle peppers, cumin and oregano — which are a wonderful combination. Add a crunchy millet crust, balanced by creamy Jack cheese, and you have a winner. All this needs is a simple green salad to complete the meal.

Makes 6 servings

TIPS

Use your favorite blend of chili powder or one from a single source, such as ancho or New Mexico chiles.

For the best flavor, toast and grind whole cumin seeds rather than buying ground cumin. Simply stir seeds in a dry skillet over medium heat until fragrant, about 3 minutes. Immediately transfer to a spice grinder or mortar and grind.

You can also make this recipe using cooked leftover chicken. Skip Steps 2 and 3, eliminating the flour and cayenne called for in the recipe. Combine 2 tbsp (25 mL) all-purpose flour and a pinch of cayenne and add in Step 4 when the reserved flour mixture is called for. Add cooked chicken in Step 4 when browned chicken is returned to the pan.

- **Preheat oven to 375°F (190°C)**
- **Shallow 10-cup (2.5 L) baking dish, greased**

MILLET CRUST

1 cup	millet	250 mL
3 cups	water or reduced-sodium chicken or vegetable stock	750 mL
	Salt and freshly ground black pepper	
1 cup	shredded Monterey Jack cheese	250 mL

FILLING

½ cup	whole wheat flour	125 mL
½ tsp	cayenne pepper	2 mL
1 lb	skinless boneless chicken breasts, cut into bite-size pieces	500 g
2 tbsp	olive oil (approx.), divided	25 mL
1	onion, finely chopped	1
4	stalks celery, diced	4
1	green bell pepper, seeded and diced	1
1	red bell pepper, seeded and diced	1
½ to 1	chipotle pepper in adobo sauce	½ to 1
2	cloves garlic, minced	2
1 tsp	finely grated lemon zest	5 mL
1 tbsp	chili powder (see Tips, left)	15 mL
1 tsp	ground cumin (see Tips, left)	5 mL
1 tsp	dried oregano leaves	5 mL
2 cups	reduced-sodium chicken stock	500 mL
2 tbsp	freshly squeezed lemon juice	25 mL

1. *Millet Crust:* In a saucepan over medium heat, toast millet, stirring constantly, until it crackles and releases its aroma, about 5 minutes. Transfer to a bowl. Add water, salt and black pepper to taste to saucepan and bring to a boil. Stir in millet. Reduce heat to low. Cover and simmer until millet is tender and all of the water is absorbed, about 20 minutes. Stir in cheese. Set aside.

2. *Filling:* Meanwhile, in a bowl or a plastic bag, combine flour and cayenne. Add chicken and toss well. Set 2 tbsp (25 mL) of excess mixture aside.

3. In a skillet, heat 1 tbsp (15 mL) of the oil over medium–high heat for 30 seconds. Add chicken, in batches, and cook, stirring, until lightly browned, about 3 minutes per batch, adding more oil, if necessary. Remove from pan and set aside.

4. Add remaining 1 tbsp (15 mL) of oil to the pan. Add onion, celery and bell peppers, and cook, stirring, until softened, about 5 minutes. Add chipotle pepper, garlic, lemon zest, chili powder, cumin and oregano and stir well Add reserved flour mixture and cook, stirring, for 2 minutes. Add stock and bring to a boil. Cook, stirring, until smooth and thickened, about 5 minutes. Return chicken to pan, stir well and transfer to prepared baking dish.

5. Spread crust evenly over filling. Bake in preheated oven until top is nicely browned, about 25 minutes.

Variation

Turkey Chile Pie with Millet Crust: Substitute an equal quantity of skinless boneless turkey for the chicken.

Nutrients per serving	
Calories	375
Protein	28.2 g
Carbohydrates	36.4 g
Fat (Total)	13.1 g
Saturated Fat	4.8 g
Monounsaturated Fat	5.6 g
Polyunsaturated Fat	1.7 g
Dietary Fiber	5.6 g
Sodium	391 mg
Cholesterol	61 mg

EXCELLENT SOURCE OF vitamin C, niacin, magnesium, manganese, copper and selenium.

GOOD SOURCE OF vitamin A, riboflavin, thiamine, folate, zinc, calcium, phosphorus and iron.

SOURCE OF vitamin E (alpha-tocopherol) and pantothenic acid.

CONTAINS a high amount of dietary fiber.

Italian-Style Chicken in White Wine with Olives and Polenta

This is a fairly straightforward recipe for chicken cooked in white wine, distinguished by the addition of fresh sage and sliced green olives, which add pleasant acidity to the sauce. Served over polenta, it makes a delicious one-dish meal.

Makes 8 servings

TIP

Have your butcher cut chicken breasts into quarters.

Nutrients per serving

Calories	365
Protein	29.8 g
Carbohydrates	19.8 g
Fat (Total)	17.9 g
Saturated Fat	4.4 g
Monounsaturated Fat	8.6 g
Polyunsaturated Fat	3.5 g
Dietary Fiber	4.0 g
Sodium	500 mg
Cholesterol	85 g

EXCELLENT SOURCE OF vitamin A, niacin, phosphorus and selenium.

GOOD SOURCE OF pantothenic acid, magnesium, manganese and zinc.

SOURCE OF vitamins C and E (alpha-tocopherol), riboflavin, thiamine, folate, iron and copper.

CONTAINS a high amount of dietary fiber.

- **Preheat oven to 350°F (180°C)**

1	batch Creamy Polenta (see Variations, page 243)	1
1 tbsp	olive oil	15 mL
3 lbs	skin-on bone-in chicken breasts, cut into serving-size pieces, rinsed and patted dry	1.5 kg
2	onions, finely chopped	2
2	carrots, peeled and diced	2
2	stalks celery, diced	2
2	cloves garlic, minced	2
2 tsp	dried Italian seasoning	10 mL
6	fresh sage leaves, chopped, or ½ tsp (2 mL) dried sage	6
½ tsp	freshly ground black pepper	2 mL
¼ tsp	cayenne pepper	1 mL
	Salt	
2 tbsp	whole barley flour	25 mL
1 cup	dry white wine	250 mL
1 cup	reduced-sodium chicken stock	250 mL
	Salt and freshly ground black pepper	
1 cup	sliced pitted green olives	250 mL
1 tbsp	freshly squeezed lemon juice	15 mL

1. In a Dutch oven, heat oil over medium heat for 30 seconds. Add chicken, in batches, and brown, turning once, about 6 minutes per batch. Transfer to a plate as completed and set aside.

2. Add onions, carrots and celery to pan and cook, stirring, until vegetables are softened, about 7 minutes. Add garlic, Italian seasoning, sage, black pepper, cayenne and salt to taste and cook, stirring for 1 minute. Add barley flour and cook, stirring, until mixture congeals, for 1 minute. Add wine and stock and bring to a boil. Cook, stirring, until mixture thickens, about 3 minutes. Return chicken to pot. Cover and bake in preheated oven until chicken is no longer pink inside, about 45 minutes. Stir in olives and lemon juice.

3. *To serve:* Spread polenta over a deep platter and top with chicken and sauce.

Southwestern-Style Chile Chicken with Wehani Rice

Bathed in a luscious sauce and served on a bed of robust red rice, perfectly braised chicken is home cooking at its finest. Complete this meal with warm tortillas and a tossed green salad.

Makes 8 servings

TIP

Wehani rice, which is grown by Lundberg Family Farms, is one of my favorite varieties of rice. It is robust and chewy and is widely available in well-stocked supermarkets or natural foods stores. Bhutanese, Thai or Camargue red rice can be substituted, although the cooking times vary. If you prefer, cook the rice in a rice cooker.

Nutrients per serving

Calories	395
Protein	31.5 g
Carbohydrates	27.6 g
Fat (Total)	17.7 g
Saturated Fat	4.3 g
Monounsaturated Fat	8.0 g
Polyunsaturated Fat	3.5 g
Dietary Fiber	4.0 g
Sodium	305 mg
Cholesterol	85 mg

EXCELLENT SOURCE OF niacin and selenium.
GOOD SOURCE OF vitamin A, riboflavin, pantothenic acid, phosphorus, iron and magnesium.
SOURCE OF vitamins C and E (alpha-tocopherol), thiamine, folate, pantothenic acid, manganese, copper and zinc.
CONTAINS a high amount of dietary fiber.

3 cups	reduced-sodium chicken stock, divided	750 mL
1 cup	Wehani rice, rinsed and drained (see Tip, left)	250 mL
4	dried ancho, mild New Mexico or guajillo chiles	4
2 cups	boiling water	500 mL
1 cup	packed coarsely chopped cilantro (stems and leaves)	250 mL
2 tbsp	red wine vinegar	25 mL
1 tbsp	extra virgin olive oil (approx.)	15 mL
3 lbs	skin-on bone-in chicken breasts, cut into serving-size pieces, rinsed and patted dry	1.5 kg
2	onions, finely chopped	2
4	cloves garlic, minced	4
1 tbsp	ground cumin (see Tips, page 134)	15 mL
1 tsp	dried oregano leaves, preferably Mexican	5 mL
½ tsp	cracked black peppercorns	2 mL
	Salt, optional	
	Finely chopped cilantro	

1. In a saucepan with a tight-fitting lid over medium–high heat, bring 2 cups (500 mL) of the stock to a boil. Add rice and stir well. Return to a rapid boil. Reduce heat to low (see Tips, page 59). Cover and cook until liquid is absorbed and rice is tender, about 45 minutes.

2. Meanwhile, in a heatproof bowl, soak dried chiles in boiling water for 30 minutes, weighing down with a cup to ensure they remain submerged. Drain, discarding soaking liquid and stems. Pat dry, chop finely and transfer to a blender. Add remaining 1 cup (250 mL) of stock, cilantro and vinegar. Purée and set aside.

3. Meanwhile, in a Dutch oven, heat oil over medium–high heat for 30 seconds. Add chicken, in batches, and cook, turning once, until skin is browned and crispy, about 10 minutes per batch, adding more oil, if necessary. Transfer to a plate and set aside. Drain off all but 1 tbsp (15 mL) fat from pan. Reduce heat to medium.

4. Add onions to pan and cook, stirring, until softened, about 3 minutes. Add garlic, cumin, oregano and peppercorns and cook, stirring, for 1 minute. Stir in reserved chile mixture. Add salt to taste, if using. Return chicken to pan, skin side up, and spoon a little sauce over each piece. Reduce heat to low. Cover and simmer until chicken is no longer pink inside, about 30 minutes, turning the chicken over to cook in the sauce for the last 5 minutes of cooking.

5. *To serve:* On a deep platter, arrange rice in a ring around the edge, leaving the center hollow. Spoon chicken and sauce into the center and garnish with additional cilantro.

Chicken Paprikash with Wheat Berry Gravy

This flavorful stew, liberally seasoned with sweet paprika and finished with sour cream, is a Hungarian classic. Normally it is topped with dumplings. Here I've added wheat berries to the luscious gravy for a delightfully different and equally delicious result.

3 cups	cooked wheat berries (see cooking instructions, page 34)	750 mL
3 lbs	skinless bone-in chicken thighs	1.5 kg
2 tbsp	freshly squeezed lemon juice	25 mL
	Salt and freshly ground black pepper	
1 tbsp	butter	15 mL
1 tbsp	extra virgin olive oil	15 mL
3	onions, thinly sliced on the vertical	3
3 tbsp	sweet paprika, preferably Hungarian	45 mL
1	can (14 oz/398 mL) no-salt-added diced tomatoes, drained	1
3 cups	reduced-sodium chicken stock	750 mL
½ cup	reduced-fat sour cream	125 mL
¼ cup	finely chopped dill	50 mL

Makes 8 servings

Nutrient Tip
Finishing this dish with a liberal serving of dill adds flavor and nutrients, such as a smattering of vitamins A and C and folate.

1. Sprinkle chicken evenly with lemon juice and season to taste with salt and pepper. Set aside.

2. In a Dutch oven or large skillet, melt butter with oil over medium heat for 30 seconds. Add onions and cook, stirring, until they begin to brown, about 10 minutes. Add paprika and cook, stirring, for 1 minute. Add chicken, in batches, and stir each piece until well coated with the mixture. Add tomatoes and stock and bring to a boil. Reduce heat to low. Cover and simmer until chicken is very tender and falling off the bone, about 1 hour.

3. Using a slotted spoon, transfer chicken to a serving dish. Stir sour cream and cooked wheat berries into sauce and cook over medium heat until heated through. Pour over chicken and garnish with dill.

Nutrients per serving

Calories	334
Protein	30.0 g
Carbohydrates	30.3 g
Fat (Total)	11.1 g
Saturated Fat	3.4 g
Monounsaturated Fat	3.9 g
Polyunsaturated Fat	2.3 g
Dietary Fiber	5.8 g
Sodium	376 mg
Cholesterol	110 mg

EXCELLENT SOURCE OF niacin, phosphorus, magnesium, manganese, zinc and selenium.

GOOD SOURCE OF vitamin A, thiamine, riboflavin, pantothenic acid, iron and copper.

SOURCE OF vitamins C and E (alpha-tocopherol), folate and calcium.

CONTAINS a high amount of dietary fiber.

Indian-Spiced Chicken and Barley

This is a great dish for Sunday dinner or when you have time on a weeknight to allow for the long slow baking. It's actually quite easy to make and the lightly spiced sauce is delectable.

- **Preheat oven to 325°F (160°C)**
- **13-by 9-inch (3 L) baking dish**

2 lbs	skinless bone-in chicken thighs	1 kg
3 tbsp	freshly squeezed lemon juice	45 mL
1 tsp	ground turmeric	5 mL
1 tbsp	olive oil	15 mL
2	onions, finely chopped	2
4	stalks celery, diced	4
4	cloves garlic, minced	4
1 tbsp	minced gingerroot	15 mL
1	long red or green chile pepper, finely chopped, or ½ tsp (2 mL) cayenne pepper	1
1 tbsp	ground cumin (see Tip, left)	15 mL
2 tsp	ground coriander	10 mL
½ tsp	ground cardamom	2 mL
½ tsp	salt	2 mL
1 cup	whole (hulled) barley, rinsed and drained	250 mL
1	can (28 oz/796 mL) no-salt-added diced tomatoes with juice	1
1 cup	reduced-sodium chicken stock	250 mL
1 cup	plain yogurt (minimum 4% M.F.)	250 mL

1. Sprinkle chicken evenly with lemon juice and turmeric and arrange over bottom of baking dish. Set aside.

2. In a skillet, heat oil over medium heat for 30 seconds. Add onions and celery and cook, stirring, until softened, about 5 minutes. Add garlic, ginger and chile pepper and cook, stirring, for 1 minute. Add cumin, coriander, cardamom and salt and cook, stirring, for 1 minute. Add barley and toss until well coated. Add tomatoes with juice and stock and bring to a rapid boil.

3. Remove from heat and stir in yogurt. Spread over chicken in baking dish. Cover with foil and bake in preheated oven until barley is tender and chicken is no longer pink inside, about 1½ hours.

Slow Cooker Method

Complete Step 1, arranging chicken over bottom of slow cooker stoneware. Complete Step 2, but do not add the chile pepper along with the garlic. Transfer mixture to slow cooker stoneware after it has come to a boil. Cover and cook on Low for 5 hours or on High for 2½ hours. Stir in chile pepper or cayenne and yogurt. Cover and cook on High for 20 minutes, until flavors meld.

Chicken with Bulgur and Walnuts

This combination of ingredients — chicken, bulgur, walnuts and parsley — is traditionally Turkish. I like to serve this with a slightly robust accompaniment, such as puréed spinach seasoned with a bit of Dijon mustard, since the flavors of the dish are pleasantly delicate. If (like my husband) you feel the need for a bit of spice, add a dollop of fruit chutney.

Makes 4 servings

TIP

I've suggested the use of cayenne pepper in this recipe because it's a pantry staple. But if you have access to Aleppo pepper, by all means substitute the cayenne with ½ tsp (2 mL) of the ground version. Aleppo is a medium-heat chile pepper from Turkey that is becoming available in North America.

1 cup	medium or coarse bulgur	250 mL
1 cup	cold water	250 mL
1 tbsp	olive oil	15 mL
2	onions, finely chopped	2
12 oz	skinless boneless chicken breasts or thighs, cut into ½-inch (1 cm) cubes	375 g
4	cloves garlic, minced	4
1 tbsp	minced gingerroot	15 mL
½ tsp	ground cinnamon	2 mL
½ tsp	ground allspice	2 mL
¼ tsp	cayenne pepper (see Tip, left)	1 mL
1 cup	reduced-sodium chicken stock	250 mL
½ cup	chopped walnuts	125 mL
¼ cup	finely chopped parsley	50 mL
	Fruit chutney, optional	

1. In a bowl, combine bulgur and cold water. Stir well and set aside. (By the time you're ready to add it to the dish, the liquid will be absorbed.)
2. Meanwhile, in a skillet, heat oil over medium heat for 30 seconds. Add onions and cook, stirring, until they begin to turn golden, about 10 minutes. Add chicken, garlic, ginger, cinnamon, allspice and cayenne and cook, stirring, until chicken is no longer pink inside, about 5 minutes. Add stock and bring to a boil. Add bulgur and cook, stirring, until bulgur is heated through and has absorbed the liquid in the pan, about 3 minutes. Transfer to a serving bowl. Sprinkle with walnuts and parsley and serve. Pass the chutney, if using.

Nutrients per serving

Calories	377
Protein	27.5 g
Carbohydrates	36.5 g
Fat (Total)	14.9 g
Saturated Fat	1.8 g
Monounsaturated Fat	4.2 g
Polyunsaturated Fat	7.8 g
Dietary Fiber	6.0 g
Sodium	211 mg
Cholesterol	50 mg

EXCELLENT SOURCE OF
magnesium, manganese, niacin, copper and selenium.

GOOD SOURCE OF thiamine, phosphorus, iron and zinc.

SOURCE OF vitamins C and E (alpha-tocopherol), folate, riboflavin, pantothenic acid and calcium.

CONTAINS a very high amount of dietary fiber.

Saffron-Scented Chicken and Barley Stew with Easy Rouille

Finished with a dollop of tasty rouille, this robust Spanish-inspired stew is a great dish to serve for a casual evening with friends. Add a tossed green salad and open a bottle of your favorite wine.

Makes 8 servings

TIPS

The brandy adds a pleasant bite to the flavor of this dish, but if you prefer, you can omit it and add 1 tbsp (15 mL) of olive oil to the rub.

For the best flavor, toast whole fennel seeds in a dry skillet, stirring over medium heat, until fragrant, about 3 minutes. Then grind them in a spice grinder or mortar.

If you prefer, omit the wine and add an additional 1 cup (250 mL) of stock.

Nutrient Tip

One serving of this dish is relatively high in calories and fat, but it is a special-occasion dish and does not require much to complete it. You can reduce the fat (and calories) by draining off all but 1 tbsp (15 mL) of the fat from the pan after browning the chicken, and reducing the quantity of extra virgin olive oil in the rub to 2 tsp (10 mL).

3 cups	cooked whole (hulled) barley (see cooking instructions, page 16)	750 mL
RUB		
2 tbsp	brandy, optional (see Tips, left)	25 mL
1 tbsp	extra virgin olive oil	15 mL
2 tsp	finely grated garlic or garlic put through a press	10 mL
2 tsp	ground fennel seeds (see Tips, left)	10 mL
1 tsp	dried thyme leaves	5 mL
1 tsp	smoked or sweet paprika	5 mL
½ tsp	freshly ground black pepper	2 mL
3 lbs	skin-on bone-in chicken breasts, cut into 8 pieces	1.5 kg
1 tbsp	olive oil	15 mL
4	leeks, white part with a bit of green, cleaned and thinly sliced (see Tips, page 74)	4
1	can (28 oz/796 mL) no-salt-added diced tomatoes, drained	1
⅛ tsp	crumbled saffron threads, dissolved in 2 tbsp (25 mL) boiling water	0.5 mL
1 cup	dry white wine (see Tips, left)	250 mL
1 cup	reduced-sodium chicken stock	250 mL
½ cup	finely chopped parsley	125 mL
EASY ROUILLE		
¼ cup	light mayonnaise	50 mL
1	roasted red pepper, peeled and chopped	1
2	cloves garlic, minced	2
Pinch	cayenne pepper	Pinch

1. *Rub:* In a small bowl, combine brandy, if using, olive oil, garlic, fennel, thyme, paprika and pepper. Rub into chicken, covering all exposed parts, and set aside in the refrigerator for at least 2 hours.

2. In a Dutch oven, heat oil over medium heat for 30 seconds. Add chicken, in batches, and brown, turning once, about 6 minutes per batch. Transfer to a plate.

3. Add leeks to pan, along with any residual marinade from the chicken, and cook, stirring, until softened, about 5 minutes. Stir in barley, tomatoes and saffron liquid. Increase heat to medium–high. Add white wine and bring to a boil. Cook, stirring, until reduced by one third, about 4 minutes. Stir in stock.

4. Return chicken to pan, skin side up, arranging evenly over barley mixture. Reduce heat to low. Cover and simmer until chicken is no longer pink inside, about 40 minutes. Garnish with parsley.

5. *Easy Rouille:* In a mini-chopper, combine mayonnaise, roasted pepper, garlic and cayenne. Process until smooth. Refrigerate until ready to use. Pass at the table.

Slow Cooker Method

Use 2 lbs (1 kg) skinless boneless chicken thighs. After removing chicken from the refrigerator, skip Step 2 and place in slow cooker stoneware. Continue with Step 3, substituting 1 cup (250 mL) raw whole barley and 2½ cups (625 mL) water or chicken stock for the cooked barley. Transfer mixture to stoneware after it is reduced. Cover and cook on Low for 6 hours or on High for 3 hours, until juices run clear when chicken is pierced with a fork.

Nutrients per serving	
Calories	439
Protein	33.3 g
Carbohydrates	31.8 g
Fat (Total)	19.8 g
Saturated Fat	4.7 g
Monounsaturated Fat	8.6 g
Polyunsaturated Fat	4.9 g
Dietary Fiber	7.2 g
Sodium	262 mg
Cholesterol	88 mg

EXCELLENT SOURCE OF vitamin C, niacin, phosphorus, iron, manganese and selenium.

GOOD SOURCE OF vitamins A and E (alpha-tocopherol), thiamine, riboflavin, folate, pantothenic acid, magnesium, zinc and copper.

SOURCE OF calcium.

CONTAINS a very high amount of dietary fiber.

Southwestern Turkey Stew with Cornmeal Dumplings

This simple stew captures the best of the Southwest — the seductive flavors of chiles, combined with luscious chunks of turkey in a tomato-based broth. Comforting cornmeal dumplings complete the theme. Serve it as a one-dish meal — there really isn't anything else you need, although you may want to add a tossed green salad.

Makes 6 servings

TIP
Chipotle peppers are dried smoked jalapeño peppers. When reconstituted and cooked in adobo sauce, they carry a lot of heat, so if you're heat averse, use only half of one.

1 tbsp	olive oil	15 mL
2	onions, finely chopped	2
4	stalks celery, chopped	4
4	cloves garlic, minced	4
1	jalapeño pepper, seeded and minced	1
1	chipotle pepper in adobo sauce, minced (see Tip, left)	1
1 tbsp	chili powder	15 mL
½ tsp	cracked black peppercorns	2 mL
1 lb	skinless boneless turkey breast, cut into ½-inch (1 cm) cubes	500 g
2 tbsp	whole wheat flour	25 mL
1	can (14 oz/398 mL) no-salt-added diced tomatoes with juice	1
2½ cups	reduced-sodium chicken stock	625 mL
2 cups	sliced green beans	500 mL

DUMPLINGS

¾ cup	stone-ground cornmeal	175 mL
½ cup	whole wheat flour	125 mL
2 tsp	baking powder	10 mL
½ tsp	salt	2 mL
1 cup	buttermilk	250 mL
1 tbsp	olive oil	15 mL

Nutrients per serving

Calories	293
Protein	23.4 g
Carbohydrates	35.8 g
Fat (Total)	7.4 g
Saturated Fat	1.1 g
Monounsaturated Fat	3.9 g
Polyunsaturated Fat	1.8 g
Dietary Fiber	7.4 g
Sodium	666 mg
Cholesterol	39 mg

EXCELLENT SOURCE OF niacin, phosphorus, magnesium and manganese.

GOOD SOURCE OF vitamin E (alpha-tocopherol), thiamine, folate, zinc, iron, copper and selenium.

SOURCE OF vitamins A and C, riboflavin, pantothenic acid and calcium.

CONTAINS a very high amount of dietary fiber.

1. In a skillet, heat oil over medium heat for 30 seconds. Add onions and celery and cook, stirring, until celery softens, about 5 minutes. Add garlic, jalapeño and chipotle peppers, chili powder and peppercorns and cook, stirring, for 1 minute. Add turkey and cook, stirring, until surface whitens, about 2 minutes. Add flour and cook, stirring, for 1 minute. Add tomatoes with juice and stock and bring to a boil. Reduce heat to low and simmer, stirring occasionally, until flavors meld, about 15 minutes. Stir in green beans.

2. *Dumplings:* In a bowl, combine cornmeal, flour, baking powder and salt. Make a well in the center. In a measuring cup, combine buttermilk and oil, mixing well. Pour into well and stir just until mixture is evenly moistened. Ensure stew is at a simmer and drop dough by heaping tablespoons (15 mL) onto simmering liquid. Cover tightly and steam until dumplings are puffed and tender, about 20 minutes.

Moroccan-Style Chicken Stew with Chickpeas and Rice

Chicken, lemon and olives are a classic Moroccan combination and are quite heavenly. This luscious stew, which is very easy to make, is a great dish for Sunday dinner or casual entertaining. It's a great one-dish meal, but you can add some sautéed bitter greens, such as rapini, or a tossed green salad. If you're a heat seeker, pass harissa at the table.

Makes 4 servings

TIPS

You can buy preserved lemons at Middle Eastern food stores. It's also very easy to make your own. If you don't have a preserved lemon, substitute 1 tbsp (15 mL) freshly squeezed lemon juice.

Harissa is a traditional North African chili paste, often added to soups or stews to add heat. If you don't have it, and crave a bit of fire, substitute your favorite hot pepper sauce.

Nutrients per serving

Calories	348
Protein	27.7 g
Carbohydrates	40.3 g
Fat (Total)	9.3 g
Saturated Fat	1.5 g
Monounsaturated Fat	5.2 g
Polyunsaturated Fat	1.7 g
Dietary Fiber	6.4 g
Sodium	493 mg
Cholesterol	50 mg

EXCELLENT SOURCE OF niacin, folate, iron, magnesium, manganese, copper and selenium.

GOOD SOURCE OF vitamin E (alpha-tocopherol), thiamine, pantothenic acid, phosphorus and zinc.

SOURCE OF vitamins A and C, riboflavin and calcium.

CONTAINS a very high amount of dietary fiber.

2 cups	cooked short-grain brown rice (see cooking instructions, page 29)	500 mL
1 tbsp	olive oil	15 mL
2	onions, finely chopped	2
12 oz	skinless boneless chicken breasts or thighs, cut into ½-inch (1 cm) cubes	375 g
4	cloves garlic, minced	4
2 tbsp	minced gingerroot	25 mL
1 tbsp	turmeric	15 mL
½ tsp	freshly ground black pepper	2 mL
1	can (14 oz/398 mL) no-salt-added diced tomatoes with juice	1
1 cup	reduced-sodium chicken stock	250 mL
	Salt, optional	
1 cup	cooked chickpeas	250 mL
1	preserved lemon, rinsed and chopped (see Tips, left)	1
½ cup	pitted green olives, chopped	125 mL
	Harissa, optional (see Tips, left)	

1. In a large saucepan or Dutch oven, heat oil over medium–high heat for 30 seconds. Add onions and cook, stirring, until softened, about 3 minutes. Add chicken and cook, stirring, just until onions begin to turn golden, about 5 minutes. Add garlic, ginger, turmeric and pepper and cook, stirring, for 1 minute. Add tomatoes with juice and stock and bring to a boil. Add salt to taste, if using.

2. Stir in rice and chickpeas. Reduce heat to low. Cover and simmer until chicken is no longer pink inside and flavors meld, about 30 minutes. Stir in preserved lemon and simmer for 5 minutes. Garnish with olives. Pass harissa at the table, if using.

Buckwheat Pilaf with Paprika-Seasoned Chicken

Smoked paprika is the secret ingredient in this flavorful chicken pilaf. The smoky and slightly nippy spice is a perfect complement to the robust flavors of buckwheat, a particularly nourishing grain, especially in cold weather when traditional wisdom suggests it warms the blood. Serve this alongside a platter of steamed carrots for a great winter meal.

Makes 4 servings

TIP

Kasha is toasted buckwheat groats. Since I find the taste of kasha quite overpowering, I prefer to buy plain buckwheat groats and toast them myself, which produces a more mildly flavored result. Place the groats in a dry skillet over high heat and cook, stirring constantly, until they are nicely fragrant, about 4 minutes. In the process, they will darken from a light shade of sand to one with a hint of brown.

Nutrients per serving

Calories	329
Protein	27.9 g
Carbohydrates	37.2 g
Fat (Total)	8.8 g
Saturated Fat	1.3 g
Monounsaturated Fat	5.0 g
Polyunsaturated Fat	1.7 g
Dietary Fiber	5.9 g
Sodium	359 mg
Cholesterol	50 mg

EXCELLENT SOURCE OF vitamin C, magnesium, manganese, niacin, copper and selenium.

GOOD SOURCE OF vitamin E (alpha-tocopherol), folate, pantothenic acid, iron and zinc.

SOURCE OF vitamin A, thiamine, riboflavin, calcium and phosphorus.

CONTAINS a high amount of dietary fiber.

1 cup	toasted buckwheat groats or kasha (see Tip, left)	250 mL
1 tbsp	olive oil	25 mL
1	onion, finely chopped	1
½	red bell pepper, seeded and finely chopped	½
2	cloves garlic, minced	2
1 tsp	smoked paprika	5 mL
½ tsp	freshly ground black pepper	2 mL
12 oz	boneless skinless chicken breasts or thighs, cut into ½-inch (1 cm) cubes	375 g
2 cups	reduced-sodium chicken stock	500 mL
¼ cup	finely chopped parsley	50 mL
¼ cup	toasted sliced almonds	50 mL

1. In a large saucepan, heat oil over medium–high heat for 30 seconds. Add onion, bell pepper and garlic and cook, stirring, until vegetables are softened, about 5 minutes. Add smoked paprika, black pepper and chicken and stir until chicken is well coated with mixture. Add stock and bring to a boil. Stir in buckwheat and return to a boil.

2. Reduce heat to low. Cover and simmer until liquid is absorbed and chicken is no longer pink inside, about 15 minutes. Remove from heat and set aside for 5 minutes. (If the pilaf still has a bit too much liquid for your taste, return to low heat and stir until it evaporates.) Transfer to a serving dish. Garnish with parsley and almonds and serve.

Turkey Cutlets in Gingery Lemon Gravy with Cranberry Rice

Delicious and easy to make, this is a great weeknight dinner so long as you allow time for cooking the rice. It's hard to believe that anything so flavorful is so easy to make. The cranberries and the hint of orange complement the nutty, slightly earthy flavor of the rice, and the luscious lemon ginger gravy unites it all. To complete the meal, the only thing you need is a steamed vegetable, such as green beans or carrots.

Makes 4 servings

TIP

If you prefer a bit of heat, use hot rather than sweet paprika when dredging the turkey.

Nutrient Tip

In addition to adding flavor to the gravy, the ginger in this recipe is very good for your digestion.

CRANBERRY RICE

1¼ cups	water or reduced-sodium chicken stock	300 mL
2 tbsp	freshly squeezed orange juice	25 mL
¾ cup	long-grain brown rice, rinsed and drained	175 mL
⅓ cup	dried cranberries	75 mL
1 tsp	grated orange zest	5 mL

TURKEY CUTLETS

3 tbsp	whole barley flour	45 mL
1 tsp	paprika	5 mL
½ tsp	freshly ground black pepper	2 mL
4	turkey cutlets (about 12 oz/375 g in total)	4
2 tbsp	olive oil, divided	25 mL
1 tbsp	butter, divided	15 mL
2	cloves garlic, minced	2
1 tbsp	minced gingerroot	15 mL
1 cup	reduced-sodium chicken stock	250 mL
1 tbsp	freshly squeezed lemon juice	15 mL

1. *Cranberry Rice:* In a heavy saucepan with a tight-fitting lid over medium heat, bring water and orange juice to a boil. Stir in rice and return to a boil. Reduce heat to low. Cover and simmer until rice is tender and water has been absorbed, about 50 minutes. Remove from heat and fluff with a fork. Stir in cranberries and orange zest and keep warm.

2. *Turkey Cutlets:* On a plate or in a plastic bag, combine flour, paprika and pepper. Add turkey and toss until well coated with mixture. Reserve any excess.

3. In a large skillet, heat 1 tbsp (15 mL) of the oil and ½ tbsp (7 mL) of the butter over medium–high heat until butter has melted. Add 2 cutlets and cook until browned, about 2 minutes. Turn and cook until no longer pink inside, about 2 minutes more. Transfer to a warm platter and keep warm. Repeat with remaining cutlets, oil and butter. Reduce heat to medium.

4. Add garlic and ginger to pan and cook, stirring, for 1 minute. Add reserved flour mixture and cook, stirring, for 1 minute. Add stock, lemon juice and any turkey juices that have accumulated on the platter and cook, stirring, until thickened, about 2 minutes. Pour over cutlets. Serve on a bed of Cranberry Rice.

Variation

Chicken Cutlets in Gingery Lemon Gravy with Cranberry Rice:
Substitute an equal quantity of chicken cutlets for the turkey.

TURKEY

Turkey is one of the best sources of complete protein because once the skin is removed, it is a very lean meat. In addition to being protein rich, turkey is also a good source of important B vitamins — niacin, B6 and B12 — as well as zinc, an immune system protector that can be challenging to obtain from dietary sources. The body can utilize the zinc in turkey and other meats more readily than that from non-meat sources. Turkey is also a good source of the trace mineral selenium, an antioxidant that supports a number of bodily functions. Research indicates that selenium intake may reduce the risk of coronary artery disease and protect the body from prostate, colorectal and lung cancers. However, a recent study published in the *Annals of Internal Medicine* found that taking selenium supplements actually increased the risk of developing Type-2 diabetes. Since recent evidence suggests that taking antioxidants as supplements may not have positive health benefits, the safest strategy is to focus on obtaining these phytonutrients by eating nutrient dense whole foods.

Nutrients per serving

Calories	378
Protein	23.7 g
Carbohydrates	42.9 g
Fat (Total)	12.6 g
Saturated Fat	3.5 g
Monounsaturated Fat	6.8 g
Polyunsaturated Fat	1.7 g
Dietary Fiber	3.4 g
Sodium	236 mg
Cholesterol	51 mg

EXCELLENT SOURCE OF niacin, phosphorus, magnesium, manganese and selenium.

GOOD SOURCE OF thiamine and zinc.

SOURCE OF vitamins A, C and E (alpha-tocopherol), riboflavin, folate, pantothenic acid, iron and copper.

CONTAINS a moderate amount of dietary fiber.

Fish and Seafood

Salmon Stew with Corn and Quinoa

Salmon Stew with Corn and Quinoa

This tasty stew is a great way to increase your intake of beneficial omega-3 rich fatty acids by including salmon in your diet. It's easy to make and, with the addition of licorice-flavored Pernod, has a uniquely sophisticated flavor. Add a simple green salad to expand the range of nutrients and bump up the amount of fiber you consume.

Makes 8 servings

Nutrient Tips

Salmon is one of the best sources of omega-3 fatty acids, which are essential to good health. Studies show that an adequate supply of omega-3 fatty acids can reduce the risk of coronary artery disease, slightly lower blood pressure and strengthen the immune system, among other benefits.

To reduce your intake of saturated fat, substitute half-and-half (10%) cream for the whipping cream.

1 tbsp	olive oil	15 mL
2 tbsp	finely chopped pancetta or bacon	25 mL
3	leeks, white part only, cleaned and thinly sliced (see Tips, page 74)	3
½ tsp	dried thyme leaves	2 mL
½ tsp	cayenne pepper	2 mL
1	bay leaf	1
½ tsp	salt	2 mL
1 cup	dry white wine	250 mL
6 cups	fish stock or 3 cups (750 mL) bottled clam juice diluted with 3 cups (750 mL) water	1.5 L
2 cups	corn kernels	500 mL
1 cup	quinoa, rinsed and drained	250 mL
1½ lbs	salmon fillets, skin removed and cut into 1-inch (2.5 cm) pieces	750 g
½ cup	whipping (35%) cream	125 mL
¼ cup	Pernod, optional	50 mL
½ cup	finely chopped chives	125 mL

1. In a Dutch oven, heat oil over medium heat for 30 seconds. Add pancetta and cook, stirring, until it begins to brown, about 3 minutes. (If you're using bacon, cook until crisp and drain off all but 1 tbsp/ 15 mL fat from pan before proceeding with recipe.)

2. Reduce heat to medium. Add leeks and cook, stirring, until softened, about 5 minutes. Add thyme, cayenne, bay leaf and salt and cook, stirring, for 1 minute. Add wine, bring to boil and boil until reduced by half, about 5 minutes. Add stock and corn and return to a boil. Stir in quinoa. Reduce heat to low. Cover and cook until quinoa is almost tender, about 15 minutes.

3. Add salmon and simmer until opaque and flakes easily with a fork, about 6 minutes. Stir in whipping cream and cook until heated through, about 2 minutes. Stir in Pernod, if using. Garnish with chives.

Nutrients per serving

Calories	373
Protein	24.1 g
Carbohydrates	26.5 g
Fat (Total)	18.6 g
Saturated Fat	5.8 g
Monounsaturated Fat	6.7 g
Polyunsaturated Fat	4.4 g
Dietary Fiber	2.8 g
Sodium	488 mg
Cholesterol	67 mg

EXCELLENT SOURCE OF thiamine, niacin, folate, pantothenic acid, phosphorus, magnesium, manganese and selenium.

GOOD SOURCE OF riboflavin, iron, zinc and copper.

SOURCE OF vitamins A, C and E (alpha-tocopherol) and calcium.

CONTAINS a moderate amount of dietary fiber.

Salmon and Wild Rice Cakes with Avocado-Chili Topping

With the addition of a big salad or an abundance of veggies, these tasty burgers make a light weeknight meal. For convenience, cook the rice ahead. The salmon mixture is quickly assembled.

TIPS

With additions such as salad, one burger makes a light meal for most people. However, hungry people might want an extra half or whole one.

I prefer to leave the salmon bones in as they add calcium, but if you prefer, remove them.

When mixed, the cakes are very wet and not easily shaped into patties. However, they dry out and solidify quickly on cooking.

Nutrients per serving	
Calories	279
Protein	15.3 g
Carbohydrates	21.1 g
Fat (Total)	15.6 g
Saturated Fat	2.7 g
Monounsaturated Fat	9.0 g
Polyunsaturated Fat	2.5 g
Dietary Fiber	4.9 g
Sodium	552 mg
Cholesterol	66 mg

EXCELLENT SOURCE OF niacin, manganese and selenium.

GOOD SOURCE OF vitamin E (alpha-tocopherol), folate, riboflavin, pantothenic acid, phosphorus, magnesium and zinc.

SOURCE OF vitamins A and C, thiamine, calcium, iron and copper.

CONTAINS a high amount of dietary fiber.

1½ cups	cooked brown and wild rice mixture, cooled	375 mL
1	can (7.5 oz/213 g) salmon, drained (see Tips, left)	1
1	egg	1
4	green onions, white part only with a bit of green, chopped	4
1 tbsp	soy sauce	15 mL
	Freshly ground black pepper	
1 tbsp	olive oil	15 mL

AVOCADO-CHILI TOPPING

1	avocado, mashed	1
1 tbsp	freshly squeezed lemon juice	15 mL
¼ tsp	salt	1 mL
	Freshly ground black pepper	
½ tsp	Asian chili sauce, such as sambal oelek	2 mL

1. In a food processor, combine salmon, egg, green onions, soy sauce and pepper to taste. Process until smooth. Add rice and pulse to blend.

2. In a skillet, heat oil over medium heat for 30 seconds. Using a large spoon, drop salmon mixture into the pan in 4 blobs (see Tips, left). Cook until crispy outside and hot in the center, about 5 minutes per side.

3. *Avocado-Chili Topping:* Meanwhile, in a bowl, combine avocado, lemon juice, salt, pepper to taste and Asian chili sauce. Mix well.

4. Serve burgers warm with a large dollop of Avocado-Chili Topping.

Indonesian-Style Shrimp Fried Rice

Serve this one-dish meal when you're in the mood for a slightly different weekday dinner. The shrimp chips are a fun and flavorful addition that should be prepared before you start the dish. Although the fried egg adds cholesterol, in my opinion, it really enhances the dish.

Makes 4 servings

TIPS

Make the rice a day ahead for convenience.

Ketjap manis, a sweet soy sauce from Indonesia, is available in Asian markets. If you can't find it, use 1 tbsp (15 mL) soy sauce combined with 1 tbsp (15 mL) pure maple syrup in this recipe.

Indonesian shrimp chips are available in Asian markets. When deep-fried, they puff up, adding flavor and texture to the fried rice.

Nutrients per serving

Calories	415
Protein	28.7 g
Carbohydrates	39.7 g
Fat (Total)	15.2 g
Saturated Fat	2.6 g
Monounsaturated Fat	7.5 g
Polyunsaturated Fat	4.0 g
Dietary Fiber	3.1 g
Sodium	490 mg
Cholesterol	352 mg

EXCELLENT SOURCE OF niacin, phosphorus, iron, magnesium, manganese, zinc and selenium.

GOOD SOURCE OF vitamins A and E (alpha-tocopherol), thiamine, riboflavin, folate, pantothenic acid and copper.

SOURCE OF vitamin C and calcium.

CONTAINS a moderate amount of dietary fiber.

FRIED SHRIMP CHIPS, OPTIONAL

	Oil for deep-frying	
	Shrimp chips	
3 cups	cooked long-grain brown rice, cooled (see cooking instructions, page 29)	750 mL
2 tbsp	oil (approx.)	25 mL
12 oz	shrimp, peeled and deveined, thawed if frozen	375 g
4	eggs	4
	Salt and freshly ground black pepper	
2 tsp	Thai red curry paste	10 mL
2 cups	shredded Napa cabbage	500 mL
2 tbsp	ketjap manis (see Tips, left)	25 mL
4	green onions, white part with a bit of green, thinly sliced	4

1. *Fried Shrimp Chips (optional):* In a wok or saucepan, pour oil to about a 1-inch (2.5 cm) depth and heat until hot but not smoking. (If the oil is too hot, the chips will curl up and cook unevenly.) Add shrimp chips, 2 at a time, and fry, turning constantly with tongs, until they are puffed all over, about 20 seconds. Transfer to a paper towel to drain.

2. In a wok or a skillet, heat 1 tbsp (15 mL) of the oil over medium-high heat for 30 seconds. Add shrimp and cook, stirring, until they turn pink and opaque, 3 to 5 minutes. Transfer to a plate. Add remaining 1 tbsp (15 mL) oil to the pan and heat just until hot but not smoking. Break an egg into the pan and season lightly with salt and pepper. Cook until edges begin to brown. Then, using a spatula, flip and continue cooking until the yolk sets, about 1 minute. Transfer to plate and repeat until all eggs are cooked. Remove wok from heat and let cool for 1 to 2 minutes.

3. Reduce heat to low. Return cooled wok to heat, adding a bit more oil, if necessary, and add curry paste. Cook, stirring, until fragrant and paste begins to separate from oil, about 5 minutes. Add cabbage and stir well until coated. Using your fingers to break up any clusters, add rice to wok. Cook, stirring constantly, until thoroughly coated with curry-cabbage mixture. Add shrimp and cook, stirring, until heated through. Add ketjap manis and stir well. Garnish with green onions.

4. *To serve:* Spoon rice onto plates and top each serving with a fried egg. Serve shrimp chips alongside, if using.

Variation

For variety, try adding some red rice to the brown rice when cooking it. Two tablespoons (25 mL) of Colusari or Camargue red rice or Wehani per cup (250 mL) of brown rice, would add a visual and textural spark to the dish.

Saffron-Scented Shrimp with Chile Rice

This dish has so much going for it, it's hard to believe it's so easy to make. Stir-fried shrimp, in a creamy sauce with a hint of saffron, are surrounded by a ring of slightly spicy rice. A garnish of toasted almonds adds texture and completes the visual effect.

Makes 6 servings

Nutrient Tip

Although coconut milk is high in saturated fat, coconut oil, the fat in the milk, contains beneficial antioxidants. Moreover, it is a medium-chain fat, which means it is quickly burned by the body. Consequently, researchers are studying its potential in weight-loss programs, and the preliminary results are encouraging.

Nutrients per serving

Calories	377
Protein	21.9 g
Carbohydrates	41.1 g
Fat (Total)	15.1 g
Saturated Fat	6.3 g
Monounsaturated Fat	4.9 g
Polyunsaturated Fat	2.9 g
Dietary Fiber	5.7 g
Sodium	412 mg
Cholesterol	147 mg

EXCELLENT SOURCE OF niacin, phosphorus, iron, magnesium, manganese, copper and selenium.

GOOD SOURCE OF vitamins A, C and E (alpha-tocopherol), thiamine, folate and zinc.

SOURCE OF riboflavin, pantothenic acid and calcium.

CONTAINS a high amount of dietary fiber.

1	batch Chile Rice (see recipe, page 234)	1
2 tbsp	olive oil, divided	25 mL
1 tbsp	minced gingerroot	15 mL
1 tsp	turmeric	5 mL
1 lb	shrimp, peeled and deveined, thawed if frozen	500 g
	Freshly ground black pepper	
1	onion, finely chopped	1
2	cloves garlic, minced	2
1	long green or red chile, seeded and minced	1
1	stick cinnamon, about 2 inches (5 cm) long	1
4	green cardamom pods, crushed	4
½ tsp	salt	2 mL
⅛ tsp	crumbled saffron threads, dissolved in 2 tbsp (25 mL) boiling water	0.5 mL
¾ cup	coconut milk (see Nutrient Tip, left)	175 mL
	Toasted slivered almonds	

1. In a skillet, heat 1 tbsp (15 mL) of the oil over medium–high heat for 30 seconds. Add ginger and turmeric and stir well. Add shrimp and cook, stirring, until they turn pink and opaque, 3 to 5 minutes. Season to taste with pepper. Transfer to a plate and set aside.

2. Reduce heat to medium. Add remaining 1 tbsp (15 mL) of oil to pan. Add onion and cook, stirring, until softened, about 3 minutes. Add garlic, chile, cinnamon, cardamom and salt and cook, stirring, for 1 minute. Add saffron liquid and coconut milk and bring to a boil. Reduce heat and simmer until flavors meld, about 5 minutes. Stir in reserved shrimp and cook until heated through, about 2 minutes.

3. *To serve:* On a deep platter, arrange rice in a ring around the edge, leaving the center hollow. Pour shrimp mixture into the hollow and garnish with toasted almonds. Serve immediately.

Peppery Shrimp with Couscous

Couscous cooked with tomatoes, onion, a bell pepper and a bit of saffron provides a bed for sautéed shrimp in this elegant dish. Simple and delicious, this is easy enough to serve on weeknights.

Makes 4 servings

Nutrient Tip

As a group, North Americans consume too much salt, largely because most of it (77%) is hidden in processed foods and restaurant meals. That's why I recommend using reduced-sodium stocks or, even better, making your own with no salt added, and canned tomatoes with no salt added, which are now widely available in supermarkets.

2 tbsp	olive oil, divided	25 mL
1	onion, diced	1
1	green bell pepper, seeded and diced	1
¼ tsp	crumbled saffron threads, dissolved in 2 tbsp (25 mL) boiling water	1 mL
½ cup	water or reduced-sodium vegetable stock	125 mL
1	can (14 oz/398 mL) no-salt-added diced tomatoes with juice	1
¾ cup	whole wheat couscous	175 mL
12 oz	shrimp, peeled and deveined, thawed if frozen	375 g
4	cloves garlic, minced	4
1 tsp	finely grated lemon zest	5 mL
¼ tsp	cayenne pepper	1 mL
	Freshly ground black pepper	
½ cup	dry white wine	125 mL
2 tbsp	freshly squeezed lemon juice	25 mL
1 cup	cooked green peas	250 mL
	Salt, optional	

1. In a saucepan, heat 1 tbsp (15 mL) of the oil over medium heat for 30 seconds. Add onion and bell pepper and cook, stirring, until softened, about 5 minutes. Add saffron liquid, water and tomatoes with juice and bring to a boil. Stir in couscous. Remove from heat and let stand, covered, for 15 minutes. Fluff with a fork.

2. In a skillet, heat remaining 1 tbsp (15 mL) of oil over medium–high heat. Add shrimp and cook, stirring, just until they turn pink and opaque, 3 to 5 minutes. Add garlic, lemon zest, cayenne and black pepper to taste. Cook, stirring, for 1 minute. Add white wine and lemon juice and bring to a boil. Stir in peas until heated through. Season to taste with salt, if using.

3. *To serve:* On a deep platter, arrange couscous in a ring around the edge, leaving the center hollow. Arrange shrimp in the center.

Variations

Peppery Shrimp with Millet: Substitute an equal quantity of millet for the couscous. For the best flavor, before using in the recipe toast it in a dry skillet, stirring until fragrant, about 5 minutes. Stir the millet into tomato mixture (Step 1) and return to a boil. Cover and simmer over low heat for 20 minutes, then remove from heat and let stand for 10 minutes.

Peppery Shrimp with Quinoa: Substitute an equal quantity rinsed quinoa for the couscous. Stir the quinoa into the tomato mixture (Step 1) and return to a boil. Cover and simmer over low heat for 15 minutes. Remove from heat, cover, and set aside for 5 minutes. Fluff with a fork before using.

Nutrients per serving

Calories	380
Protein	27.3 g
Carbohydrates	48.1 g
Fat (Total)	8.8 g
Saturated Fat	1.2 g
Monounsaturated Fat	5.2 g
Polyunsaturated Fat	1.3 g
Dietary Fiber	9.1 g
Sodium	254 mg
Cholesterol	166 mg

EXCELLENT SOURCE OF vitamin C, niacin, iron, manganese and selenium.

GOOD SOURCE OF vitamins A and E (alpha-tocopherol), thiamine, folate, magnesium, phosphorus, zinc and copper.

SOURCE OF riboflavin, pantothenic acid and calcium.

CONTAINS a very high amount of dietary fiber.

Peppery Quinoa Stew with Corn and Crispy Snapper

This zesty stew is chock-full of lip-smacking flavor. It's a meal-in-a-bowl, although you may want to add some whole-grain bread to soak up the tasty broth.

Makes 6 servings

TIPS

For the best flavor, toast and grind whole cumin seeds rather than buying ground cumin. Simply stir seeds in a dry skillet over medium heat until fragrant, about 3 minutes. Immediately transfer to a spice grinder or mortar and grind.

Chipotle peppers pack a lot of wallop. If you're not a heat seeker, err on the side of caution and use half of one here. You can always add a little hot sauce if you find the result too tame.

Nutrients per serving

Calories	357
Protein	30.6 g
Carbohydrates	41.7 g
Fat (Total)	8.6 g
Saturated Fat	0.9 g
Monounsaturated Fat	3.6 g
Polyunsaturated Fat	2.9 g
Dietary Fiber	6.1 g
Sodium	111 mg
Cholesterol	42 mg

EXCELLENT SOURCE OF vitamin C, phosphorus, iron, magnesium, manganese, copper and selenium.

GOOD SOURCE OF vitamins A and E (alpha-tocopherol), thiamine, niacin, folate, pantothenic acid and zinc.

SOURCE OF riboflavin and calcium.

CONTAINS a very high amount of dietary fiber.

2 tbsp	olive oil, divided	25 mL
2	onions, finely chopped	2
4	stalks celery, diced	4
1	red bell pepper, seeded and chopped	1
1	green bell pepper, seeded and chopped	1
2	cloves garlic, minced	2
2 tsp	ground cumin (see Tips, left)	10 mL
1 tsp	dried oregano leaves	5 mL
	Salt and freshly ground black pepper	
½ to 1	chipotle pepper in adobo sauce, minced (see Tips, left)	½ to 1
4 cups	reduced-sodium vegetable or chicken stock	1 L
1	can (14 oz/398 mL) no-salt-added diced tomatoes with juice	1
1 cup	corn kernels	250 mL
1 cup	quinoa, rinsed and drained	250 mL
½ cup	whole wheat or barley flour	125 mL
1 tsp	chili powder	5 mL
1½ lbs	skinless snapper or other firm white fish fillets, cut into 1-inch (2.5 cm) cubes	750 g
	Finely chopped cilantro	

1. In a stockpot, heat 1 tbsp (15 mL) of the oil over medium heat. Add onions, celery, bell peppers and garlic and stir well. Reduce heat to low. Cover and cook until vegetables are softened, about 10 minutes. Increase heat to medium. Add cumin, oregano, salt and black pepper to taste and cook, stirring, for 1 minute. Add chipotle pepper, stock, tomatoes with juice and corn and bring to a boil. Stir in quinoa. Reduce heat to low. Cover and simmer until quinoa is tender, about 15 minutes. Remove from heat and set aside.

2. On a plate or in a plastic bag, combine whole wheat flour and chili powder. Add snapper and roll until coated. Discard excess flour. In a skillet, heat remaining 1 tbsp (15 mL) of oil over medium–high heat for 30 seconds. Add dredged snapper and sauté until fish is nicely browned on both sides and cooked to desired doneness, about 4 minutes.

3. *To serve:* Ladle stew into soup plates and layer snapper on top. Garnish with cilantro.

Variation

Peppery Millet Stew with Corn and Crispy Snapper: Substitute toasted millet (see page 23) for the quinoa. Add ½ cup (125 mL) water along with the stock and increase cooking time to 25 minutes.

Mussels in Spicy Lemongrass Broth with Chinese Black Rice

This dish was inspired by a favorite recipe from New World Noodles by Bill Jones and Stephen Wong. If you're organized, you can make this for a great weeknight dinner. Prepare the broth and rice ahead of time and refrigerate overnight. Just add a salad, such as sliced tomatoes tossed in vinaigrette. If you're entertaining, this makes a smashing first course for as many as eight people.

Makes 4 servings

TIPS

To cook Chinese black rice, bring 1¾ cups (425 mL) water to a rapid boil. Add salt to taste, if desired. Stir in 1 cup (250 mL) rice and return to a rapid boil. Reduce heat to low and simmer until rice is tender and water is absorbed, about 30 minutes. Remove from heat and let stand, covered, for 5 minutes.

For convenience, cook the broth to the 25-minute mark in Step 2 and refrigerate for up to 2 days. The flavors will improve with standing. Strain out the solids and reheat broth when you're ready to finish the dish.

Nutrients per serving

Calories	254
Protein	12.1 g
Carbohydrates	38.0 g
Fat (Total)	6.0 g
Saturated Fat	0.6 g
Monounsaturated Fat	2.5 g
Polyunsaturated Fat	1.5 q
Dietary Fiber	0.3 g
Sodium	150 mg
Cholesterol	19 mg

EXCELLENT SOURCE OF iron, manganese and selenium.

GOOD SOURCE OF niacin, thiamine, folate and phosphorus.

SOURCE OF vitamins A, C and E (alpha-tocopherol), riboflavin, pantothenic acid, magnesium, copper and zinc.

2 cups	cooked Chinese black rice (see Tips, left)	500 mL
1 tbsp	olive oil	15 mL
1	onion, chopped	1
2	cloves garlic, minced	2
1 tbsp	minced gingerroot	15 mL
2 tsp	coriander seeds	10 mL
1	stick cinnamon, about 2 inches (5 cm) long	1
2	stalks lemongrass, coarsely chopped	2
½ tsp	cracked black peppercorns	2 mL
¼ tsp	hot pepper flakes	1 mL
¼ cup	tomato paste	50 mL
4 cups	reduced-sodium vegetable stock	1 L
2 lbs	mussels, cleaned	1 kg
	Finely chopped cilantro	

1. In a large saucepan, heat oil over medium heat for 30 seconds. Add onion and cook, stirring, until softened, about 3 minutes. Add garlic, ginger, coriander seeds, cinnamon stick, lemongrass, peppercorns and hot pepper flakes and cook, stirring, for 1 minute. Add tomato paste and stock and bring to a boil. Reduce heat to low. Cover and simmer until flavors meld, about 25 minutes (see Tips, left). Strain through a fine mesh strainer and, to maximize the flavor, gently press out the liquid using a wooden spoon. Discard solids.

2. Transfer strained broth to a large saucepan and bring to a boil. Add cooked rice and mussels. Cover and cook until mussels open. Discard any that do not open. Ladle mussels and broth into bowls. Garnish with cilantro and serve.

Variation

Substitute any non-glutinous rice for the Chinese black rice. Italian Black Venere, Kalijira brown or long-grain brown rice would work well in this recipe.

Mexican-Style Seafood Stew with Hominy

This rustic dish has an abundance of interesting flavors that combine in intriguing ways. The chiles add depth with just a hint of heat, and the hominy and clams add robustness. I like to finish this with a garnish of avocado cubes drizzled with lime juice, which inserts creaminess and a hit of acidity into the mix.

Makes 6 servings

TIPS

Fish stock provides the best flavor base, but you can substitute an equal quantity of vegetable stock or equal parts bottled clam juice and water.

If using the avocado, you can cut it a few minutes ahead if you toss it with about 1 tbsp (15 mL) freshly squeezed lime juice, which will prevent browning.

Nutrients per serving

Calories	219
Protein	25.8 g
Carbohydrates	15.5 g
Fat (Total)	5.9 g
Saturated Fat	1.0 g
Monounsaturated Fat	2.4 g
Polyunsaturated Fat	1.4 g
Dietary Fiber	3.3 g
Sodium	480 mg
Cholesterol	66 mg

EXCELLENT SOURCE OF niacin, iron, folate, phosphorus, manganese and selenium.

GOOD SOURCE OF vitamin A, riboflavin, pantothenic acid, magnesium, zinc and copper.

SOURCE OF vitamins C and E (alpha-tocopherol), thiamine and calcium.

CONTAINS a moderate amount of dietary fiber.

2	dried ancho, guajillo or mild New Mexico chiles	2
1 cup	packed cilantro leaves	250 mL
4 cups	fish stock, divided (see Tips, left)	1 L
1 tbsp	olive oil	15 mL
2	onions, finely chopped	2
3	cloves garlic, minced	3
1 tsp	ground cumin	5 mL
1 tsp	dried oregano leaves, preferably Mexican	5 mL
1	can (14 oz/398 mL) diced tomatoes with juice	1
1	can (15 oz/412 mL) hominy, drained and rinsed	1
12	clams, thoroughly scrubbed and rinsed	12
12 oz	skinless snapper fillets or other firm white fish, cut into bite-size pieces	375 g
6 oz	medium shrimp, peeled and deveined	175 g
	Salt and freshly ground black pepper	
	Finely chopped cilantro	
	Avocado cubes, optional (see Tips, left)	
	Lime wedges	

1. In a heatproof bowl, soak chiles in boiling water for 30 minutes, weighing down with a cup to ensure they remain submerged. Drain, discarding soaking liquid and stems, and chop coarsely. Transfer to a blender. Add cilantro and 1 cup (250 mL) of the stock. Purée and set aside.

2. In a large saucepan or stockpot, heat oil over medium heat for 30 seconds. Add onions and cook, stirring, until softened, about 3 minutes. Add garlic, cumin and oregano and cook, stirring, for 1 minute. Add tomatoes with juice, reserved chile mixture, remaining 3 cups (750 mL) of the stock and hominy. Season to taste with salt and black pepper and bring to a boil. Reduce heat to low. Cover and simmer until flavors meld, about 30 minutes.

3. Increase heat to medium–high. Return mixture to a full boil. Add clams. Cover and cook, shaking the pot, until all the clams open, about 5 minutes. Discard any that do not open. Add snapper and shrimp and cook, stirring, until fish is tender and shrimp turn pink and are cooked through, 3 to 5 minutes.

4. *To serve:* Ladle stew into soup plates. Garnish with cilantro and avocado, if using. Pass lime wedges at the table.

Variation

If fresh clams aren't available, substitute 2 cans (each 5 oz/142 g) baby clams, drained and rinsed. Stir into stew along with shrimp.

Mexican-Style Millet and Shrimp

If you're tired of simple stir-fries, try this for a welcome change of pace. The millet pilaf, lightly flavored with chipotle pepper, forms a bed for tasty stir-fried shrimp bathed in gently warmed tomatoes and avocado, and finished with a liberal sprinkling of cilantro.

Makes 6 servings

Nutrient Tip

Although avocados are high in calories, ounce for ounce, they are extremely nutritious. Moreover, avocados help your body make better use of antioxidants, such as the lycopene in tomatoes. For instance, one recent study showed that when avocado was added to tomato salsa, lycopene absorption was increased by 4.4 times.

Nutrients per serving

Calories	319
Protein	21.1 g
Carbohydrates	33.6 g
Fat (Total)	11.5 g
Saturated Fat	1.8 g
Monounsaturated Fat	7.0 g
Polyunsaturated Fat	2.0 g
Dietary Fiber	6.5 g
Sodium	185 mg
Cholesterol	147 mg

EXCELLENT SOURCE OF niacin, iron, magnesium, manganese and selenium.

GOOD SOURCE OF vitamin E (alpha-tocopherol), folate, thiamine, zinc, phosphorus and copper.

SOURCE OF vitamins A and C, riboflavin, pantothenic acid and calcium.

CONTAINS a very high amount of dietary fiber.

1 cup	millet	250 mL
2 tbsp	olive oil, divided	25 mL
1	onion, diced	1
4	cloves garlic, minced	4
1 tsp	dried oregano leaves, preferably Mexican	5 mL
	Freshly ground black pepper	
½ to 1	chipotle pepper in adobo sauce, minced	½ to 1
2 cups	reduced-sodium vegetable or chicken stock	500 mL
½ cup	water	125 mL
1 lb	shrimp, peeled and deveined, thawed if frozen	500 g
2 cups	diced tomatoes	500 mL
2 tbsp	freshly squeezed lime juice	25 mL
1	avocado, diced	1
	Salt	
¼ cup	finely chopped cilantro	50 mL

1. In a saucepan over medium heat, toast millet, stirring constantly, until it crackles and releases its aroma, about 5 minutes. Transfer to a bowl and set aside.

2. In same saucepan, heat 1 tbsp (15 mL) of the oil over medium heat for 30 seconds. Add onion and cook, stirring, until softened, about 3 minutes. Add garlic, oregano and black pepper to taste and cook, stirring, for 1 minute. Add chipotle pepper and stir well. Add stock and water and bring to a boil. Stir in millet. Return to a boil. Reduce heat to low. Cover tightly and simmer until liquid is absorbed, about 25 minutes. Set aside. Just before you're ready to serve, fluff millet with a fork and spread over a deep platter.

3. In a wok, heat remaining 1 tbsp (15 mL) of the oil over medium-high heat for 30 seconds. Add shrimp and cook, stirring, until they turn pink and opaque, 2 to 5 minutes. Using tongs, arrange shrimp over top of millet. Add tomatoes and lime juice to pan and toss well. Add avocado and cook until heated through. Season to taste with salt and pepper. Arrange mixture over shrimp and garnish with cilantro.

Variation

Mexican-Style Quinoa and Shrimp: Substitute an equal quantity of quinoa for the millet. Rinse quinoa thoroughly and skip Step 1. Omit water and reduce cooking time to about 20 minutes.

Beef

Whole-Grain Spaghetti with Bulgur-Laced Meatballs

Whole-Grain Spaghetti with Bulgur-Laced Meatballs

Here's an updated version of a great comfort food dish that maintains every bit of flavor while transitioning to healthier status. Substituting bulgur for some of the meat, using whole wheat rather than all-purpose flour to dredge the meatballs and serving the luscious sauce over whole-grain pasta results in a whopping 11.7 grams of fiber per serving. For a change, serve the meatballs and sauce over polenta, cooked wheat, spelt or Kamut berries or even whole-grain couscous. Yum!

Makes 8 servings

TIPS

Chicken, beef or vegetable stock work well in this recipe in place of the wine.

If you prefer a thick tomato sauce, add 2 tbsp (25 mL) of tomato paste along with the tomatoes.

Nutrient Tip

One serving of this dish is fairly high in calories because it is a substantial portion. Keep the sides to a minimum or omit them entirely. It makes a very nutritious one-dish meal.

MEATBALLS

¾ cup	bulgur	175 mL
¾ cup	skim milk	175 mL
1 lb	lean ground beef	500 g
¼ cup	basil pesto	50 mL
¼ cup	freshly grated Parmesan cheese	50 mL
4	cloves garlic, minced	4
1	egg, beaten	1
1 tsp	freshly grated lemon zest	5 mL
1 tsp	salt	5 mL
	Freshly ground black pepper	
¼ cup	whole wheat flour	50 mL

TOMATO SAUCE

2 tbsp	olive oil	25 mL
1	onion, finely chopped	1
2	stalks celery, diced	2
1	carrot, peeled and diced	1
4	cloves garlic, minced	4
1 cup	dry white wine or stock (see Tips, left)	250 mL
2	cans (each 28 oz/796 mL) no-salt-added tomatoes with juice, coarsely chopped (see Tips, left)	2
1	package (16 oz/454 g) whole wheat, spelt or Kamut spaghetti	1
	Finely chopped parsley, optional	

1. *Meatballs:* In a large bowl, combine bulgur and milk, stirring until combined. Let stand until milk is absorbed, about 10 minutes. Add ground beef, pesto, Parmesan, garlic, egg, lemon zest, salt and pepper to taste. Shape into meatballs about 1 inch (2.5 cm) in diameter. Roll in flour and shake off excess.

2. *Tomato Sauce:* In a skillet, heat oil over medium heat for 30 seconds. Add meatballs, in batches, and cook, stirring, until evenly browned. Transfer to a plate. Drain off all but 1 tbsp (15 mL) fat from skillet. Add onion, celery and carrot to pan and cook, stirring, until carrot is softened, about 7 minutes. Add garlic and cook, stirring, for 1 minute. Add white wine and tomatoes with juice and bring to a boil. Return meatballs and any accumulated juices to pan. Reduce heat to low. Cover and simmer until sauce thickens and meatballs are no longer pink inside, about 20 minutes.

3. Meanwhile, in a large pot of boiling salted water, cook spaghetti until tender to the bite, about 11 minutes. Drain in a colander and place in a large deep platter or shallow serving bowl. Arrange sauce and meatballs over top. Sprinkle with parsley, if using.

TOMATOES

This delicious dish is loaded with nutrients, many of which are found in tomatoes. Tomatoes are loaded with vitamin C and also provide a goodly amount of vitamin A (derived from beta-carotene), as well as folate. They also contain fiber and the antioxidant lycopene, which gives them their bright red color. Lycopene, which appears to be a potent cancer fighter, is a fat-soluble carotenoid. That means its disease-fighting abilities are empowered when it is consumed with a little fat, such as olive oil, as it is in this recipe.

Nutrients per serving

Calories	546
Protein	28.5 g
Carbohydrates	75 g
Fat (Total)	15.3 g
Saturated Fat	4.8 g
Monounsaturated Fat	6.2 g
Polyunsaturated Fat	2.3 g
Dietary Fiber	11.7 g
Sodium	716 mg
Cholesterol	61 mg

EXCELLENT SOURCE OF vitamin A, thiamine, riboflavin, niacin, phosphorus, iron, magnesium, manganese, zinc, copper and selenium.

GOOD SOURCE OF vitamins C and E (alpha-tocopherol), folate, pantothenic acid and calcium.

CONTAINS a very high amount of dietary fiber.

Barley-Stuffed Peppers with Crispy Bread Crumbs

Here's a perfect weeknight meal with wide appeal — just add a salad and some whole-grain bread. If you're pressed for time, make the filling the night before and refrigerate until you're ready to fill the peppers (see Tips, below). The flavors will develop more fully.

Makes 6 servings

TIPS

If your filling has been refrigerated, add 10 minutes to the baking time.

For the best flavor, toast whole cumin seeds and grind them yourself (see page 152).

Chipotle pepper powder is available in well-stocked supermarkets or specialty food shops. You can make your own by grinding a dried chipotle pepper in a spice grinder. Or, you can substitute 1 jalapeño or chipotle pepper in abodo sauce, finely chopped. Add along with the garlic.

Nutrients per serving

Calories	352
Protein	21.0 g
Carbohydrates	30.3 g
Fat (Total)	14.7 g
Saturated Fat	5.1 g
Monounsaturated Fat	6.8 g
Polyunsaturated Fat	1.1 g
Dietary Fiber	6.7 g
Sodium	726 mg
Cholesterol	47 mg

EXCELLENT SOURCE OF vitamin C, niacin, iron, manganese, zinc and selenium.

GOOD SOURCE OF thiamine, riboflavin, folate, phosphorus, magnesium and copper.

SOURCE OF vitamins A and E (alpha-tocopherol), pantothenic acid and calcium.

CONTAINS a very high amount of dietary fiber.

* **Preheat oven to 350°F (180°C)**
* **13-by 9-inch (3 L) baking dish, greased**

1½ cups	cooked whole (hulled) barley (see cooking instructions, page 16)	375 mL
6	green or red bell peppers, halved lengthwise, seeded and deveined	6
1 tbsp	olive oil	15 mL
1 lb	lean ground beef	500 g
1	onion, finely chopped	1
4	cloves garlic, minced	4
1 tbsp	ground cumin (see Tips, page left)	15 mL
2 tsp	sweet paprika	10 mL
½ tsp	dried oregano leaves	2 mL
½ tsp	chipotle pepper powder (see Tips, left)	2 mL
½ tsp	salt	2 mL
½ tsp	freshly ground black pepper	2 mL
2 tbsp	tomato paste	25 mL
1 cup	reduced-sodium beef stock	250 mL
½ cup	whole wheat bread crumbs	125 mL
2 tbsp	freshly grated Parmesan cheese	25 mL
	Extra virgin olive oil	

1. In a large pot of boiling water, blanch bell peppers for 5 minutes. Drain well and set aside.

2. In a skillet, heat oil over medium heat for 30 seconds. Add ground beef and onion and cook, breaking up with a spoon, until beef is no longer pink, about 5 minutes. Add garlic, cumin, paprika, oregano, chipotle pepper powder, salt and black pepper and cook, stirring, for 1 minute. Stir in tomato paste. Add stock and bring to a boil. Stir in barley.

3. In a bowl, combine bread crumbs and Parmesan cheese. Mix well.

4. Arrange bell peppers, cut side up, in prepared baking dish. Fill with barley mixture. Sprinkle with bread crumb mixture. Drizzle with olive oil. Bake in preheated oven until piping hot and bread crumbs are lightly browned, about 35 minutes.

Variations

Substitute an equal quantity of wheat, spelt or Kamut berries or farro for the barley.

Add a pinch of chipotle or another chili powder to the bread crumb mixture.

Chili Con Wheat Berries

Here's a nicely spiced chili that is perfect for a weekday meal. It makes a large quantity, but you can freeze half and have dinner ready for a busy day. Chili with toast is a dish I remember fondly from my childhood, so I serve this with toast made from whole-grain bread and complete the meal with a simple green salad.

Makes 8 servings

TIPS
One jalapeño produces a nicely spiced chili. Use the second if you like heat.

If you don't have jalapeños, substitute ¼ to ½ tsp (1 to 2 mL) cayenne pepper.

Nutrients per serving

Calories	262
Protein	18.7 g
Carbohydrates	34.0 g
Fat (Total)	7.0 g
Saturated Fat	2.2 g
Monounsaturated Fat	3.3 g
Polyunsaturated Fat	0.8 g
Dietary Fiber	7.5 g
Sodium	176 mg
Cholesterol	32 mg

EXCELLENT SOURCE OF niacin, phosphorus, iron, magnesium, manganese, zinc and selenium.

GOOD SOURCE OF vitamins C and E (alpha-tocopherol), folate, thiamine, riboflavin and copper.

SOURCE OF vitamin A, pantothenic acid and calcium.

CONTAINS a very high amount of dietary fiber.

3 cups	cooked wheat, spelt or Kamut berries (see cooking instructions, page 34)	750 mL
1 tbsp	olive oil	15 mL
1 lb	extra lean ground beef	500 g
2	onions, finely chopped	2
4	stalks celery, diced	4
1	green bell pepper, seeded and diced	1
1 to 2	jalapeño peppers, seeded and diced (see Tips, left)	1 to 2
4	cloves garlic, minced	4
1 tbsp	chili powder	15 mL
1 tsp	caraway seeds	5 mL
½ tsp	cracked black peppercorns	5 mL
1	can (28 oz/796 mL) no-salt-added diced tomatoes with juice	1
1 cup	reduced-sodium beef stock	250 mL
1 cup	drained, cooked red kidney beans	250 mL
	Salt, optional	

1. In a Dutch oven, heat oil over medium–high heat for 30 seconds. Add ground beef and onions and cook, stirring and breaking up beef with a spoon, until beef is no longer pink, about 6 minutes.

2. Add celery, bell pepper, jalapeño and garlic, and cook, stirring, until vegetables begin to soften, about 3 minutes. Add chili powder, caraway seeds and peppercorns and cook, stirring, for 1 minute. Add tomatoes with juice, stock, kidney beans and wheat berries and bring to a boil. Reduce heat to low. Cover and simmer until flavors blend, about 30 minutes. Season to taste with salt, if using.

Variations
Chili Con Barley: Substitute an equal quantity of whole (hulled) barley for the wheat berries.

Tailgaters' Favorite Stew

I can't imagine anything more appealing on a blustery day than a big serving of this ambrosial stew. It's great for potlucks and outdoor get-togethers because it's easily transportable and there is nothing to add.

Makes 8 servings

TIPS

The orange juice and zest add wonderful depth to this stew. If you like heat, increase the cayenne to as much as ½ tsp (2 mL).

Browning the beef takes about 5 minutes per batch.

You'll need to simmer the stew for about 1½ hours to ensure the wheat berries are tender.

6	slices bacon (about 4 oz/125 g)	6
¼ cup	whole wheat flour	50 mL
1 tsp	salt	5 mL
½ tsp	cracked black peppercorns	2 mL
¼ tsp	cayenne pepper	1 mL
2 lbs	trimmed stewing beef, cut into 1-inch (2.5 cm) chunks	1 kg
2	onions, finely chopped	2
2	stalks celery, diced	2
2	carrots, peeled and diced	2
4	cloves garlic, minced	4
2	bay leaves	2
½ tsp	freshly grated nutmeg	2 mL
	Grated zest and juice of 1 orange	
1½ cups	wheat, spelt or Kamut berries, rinsed and drained	375 mL
1 cup	dry red wine	250 mL
1	can (5½ oz/156 mL) tomato paste	1
2 cups	reduced-sodium beef stock	500 mL

1. In a Dutch oven over medium–high heat, sauté bacon until crisp. Transfer to a paper towel–lined plate to drain. When cool, crumble and set aside. Drain off all but 2 tbsp (25 mL) fat from pan, reserving extra.

2. On a plate, combine flour, salt, peppercorns and cayenne. Dredge beef in mixture until coated. Discard any excess. Add beef to pan, in batches, and cook, stirring, until nicely browned on all sides. Add more bacon drippings, if required. Remove beef to a plate and reserve. Reduce heat to medium.

3. Add onions, celery and carrots to pan and cook, stirring, until carrots are softened, about 7 minutes. Add garlic, bay leaves, nutmeg and orange zest and cook, stirring, for 1 minute. Add wheat berries, orange juice, red wine, tomato paste, stock and 1½ cups (375 mL) water and bring to a boil. Return beef and bacon to pot and bring to a boil. Reduce heat to low. Cover and simmer until wheat berries are tender.

Variations

Substitute an equal quantity of barley or farro for the wheat berries.

Slow Cooker Method

Follow Steps 1 through 3, then transfer mixture to slow cooker stoneware, adding just 1 cup (250) mL of water along with the wheat berries. Cover and cook on Low for 8 hours or on High for 4 hours, until wheat berries are tender.

Nutrients per serving

Calories	398
Protein	32.9 g
Carbohydrates	37.3 g
Fat (Total)	13.3 g
Saturated Fat	4.7 g
Monounsaturated Fat	5.2 g
Polyunsaturated Fat	1.2 g
Dietary Fiber	6.9 g
Sodium	552 mg
Cholesterol	63 mg

EXCELLENT SOURCE OF vitamin A, niacin, phosphorus, iron, magnesium, manganese, zinc and selenium.

GOOD SOURCE OF thiamine, riboflavin and copper.

SOURCE OF vitamins C and E (alpha-tocopherol), folate, pantothenic acid and calcium.

CONTAINS a very high amount of dietary fiber.

Ropa Vieja with Wheat Berries

This zesty mélange makes a great filling for warm tortillas — just add toppings to suit your taste. My favorites include chopped red onion or radishes, shredded cheese or sour cream. Leave the tortillas and garnishes out so people can help themselves. Because it benefits from being made a day ahead and reheated, this is a great dish to make at home and bring to the country for a weekend.

Makes 6 servings

TIPS

If you like heat, add ¼ tsp (1 mL) cayenne along with the paprika.

The meat mixture needs to cool a bit so it can be served in tortillas. In the process, the wheat berries will soak up additional liquid.

2 tbsp	olive oil, divided	25 mL
1½ lbs	trimmed flank steak	750 g
1 cup	wheat, spelt or Kamut berries, rinsed and drained	250 mL
2½ cups	water	625 mL
1 cup	reduced-sodium beef stock	250 mL
2	onions, finely chopped	2
4	cloves garlic, minced	4
1	red bell pepper, seeded and diced	1
1	green bell pepper, seeded and diced	1
1 to 2	jalapeño peppers, seeded and diced	1 to 2
2 tsp	sweet or smoked paprika (see Tips, left)	10 mL
2 tsp	dried oregano leaves, crumbled	10 mL
2 tsp	ground cumin	10 mL
1 tsp	ground allspice	5 mL
½ tsp	salt or to taste	2 mL
½ tsp	cracked black peppercorns	2 mL
1	can (14 oz/398 mL) diced tomatoes with juice	1
2 tbsp	red wine vinegar	25 mL

1. In a Dutch oven or a large skillet with lid, heat 1 tbsp (15 mL) of the oil over medium heat for 30 seconds. Add steak and brown lightly on both sides, about 5 minutes. Add wheat berries, water and beef stock. Bring to a boil over medium heat. Reduce heat to low. Cover and simmer until wheat berries are tender, about 1 hour. Let cool (see Tips, left).

2. Transfer cooled meat to a cutting board and shred. Set wheat berries with any residual liquid aside.

3. Wipe skillet clean. Add remaining 1 tbsp (15 mL) of oil and heat over medium heat for 30 seconds. Add onions, garlic, bell peppers and jalapeño and cook, stirring, until vegetables begin to brown, about 10 minutes. Add paprika, oregano, cumin, allspice, salt and peppercorns and cook, stirring, for 1 minute. Add shredded beef, wheat berries with liquid, tomatoes with juice and red wine vinegar. Reduce heat to low. Cover and simmer until flavors meld, about 30 minutes. Let cool slightly before serving.

Variations

Substitute an equal quantity of whole (hulled) barley or farro for the wheat berries.

Slow Cooker Method

You can use your slow cooker to complete the preliminary cooking of this dish. Proceed with Step 1, but after the mixture comes to a boil, transfer to slow cooker stoneware. Cover and cook on Low for 8 hours or on High for 4 hours, until wheat berries are tender. Continue with Steps 2 and 3, using a clean skillet.

CHILE PEPPERS

The jalapeño peppers in this recipe are just one of hundreds of varieties of chile peppers, which vary dramatically in terms of flavor and heat. Jalapeños are mildly hot (according to the Scoville scale, which measures the heat in hot peppers) and have an earthy flavor, which works well in this dish. Like all chile peppers, they contain capsaicin, a substance that is being studied for its anti-inflammatory properties. Applied topically, capsaicin, may alleviate the discomfort associated with arthritis and psoriasis, among other ailments. A recent study in the *Journal of Agricultural and Food Chemistry* found that in a laboratory situation, capsaicin prevented burgeoning fat cells from becoming mature, suggesting that spicing up your dinner may be a strategy for battling obesity.

Nutrients per serving

Calories	386
Protein	29.6 g
Carbohydrates	31.7 g
Fat (Total)	15.5 g
Saturated Fat	4.9 g
Monounsaturated Fat	7.3 g
Polyunsaturated Fat	1.7 g
Dietary Fiber	6.1 g
Sodium	459 mg
Cholesterol	48 mg

EXCELLENT SOURCE OF vitamin C, niacin, phosphorus, iron, magnesium, manganese, zinc and selenium.

GOOD SOURCE OF vitamin E (alpha-tocopherol), thiamine, pantothenic acid and copper.

SOURCE OF vitamin A, folate, riboflavin and calcium.

CONTAINS a very high amount of dietary fiber.

Sloppy Joes Zucchini

There's so much tasty filling in these zucchini, they remind me of Sloppy Joe burgers spilling out of a bun. They aren't fancy, but they make a delicious weeknight meal and are particularly good to make in the late summer and fall when zucchini are abundant. All you need to add is a simple salad — perhaps sliced cucumbers or some tossed greens.

Makes 6 servings

Nutrient Tip

This recipe is relatively high in sodium, virtually all of which comes from three sources: the regular canned tomatoes (279 mg), the added salt (172 mg) and last, but certainly not least, the feta cheese (279 mg). If you're watching your sodium intake, you can omit the added salt, use canned tomatoes with no salt added, and/or substitute low-salt feta cheese for the regular version.

Nutrients per serving

Calories	298
Protein	18.0 g
Carbohydrates	35.2 g
Fat (Total)	11.2 g
Saturated Fat	5.5 g
Monounsaturated Fat	4.2 g
Polyunsaturated Fat	0.7 g
Dietary Fiber	7.0 g
Sodium	893 mg
Cholesterol	45 mg

EXCELLENT SOURCE OF vitamins A and C, riboflavin, niacin, phosphorus, iron, magnesium, manganese and zinc.

GOOD SOURCE OF folate, thiamine, pantothenic acid, calcium, selenium and copper.

SOURCE OF vitamin E (alpha-tocopherol).

CONTAINS a very high amount of dietary fiber.

- **Preheat oven to 375°F (190°C)**
- **13-by 9-inch (3 L) baking dish**

2 cups	reduced-sodium beef stock	500 mL
1 cup	coarse or medium bulgur	250 mL
3	medium zucchini (each about 12 oz/375 g)	3
1 tbsp	olive oil	15 mL
8 oz	extra lean ground beef	250 g
2	onions, finely chopped	2
4	cloves garlic, minced	4
1 tbsp	dried oregano leaves, crumbled	15 mL
½ tsp	salt	2 mL
½ tsp	ground cinnamon	2 mL
	Freshly ground black pepper	
1	can (28 oz/796 mL) tomatoes with juice, coarsely chopped	1
½ cup	chopped parsley	125 mL
1 cup	crumbled feta	250 mL

1. In a saucepan over medium–high heat, bring stock to a boil. Remove from heat. Add bulgur in a steady stream, stirring constantly. Cover and let stand until bulgur is softened, about 20 minutes.

2. Cut zucchini in half lengthwise and, using a large spoon, scoop out the centers, leaving a solid frame. Finely chop pulp and set aside. Place halves in baking dish.

3. In a skillet, heat oil over medium heat for 30 seconds. Add ground beef and onions and cook, stirring and breaking up with a spoon, until beef is no longer pink, about 8 minutes. Add garlic, oregano, salt, cinnamon and pepper to taste and cook, stirring, for 1 minute. Add reserved zucchini pulp and cook, stirring, for 2 minutes. Stir in reserved bulgur and tomatoes with juice and bring to a boil. Stir in parsley.

4. Spoon tomato mixture over zucchini, filling the shells. (Don't worry about spillover; it will cook nicely, too.) Bake in preheated oven until mixture is hot and bubbly and zucchini shells are tender but still a bit firm, about 45 minutes. Sprinkle feta over top of shells and bake just until the cheese begins to melt, about 5 minutes.

Variation

Substitute ground lamb for the beef.

Southwestern-Style Rice-Stuffed Peppers

The addition of corn and chili powder adds a nice Southwestern touch to this classic preparation. It's filling enough to be a meal in itself and it has enough nutrients, including a very high amount of dietary fiber, to justify being a complete meal. It's a great dish for those evenings when everyone is coming and going, as you can keep it warm and people can help themselves.

Makes 4 servings

TIPS

I prefer to use chili powder made from ground ancho or New Mexico chiles in this recipe but a good blend works well, too.

A grapefruit spoon makes easy work of scraping out the veins in the pepper.

Blanching the peppers in salted water adds a significant amount (387 mg per serving) of sodium to this recipe. If you're watching your sodium intake, blanch them in unsalted water.

Nutrients per serving

Calories	502
Protein	21.5 g
Carbohydrates	72.1 g
Fat (Total)	13.2 g
Saturated Fat	4.0 g
Monounsaturated Fat	6.5 g
Polyunsaturated Fat	1.4 g
Dietary Fiber	14.7 g
Sodium	817 mg
Cholesterol	34 mg

EXCELLENT SOURCE OF vitamins A and C, niacin, phosphorus, magnesium, manganese, zinc and selenium.

GOOD SOURCE OF folate, thiamine, riboflavin, iron and copper.

SOURCE OF vitamin E (alpha-tocopherol), pantothenic acid and calcium.

CONTAINS a very high amount of dietary fiber.

- **Preheat oven to 350°F (180°C)**
- **Baking dish, lightly greased**

2 cups	cooked brown rice (see cooking instructions, page 29)	500 mL
4	large green bell peppers	4
1 tbsp	olive oil	15 mL
1	onion, finely chopped	1
2	stalks celery, diced	2
8 oz	lean ground beef	250 g
4	cloves garlic, minced	4
1 tbsp	chili powder (see Tips, left)	15 mL
2 tsp	dried oregano leaves	10 mL
½ tsp	salt	2 mL
½ tsp	cracked black peppercorns	2 mL
1½ cups	cooked corn kernels	375 mL
2 cups	reduced-sodium tomato sauce	500 mL

1. Cut a thin slice off the top of bell peppers and remove the stems, seeds and veins (see Tips, left). Place peppers in a large pot of boiling salted water. Return to a boil and blanch for 10 minutes. Set aside to drain upside down on several layers of paper towels.

2. In a skillet, heat oil over medium heat for 30 seconds. Add onion, celery and ground beef and cook, stirring and breaking up beef with a spoon, until beef is no longer pink, about 6 minutes. Add garlic, chili powder, oregano, salt and peppercorns and cook, stirring for 1 minute. Remove from heat. Stir in cooked rice and corn.

3. Fill peppers and place in prepared baking dish. Cover with tomato sauce. Cover loosely with foil and bake in preheated oven until hot and steamy, about 45 minutes.

Pot Roast with Wheat Berries and Cumin-Spiked Gravy

Here's a dish that's reminiscent of old-fashioned country kitchens with a difference — nutritious wheat berries stand in for potatoes, shifting the flavor profile and adding a pleasant bit of crunch, along with valuable nutrients. This makes a fabulous Sunday dinner, especially when it's cold outside. Just add some sliced green beans and, perhaps, hot whole-grain rolls to soak up the gravy.

Makes 10 servings

TIP

For the best flavor, toast and grind whole cumin seeds rather than buying ground cumin. Simply stir seeds in a dry skillet over medium heat until fragrant, about 3 minutes. Immediately transfer to a spice grinder or mortar and grind.

Nutrient Tip

Like most spices, cumin does more than add flavor to a dish. It also helps to keep you healthy. Cumin contains iron, an essential mineral, and may have anti-carcinogenic properties. In one laboratory study, cumin was shown to protect against the development of tumors in the stomach and liver. Long recognized as a digestive, cumin accomplishes this result by stimulating the pancreas, producing enzymes that help the body digest food and assimilate nutrients.

• **Preheat oven to 325°F (160°C)**

¼ cup	all-purpose flour	50 mL
1 tsp	dried thyme leaves	5 mL
½ tsp	salt	2 mL
½ tsp	freshly ground black pepper	2 mL
3 lbs	boneless beef pot roast	1.5 kg
2 tbsp	olive oil (approx.)	25 mL
2	onions, finely chopped	2
4	stalks celery, diced	4
4	cloves garlic, minced	4
2 tbsp	ground cumin seeds (see Tip, left)	25 mL
1	bay leaf	1
1¼ cups	wheat, spelt or Kamut berries, rinsed and drained	300 mL
2 cups	water	500 mL
2 cups	reduced-sodium beef stock	500 mL
1 cup	dry red wine	250 mL
3 cups	thinly sliced peeled carrots	750 mL
	Salt and freshly ground black pepper	
½ cup	finely chopped parsley	125 mL

1. On a plate, combine flour, thyme, salt and pepper. Mix well. Dredge roast, covering all sides, and set any remaining mixture aside.

2. In a Dutch oven, heat 1 tbsp (15 mL) of the oil over medium heat for 30 seconds. Add dredged roast and brown on all sides, about 8 minutes. Transfer meat to a plate and set aside. Add more oil to pot, if required.

3. Add onions and celery and cook, stirring, until celery is softened, about 5 minutes. Add garlic, cumin and bay leaf and cook, stirring, for 1 minute. Add wheat berries and toss to coat. Add water, stock and red wine and bring to a boil. Return roast to pot.

4. Cover, place in preheated oven and cook for 2 hours. Turn beef over and add carrots. Cover and continue cooking until carrots are tender, for 1½ hours. Taste and add salt and pepper, if necessary.

5. *To serve:* Transfer meat to a deep platter or serving dish and slice thinly. Cover with sauce and garnish with parsley.

Variations

Pot Roast with Barley and Cumin-Spiked Gravy: Substitute an equal quantity of whole (hulled) barley for the wheat berries.

If you have access to farro, consider substituting it for the wheat berries. Check the package, as most of the farro sold in North America is pearled (it will be labeled perlato). A less pearled version (semi-perlato) is close enough to a whole grain to be acceptable. The advantage to using farro (like spelt, Kamut and barley) is that is can often be tolerated by people who are sensitive to wheat.

Nutrients per serving	
Calories	343
Protein	27.6 g
Carbohydrates	25.3 g
Fat (Total)	14.8 g
Saturated Fat	5.1 g
Monounsaturated Fat	7.1 g
Polyunsaturated Fat	0.9 g
Dietary Fiber	4.6 g
Sodium	325 mg
Cholesterol	67 mg

EXCELLENT SOURCE OF vitamin A, phosphorus, iron, manganese, zinc and selenium.

GOOD SOURCE OF thiamine, riboflavin, niacin, magnesium and copper.

SOURCE OF vitamin C, vitamin E (alpha-tocopherol), folate, pantothenic acid and calcium.

CONTAINS a high amount of dietary fiber.

Cuban-Style Hash with Fried Plantains

This take on picadillo, a classic Cuban dish, is a fabulous weeknight meal — it makes a large serving and you don't need to serve anything else. Make it the night before you intend to serve it because the flavors will improve. (Complete Steps 1 and 2, but don't add the olives.)

Makes 6 servings

TIP

According to my friend Ana Thompson, who is Cuban, plantains should have black skins before they are cooked. In Cuba, they are usually fried in copious amounts of vegetable oil, but I find my method produces a very acceptable result.

Nutrients per serving

Calories	428
Protein	16.6 g
Carbohydrates	65.6 g
Fat (Total)	13.5 g
Saturated Fat	5.0 g
Monounsaturated Fat	6.2 g
Polyunsaturated Fat	1.0 g
Dietary Fiber	6.5 g
Sodium	646 mg
Cholesterol	41 mg

EXCELLENT SOURCE OF vitamin C, niacin, iron, magnesium, manganese, zinc and selenium.

GOOD SOURCE OF vitamins A and E (alpha-tocopherol), thiamine, riboflavin, folate, pantothenic acid, phosphorus and copper.

SOURCE OF calcium.

CONTAINS a very high amount of dietary fiber.

2 cups	cooked brown or red rice (see cooking instructions, page 29)	500 mL
1 tbsp	olive oil	15 mL
1	onion, finely chopped	1
1	green bell pepper, seeded and diced	1
1	jalapeño pepper, seeded and diced	1
4	cloves garlic, minced	4
12 oz	extra lean ground beef	375 g
2 tsp	dried oregano leaves	10 mL
½ tsp	salt	2 mL
½ tsp	freshly ground black pepper	2 mL
1	stick cinnamon, about 2 inches (5 cm) long	1
1	bay leaf	1
1	can (28 oz/796 mL) no-salt-added diced tomatoes with juice	1
2 tbsp	each tomato paste and red wine vinegar	25 mL
8	large pimento-stuffed olives, sliced	8

FRIED PLANTAINS

2 tbsp	butter	25 mL
4	very ripe plantains, thinly sliced (see Tip, left)	4
2 tbsp	freshly squeezed lime or lemon juice	25 mL
4	hot runny fried or poached eggs, optional	4

1. In a large skillet or saucepan, heat oil over medium heat for 30 seconds. Add onion, bell pepper, jalapeño and garlic and stir well. Reduce heat to low. Cover and cook until vegetables are softened, about 10 minutes.

2. Increase heat to medium-high. Add ground beef, oregano, salt, black pepper, cinnamon stick and bay leaf and cook, stirring and breaking up beef with a spoon, until beef is browned and no longer pink, about 5 minutes. Add tomatoes with juice, tomato paste and vinegar and stir well. Stir in rice and season to taste with salt and black pepper. Reduce heat to low. Cover and simmer until flavors meld, about 15 minutes. Stir in sliced olives and remove from heat.

3. *Meanwhile, make Fried Plantains:* In a skillet, melt butter over low heat. Add plantains and cook, stirring occasionally, until caramelized, about 25 minutes. Pour lime juice over top. Serve hot.

4. *To serve:* Spoon picadillo onto a plate and top with a fried egg, if using. Serve fried plantains alongside.

Meatballs with Couscous in Spinach Sauce

It may seem like this recipe has a lot of steps, but they are all easy and it is actually quite efficient since you can work on the couscous and sauce while the meatballs cook. The result of your labor is an extremely nutritious and delicious one-dish meal — just the thing to inspire taste buds that have grown tired of the same old thing.

Makes 8 servings

Nutrient Tip

If you're concerned about the quantity of fat in this recipe, reduce the quantities of pesto and tahini. However, most of the fat is unsaturated, which is associated with healthful benefits. For instance, unsaturated fat raises HDL (good) cholesterol, while lowering LDL (bad) cholesterol.

- **Preheat oven to 350°F (180°C)**
- **Rimmed baking sheet, lightly greased**

MEATBALLS

½ cup	bulgur	125 mL
¾ cup	ice cold water	175 mL
1 lb	lean ground beef	500 g
¼ cup	sun-dried tomato pesto	50 mL
1	egg, beaten	1
	Salt and freshly ground black pepper	

COUSCOUS

2 cups	vegetable stock or water	500 mL
1 cup	whole wheat couscous	250 mL
	Salt, optional	

SPINACH SAUCE

1 lb	fresh spinach, stems removed, or 1 package (10 oz/300 g) spinach leaves, thawed if frozen	500 g
⅓ cup	tahini	75 mL
2 tbsp	freshly squeezed lemon juice	25 mL
2	green onions, white part only, chopped	2
2	cloves garlic, minced	2
½ tsp	ground cumin	2 mL
	Salt and freshly ground black pepper	

1. *Meatballs:* In a bowl, combine bulgur and water. Stir well and set aside for 5 minutes. Drain and squeeze out excess liquid and return to bowl. Add ground beef, pesto, egg, salt and pepper to taste and soaked bulgur. Using your hands, mix well. Shape into 12 meatballs, each about ¼ cup (50 mL). Place on prepared baking sheet and bake in preheated oven for 15 minutes. Turn and bake until beef is no longer pink, about 15 minutes more.

2. *Couscous:* Meanwhile, in a saucepan, bring stock to a boil. Gradually add couscous, stirring well. Season to taste with salt, if using. Remove from heat, cover and let stand for at least 15 minutes. Fluff with a fork before using.

3. *Spinach Sauce:* Meanwhile, in a large pot, cook spinach until wilted, about 5 minutes (or just until heated through if using frozen). (Drain spinach but don't squeeze the water out. Otherwise, your sauce will not have enough liquid.) Transfer to a food processor. Add tahini, lemon juice, green onions, garlic and cumin. Season to taste with salt and pepper.

4. *To serve:* Spoon couscous onto a deep platter and top with spinach sauce. Arrange meatballs over top.

ANTIOXIDANTS

The plant foods in this recipe (bulgur, couscous, tomatoes, spinach, tahini, lemon juice, onions, garlic and cumin) are a great source of antioxidants, which may help to delay the development of many age-related diseases when consumed as part of a nutritious diet. Nutrients with antioxidant activity include vitamins A, C and E, as well as selenium. Researchers now believe that eating fruits and vegetables in combination increases their antioxidant power. The fat in this recipe also contributes to the disease-fighting abilities of those nutrients that are fat-soluble (vitamins A and E). The tomatoes and spinach also provide the antioxidants beta-carotene, lycopene, lutein and zeaxanthin.

Nutrients per serving

Calories	409
Protein	20.7 g
Carbohydrates	33.2 g
Fat (Total)	20.9 g
Saturated Fat	4.7 g
Monounsaturated Fat	9.3 g
Polyunsaturated Fat	4.9 g
Dietary Fiber	6.6 g
Sodium	394 mg
Cholesterol	58 mg

EXCELLENT SOURCE OF vitamin A, niacin, folate, iron, magnesium, manganese and zinc.

GOOD SOURCE OF riboflavin, thiamine, phosphorus, copper and selenium.

SOURCE OF vitamins C and E (alpha-tocopherol), pantothenic acid and calcium.

CONTAINS a very high amount of dietary fiber.

Beef Stew with Rye Berries, Sauerkraut and Dill

With its robust flavors, this is the perfect antidote to a bone-chilling day. It's a great one-dish meal, just the thing for après ski. Make it in your slow cooker and it will be ready and waiting when you arrive home.

Makes 8 servings

TIPS

Be sure to rinse sauerkraut in several changes of cold water to remove the sour taste. I rinse, then soak mine in fresh water in the refrigerator for 6 to 8 hours before using.

If you like the taste of caraway, increase the quantity of seeds to as much as 1½ tbsp (22 mL).

Nutrient Tip

This recipe is high in sodium, but most (774 mg) comes from the sauerkraut. Make sure to soak and rinse your sauerkraut to remove as much salt as possible.

Nutrients per serving

Calories	277
Protein	24.5 g
Carbohydrates	26.9 g
Fat (Total)	8.7 g
Saturated Fat	2.5 g
Monounsaturated Fat	3.7 g
Polyunsaturated Fat	0.9 g
Dietary Fiber	7.5 g
Sodium	1125 mg
Cholesterol	42 mg

EXCELLENT SOURCE OF vitamin A, niacin, phosphorus, iron, manganese and zinc.

GOOD SOURCE OF vitamin C, riboflavin, folate, magnesium, copper and selenium.

SOURCE OF vitamin E (alpha-tocopherol), thiamine, pantothenic acid and calcium.

CONTAINS a very high amount of dietary fiber.

• **Preheat oven to 350°F (180°C)**

4 cups	sauerkraut, rinsed, soaked and drained (see Tips, left)	1 L
1 tbsp	olive oil	15 mL
1½ lbs	trimmed stewing beef, cut into 1-inch (2.5 cm) cubes	750 g
2	onions, finely chopped	2
2	carrots, peeled and diced	2
2	stalks celery, diced	2
4	cloves garlic, minced	4
1 tbsp	caraway seeds (see Tips, left)	15 mL
½ tsp	cracked black peppercorns	2 mL
1 cup	rye berries, rinsed and drained	250 mL
2 cups	reduced-sodium beef stock	500 mL
2 cups	water	500 mL
	Salt, optional	
½ cup	finely chopped dill	125 mL
	Sour cream, optional	

1. In a Dutch oven, heat oil over medium–high heat for 30 seconds. Add beef, in batches, and brown, about 4 minutes per batch. Transfer to a plate and set aside. Reduce heat to medium.

2. Add onions, carrots and celery to pot and cook, stirring, until softened, about 7 minutes. Add garlic, caraway seeds and peppercorns and cook, stirring, for 1 minute. Add rye berries, stock, water, sauerkraut and reserved beef and any accumulated juices and bring to a rapid boil. Season to taste with salt, if using.

3. Cover and bake in preheated oven until rye berries are tender, about 2 hours.

4. *To serve:* Ladle into soup plates and garnish with dill. Pass the sour cream at the table, if using.

Slow Cooker Method
Complete Steps 1 and 2. Transfer mixture to slow cooker stoneware. Cover and cook on Low for 8 hours or on High for 4 hours, until rye berries and beef are tender.

Asian-Spiced Beef with Soba Noodles

Although the flavorings lean toward being Chinese, and the soba noodles are traditionally Japanese, this is a variation on the theme of Vietnamese pho, a meal of beef and noodles cooked in an abundance of flavorful broth. Serve this on those days when you want something substantial and satisfying — it's all you'll need.

Makes 6 servings

TIP
Depending upon the size of your baby bok choy, you may have trouble fitting them all in the pan. If so, stir in gradually.

Nutrient Tip
Most of the sodium in this dish comes from beef stock, which contributes 852 mg. So, if you're concerned about your sodium intake, make your own beef stock with no salt added.

Nutrients per serving

Calories	504
Protein	41.4 g
Carbohydrates	50.3 g
Fat (Total)	15.9 g
Saturated Fat	5.1 g
Monounsaturated Fat	7.8 g
Polyunsaturated Fat	1.4 g
Dietary Fiber	5.6 g
Sodium	1317 mg
Cholesterol	51 mg

EXCELLENT SOURCE OF vitamins A and C, thiamine, niacin, folate, phosphorus, iron, manganese, zinc and selenium.

GOOD SOURCE OF riboflavin, pantothenic acid, magnesium and calcium.

SOURCE OF vitamin E (alpha-tocopherol) and copper.

CONTAINS a high amount of dietary fiber.

2 tbsp	extra virgin olive oil, divided	25 mL
1	flank steak, about 1½ lbs (750 g)	1
1	whole star anise	1
2 tsp	Szechuan peppercorns	10 mL
1 tsp	fennel seeds	5 mL
1 tsp	cracked black peppercorns	5 mL
1	stick cinnamon, about 2 inches (5 cm) long	1
1	piece (2 inches/5 cm) gingerroot, coarsely chopped	1
8 cups	reduced-sodium beef stock	2 L
¼ cup	dry sherry, dry white wine or Shaoxing wine	50 mL
2 tbsp	reduced-sodium soy sauce	25 mL
12 oz	soba noodles	375 g
1 tsp	sesame oil	5 mL
2	cloves garlic, minced	2
8 oz	sliced fresh shiitake mushroom caps	250 g
2 cups	shredded peeled carrots	500 mL
12	baby bok choy, halved lengthwise	12
2 tbsp	thinly sliced green onions	25 mL
	Minced Thai chiles, optional	
	Lime wedges, optional	

1. In a skillet, heat 1 tbsp (15 mL) of the oil over medium heat for 30 seconds. Add steak and brown well on both sides, about 5 minutes. Transfer to a large saucepan set over medium heat. Add star anise, Szechuan peppercorns, fennel seeds, cracked peppercorns, cinnamon stick, ginger, stock and sherry. Bring to a boil. Reduce heat to low. Cover and simmer until meat is very tender, about 1 hour. Lift out meat and shred. Strain liquid, discarding solids. Stir in soy sauce and keep stock warm.

2. Meanwhile, cook soba noodles according to package instructions. Drain and rinse under cold running water. Toss with sesame oil and set aside.

3. In a large wok or skillet, heat remaining 1 tbsp (15 mL) of oil over medium-high heat for 30 seconds. Add garlic, shredded meat and mushrooms and cook, stirring, until mushrooms have softened. Add carrots and bok choy and cook, stirring, until bok choy is slightly wilted.

4. *To serve:* Divide steak mixture and cooked noodles evenly among soup bowls. Pour stock over. Sprinkle with green onions and chile pepper, if using. Serve with lime wedges to squeeze over top, if using.

Peppery Meat Loaf with Couscous

I love the range of mouthwatering tastes in this recipe, which combines old-fashioned meat loaf with Mediterranean flavors such as red peppers, paprika, cumin and coriander. Serve this with baked potatoes in their skins and a tossed salad.

Makes 8 servings

TIP

For the best flavor, toast whole cumin and coriander seeds and grind them yourself. To toast seeds, spread in a dry skillet over medium heat and cook, stirring, until fragrant, about 3 minutes. Transfer to a mortar or a spice grinder and grind.

Nutrients per serving

Calories	299
Protein	21.8 g
Carbohydrates	24.0 g
Fat (Total)	12.9 g
Saturated Fat	4.3 g
Monounsaturated Fat	5.2 g
Polyunsaturated Fat	1.2 g
Dietary Fiber	5.3 g
Sodium	444 mg
Cholesterol	93 mg

EXCELLENT SOURCE OF vitamin C, zinc and selenium.

GOOD SOURCE OF vitamin A niacin, riboflavin, phosphorus and iron.

SOURCE OF vitamin E (alpha-tocopherol), thiamine, folate, pantothenic acid, magnesium, manganese and copper.

CONTAINS a high amount of dietary fiber.

- **Preheat oven to 350°F (180°C)**
- **9-by 5-inch (2 L) loaf pan**
- **Instant-read thermometer**

¾ cup	water	175 mL
½ cup	reduced-sodium beef stock or water	125 mL
¾ cup	whole wheat couscous	175 mL
1 lb	extra lean ground beef	500 g
8 oz	Italian sausage, removed from casings and crumbled	250 mL
1	onion, diced	1
1	red bell pepper, seeded and diced	1
½ cup	finely chopped parsley	125 mL
2	eggs, beaten	2
1 cup	reduced-sodium tomato sauce, divided	250 mL
1 tbsp	sweet paprika	15 mL
1 tbsp	ground cumin (see Tip, left)	15 mL
1 tsp	ground coriander	5 mL
½ tsp	salt	2 mL
¼ tsp	cayenne pepper	1 mL

1. In a saucepan, bring water and beef stock to a boil. Gradually stir in couscous. Cover, remove from heat and set aside or let stand until couscous is tender and water is absorbed, about 15 minutes. Fluff with a fork before using.

2. In a large bowl, combine ground beef, sausage, onion, bell pepper, parsley, eggs, all but 2 tbsp (25 mL) of the tomato sauce, paprika, cumin, coriander, salt, cayenne and couscous. Using your hands, mix until well blended. Transfer to loaf pan and spread remaining 2 tbsp (25 mL) of tomato sauce over top. Bake in preheated oven until temperature reaches 165°F (75°C) on a thermometer, about 1 hour.

Variation

Substitute spelt or barley couscous for the whole wheat version.

Steak and Mushroom Pie with Barley in Whole Wheat Crust

This is one of my favorite Sunday dinners — there is something extremely comforting about meat pies and the house smells so appetizing while they bake in the oven. This doesn't need much more than a tossed green salad or a steamed green vegetable such as broccoli or beans.

- **10-inch (25 cm) deep dish pie plate**

1 cup	cooked whole (hulled) barley (see cooking instructions, page 16)	250 mL
¼ cup	whole barley or wheat flour	50 mL
1 tsp	salt	5 mL
½ tsp	cracked black peppercorns	2 mL
¼ tsp	cayenne pepper	1 mL
1½ lbs	boneless top round steak, cut into bite-size pieces	750 g
2 tbsp	butter, divided	25 mL
1 tbsp	olive oil (approx.)	15 mL
1 lb	sliced mushrooms caps (see Tips, left)	500 g
½ cup	diced shallots	125 mL
½ tsp	dried thyme leaves (see Tips, left)	2 mL
½ tsp	cracked black peppercorns	2 mL
1 tbsp	brandy or cognac, optional	15 mL
2 cups	reduced-sodium beef stock	500 mL
2 tbsp	finely chopped parsley	25 mL
1 tbsp	Worcestershire sauce	15 mL
	Double-batch Whole Wheat Pie Crust (see recipe, page 245)	

1. In a resealable bag, combine barley flour, salt, peppercorns and cayenne. Add steak and toss until well coated. Set aside excess flour mixture.

2. In a skillet, heat 1 tbsp (15 mL) of the butter and oil over medium–high heat for 30 seconds. Add steak, in batches, and cook, stirring, until browned, about 4 minutes per batch, adding more oil if necessary. Transfer to a plate.

3. Add remaining butter and mushrooms to pan. Cook, stirring, until they start to brown, about 5 minutes. Remove with a slotted spoon and set aside. Add shallots to pan and cook, stirring, just until they begin to turn golden, about 4 minutes. Add thyme and peppercorns and cook, stirring, for 1 minute. Add reserved flour mixture and cook, stirring, for 1 minute. Add brandy, if using, and cook until it evaporates. Add stock and bring to a boil. Return beef with any accumulated juices and mushrooms to pan and stir well. Remove from heat and stir in parsley, Worcestershire sauce and barley. Set aside and let cool until lukewarm, about 30 minutes

4. Preheat oven to 425°F (220°C). Roll out bottom crust. Place in pie plate and fill with mixture. Roll out top crust and place over bottom crust, then flute. The pie will be very full; place it on a baking sheet to prevent spillage. Bake in preheated oven for 15 minutes. Reduce heat to 350°F (180°C) and bake for 30 minutes more.

Variations

Substitute cooked wheat, spelt or Kamut berries for the barley.

Nutrients per serving	
Calories	219
Protein	22.3 g
Carbohydrates	13.7 g
Fat (Total)	8.4 g
Saturated Fat	3.5 g
Monounsaturated Fat	3.7 g
Polyunsaturated Fat	0.7 g
Dietary Fiber	3.1 g
Sodium	544 mg
Cholesterol	52 mg

EXCELLENT SOURCE OF niacin, zinc and selenium.

GOOD SOURCE OF riboflavin, pantothenic acid, phosphorus, iron, manganese and copper.

SOURCE OF vitamins A, C and E (alpha-tocopherol), folate, thiamine and magnesium.

CONTAINS a moderate amount of dietary fiber.

Beef Biriyani

This is a classic Indian dish made with layers of basmati rice, a curry filling and yogurt. It makes a large quantity and is perfect to add interest to a buffet. If you're cooking for your family, it's a great Sunday dinner with the addition of puréed spinach or a salad. Don't be daunted by the quantity if you're cooking for fewer people — just cut the recipe in half.

Makes 10 servings

TIPS

I prefer to toast and grind cumin and coriander seeds myself and it produces better flavor. However, if you prefer, you can substitute 2 tsp (10 mL) ground cumin and 1½ tsp (7 mL) ground coriander and skip the toasting.

You can marinate the meat for up to 2 days ahead of cooking, if you prefer. Or you can make the components ahead and assemble just before you're ready to serve. Complete Steps 1 through 4. Cover and refrigerate meat mixture for up to 2 days. Complete Step 5. Transfer cooked rice to a shallow container and let cool slightly. Immediately cover and refrigerate separate from the meat mixture for up to 2 days.

MARINADE

1 tbsp	cumin seeds (see Tips, left)	15 mL
2 tsp	coriander seeds	10 mL
2	onions, finely chopped	2
2 tbsp	minced gingerroot	25 mL
2 tbsp	minced garlic	25 mL
1 cup	plain yogurt (minimum 4% M.F.)	250 mL
2 lbs	trimmed stewing beef, cut into bite-size pieces	1 kg

FILLING

1 tbsp	olive oil	15 mL
2	onions, thinly sliced on the vertical	2
2 tsp	curry powder	10 mL
½ tsp	cracked black peppercorns	2 mL
¼ tsp	cayenne pepper, optional	1 mL
½ tsp	crumbled saffron threads, dissolved in ½ cup (125 mL) boiling water	2 mL
	Salt	
2 cups	reduced-sodium beef stock	500 mL
2 cups	water	500 mL
1	stick cinnamon, about 2 inches (5 cm) long	1
2 cups	brown basmati or brown long-grain rice, rinsed and drained	500 mL
1 to 2	long red or green chiles, seeded and minced	1 to 2
1 cup	plain yogurt (minimum 4% M.F.)	250 mL

1. In a dry skillet over medium heat, toast cumin and coriander seeds, stirring constantly, until fragrant, about 3 minutes. Transfer to a mortar or a spice grinder and grind. Set aside.

2. *Marinade:* In a bowl, combine onions, ginger, garlic, yogurt and reserved spices. Add beef and toss well. Cover and marinate in the refrigerator for at least 2 hours (see Tips, left).

3. *Filling:* Using a slotted spoon, remove beef from marinade and pat dry. Set marinade aside. In a skillet, heat oil over medium–high heat for 30 seconds. Add beef, in batches, and cook, stirring, until browned, about 4 minutes per batch. Transfer to a plate and set aside.

4. Add onions to pan and cook, stirring, until golden, about 15 minutes. Add curry powder, peppercorns and cayenne, if using, and cook, stirring for 1 minute. Return beef and any accumulated juices to pan and stir well. Add reserved marinade and saffron liquid. Stir well and bring to a boil. Season to taste with salt. Reduce heat to low. Cover and simmer, watching carefully and stirring occasionally to ensure mixture doesn't scorch, until beef is fork tender, about 45 minutes.

5. Meanwhile, in a heavy pot with a tight-fitting lid over medium-high heat, bring stock, water and cinnamon stick to a boil. Add rice and return to a boil. Reduce heat to low. Cover and simmer until rice is tender and liquid has been absorbed, about 50 minutes. Remove cinnamon stick and stir in chiles.

6. *Assembly:* Fifteen minutes before you're ready to bake, preheat oven to 350°F (180°C). Spread approximately one third of rice evenly over bottom of baking dish, ensuring it's completely covered. Add beef mixture. Spread one third of rice over beef and spread yogurt over rice. Spread remaining rice evenly over yogurt. Cover and bake in preheated oven until piping hot, about 30 minutes.

Variation

Lamb Biriyani: Substitute an equal quantity of stewing lamb for the beef. Eliminate the beef stock and cook the rice in 4 cups (1 L) water.

Nutrients per serving	
Calories	361
Protein	26.7 g
Carbohydrates	39.1 g
Fat (Total)	10.5 g
Saturated Fat	3.6 g
Monounsaturated Fat	4.3 g
Polyunsaturated Fat	0.9 g
Dietary Fiber	3.4 g
Sodium	219 mg
Cholesterol	49 mg

EXCELLENT SOURCE OF niacin, phosphorus, magnesium, manganese and zinc.

GOOD SOURCE OF riboflavin, thiamine, pantothenic acid and iron.

SOURCE OF vitamins A and C, folate, calcium and copper.

CONTAINS a moderate amount of dietary fiber.

MAGNESIUM

One serving of this recipe is an excellent source of magnesium, a mineral that supports every major system in our bodies. Among its most important functions, magnesium helps to keep bones strong, and an insufficient intake of this mineral may increase the risk of osteoporosis in older women. It also supports the nervous system, working with calcium to help keep nerves relaxed and healthy. Without an adequate supply of magnesium, muscles may react, triggering cramps and spasms. Muscle tension, anxiety and heart disease are among the ailments linked with a magnesium deficiency.

Pork and Lamb

Pork Pozole

Pork Pozole

I love the robust flavors in this traditional Mexican dish, which is perfect for a casual evening with friends. Add the chipotle pepper if you like heat and a bit of smoke. To continue the Mexican theme, serve with a tossed green salad that includes a diced avocado, and warm fresh tortillas.

Makes 8 servings

TIP

Poblano peppers, one of the mildest chile peppers, are becoming increasingly available in markets. Triangular in shape, they are a deep shade of green and have a wonderful hot-fruity flavor that is lovely in this dish. However, if you can't find them, green bell peppers make a more than acceptable substitute. In their dried form, poblano peppers are known as ancho peppers.

4	slices bacon	4
2 lbs	trimmed pork shoulder, cut into 1-inch (2.5 cm) cubes	1 kg
2	onions, finely chopped	2
4	cloves garlic, minced	4
1 tbsp	dried oregano leaves	15 mL
½ tsp	cracked black peppercorns	2 mL
2 tsp	finely grated lime zest	10 mL
1	can (14 oz/398 mL) no-salt-added diced tomatoes with juice	1
2 cups	reduced-sodium chicken stock	500 mL
1	can (29 oz/824 mL) hominy, drained and rinsed	1
2	poblano or green bell peppers, seeded and diced (see Tip, left)	2
2	dried ancho or guajillo chiles	2
2 cups	boiling water	500 mL
2 tbsp	freshly squeezed lime juice	25 mL
2 tbsp	finely chopped cilantro	25 mL
1	chipotle pepper in adobo sauce, optional	1
	Salt	
	Shredded lettuce, optional	
	Chopped radish, optional	
	Chopped red or green onion, optional	
	Fried tortilla strips, optional	
	Lime wedges	

1. In a Dutch oven, cook bacon over medium–high heat until crisp. Drain on paper towel and crumble. Cover and refrigerate until ready to use. Drain all but 2 tbsp (25 mL) fat from pan. Add pork, in batches, and brown, about 3 minutes per batch. Transfer to a plate. Reduce heat to medium.

2. Add onions to pan and cook, stirring, until softened, about 3 minutes. Add garlic, oregano, peppercorns and lime zest and cook, stirring, for 1 minute. Add tomatoes with juice, stock, hominy and reserved pork and any accumulated juices and return to a boil.

3. Reduce heat to low. Cover and simmer until pork is almost tender, for 1½ hours. Stir in reserved bacon and poblano peppers.

4. Meanwhile, in a heatproof bowl, soak ancho chiles in boiling water for 30 minutes, weighing down with a cup to keep submerged. Drain and discard soaking liquid and stems. Chop chiles coarsely. Transfer to a blender. Scoop out ½ cup (125 mL) cooking liquid from the pozole and add to blender along with lime juice, cilantro and chipotle pepper, if using. Purée and stir into pozole. Add salt to taste and continue cooking until pork is tender and flavors meld, about 30 minutes.

5. *To serve:* Ladle into soup plates and top with the garnishes of your choice. Season to taste with lime juice.

Slow Cooker Method

Complete Steps 1 and 2, reducing the quantity of chicken stock to 1½ cups (375 mL). Cover and cook on Low for 8 to 10 hours or on High for 4 to 5 hours, until pork is tender. Stir in reserved bacon, poblano pepper and ancho chile mixture and adjust seasoning. Cover and cook on High for 30 minutes, until peppers are tender.

FOLATE

One serving of this dish is an excellent source of folate, a B vitamin that has long been known to prevent neural tube defects in babies. Now information from the Harvard Nurses' Study suggests that an adequate supply of folate has more wide-ranging effects. Consumption of folate may help to prevent high blood pressure and keep homocysteine levels under control, protecting blood vessels from plaque. And Finnish researchers found a link between the consumption of folate and a reduced risk of depression. Although previous information linked folate intake with a decreased risk of colon cancer, a recent study published in *The Journal of the American Medical Association* reported that large daily doses of the nutrient actually seemed to increase the risk of the disease. Once again, it appears that supplementation, not the nutrient itself, may be the problem. Folate is not easily obtained in a typical North American diet. Sources include leafy greens, legumes, nuts and whole grains.

Nutrients per serving

Calories	242
Protein	22.9 g
Carbohydrates	19.6 g
Fat (Total)	8.4 g
Saturated Fat	2.9 g
Monounsaturated Fat	3.5 g
Polyunsaturated Fat	1.4 g
Dietary Fiber	4.4 g
Sodium	371 mg
Cholesterol	63 mg

EXCELLENT SOURCE OF vitamin C, thiamine, niacin, folate and zinc.

GOOD SOURCE OF pantothenic acid, riboflavin, phosphorus, iron, magnesium, manganese and copper.

SOURCE OF vitamins A and E (alpha-tocopherol), calcium and selenium.

CONTAINS a high amount of dietary fiber.

Sausage-Spiked Peas 'n' Rice

What could be easier than this combination of brown and wild rice and split peas, seasoned with sausage and fennel? The flavors are fantastic and I love the way the split peas dissolve into the sauce, creating a luscious texture that I find extremely satisfying. Add a simple green salad or some steamed green beans and enjoy.

Makes 6 servings

TIPS

You can cook the split peas yourself, reserving ¼ cup (50 mL) of the cooking liquid or you can use a can (14 to 19 oz/398 to 540 mL) yellow split peas, rinsed and drained, plus ¼ cup (50 mL) water, instead. Be aware that the canned peas will be much higher in sodium than those you cook yourself.

If you have fresh thyme on hand, substitute 2 whole sprigs, stem and all, for the dried. Remove and discard before serving.

2 cups	cooked yellow split peas, with ¼ cup (50 mL) cooking liquid (see Tips, left)	500 mL
1 tbsp	olive oil	15 mL
12 oz	hot or mild Italian sausage, removed from casings	375 g
1	bulb fennel, cored and chopped	1
1	onion, finely chopped	1
4	cloves garlic, minced	4
1 tsp	dried thyme leaves (see Tips, left)	5 mL
	Freshly ground black pepper	
1 cup	brown and wild rice mixture, rinsed and drained	250 mL
2 cups	reduced-sodium chicken stock	500 mL

1. In a large saucepan with a tight-fitting lid or Dutch oven, heat oil over medium heat for 30 seconds. Add sausage, fennel and onion and cook, stirring and breaking sausage up with a spoon, until meat is cooked through, about 6 minutes. Add garlic, thyme, pepper to taste and rice and cook, stirring, for 1 minute. Stir in peas with reserved liquid and stock and bring to a boil.

2. Reduce heat to low. Cover tightly and simmer until grains of wild rice begin to split, about 50 minutes. Ladle into soup plates.

Slow Cooker Method
Complete Step 1. Transfer mixture to slow cooker stoneware. Cover and cook on Low for 8 hours or on High for 4 hours, until wild rice is tender and grains begin to split.

Nutrients per serving

Calories	385
Protein	18.7 g
Carbohydrates	41.7 g
Fat (Total)	16.5 g
Saturated Fat	4.6 g
Monounsaturated Fat	7.3 g
Polyunsaturated Fat	2.1 g
Dietary Fiber	5.1 g
Sodium	606 mg
Cholesterol	30 mg

EXCELLENT SOURCE OF thiamine, magnesium and manganese.
GOOD SOURCE OF niacin, folate, zinc, selenium, phosphorus, iron and copper.
SOURCE OF vitamin C, riboflavin, pantothenic acid and calcium.
CONTAINS a high amount of dietary fiber.

Baked Beans 'n' Barley

If you're a fan of Boston baked beans, this dish is for you. It's every bit as delicious as the best versions of the original. This is the perfect dish for a blustery day, potluck or a tailgating party. If you're serving it for dinner, complete the meal with warm whole-grain rolls and a tossed green salad.

Makes 8 servings

TIPS

Although any kind of maple syrup works well in this recipe, I like to use the dark amber or grade B versions, which are more strongly flavored. They are also more economical than the lighter kinds.

If you like heat, the chile pepper adds a pleasant note, but it is not essential.

1 cup	whole (hulled) barley, rinsed and drained	250 mL
1 cup	dried navy beans	250 mL
¾ cup	ketchup	175 mL
⅔ cup	pure maple syrup (see Tips, left)	150 mL
4	cloves garlic, minced	4
1 tbsp	minced gingerroot	15 mL
1 tsp	dry mustard	5 mL
1 tsp	salt	5 mL
1 tsp	cracked black peppercorns	5 mL
1	dried red chile pepper, optional (see Tips, left)	1
4 oz	chunk pancetta or salt pork, diced	125 g
2	onions, halved and thinly sliced on the vertical	2

1. In a bowl, combine barley and 2½ cups (625 mL) water. Set aside. In a large saucepan, combine beans and 4 cups (1 L) water. Cover and bring to a boil over medium-high heat. Boil rapidly for 3 minutes. Set barley and beans aside for 1 hour. Drain beans, discarding liquid, and rinse thoroughly under cold running water.

2. Return drained beans to saucepan. Add reserved barley with soaking liquid and 4 cups (1 L) more water. Bring to a boil over medium–high heat. Reduce heat to low. Cover and simmer until beans are tender, about 1 hour. Drain, reserving liquid.

3. Preheat oven to 325°F (160°C). In a bowl, combine ketchup, maple syrup, garlic, ginger, dry mustard, salt, peppercorns and chile pepper, if using. Set aside.

4. In a Dutch oven, combine pancetta, onions, barley-bean and ketchup mixtures. Stir well. Add reserved bean liquid barely to cover, setting remainder aside. Cover and bake in preheated oven for 2½ hours. Remove cover and add more bean liquid, if necessary. Bake until top is crusty, about 30 minutes. Remove and discard chile pepper.

Nutrients per serving

Calories	290
Protein	9.2 g
Carbohydrates	59.9 g
Fat (Total)	2.8 g
Saturated Fat	1.2 g
Monounsaturated Fat	1.3 g
Polyunsaturated Fat	0.8 g
Dietary Fiber	8.9 g
Sodium	570 mg
Cholesterol	2 mg

EXCELLENT SOURCE OF folate and manganese.

GOOD SOURCE OF phosphorus, iron, magnesium, thiamine, zinc, copper and selenium.

SOURCE OF vitamins C and E (alpha-tocopherol), calcium, niacin and riboflavin.

CONTAINS a very high amount of dietary fiber.

Slow Cooker Method

You can make this recipe using your slow cooker if it has a removable stoneware insert that is ovenproof. Complete Steps 1 through 3, but do not precook or soak the barley. Simply add it to the stoneware along with the pancetta and other ingredients in Step 4. Place two tea towels, folded in half, over the top of the stoneware before putting the lid in place. Fold any towel that is hanging down back up over the lid to prevent it from becoming too hot from contact with the casing. Cook on Low for 8 hours or on High for 4 hours before removing the lid and towels and transferring the insert to bake until top is crusty.

Fragrant Lamb Curry with Barley

Make this delicious curry any time you have a craving for something lusciously different. It's a great Sunday night dinner and is perfect for a potluck or on a buffet.

- **Preheat oven to 325°F (160°C)**
- **13-by 9-inch (3 L) baking dish**

2 tbsp	olive oil, divided	25 mL
1 lb	trimmed stewing lamb	500 g
2	onions, finely chopped	2
4	cloves garlic, minced	4
1 tbsp	minced gingerroot	15 mL
1 to 2	long red or green chile peppers, seeded and diced	1 to 2
1 tsp	sweet paprika	5 mL
1 tsp	turmeric	5 mL
1 tsp	salt	5 mL
½ tsp	cracked black peppercorns	2 mL
¼ tsp	cayenne pepper	1 mL
2	black cardamom pods, crushed	2
4	whole cloves	4
1	stick cinnamon, about 3 inches (7.5 cm) long	1
2	bay leaves	2
1 cup	whole (hulled) barley, rinsed and drained	250 mL
2 cups	reduced-sodium chicken stock or water	500 mL
1½ cups	plain yogurt (minimum 4% M.F.)	375 mL
¼ cup	finely chopped cilantro	50 mL

1. In a skillet, heat 1 tbsp (15 mL) of the oil over medium heat for 30 seconds. Add lamb, in batches, and cook, stirring, until browned, about 4 minutes per batch. Transfer to a plate and set aside.

2. Add remaining 1 tbsp (15 mL) of oil to pan. Add onions and cook, stirring, until softened, about 3 minutes. Add garlic, ginger, chile peppers, paprika, turmeric, salt, peppercorns, cayenne, cardamom, cloves, cinnamon stick and bay leaves and cook, stirring, for 2 minutes. Add barley and toss until coated with mixture. Stir in stock and bring to a boil.

3. Return lamb and any accumulated juices to pan and stir well. Transfer to baking dish and stir in yogurt. Cover with foil and bake in preheated oven until barley and lamb are tender, about 1 hour. Garnish with cilantro.

Variation

Spicy Beef Curry with Barley: Substitute an equal quantity of stewing beef for the lamb.

Chinese-Style Pork Fried Rice

This zesty rice is a perfect weekday meal, ideal for those days when everyone is coming and going at different times. Just keep it warm and set out the fixins' for salad.

TIP

Shaoxing wine is a Chinese rice wine. Look for it in Chinese markets rather than liquor stores, as the varieties available in North America are usually cooking, not drinking, quality.

2 cups	cooked brown rice (see cooking instructions, page 29)	500 mL
MARINADE		
2 tbsp	reduced-sodium soy sauce	25 mL
2 tbsp	Shaoxing wine, dry sherry or vodka (see Tip, left)	25 mL
1 tbsp	minced gingerroot	15 mL
1 tsp	sesame oil	5 mL
1 lb	pork tenderloin, thinly sliced	500 g
SAUCE		
2 tbsp	reduced-sodium chicken stock	25 mL
2 tbsp	Shaoxing wine, dry sherry or vodka	25 mL
1 tbsp	reduced-sodium soy sauce	15 mL
2 tsp	sesame oil	10 mL
2 tbsp	vegetable oil, divided	25 mL
1 tsp	red curry paste, optional	5 mL
2	eggs, beaten	2
6	green onions, white part with a bit of green, thinly sliced	6
2	cloves garlic, minced	2
2 cups	sliced green beans, cooked until just tender to the bite	500 mL
1	red bell pepper, seeded and diced	1
¼ cup	roasted peanuts	50 mL

Nutrients per serving

Calories	325
Protein	25.1 g
Carbohydrates	23.0 g
Fat (Total)	14.1 g
Saturated Fat	2.4 g
Monounsaturated Fat	6.8 g
Polyunsaturated Fat	3.9 g
Dietary Fiber	3.3 g
Sodium	404 mg
Cholesterol	107 mg

EXCELLENT SOURCE OF vitamin C, thiamine, niacin, phosphorus, magnesium, manganese and selenium.

GOOD SOURCE OF vitamin E (alpha-tocopherol), riboflavin, folate, zinc and iron.

SOURCE OF vitamin A, pantothenic acid, calcium and copper.

CONTAINS a moderate amount of dietary fiber.

1. *Marinade:* In a bowl, combine soy sauce, Shaoxing wine, ginger and sesame oil. Stir will. Add pork and toss until well coated. Cover and set aside at room temperature for 20 minutes.

2. *Sauce:* In a small bowl, combine stock, Shaoxing wine, soy sauce and sesame oil. Set aside.

3. In a large skillet or wok, heat 1 tbsp (15 mL) of the oil over medium-high heat for 30 seconds. Add pork with marinade and cook, stirring, until cooked through, about 4 minutes. Transfer to a plate and wipe skillet clean.

4. Add remaining 1 tbsp (15 mL) of oil to skillet. Add curry paste, if using, and cook, stirring and watching carefully to ensure it doesn't burn, until fragrant, about 30 seconds. Add eggs and cook, stirring, until scrambled, about 30 seconds. Add green onions, garlic, green beans and bell pepper and cook, stirring, until fragrant and pepper begins to soften, about 3 minutes. Add rice, breaking it up with your fingers while dropping it into the pan, and cook, stirring, until well combined and heated through, for 3 minutes. Add cooked pork and any accumulated juices and stir well. Add sauce and toss well. Garnish with peanuts and serve.

Millet-Crusted Tamale Pie

This is a great weeknight meal — the perfect thing to serve on a night your teenager spontaneously invites a friend or two for dinner. If you have a can of beans in the pantry and cooked rice in the freezer, you can quickly defrost the ingredients, toss a salad and in less than an hour produce a nutritious dinner the kids will rave about.

Makes 6 servings

TIPS

If you don't have a deep-dish pie dish, use an 8- or 9-inch (2 or 2.5 L) square baking dish.

Use spicy or not-so-spicy salsa.

Nutrient Tip

Much of the fat in this dish comes from the regular-fat cheese (5.7 g) and the Italian sausage, which contributes a total of 9.3 grams. To reduce your consumption of fat, use lower-fat cheese and reduce the quantity of sausage in the dish.

Nutrients per serving

Calories	437
Protein	20.8 g
Carbohydrates	46.5 g
Fat (Total)	19.1 g
Saturated Fat	7.5 g
Monounsaturated Fat	8.0 g
Polyunsaturated Fat	2.4 g
Dietary Fiber	6.5 g
Sodium	768 mg
Cholesterol	43 mg

EXCELLENT SOURCE OF thiamine, phosphorus, magnesium, manganese and selenium.

GOOD SOURCE OF niacin, riboflavin, folate, calcium, iron, copper and zinc.

SOURCE OF vitamins A and E (alpha-tocopherol) and pantothenic acid.

CONTAINS a very high amount of dietary fiber.

- **Preheat oven to 375°F (190°C)**
- **10-inch (25 cm) deep-dish glass pie dish (see Tips, left)**

1 cup	cooked brown rice (see cooking instructions, page 29)	250 mL
TOPPING		
1 cup	millet	250 mL
3 cups	water or chicken or vegetable stock	750 mL
	Salt and freshly ground black pepper	
1 cup	shredded Monterey Jack cheese	250 mL
FILLING		
1 tbsp	olive oil	15 mL
12 oz	hot or mild Italian sausage, casings removed	375 g
2 tsp	chili powder	10 mL
¾ cup	tomato salsa (see Tips, left)	175 mL
1 cup	corn kernels	250 mL
1 cup	cooked pinto beans, drained and rinsed (see Variation, below)	250 mL

1. *Topping:* In a saucepan over medium heat, toast millet, stirring constantly, until it crackles and releases its aroma, about 5 minutes. Add water, salt and pepper to taste and bring to a boil. Reduce heat to low. Cover and cook until millet is tender and all of the water is absorbed, about 20 minutes. Stir in cheese.

2. *Filling:* Meanwhile, in a skillet, heat oil over medium heat for 30 seconds. Add sausage and cook, breaking up with a spoon, until no longer pink, about 8 minutes. Drain off all but 1 tbsp (15 mL) fat from pan, if necessary. Add chili powder and cook, stirring, for 1 minute. Add salsa and stir well. Stir in corn, beans and rice and cook, stirring, until heated through. Place in pie dish.

3. Spread topping evenly over filling. Bake in preheated oven until top is nicely browned, about 25 minutes.

Variation

If you don't have pinto beans, substitute an equal quantity of red kidney beans, small red beans or cranberry beans. Be aware that although you can use canned beans, rinse them well because many brands are very high in sodium, or you can cook dried beans yourself with no salt added.

Roast Pork with Red Rice and Beans

This is a great dish for entertaining or for a special family meal. The recipe was inspired by one in the book Spice by chef Ana Sortin. It's a Mediterranean spin on down-home red beans and rice, and in that spirit I like to serve it with a big platter of collard greens, seasoned with a bit of cider vinegar, but any green vegetable makes a nice accompaniment.

Makes 10 servings

TIPS

The cooking time for red rice depends upon the variety you use. These instructions work for longer-cooking varieties, such as Camargue and Wehani. I've also made this using Thai red rice, which should be added to the beans after they have cooked for 30 minutes in total. If you're using quick-cooking Bhutanese red rice, add it to the beans after they have cooked for 45 minutes in total.

I like to use coarse sea salt when making this recipe, which I crush in a mortar with a pestle until it is fine enough to rub evenly over the meat, while retaining its chunky texture. Kosher salt works well, too, and, depending upon the brand, may or may not need to be lightly crushed before combining with the other ingredients.

You can also make this recipe using a single-loin roast of the same weight, in which case it will cook more quickly, in about 1 hour.

Demi-glace concentrate is available in specialty stores and well-stocked supermarkets. This dish is tasty without it, but it adds luscious depth to the rice and bean mixture.

- Roasting pan
- Instant-read thermometer

1½ cups	red rice, rinsed and drained (see Tips, left)	375 mL
1½ cups	dried navy beans (see Variation, page 193)	375 mL
5 cups	reduced-sodium chicken stock, divided	1.25 L
1 tbsp	coarse salt (see Tips, left)	15 mL
1 tbsp	herbes de Provence	15 mL
6	cloves garlic, finely grated or put through a press	6
1 tsp	cracked black peppercorns	5 mL
1 tbsp	olive oil (approx.)	15 mL
3 lbs	boneless pork double-loin roast, trimmed and tied (see Tips, left)	1.5 kg
3	leeks, cleaned and thinly sliced (see Tips, page 196)	3
6	stalks celery, diced	6
30	fresh sage leaves, finely chopped	30
2 tsp	poultry seasoning	10 mL
1 tsp	paprika	5 mL
1 cup	dry white wine	250 mL
1 tbsp	demi-glace concentrate, optional (see Tips, left)	15 mL
	Salt and freshly ground black pepper	

1. In a bowl, combine red rice with 2½ cups (625 mL) water. Set aside for 1 hour.

2. In a large saucepan over medium–high heat, combine beans and 4 cups (1 L) water. Bring to boil and boil rapidly for 3 minutes. Remove from heat and let stand for 1 hour. Drain and rinse thoroughly under cold running water. Return to saucepan and add 4 cups (1 L) of the chicken stock. Bring to a boil. Reduce heat to low and simmer, uncovered, for 15 minutes. Add red rice with soaking liquid and bring to boil. Cover and cook until rice and beans are tender, about 50 minutes.

3. In a separate bowl, combine coarse salt, herbes de Provence, garlic and peppercorns. Mix well and stir in 1 tbsp (15 mL) olive oil. Rub all over pork. Place pork in a roasting pan and set aside at room temperature for 30 minutes.

4. Meanwhile, preheat oven to 350°F (180°C). Roast pork in preheated oven until a meat thermometer inserted into the thickest part of the meat registers 160°F (71°C), about 1 hour and 15 minutes. Transfer to a platter, cover loosely with foil and keep warm. Drain off all but 2 tbsp (25 mL) of the fat in roasting pan (or, if necessary add olive oil to make 2 tbsp/25 mL), and place roasting pan on stove over medium heat.

5. Add leeks, celery and sage to roasting pan and cook, stirring, until vegetables are very soft, about 10 minutes. Add poultry seasoning and paprika and stir well. Increase heat to high and add wine and remaining 1 cup (250 mL) of chicken stock. Cook, stirring, until reduced by half, about 3 minutes. Add demi-glace concentrate, if using, and any juice from the pork that has collected on the platter and cook, stirring, until concentrate has completely dissolved. Add beans and rice with cooking liquid and cook, stirring, to meld flavors, about 5 minutes. Season to taste with salt and pepper.

6. *To serve:* Spread rice and beans on a large deep platter. Slice pork thinly and lay on top.

Variation

Substitute an equal quantity of dried flageolet for the navy beans. They are slightly sweeter and more buttery and are available in well-stocked supermarkets and specialty stores.

Nutrients per serving	
Calories	426
Protein	38.9 g
Carbohydrates	47.0 g
Fat (Total)	8.1 g
Saturated Fat	2.6 g
Monounsaturated Fat	3.8 g
Polyunsaturated Fat	1.4 g
Dietary Fiber	7.6 g
Sodium	859 mg
Cholesterol	65 mg

EXCELLENT SOURCE OF thiamine, niacin, folate, phosphorus, iron, magnesium and manganese.

GOOD SOURCE OF riboflavin, pantothenic acid, zinc and copper.

SOURCE OF vitamins C and E (alpha-tocopherol), calcium and selenium.

CONTAINS a very high amount of dietary fiber.

Savory Lamb Shanks with Eggplant and Barley

Here's a rich, delicious Mediterranean-inspired stew that will warm the cockles of your heart on a chilly night. Although lamb shanks are fatty, they are succulent and the dish is loaded with nutrients, including fiber. If you're watching your weight, treat it as a dietary splurge. Lamb shanks are at their best when cooked slowly in moist heat, so if you have a slow cooker, by all means use it to make this dish.

Makes 8 servings

TIPS

You'll need an eggplant that weighs about 1½ lbs (750 g).

Have your butcher slice the shanks for you. Depending on their size, you'll get from 2 to 4 pieces from each shank.

After adding the lamb to the casserole, make sure you arrange it so all the meat is submerged in the cooking liquid.

1	large eggplant, peeled, cut into 2-inch (5 cm) cubes (see Tips, left)	1
4 lbs	sliced lamb shanks (see Tips, left)	2 kg
½ tsp	salt	2 mL
½ tsp	cracked black peppercorns	2 mL
2 tbsp	olive oil (approx.), divided	25 mL
2	onions, thinly sliced on the vertical	2
4	cloves garlic, minced	4
2	bay leaves	2
1 tbsp	finely grated lemon zest	15 mL
1	stick cinnamon, about 2 inches (5 cm) long	1
1 cup	whole (hulled) barley, drained and rinsed	250 mL
1 cup	red wine	250 mL
1	can (28 oz/796 mL) no-salt-added tomatoes with juice	1
¼ cup	finely chopped parsley	50 mL

1. Sprinkle the eggplant pieces with salt and set aside in a colander for 1 to 2 hours. (If time is short, blanch them in heavily salted water.) In either case, rinse thoroughly in fresh cold water and, using your hands, squeeze out the excess moisture. Pat dry with paper towels.

2. Preheat oven to 325°F (160°C). Pat shanks dry with paper towel and season with salt and peppercorns. In a Dutch oven, heat 1 tbsp (15 mL) of the oil over medium–high heat for 30 seconds. Add lamb shanks, in batches, and brown well on all sides, about 4 minutes per batch. Transfer to a plate as completed and set aside. Drain off all but 2 tbsp (15 mL) fat from pan, if necessary. (If your lamb is very lean, you may not have enough oil left in the pan and may need to add a bit here.)

3. Add eggplant, in batches, and cook, stirring, until lightly browned, adding more oil, if needed. Remove and set aside. Add onions to pan and cook, stirring, until lightly browned, about 7 minutes. Add garlic, bay leaves, lemon zest and cinnamon stick and cook, stirring, for 1 minute. Add barley and toss to coat. Add wine and tomatoes with juice, reserved lamb shanks and any accumulated juices and eggplant and bring to a boil.

4. Cover and bake in preheated oven until meat is tender and falling off the bone, about 2½ hours. Garnish with parsley.

Variation

If you like the flavor of lemon and want to give this recipe a Moroccan spin, substitute a finely chopped preserved lemon for the lemon zest. Add it along with the tomatoes.

Slow Cooker Method

Complete Steps 1, 2 and 3. Transfer mixture to slow cooker stoneware, cover and cook on Low for 10 to 12 hours or on High for 5 to 6 hours, until the meat is falling off the bone.

DIETARY FIBER

One serving of this dish contains a very high amount of fiber, more than half of which comes from the whole-grain barley (most of the remainder is provided by the eggplant and tomatoes). You can nurture your heart and help to keep your weight under control by regularly adding fiber-rich whole grains, such as barley, to your diet. Not only does barley contain a high amount of dietary fiber, it is particularly high in soluble fiber. In fact, the U.S. Food and Drug Administration has allowed a health claim for the beta-glucan soluble fiber in barley — it can reduce the risk of coronary heart disease by helping to keep cholesterol under control. Studies also show that a high intake of fiber-rich foods protects against obesity because they make you feel full before you have consumed a lot of calories.

Nutrients per serving

Calories	456
Protein	34.6 g
Carbohydrates	31.9 g
Fat (Total)	21.3 g
Saturated Fat	7.3 g
Monounsaturated Fat	9.9 g
Polyunsaturated Fat	1.9 g
Dietary Fiber	7.4 g
Sodium	415 mg
Cholesterol	107 mg

EXCELLENT SOURCE OF niacin, phosphorus, iron, manganese, zinc and selenium.

GOOD SOURCE OF vitamins C and E (alpha-tocopherol), thiamine, riboflavin, folate, magnesium and copper.

SOURCE OF pantothenic acid and calcium.

CONTAINS a very high amount of dietary fiber.

Coconut-Spiked Pork with Quinoa and Peanuts

I love the unusual combination of flavors in this one-dish meal. It's easy enough to make for a weeknight dinner and particularly colorful if made with red quinoa.

Makes 6 servings

TIPS

To clean leeks: Fill sink full of lukewarm water. Split leeks in half lengthwise and submerge in water, swishing them around to remove all traces of dirt. Transfer to a colander and rinse under cold water.

Use the kind of chile pepper you have on hand. Jalapeño, long red or green or even habanero (if you only use half) will work well in this recipe.

1½ cups	reduced-sodium chicken or vegetable stock or water	375 mL
½ cup	coconut milk	125 mL
¼ cup	dry-roasted peanuts	50 mL
1 tbsp	olive oil	15 mL
12 oz	pork tenderloin, thinly sliced	375 g
2	leeks, white part only, cleaned and sliced (see Tips, left)	2
4	cloves garlic, minced	4
1	chile pepper, minced (see Tips, left)	1
2 tsp	ground cumin	10 mL
½ tsp	salt	2 mL
	Freshly ground black pepper	
1	can (14 oz/398 mL) no-salt-added diced tomatoes with juice	1
1 cup	quinoa, rinsed and drained	250 mL
1 cup	sliced green beans	250 mL

1. In a blender, combine stock, coconut milk and peanuts. Process until smooth. Set aside.

2. In a skillet, heat oil over medium–high heat for 30 seconds. Add pork, in batches if necessary, and cook until lightly browned, about 1 minute per side. Transfer to a plate and set aside.

3. Add leeks to pan and cook, stirring, until softened, about 5 minutes. Add garlic, chile pepper, cumin, salt and black pepper to taste and cook, stirring, for 1 minute. Add tomatoes with juice and reserved peanut mixture and bring to a boil. Stir in quinoa and green beans and return to a boil. Reduce heat to low. Stir in pork and any accumulated juices. Cover and simmer until quinoa is tender, about 20 minutes.

Nutrients per serving

Calories	320
Protein	21.8 g
Carbohydrates	32.0 g
Fat (Total)	12.9 g
Saturated Fat	5.0 g
Monounsaturated Fat	4.6 g
Polyunsaturated Fat	2.2 g
Dietary Fiber	5.1 g
Sodium	455 mg
Cholesterol	34 mg

EXCELLENT SOURCE OF thiamine, niacin, phosphorus, iron, magnesium, manganese, copper and selenium.

GOOD SOURCE OF vitamin E (alpha-tocopherol), riboflavin, folate and zinc.

SOURCE OF vitamins A and C, pantothenic acid and calcium.

CONTAINS a high amount of dietary fiber.

Home-Style Skillet Rice with Tomato Crust

Here's a great dish to serve if your kids call to say they are bringing friends home after soccer practice. It has great robust flavor and is very quick to make so long as you have some precooked rice on hand. Add the cheese for a creamy mellow finish. Serve a tossed green salad and warm sourdough bread to complete the meal.

Makes 6 servings

TIPS

Lundberg sells a variety of brown rice mixes, all of which would work well in this recipe. Their Jubilee blend, which includes Wehani and Black Japonica, is particularly nice in this dish.

Use hot or mild Italian sausage to suit your taste.

Nutrients per serving

Calories	318
Protein	11.6 g
Carbohydrates	37.7 g
Fat (Total)	14.0 g
Saturated Fat	3.7 g
Monounsaturated Fat	6.1 g
Polyunsaturated Fat	1.7 g
Dietary Fiber	4.8 g
Sodium	509 mg
Cholesterol	82 mg

EXCELLENT SOURCE OF vitamin C and folate.

GOOD SOURCE OF vitamin E (alpha-tocopherol), thiamine, niacin, iron and selenium.

SOURCE OF vitamin A, riboflavin, pantothenic acid, phosphorus, magnesium, manganese, copper, calcium and zinc.

CONTAINS a high amount of dietary fiber.

• **Preheat oven to 350°F (180°C)**

3 cups	cooked red, brown or brown and wild rice mixture (see cooking instructions, page 29, and Tips, left)	750 mL
1 tbsp	olive oil	15 mL
8 oz	Italian sausage, removed from casings (see Tips, left)	250 g
1	onion, finely chopped	1
4	stalks celery, diced	4
2	green bell peppers, seeded and diced	2
4	cloves garlic, minced	4
1 tbsp	chili powder	15 mL
2 tsp	caraway seeds	10 mL
1 tsp	dried oregano leaves	5 mL
½ tsp	salt or to taste	2 mL
	Freshly ground black pepper	
1½ cups	reduced-sodium tomato sauce	375 mL
2	eggs, beaten	2
8 oz	sliced mozzarella, optional	250 g

1. In a cast-iron or other ovenproof skillet, heat oil over medium heat for 30 seconds. Add sausage, onion, celery and bell peppers and cook, stirring and breaking up sausage with a spoon, until vegetables are very tender and sausage is no longer pink, about 7 minutes. Add garlic, chili powder, caraway seeds, oregano, salt and black pepper to taste and cook, stirring, for 1 minute. Add cooked rice and cook, stirring, until heated through. Remove from heat.

2. In a bowl, beat tomato sauce and eggs until blended. Spread evenly over rice in skillet. Lay sliced mozzarella, if using, evenly over top. Place skillet in preheated oven and bake until top is crusty and cheese, if using, is melted, about 15 minutes.

Mushroom, Sausage and Wild Rice Stir-Fry

This is a great weekday dinner. If you've precooked the rice, it's perfect for those evenings when you want to put a nutritious meal on the table and are pressed for time. In season, a simple salad of sliced tomatoes makes a perfect finish.

Makes 6 servings

TIPS

Use half long-grain brown and half wild rice or a packaged blend of brown and wild rice.

Use hot or mild Italian sausage to suit your taste.

3 cups	cooked brown and wild rice mixture (see cooking instructions, page 29, and Tips, left)	750 mL
1 tbsp	butter	15 mL
1 lb	mushrooms, thinly sliced	500 g
	Salt and freshly ground black pepper	
1 tbsp	freshly squeezed lemon juice	15 mL
1 tbsp	olive oil	15 mL
8 oz	Italian sausage, removed from casings (see Tips, left)	250 g
1	onion, finely chopped	1
2	red bell peppers, seeded and diced	2
4	cloves garlic, minced	4
1 tbsp	dried Italian seasoning	15 mL
½ cup	dry white wine or chicken stock	125 mL

1. In a large skillet, melt butter over medium–high heat. Add mushrooms and cook, stirring, until they release their liquid, about 7 minutes. Continue to cook until most of the liquid evaporates, about 2 minutes. Remove from heat. Season to taste with salt and black pepper and stir in lemon juice. Transfer to a bowl. Return skillet to medium heat.

2. Add oil to pan and heat for 30 seconds. Add sausage, onion, bell peppers and garlic. Cook, stirring and breaking sausage up with a spoon, until vegetables are very tender and sausage is no longer pink, about 7 minutes. Add Italian seasoning and cook, stirring, for 1 minute. Add wine and bring to a boil. Cook until reduced by half, about 2 minutes. Stir in rice and reserved mushrooms and cook until heated through, about 3 minutes.

Nutrients per serving

Calories	286
Protein	11.5 g
Carbohydrates	28.6 g
Fat (Total)	13.9 g
Saturated Fat	4.5 g
Monounsaturated Fat	5.9 g
Polyunsaturated Fat	1.7 g
Dietary Fiber	3.7 g
Sodium	280 mg
Cholesterol	25 mg

EXCELLENT SOURCE OF vitamin C, riboflavin, niacin, manganese and selenium.

GOOD SOURCE OF vitamin A, thiamine, pantothenic acid, phosphorus, magnesium, zinc and copper.

SOURCE OF vitamin E (alpha-tocopherol), folate and iron.

CONTAINS a moderate amount of dietary fiber.

Peppery Polenta Bake with Mushrooms and Sausages

I have a real weakness for this combination of ingredients and flavors: the zesty sausage, sweet peppers and mushrooms surrounded by creamy polenta and cheese is a marriage made in heaven. I love having leftovers so I can heat some up for an afternoon snack.

Makes 8 servings

TIPS

Creamy Polenta contains a bit of milk and Parmesan cheese, which works nicely with this recipe.

For convenience, cool both the polenta and the sausage mixture separately, assemble the dish without the cheese and refrigerate for up to 2 days, until ready to cook. Bake until hot, about 40 minutes, adding cheese for the last 10 minutes.

Nutrients per serving

Calories	278
Protein	14.8 g
Carbohydrates	21.8 g
Fat (Total)	15.4 g
Saturated Fat	6.8 g
Monounsaturated Fat	6.2 g
Polyunsaturated Fat	1.5 g
Dietary Fiber	4.0 g
Sodium	474 mg
Cholesterol	43 mg

EXCELLENT SOURCE OF vitamin C and selenium.

GOOD SOURCE OF vitamin A, thiamine, calcium, phosphorus, magnesium, zinc and copper.

SOURCE OF vitamin E (alpha-tocopherol), riboflavin, folate, pantothenic acid, manganese and iron.

CONTAINS a high amount of dietary fiber.

- 10-cup (2.5 L) baking dish, greased

1	batch Creamy Polenta (see Variation, page 243)	1
1 tbsp	extra virgin olive oil	15 mL
12 oz	Italian sausage, removed from casings	375 g
1	onion, finely chopped	1
1	red bell pepper, seeded and diced	1
1	green bell pepper, seeded and diced	1
2	cloves garlic, minced	2
2 tbsp	crumbled dried mushrooms, such as porcini or portobello	25 mL
2 tsp	dried Italian seasoning	10 mL
1	can (14 oz/398 mL) no-salt-added diced tomatoes with juice	1
	Salt and freshly ground black pepper	
2 cups	shredded mozzarella cheese	500 mL

1. Spread warm polenta evenly over the bottom of baking dish and set aside to firm up.

2. Meanwhile, in a skillet, heat oil over medium heat for 30 seconds. Add sausage, onion and bell peppers and cook, breaking sausage up with a spoon, until vegetables are quite soft and sausage is no longer pink, about 7 minutes. Drain off all fat from pan. Add garlic, mushrooms and Italian seasoning and cook, stirring, for 1 minute. Add tomatoes with juice and bring to a boil. Season to taste with salt and black pepper. Reduce heat to low. Cover and simmer until flavors meld, about 10 minutes.

3. Meanwhile, preheat oven to 350°F (180°C). Spread sausage mixture evenly over polenta. Sprinkle cheese evenly over top. Bake in preheated oven until cheese is melted and mixture is bubbly, about 15 minutes.

Citrus Lamb with Spinach and Couscous

In the Middle East, sun-dried limes often add pleasant pungency to dishes. Here I've tried to capture some of their unique character. Prominent citrus flavors balance the richness of the saffron and lamb, and slightly bitter spinach adds to the pleasing complexity. Couscous makes the perfect finish.

Makes 6 servings

TIP

Spinach that hasn't been pre-washed can be quite gritty, so pay extra attention when washing. I always swish the leaves around in a basin of lukewarm water to remove any grit, then rinse thoroughly under cold running water before using.

Nutrients per serving

Calories	376
Protein	30.7 g
Carbohydrates	33.7 g
Fat (Total)	14 g
Saturated Fat	3.7 g
Monounsaturated Fat	6.9 g
Polyunsaturated Fat	1.3 g
Dietary Fiber	6.3 g
Sodium	722 mg
Cholesterol	77 mg

EXCELLENT SOURCE OF vitamin A, niacin, folate, iron, magnesium, manganese, zinc and selenium.

GOOD SOURCE OF vitamin E (alpha-tocopherol), riboflavin and phosphorus.

SOURCE OF vitamin C, thiamine, pantothenic acid, calcium and copper.

CONTAINS a very high amount of dietary fiber.

2 tbsp	olive oil (approx.)	25 mL
1½ lbs	trimmed lamb shoulder, cut into 1-inch (2.5 cm) cubes	750 g
2	onions, thinly sliced on the vertical	2
4	cloves garlic, minced	4
1 tbsp	finely grated lime zest	15 mL
1 tsp	cracked black peppercorns	5 mL
½ tsp	salt	2 mL
¼ cup	freshly squeezed lime juice	50 mL
½ tsp	crumbled saffron threads, dissolved in ¼ cup (50 mL) boiling water	2 mL
3½ cups	reduced-sodium chicken stock, divided	875 mL
1 lb	spinach leaves, stems removed, and finely chopped (see Tip, left)	500 g
1 cup	whole wheat, spelt or barley couscous	250 mL

1. In a Dutch oven, heat oil over medium–high heat for 30 seconds. Add lamb, in batches, and brown well on all sides, about 4 minutes per batch, adding more oil, if necessary. Transfer to a plate as completed and set aside.

2. Add onions to pan and cook, stirring, just until they begin to brown, about 7 minutes. Add garlic, lime zest, peppercorns and salt and cook, stirring, for 30 seconds. Add lime juice, saffron liquid and 2 cups (500 mL) of the stock and bring to a boil. Return lamb and any accumulated juices to pot.

3. Reduce heat to low. Cover and simmer until meat is tender, 1½ to 2 hours. Stir in spinach and cook until wilted, about 5 minutes.

4. Meanwhile, in a saucepan over medium heat, bring remaining 1½ cups (375 mL) of stock to a boil. Add couscous in a steady stream, stirring constantly. Remove from heat. Cover and let stand until liquid is absorbed, about 15 minutes. Fluff with a fork.

5. *To serve:* Spread couscous over a deep platter. Arrange lamb mixture evenly over top, leaving a border around the edges.

Slow Cooker Method

Complete Steps 1 and 2. Transfer mixture to slow cooker stoneware. Cover and cook on Low for 8 hours or on High for 4 hours, until lamb is tender. Stir in spinach. Cover and cook on High for 10 minutes, until nicely wilted.

Meatless Mains

Soba Noodles with Broccoli Sauce

Soba Noodles with Broccoli Sauce

This flavorful combination makes a great light weekday dinner. You can also serve smaller portions as a side dish. It is particularly enjoyable alongside miso-glazed tofu or fish.

Makes 4 servings

TIPS

If you are a heat seeker, increase the quantity of chili sauce to suit your taste.

I make this using sambal oelek, which is widely available, but other Asian chili sauces, such as chili-garlic and Sriracha, will also work.

| 8 oz | dried soba noodles | 250 g |
| 1 tsp | sesame oil | 5 mL |

BROCCOLI SAUCE

3 tbsp	reduced-sodium soy sauce	45 mL
1 tbsp	sake or vodka	15 mL
1 tbsp	cornstarch	15 mL
½ tsp	granulated sugar	2 mL
½ tsp	Asian chili sauce (see Tips, left)	2 mL
	Freshly ground black pepper	
1 tbsp	vegetable oil	15 mL
2	cloves garlic, minced	2
1 tbsp	minced gingerroot	15 mL
4 cups	broccoli florets	1 L
2 tbsp	reduced-sodium vegetable or chicken stock or water	25 mL
2	green onions, white part with a bit of green, thinly sliced	2
	Sesame oil	

1. In a large pot of boiling salted water, cook noodles until tender to the bite, about 7 minutes. Drain, rinse well in cold running water and drain again. Toss with sesame oil. Transfer to a serving bowl or deep platter and set aside.

2. *Broccoli Sauce:* In a small bowl, combine soy sauce, sake, cornstarch, sugar, chili sauce and pepper to taste. Mix well and set aside.

3. In a skillet or wok, heat oil over medium heat for 30 seconds. Add garlic and ginger and cook, stirring, for 1 minute. Add broccoli and toss to coat. Sprinkle with stock. Reduce heat to low. Cover and cook until broccoli is tender, about 5 minutes. Add soy sauce mixture and cook, stirring, until thickened, about 30 seconds.

4. Arrange broccoli mixture over noodles, sprinkle with green onions and drizzle with sesame oil. Serve immediately or let cool to room temperature.

Nutrients per serving

Calories	375
Protein	12.9 g
Carbohydrates	75.0 g
Fat (Total)	5.0 g
Saturated Fat	0.5 g
Monounsaturated Fat	2.5 g
Polyunsaturated Fat	1.7 g
Dietary Fiber	2.5 g
Sodium	781 mg
Cholesterol	0 mg

EXCELLENT SOURCE OF vitamin C and manganese.

GOOD SOURCE OF vitamin A, thiamine, niacin, folate and magnesium.

SOURCE OF vitamin E (alpha-tocopherol), calcium, phosphorus, riboflavin, pantothenic acid, iron, zinc and selenium.

CONTAINS a moderate amount of dietary fiber.

Quinoa-Stuffed Tomatoes

Here's a delightfully different main course. Make this in late summer or early fall when field tomatoes are in season and use the largest reddest tomatoes you can find for a spectacular presentation.

Makes 6 servings

TIPS

A grapefruit spoon makes easy work of scooping out the tomato pulp.

If you're shredding your own cheese, you'll need about a 6-oz (175 g) block.

If you enjoy a bit of heat, include an additional 1 tsp (5 mL) of the adobo sauce in the mixture.

• **Preheat oven to 350°F (180°C)**

6	large firm tomatoes	6
	FILLING	
2 cups	cooked quinoa (see cooking instructions, page 26)	500 mL
2 cups	shredded Cheddar cheese, divided (see Tips, left)	500 mL
¼ cup	finely chopped red onion	50 mL
1	finely chopped chipotle pepper in adobo sauce (see Tips, left)	1
1 tsp	sweet paprika	5 mL
½ tsp	salt	2 mL
	Freshly ground black pepper	

1. Cut ½ inch (1 cm) off tops of tomatoes. Remove the core and discard. Carefully scoop out remaining pulp, leaving a thin wall and being careful not to puncture the shell. Place tomatoes in a baking dish. Finely chop pulp and set aside.

2. *Filling:* In a bowl, combine quinoa, 1½ cups (375 mL) of the cheese, onion, chipotle pepper with sauce, paprika, salt, pepper to taste and reserved tomato pulp. Mix well. Spoon into tomato shells. Sprinkle remaining cheese over top. Bake in preheated oven until cheese is melted and browned and tomatoes are tender, about 30 minutes. Serve hot.

Variation

Millet-Stuffed Tomatoes: Substitute an equal quantity of toasted cooked millet (see cooking instructions, page 23) for the quinoa.

Nutrients per serving

Calories	257
Protein	13.5 g
Carbohydrates	21.1 g
Fat (Total)	14.0 g
Saturated Fat	8.1 g
Monounsaturated Fat	3.9 g
Polyunsaturated Fat	1.1 g
Dietary Fiber	3.6 g
Sodium	453 mg
Cholesterol	40 mg

EXCELLENT SOURCE OF vitamin A, calcium, phosphorus and manganese.

GOOD SOURCE OF vitamin C, riboflavin, iron, magnesium and zinc.

SOURCE OF vitamin E (alpha-tocopherol), niacin, folate, thiamine, pantothenic acid, copper and selenium.

CONTAINS a moderate amount of dietary fiber.

Whole Wheat Mac and Cheese

This is an adaptation of a luscious mac and cheese I sampled at an artisanal cheese store in Seattle's Pike Place Market. Although I couldn't use their fabulous cheese, I think this combination of Swiss, Cheddar and Parmesan does the trick and using whole wheat pasta increases the nutritional value of the dish. This is so good, people will want seconds, so just serve it with a tossed green salad and whole-grain rolls. It is high in saturated fat, so treat it as a well-deserved splurge.

Makes 8 servings

TIPS

To make fresh bread crumbs, slice bread, cut off the crusts, break into chunks and process in a food processor fitted with a metal blade until desired consistency is reached.

Chipotle pepper powder is available in well-stocked supermarkets or specialty stores. Or you can make your own by grinding a dried chipotle pepper in a spice grinder. For a milder result, use ancho, New Mexico or a traditional blended chili powder.

Nutrient Tip

Although this dish is delicious, I don't make it very often because it is high in saturated fat. If you are concerned about the quantity of saturated fat, substitute lower-fat Cheddar cheese for the full-fat version used and skim milk for the 2% the nutritional analysis is based upon. Use 3 tbsp (45 mL) of butter to make the sauce (Step 3) and substitute 1 tbsp (15 mL) olive oil for the melted butter drizzle in Step 1.

- **Preheat oven to 375°F (190°C)**
- **8-cup (2 L) baking dish, greased**

2 cups	whole wheat penne (see Variation, page 207)	500 mL
1 tbsp	extra virgin olive oil	15 mL
2 cups	shredded old Cheddar cheese, divided (about 6 oz/175 g)	500 mL
½ cup	freshly grated Parmesan cheese, divided	125 mL
1 cup	fresh whole wheat bread crumbs (see Tips, left)	250 mL
¼ cup	butter, divided	50 mL
¼ cup	whole wheat or all-purpose flour	50 mL
1½ tsp	chipotle pepper powder (see Tips, left)	7 mL
1 tsp	dried oregano leaves, crumbled	5 mL
3 cups	warm milk	750 mL
1 tbsp	Dijon mustard	15 mL
1 cup	reduced-fat Swiss or Gruyère cheese, shredded	250 mL
	Salt and freshly ground black pepper	
3	tomatoes, thinly sliced, optional	3

1. In a pot of boiling salted water, cook penne until tender to the bite, about 12 minutes. Drain and rinse well under cold running water. Toss with olive oil and set aside.

2. In a bowl, mix together ¼ cup (50 mL) of the Cheddar, 2 tbsp (25 mL) of the Parmesan and bread crumbs. Set aside.

3. In a large saucepan, melt 3 tbsp (45 mL) of the butter over medium heat. Add flour and cook, stirring, until foamy. Continue cooking and stirring, without browning, for 1 minute. Stir in chipotle pepper powder and oregano. Gradually add warm milk, whisking until blended. Continue to cook, stirring, until mixture comes to a boil and thickens, about 7 minutes. Whisk in mustard.

4. Reduce heat to low. Add Swiss, remaining Cheddar and Parmesan cheeses and cook, stirring, until melted and smooth. Season to taste with salt and pepper. Remove from heat and stir in reserved pasta.

5. Transfer pasta mixture to prepared dish, spreading evenly. Arrange tomatoes, if using, evenly over top, in layers, as necessary. Sprinkle bread crumb mixture evenly over top. Melt remaining 1 tbsp (15 mL) of butter and drizzle over top. Bake in preheated oven until hot and bubbly, for 25 minutes. Preheat broiler and broil until crumbs are crisp and browned, about 2 minutes.

Variation

Substitute Kamut, farro or spelt penne for the whole wheat version if you prefer. Check the package for cooking times.

CALCIUM

While the milk and cheese in this recipe are a source of fat, they also provide an ample amount of calcium. Nowadays, most of us are aware of how much our bodies need calcium to maintain healthy bones and keep osteoporosis at bay. But this essential mineral also supports a wide range of important body functions, from your nervous system to how your muscles function. Recent research also suggests it may help to prevent many ailments, from high blood pressure and PMS to inflammatory bowel disease. A recent study involving more than 45,000 American women found a link between calcium intake and a reduced risk of colon cancer.

Nutrients per serving

Calories	370
Protein	19.8 g
Carbohydrates	30.6 g
Fat (Total)	19.7 g
Saturated Fat	11.1 g
Monounsaturated Fat	6.1 g
Polyunsaturated Fat	1.1 g
Dietary Fiber	3.5 g
Sodium	475 mg
Cholesterol	55 mg

EXCELLENT SOURCE OF calcium, phosphorus, manganese and selenium.

GOOD SOURCE OF vitamin A, riboflavin, zinc and magnesium.

SOURCE OF vitamin E (alpha-tocopherol), niacin, thiamine, folate, pantothenic acid, iron and copper.

CONTAINS a moderate amount of dietary fiber.

Wheat Berries with Cauliflower and Crispy Bread Crumbs

This Mediterranean-inspired dish combines slightly crunchy wheat berries with cauliflower, onions, sun-dried tomatoes, pine nuts and a crispy bread crumb topping. The addition of saffron and a good hit of lemon add a Middle Eastern note. Serve this with a shredded carrot and currant salad to complete the theme.

Makes 6 servings

TIP

To toast pine nuts, cook in a skillet over medium heat, stirring, until browned and fragrant, about 5 minutes. Immediately transfer to a bowl, as once the nuts start to brown, they can quickly burn.

2 cups	cooked hot wheat, spelt or Kamut berries (see cooking instructions, page 34)	500 mL
1 tbsp	olive oil	15 mL
1	onion, finely chopped	1
4	cloves garlic, minced	4
½ tsp	salt	2 mL
¼ tsp	hot pepper flakes	1 mL
¼ cup	drained oil-packed sun-dried tomatoes, finely chopped	50 mL
6 cups	cauliflower florets	1.5 L
¼ tsp	crumbled saffron threads, dissolved in ¼ cup (50 mL) boiling water	1 mL
2 tbsp	freshly squeezed lemon juice	25 mL
2 tbsp	butter	25 mL
1 cup	dry whole wheat bread crumbs	250 mL
¼ cup	finely chopped parsley	50 mL
2 tbsp	toasted pine nuts (see Tip, left)	25 mL
½ cup	freshly grated Parmesan cheese	125 mL
	Freshly ground black pepper	

Nutrients per serving

Calories	299
Protein	10.8 g
Carbohydrates	38.5 g
Fat (Total)	12.8 g
Saturated Fat	4.8 g
Monounsaturated Fat	4.5 g
Polyunsaturated Fat	2.3 g
Dietary Fiber	8.6 g
Sodium	509 mg
Cholesterol	18 mg

EXCELLENT SOURCE OF vitamin C, thiamine, folate, manganese and selenium.

GOOD SOURCE OF niacin, magnesium, calcium, phosphorus, iron and zinc.

SOURCE OF vitamins A and E (alpha-tocopherol), riboflavin, pantothenic acid and copper.

CONTAINS a very high amount of dietary fiber.

1. In a large skillet, heat oil over medium heat for 30 seconds. Add onion and cook, stirring, until softened, about 3 minutes. Add garlic, salt and hot pepper flakes and cook, stirring for 1 minute. Stir in sun-dried tomatoes. Add cauliflower, stir well and sprinkle with saffron liquid and lemon juice. Reduce heat to low. Cover and cook until cauliflower is tender, about 7 minutes. Remove from heat.

2. In a separate skillet, melt butter over medium heat. Add bread crumbs and parsley and toss until evenly coated. Cook, stirring, until crumbs are crisped and browned, about 5 minutes. Remove from heat and stir in toasted pine nuts and Parmesan.

3. Spread wheat berries over a deep platter. Arrange cauliflower mixture evenly over top and sprinkle evenly with crumb mixture. Season to taste with black pepper. Serve immediately.

Variation

Barley with Cauliflower and Crispy Bread Crumbs: Substitute an equal quantity of cooked whole (hulled) barley (see cooking instructions, page 16) for the wheat berries.

Roasted Mushrooms with Millet and Goat Cheese

Accompanied by a salad, this makes a nice light dinner. In season, I like to serve this with a sliced tomato salad, but tossed greens work well, too.

Makes 4 servings

TIPS

Depending upon the size of your mushrooms, you may need a bit more olive oil to complete the brushing.

Try to time this so the preliminary baking of the mushrooms is completed at about the same time as the filling.

The mushrooms will be rather flat after roasting, so be aware that you will be piling on the filling rather than filling the tops.

Nutrients per serving

Calories	310
Protein	13.4 g
Carbohydrates	28.8 g
Fat (Total)	17.2 g
Saturated Fat	5.8 g
Monounsaturated Fat	7.4 g
Polyunsaturated Fat	2.7 g
Dietary Fiber	5.3 g
Sodium	156 mg
Cholesterol	14 mg

EXCELLENT SOURCE OF vitamin A, riboflavin, niacin, folate, pantothenic acid, phosphorus, iron, magnesium, manganese, copper and selenium.

GOOD SOURCE OF vitamin E (alpha-tocopherol), thiamine and zinc.

SOURCE OF vitamin C and calcium.

CONTAINS a high amount of dietary fiber.

- **Preheat oven to 400°F (200°C)**
- **Rimmed baking sheet, lightly greased**

1½ cups	cooked toasted millet (see cooking instructions, page 23)	375 mL
4	large portobello mushrooms, stems and gills removed (each about 6 oz/175 g, after stemming)	4
2 tbsp	extra virgin olive oil, divided	25 mL
	Salt and freshly ground black pepper	
2 tbsp	freshly squeezed lemon juice	25 mL
½ cup	finely chopped shallots	125 mL
2	cloves garlic, minced	2
6 cups	loosely packed chopped spinach leaves	1.5 L
½ cup	soft goat cheese	125 mL
2 tbsp	pine nuts	25 mL
2 tsp	balsamic vinegar	10 mL

1. Brush mushrooms all over with 1 tbsp (15 mL) of the olive oil and place on prepared baking sheet, gill side down. Roast in preheated oven until the edges are browning, about 15 minutes. Remove from oven and turn over. Season to taste with salt and pepper and drizzle with lemon juice. Set aside. Preheat broiler.

2. Meanwhile, in a skillet, heat remaining 1 tbsp (15 ml) of olive oil over medium heat for 30 seconds. Add shallots and cook, stirring, until softened, about 3 minutes. Add garlic and cook, stirring, for 1 minute. Add spinach and toss until wilted, about 2 minutes. Add millet and cook, stirring, until heated through, about 1 minute. Spoon mixture evenly into warm mushroom caps (see Tips, left).

3. Spoon 2 tbsp (25 mL) of goat cheese over each filled mushroom, evening out as best you can. Sprinkle with pine nuts. Heat under broiler until pine nuts brown, about 4 minutes. Drizzle balsamic vinegar evenly over mushrooms.

Variation

Roasted Mushrooms with Quinoa and Goat Cheese: Substitute an equal quantity of cooked quinoa (see cooking instructions, page 26) for the millet.

Korean-Style Rice Bowl

This version of a Korean dish known as bibimbap makes a deliciously different vegetarian meal. Traditionally, an assortment of vegetables, sticky rice and often meat, topped with a runny fried egg, is served in a hot stone bowl called a tukbaege. Vegans can feel free to omit the egg.

Makes 4 servings

TIPS

If you're not concerned about using butter, brush the rice with about 2 tsp (10 mL) melted butter instead of the vegetable oil prior to baking to ensure a nicely crusted top.

This quantity of chili paste and sesame oil likely makes more hot sauce than you will need to satisfy most palates, but if you have heat seekers among your diners, you may require this amount. For subsequent meals, just combine an equal quantity of Asian chili paste and sesame oil to suit your needs.

Nutrients per serving

Calories	315
Protein	6.3 g
Carbohydrates	47.7 g
Fat (Total)	11.8 g
Saturated Fat	1.3 g
Monounsaturated Fat	5.8 g
Polyunsaturated Fat	4.0 g
Dietary Fiber	6.2 g
Sodium	63 mg
Cholesterol	0 mg

EXCELLENT SOURCE OF vitamins A and C, magnesium and manganese.

GOOD SOURCE OF vitamin E (alpha-tocopherol), thiamine, niacin, folate, pantothenic acid, phosphorus, iron, zinc and copper.

SOURCE OF riboflavin and calcium.

CONTAINS a very high amount of dietary fiber.

- Preheat oven to 400°F (200°C)
- 13-by 9-inch (3 L) baking pan, lightly greased

3 cups	hot cooked short-grain brown rice (see cooking instructions, page 29)	750 mL
3 tbsp	vegetable oil, divided (approx.) (see Tips, left)	45 mL
8 oz	shiitake mushrooms, stems removed and sliced	250 g
2	cloves garlic, minced	2
	Salt and freshly ground black pepper	
1 tbsp	freshly squeezed lemon juice	15 mL
1 cup	sliced green beans, blanched	250 mL
1 cup	diced carrots, blanched	250 mL
1	red bell pepper, seeded and diced	1
6	green onions, white part with a bit of green, thinly sliced	6
1 cup	diced English cucumber	250 mL
1 tsp	rice vinegar	5 mL
1 tbsp	Asian chili paste, such as sambal oelek (see Tips, left)	15 mL
1 tbsp	sesame oil	15 mL
4	eggs, optional	4
	Kimchi, optional	

1. Spread rice in a thin layer in prepared pan. Brush lightly with 2 tsp (10 mL) vegetable oil and bake in preheated oven until crusty, about 15 minutes. Set aside.

2. Meanwhile, in a wok, heat 1 tbsp (15 mL) of the oil over medium–high heat for 30 seconds. Add mushrooms and garlic and cook, stirring, until mushrooms lose their liquid, about 8 minutes. Season to taste with salt and pepper. Sprinkle with lemon juice. Transfer to a bowl and set aside.

3. Add 1 tbsp (15 mL) of oil to wok. Add green beans, carrots and bell pepper and cook, stirring, until vegetables are softened, about 5 minutes. Remove from heat and set aside.

4. In a bowl, combine green onions and cucumber. Toss with rice vinegar. Season to taste with salt and pepper and set aside.

5. In a small bowl, combine chili paste and sesame oil. Set aside.

6. Divide baked rice into 4 bowls. Arrange mushroom, green bean and cucumber mixtures over top. Drizzle with a small amount of chili–sesame oil and place remainder in a small dish to pass at the table.

7. If using eggs, heat remaining 1 tbsp (15 mL) of oil in wok. Add eggs, 2 at a time, and fry until crispy brown around the edges. Top each rice bowl with a fried egg and serve immediately. Serve with kimchi, if using.

Wild Rice Cakes

These make a nice light dinner accompanied by a salad or you can serve them as a substantial side dish. I top them with homemade ketchup or the red pepper coulis, both of which are delicious, but chili sauce, tomato sauce, or even a dab of pesto, also work quite well.

Makes 4 main servings or 8 side servings

TIPS

Be careful when turning the cakes, as they have a tendency to fall apart until they are thoroughly cooked.

The basil adds a nice note to the coulis, but if you can't get fresh leaves, omit it — the coulis will be quite tasty, anyway.

Nutrients per serving

Calories	386
Protein	21.4 g
Carbohydrates	41.9 g
Fat (Total)	14.7 g
Saturated Fat	4.4 g
Monounsaturated Fat	7.8 g
Polyunsaturated Fat	1.7 g
Dietary Fiber	3.5 g
Sodium	547 mg
Cholesterol	113 mg

EXCELLENT SOURCE OF vitamin C, calcium, phosphorus, magnesium, manganese, riboflavin, zinc and selenium.

GOOD SOURCE OF vitamins A and E (alpha-tocopherol), folate and niacin.

SOURCE OF thiamine, pantothenic acid, iron and copper.

CONTAINS a moderate amount of dietary fiber.

- **Preheat oven to 400°F (200°C)**
- **Large rimmed baking sheet, lightly greased**

2½ cups	water	625 mL
1 cup	wild and brown rice mixture, rinsed and drained	250 mL
½ tsp	salt	2 mL
1½ cups	shredded reduced-fat Swiss cheese	375 mL
½ cup	plain yogurt, preferably full fat	125 mL
¼ cup	chopped red or green onion	50 mL
¼ cup	finely chopped parsley	50 mL
2	eggs, beaten	2
	Freshly ground black pepper	

RED PEPPER COULIS

2	roasted red peppers	2
3	drained oil-packed sun-dried tomatoes, chopped	3
2 tbsp	extra virgin olive oil	25 mL
1 tbsp	balsamic vinegar	15 mL
10	fresh basil leaves, optional	10

1. In a large saucepan, bring water to a rolling boil. Add rice and salt. Return to a boil. Reduce heat, cover and simmer until rice is tender and about half of the wild rice grains have split, about 1 hour. Set aside until cool enough to handle, about 20 minutes.

2. In a bowl, combine rice, Swiss cheese, yogurt, red onion, parsley, eggs and pepper to taste. Mix well. Using a large spoon, drop mixture in 8 batches, onto prepared baking sheet. Flatten lightly with a spatula or large spoon.

3. Bake in preheated oven for 15 minutes, then flip and cook until lightly browned and heated through, for 5 minutes. Let cool on pan for 5 minutes before serving. Top with Red Pepper Coulis, if using.

4. *Red Pepper Coulis:* In a food processor, combine roasted peppers, sun-dried tomatoes, oil, balsamic vinegar and basil, if using, and process until smooth.

Quinoa Chili

This chili is easy to make, very tasty and different enough to perk up your taste buds if they have grown tired of the same old thing. Like most whole-grain dishes, it soaks up liquid if left to sit, so keep some extra vegetable stock on hand to add if you're reheating leftovers. I like to serve this with a tossed green salad.

Makes 6 servings

TIP

In all the recipes calling for beans (as in legumes, not green beans), you can cook dried beans from scratch, in which case soak and cook 1 cup (250 mL) of dried beans. Or use canned beans, which are already cooked, and thoroughly rinse and drain.

1 tbsp	olive oil	15 mL
2	onions, finely chopped	2
2	stalks celery, diced	2
1	carrot, peeled and diced	1
1	green bell pepper, seeded and diced	1
4	cloves garlic, minced	4
2 tbsp	chili powder	25 mL
1	chipotle pepper in adobo sauce, minced	1
1	can (28 oz/796 mL) no-salt-added diced tomatoes with juice	1
2 cups	reduced-sodium vegetable stock	500 mL
	Salt and freshly ground black pepper	
1 cup	quinoa, rinsed and drained	250 mL
2 cups	drained, rinsed cooked or canned pinto beans (see Tip, left)	500 mL
1 cup	corn kernels	250 mL

1. In a large deep skillet with a tight-fitting lid, heat oil over medium heat for 30 seconds. Add onions, celery, carrot, bell pepper and garlic and stir well. Reduce heat to low. Cover and cook until vegetables are softened, about 10 minutes.

2. Increase heat to medium. Add chili powder and chipotle pepper and cook, stirring, for 1 minute. Add tomatoes with juice and stock and bring to a boil. Season to taste with salt and black pepper. Add quinoa, beans and corn and cook, stirring, until mixture returns to a boil. Reduce heat to low. Cover and simmer until quinoa is tender, about 25 minutes.

Variations

Millet Chili: Substitute an equal quantity of toasted millet for the quinoa. Increase the quantity of vegetable stock to 2½ cups (625 mL) and increase cooking time to about 25 minutes.

Substitute red kidney, cranberry or small red beans for the kidney beans.

Nutrients per serving

Calories	293
Protein	11.5 g
Carbohydrates	55.1 g
Fat (Total)	5.3 g
Saturated Fat	0.7 g
Monounsaturated Fat	2.4 g
Polyunsaturated Fat	1.5 g
Dietary Fiber	10.6 g
Sodium	303 mg
Cholesterol	0 mg

EXCELLENT SOURCE OF vitamins A and C, folate, iron, magnesium, manganese and copper.

GOOD SOURCE OF vitamin E (alpha-tocopherol), thiamine, riboflavin, niacin, phosphorus and zinc.

SOURCE OF pantothenic acid, calcium and selenium.

CONTAINS a very high amount of dietary fiber.

Rice-Stuffed Eggplant

This one-dish meal is very tasty and particularly handy for those nights when everyone is coming and going at different times. Cover the cooked eggplants and leave them out so people can help themselves, and leave the fixins' for salad alongside. If you roast the eggplant in the oven while you're chopping the vegetables, it's actually quite time-efficient.

Makes 6 servings

TIP

Herbes de Provence is a traditional French combination of dried herbs such as thyme, marjoram, tarragon and parsley. It is available premixed or you can make your own simplified version by combining 2 tsp (10 mL) dried thyme leaves with 1 tsp (5 mL) each marjoram and dried parsley.

Nutrients per serving

Calories	281
Protein	8.9 g
Carbohydrates	42.4 g
Fat (Total)	10.6 g
Saturated Fat	2.6 g
Monounsaturated Fat	6.0 g
Polyunsaturated Fat	1.3 g
Dietary Fiber	8.0 g
Sodium	556 mg
Cholesterol	7 mg

EXCELLENT SOURCE OF vitamin C, magnesium and manganese.

GOOD SOURCE OF vitamins A and E (alpha-tocopherol), thiamine, niacin, folate, calcium, phosphorus, iron, copper and selenium.

SOURCE OF riboflavin, pantothenic acid and zinc.

CONTAINS a very high amount of dietary fiber.

- **Preheat oven to 350°F (180°C)**
- **Rimmed baking sheet**

2 cups	cooked brown or red rice, cooled	500 mL
3	eggplants (each about 10 oz/300 g)	3
3 tbsp	olive oil (approx.), divided	45 mL
1	onion, finely chopped	1
1	green bell pepper, seeded and diced	1
1	red bell pepper, seeded and diced	1
4	cloves garlic, minced	4
1 tbsp	herbes de Provence (see Tip, left)	15 mL
1 tsp	salt	5 mL
	Freshly ground black pepper	
1	can (28 oz/796 mL) no-salt-added diced tomatoes, drained	1
½ cup	freshly grated Parmesan cheese	125 mL

1. Halve eggplants lengthwise and brush cut sides liberally with about 2 tbsp (25 mL) of the olive oil. Place cut side down on baking sheet and roast in preheated oven until softened, about 35 minutes. Let cool. Scoop out flesh, leaving about ½ inch (1 cm) of the shell, and return to baking sheet, hollow side up. Chop flesh finely. Set both parts aside.

2. In a large skillet, heat remaining 1 tbsp (15 mL) of olive oil over medium heat for 30 seconds. Add onion, bell peppers and garlic and stir well. Reduce heat to low. Cover and cook until vegetables are softened, about 10 minutes. Increase heat to medium. Add herbes de Provence, salt and black pepper to taste and cook, stirring, for 1 minute. Add reserved eggplant flesh, cooked rice and diced tomatoes and cook, stirring, until heated through.

3. Spoon filling into eggplant shells to form a generous mound. Bake in preheated oven for 20 minutes. Sprinkle Parmesan evenly over tops and bake until cheese is melted and slightly crusty, about 10 minutes.

VEGAN FRIENDLY

Khitchuri with Tomatoes and Green Peppers

This traditional Indian dish of rice and lentils makes a delicious main course when topped off with a mélange of peppers and tomatoes, so expect requests for seconds. I like to use red lentils because they dissolve in the liquid, adding creaminess to the sauce. The pilaf will be liquidy when the rice is cooked, so serve this in soup plates. You don't need to add much — a simple green salad and perhaps some whole-grain bread to soak up the sauce.

Makes 6 servings

TIPS

For the best flavor, toast and grind whole cumin seeds rather than buying ground cumin. Simply stir seeds in a dry skillet over medium heat until fragrant, about 3 minutes. Immediately transfer to a spice grinder or mortar and grind.

Substitute 2 cups (500 mL) halved cherry tomatoes for the chopped tomatoes, if you prefer.

Nutrients per serving

Calories	310
Protein	12.2 g
Carbohydrates	54.0 g
Fat (Total)	6.1 g
Saturated Fat	0.9 g
Monounsaturated Fat	3.8 g
Polyunsaturated Fat	1.1 g
Dietary Fiber	7.9 g
Sodium	347 mg
Cholesterol	0 mg

EXCELLENT SOURCE OF vitamins A and C, thiamine, folate, riboflavin, phosphorus, iron, magnesium and manganese.

GOOD SOURCE OF niacin, pantothenic acid, zinc and copper.

SOURCE OF vitamin E (alpha-tocopherol), calcium and selenium.

CONTAINS a very high amount of dietary fiber.

2 tbsp	olive oil, divided	25 mL
1	onion, finely chopped	1
2	cloves garlic, minced	2
2 tsp	curry powder	10 mL
1	bay leaf	1
1 cup	brown basmati or brown long-grain rice, rinsed and drained	250 mL
1 cup	dried red lentils	250 mL
4 cups	reduced-sodium vegetable stock	1 L
2	green bell peppers, seeded and diced	2
½ tsp	ground cumin (see Tips, left)	2 mL
½ tsp	salt	2 mL
½ tsp	freshly ground black pepper	2 mL
1	hot pepper, long red or green or Thai chile pepper, optional	1
4	small tomatoes, peeled and chopped (see Tips, left)	4
⅓ cup	ketchup	75 mL
3	hard-cooked eggs, sliced, optional	3

1. In a saucepan, heat 1 tbsp (15 mL) of the oil over medium heat. Add onion and garlic and cook, stirring, until onion softens, about 3 minutes. Stir in curry powder and bay leaf. Add rice and lentils and stir until coated. Add stock and bring to a boil. Reduce heat to low. Cover and simmer until rice is tender, about 50 minutes.

2. Meanwhile, in a skillet, heat remaining 1 tbsp (15 mL) of oil over medium heat. Add bell peppers, cumin, salt, black pepper and chile pepper, if using, and cook, stirring, until peppers are softened, about 5 minutes. Add tomatoes and cook, stirring, for 1 minute. Stir in ketchup. Reduce heat to low and simmer, stirring occasionally, until flavors meld, about 10 minutes.

3. *To serve:* Spread rice mixture evenly over a large deep platter. Arrange pepper mixture over top and garnish with eggs, if using.

Zuni Stew

Zuni stew, which is often made with meat, has its roots firmly in New Mexico, where the key ingredients, corn and chile peppers, thrive. It also happens to be home to the Zuni people, who make it from whatever they have on hand. My version introduces a novel ingredient, wheat berries, which although not indigenous seem right at home in this ambrosial mix. Serve this with warm tortillas and, if you're feeling festive, a dollop of guacamole.

Makes 8 servings

TIPS

If you've cooked your own beans, save the cooking liquid and use it to moisten the stew instead of water or stock (Step 3).

I like to use a single-source chili powder (ancho or New Mexico) that differs from the variety of dried chile reconstituted for the stew, but your favorite blend will work well, too.

For the best flavor, toast and grind whole cumin seeds rather than buying ground cumin. Simply stir seeds in a dry skillet over medium heat until fragrant, about 3 minutes. Immediately transfer to a spice grinder or mortar and grind.

Substitute red kidney beans, cranberry beans or small red beans for the pinto beans.

4 cups	cooked wheat, spelt or Kamut berries (see cooking instructions, page 34)	1 L
1 cup	drained, rinsed cooked or canned pinto beans (see Tips, left)	250 mL
2	dried ancho, New Mexico or guajillo chiles	2
2 cups	boiling water	500 mL
1 tbsp	olive oil	15 mL
2	onions, finely chopped	2
4	stalks celery, diced	4
1	green bell pepper, seeded and diced	1
2	cloves garlic, minced	2
2 tbsp	chili powder (see Tips, left)	25 mL
2 tsp	ground cumin (see Tips, left)	10 mL
1 tsp	dried oregano leaves	5 mL
½ tsp	salt	2 mL
	Freshly ground black pepper	
1	chipotle pepper in adobo sauce, minced	1
1	can (28 oz/796 mL) no-salt-added diced tomatoes with juice	1
2 cups	corn kernels	500 mL
2	small zucchini (each about 8 oz/250 g), cut into ½-inch (1 cm) cubes	2
1 cup	sliced green beans	250 mL
	Water or reduced-sodium vegetable stock	
2 cups	shredded reduced-fat Monterey Jack cheese	500 mL

1. In a heatproof bowl, soak dried chiles in boiling water, weighing down with a cup to keep submerged, for 30 minutes. Drain, discarding soaking liquid and stems. Pat chiles dry, chop finely and set aside.

2. In a Dutch oven, heat oil over medium heat for 30 seconds. Add onions, celery, bell pepper and garlic and stir well. Reduce heat to low. Cover and cook until vegetables are softened, for 10 minutes. Add chili powder, cumin, oregano leaves, salt, black pepper to taste, reserved chiles and chipotle pepper. Cook, stirring, for 1 minute. Add wheat berries and pinto beans and stir well.

3. Add tomatoes with juice and bring to a boil. Stir in corn, zucchini and green beans. Add water or stock barely to cover. Cover and simmer until vegetables are tender and flavors meld, about 30 minutes. Ladle into soup plates and pass the cheese at the table for sprinkling.

Variations

Substitute an equal quantity of cooked barley or rye berries for the wheat berries.

If you prefer, use a sliced roasted red pepper — or two — instead of, or in addition to, the green bell pepper. Add after the stew has cooked and simmer for a minute or two, just until heated through.

VITAMIN A

One serving of this dish is an excellent source of vitamin A. Although this vitamin is famous for keeping your eyes healthy, it has other important functions, such as contributing to your ability to see at night, supporting bone growth and keeping cells functioning well. Dietary intake studies suggest that diets rich in beta-carotene (which the body makes into vitamin A) and vitamin A may lower the risk of many types of cancer. However, studies testing beta-carotene supplements found no such correlation.

Nutrients per serving	
Calories	360
Protein	17.9 g
Carbohydrates	56.2 g
Fat (Total)	10.0 g
Saturated Fat	4.5 g
Monounsaturated Fat	3.2 g
Polyunsaturated Fat	1.3 g
Dietary Fiber	12.3 g
Sodium	387 mg
Cholesterol	18 mg

EXCELLENT SOURCE OF vitamin A, niacin, folate, calcium, phosphorus, iron, magnesium, manganese, copper and selenium.

GOOD SOURCE OF vitamins C and E (alpha-tocopherol), thiamine, riboflavin and zinc.

SOURCE OF pantothenic acid.

CONTAINS a very high amount of dietary fiber.

Mushroom and Barley Ragoût

You can't go wrong with the combination of mushrooms and barley. The addition of Chinese seasonings and lentils adds interesting flavors and expands the range of nutrients in the dish. Just add a sliced tomato or green salad to complete the meal.

Makes 8 servings

TIP

Be careful not to use more Chinese 5-slice powder than the quantity called for. It has a very pronounced flavor and will overpower the dish.

3 cups	cooked whole (hulled) barley (see cooking instructions, page 16)	750 mL
4	dried shiitake mushrooms	4
2 cups	hot water	500 mL
1 tbsp	butter	15 mL
8 oz	cremini mushrooms, stemmed and sliced	250 g
1 tbsp	olive oil	15 mL
2	onions, finely chopped	2
4	stalks celery, diced	4
2	carrots, diced	2
4	cloves garlic, minced	4
2 tbsp	minced gingerroot	25 mL
1 tsp	cracked black peppercorns	5 mL
½ tsp	Chinese 5-spice powder (see Tip, left)	2 mL
1 cup	dried brown lentils, rinsed and drained	250 mL
4 cups	reduced-sodium vegetable stock	1 L
¼ cup	reduced-sodium soy sauce	50 mL
	Finely chopped green onions	

1. In a bowl, combine dried shiitake mushrooms with hot water. Stir well. Let stand for 30 minutes. Strain through a fine sieve, reserving mushrooms and liquid separately. Pat mushrooms dry, remove stems and chop finely.

2. Meanwhile, in a deep skillet, melt butter over medium heat. Add cremini mushrooms and cook, stirring, until they begin to release liquid, about 5 minutes. Transfer to a bowl.

3. Add oil to pan and heat for 30 seconds. Add onions, celery and carrots and cook, stirring, until vegetables are softened, about 7 minutes. Add garlic, ginger, peppercorns and 5-spice powder and cook, stirring, for 1 minute. Stir in reconstituted and fresh mushrooms. Add barley and lentils and stir well. Stir in stock and reserved mushroom soaking liquid. Bring to a boil. Reduce heat to low. Cover and simmer until lentils are tender, about 40 minutes. Stir in soy sauce. Garnish with green onions.

Variation

Mushroom and Rice Ragoût: Substitute an equal quantity of cooked brown or red rice for the barley.

Nutrients per serving

Calories	251
Protein	11.4 g
Carbohydrates	45.6 g
Fat (Total)	4.2 g
Saturated Fat	1.4 g
Monounsaturated Fat	1.8 g
Polyunsaturated Fat	0.7 g
Dietary Fiber	9.7 g
Sodium	315 mg
Cholesterol	4 mg

EXCELLENT SOURCE OF vitamin A, thiamine, folate, pantothenic acid, iron, manganese, copper and selenium.

GOOD SOURCE OF niacin, riboflavin, zinc, phosphorus and magnesium.

SOURCE OF vitamins C and E (alpha-tocopherol) and calcium.

CONTAINS a very high amount of dietary fiber.

Mushroom Varnishkes

This traditional dish of buckwheat groats with bowtie pasta and mushrooms can be categorized as Jewish comfort food. I've embellished it a bit with celery and spice, and specified whole wheat farfalle to bump up the whole-grain content, but haven't strayed far from its roots. This is a substantial but simple dish deeply rooted in Eastern European cuisine. Serve it with steamed green beans or a tossed green salad.

Makes 6 servings

TIP

Buckwheat groats that are already toasted are known as kasha. If you prefer a milder buckwheat flavor, use groats rather than kasha in this dish. Cooking them with the egg serves the same purpose as toasting — to bring out the flavor.

1	egg	1
½ tsp	salt	2 mL
¼ tsp	cayenne pepper	1 mL
	Freshly ground black pepper	
1 cup	buckwheat groats or kasha (see Tip, left)	250 mL
2 tbsp	olive oil, divided	25 mL
2 tbsp	butter, divided	25 mL
8 oz	cremini mushrooms, stems removed and thinly sliced	250 g
2 tbsp	freshly squeezed lemon juice	25 mL
1	onion, finely chopped	1
2	stalks celery, diced	2
2	cloves garlic, minced	2
1 tsp	sweet paprika	5 mL
2 cups	reduced-sodium vegetable stock or water	500 mL
1 cup	whole wheat bowtie pasta (farfalle)	250 mL
½ cup	finely chopped parsley or dill	125 mL

1. In a bowl, beat egg, salt, cayenne and black pepper to taste until eggs are frothy. Add groats and stir to coat. Heat a skillet over medium heat for 30 seconds. Add groat mixture, stirring, until egg sets and grains separate, about 3 minutes. Transfer to a bowl and wipe skillet clean.

2. In same skillet, heat 1 tbsp (15 mL) each of the oil and butter over medium-high heat. Add mushrooms and cook, stirring, until their liquid evaporates, about 8 minutes. Sprinkle with lemon juice and, using a slotted spoon, transfer to a bowl and set aside.

3. Add remaining 1 tbsp (15 mL) of oil to pan. Add onion, celery, garlic and paprika and cook, stirring, until celery is softened, about 5 minutes. Add cooled groats and egg mixture and reserved mushrooms and toss well. Add stock and bring to a boil. Reduce heat to low. Cover and simmer for 5 minutes. Remove from heat and set aside until groats are tender and liquid is absorbed, about 10 minutes.

4. Meanwhile, in a large pot of boiling salted water, cook bowtie pasta until tender to the bite, about 12 minutes. Toss with remaining 1 tbsp (15 mL) of butter. Add to cooked groats and mix well. Garnish with parsley.

Nutrients per serving

Calories	250
Protein	7.8 g
Carbohydrates	35.7 g
Fat (Total)	10.2 g
Saturated Fat	3.5 g
Monounsaturated Fat	4.9 g
Polyunsaturated Fat	1.1 g
Dietary Fiber	5.4 g
Sodium	250 mg
Cholesterol	41 mg

EXCELLENT SOURCE OF manganese and selenium.

GOOD SOURCE OF riboflavin, niacin, folate, pantothenic acid, magnesium, phosphorus, zinc and copper.

SOURCE OF vitamins A, C and E (alpha-tocopherol), thiamine and iron.

CONTAINS a high amount of dietary fiber.

Chile-Spiked Quinoa Pudding with Corn

This is a tasty and versatile dish. I like to serve it on weekdays as a main course, accompanied by a salad of bibb lettuce, green onions and diced avocado in a white wine vinaigrette. If you're having a large number of guests for dinner and looking to stretch the meal, it also works as an unusual side, serving eight to ten.

Makes 6 servings

TIP
If you are a heat seeker, add an extra half chipotle pepper in adobo sauce.

- Preheat oven to 375°F (190°C)
- Shallow 8-cup (2 L) baking dish, lightly greased

3 cups	cooked quinoa (see cooking instructions, page 26)	750 mL
1 tbsp	olive oil	15 mL
1	onion, finely chopped	1
1	red bell pepper, seeded and diced	1
1	clove garlic, minced	1
2 tsp	dried oregano leaves	10 mL
½ tsp	salt	2 mL
½ tsp	freshly ground black pepper	2 mL
1	chipotle pepper in adobo sauce, minced	1
1	can (14 oz/398 mL) diced tomatoes with juice	1
1 cup	corn kernels	250 mL
3	eggs, beaten	3

1. In a large saucepan, heat oil over medium heat for 30 seconds. Add onion and bell pepper. Reduce heat to low. Cover and cook until vegetables are softened, about 10 minutes.

2. Add garlic, oregano, salt and black pepper and cook, stirring, for 1 minute. Stir in chipotle pepper. Add quinoa and mix well. Stir in tomatoes with juice and corn. Remove from heat.

3. In a small bowl, combine beaten eggs with about ½ cup (125 mL) of the hot mixture, beating until combined. Gradually return to pot, mixing well. Transfer to prepared baking dish. Bake in preheated oven until pudding sets and top is crispy and browned, about 45 minutes.

Variation
Chile-Spiked Millet Pudding with Corn: Substitute an equal quantity of cooked toasted millet (see cooking instructions, page 23) for the quinoa.

Nutrients per serving
Calories	212
Protein	8.5 g
Carbohydrates	31.4 g
Fat (Total)	6.8 g
Saturated Fat	1.3 g
Monounsaturated Fat	3.2 g
Polyunsaturated Fat	1.4 g
Dietary Fiber	3.8 g
Sodium	331 mg
Cholesterol	93 mg

EXCELLENT SOURCE OF vitamin C, iron, magnesium and manganese.

GOOD SOURCE OF riboflavin, niacin, thiamine, folate, phosphorus, zinc, copper and selenium.

SOURCE OF vitamins A and E (alpha-tocopherol), pantothenic acid and calcium.

CONTAINS a moderate amount of dietary fiber.

Best-Ever Buckwheat Burgers with Bulgur in Tomato-Mushroom Gravy

Topped with the colorful gravy, these "burgers" are visually appealing, in addition to being tasty and nutritious. They make an interesting and unusual main course. A simple green salad completes the meal.

Makes 4 servings

TIPS

If you're using buckwheat groats rather than kasha, which has already been toasted, toast them in a dry skillet over medium-high heat, stirring constantly, until fragrant, about 4 minutes. Then cook according to instructions.

To sweat eggplant for this recipe, drop the pieces into rapidly boiling heavily salted water and blanch for 2 minutes. Rinse thoroughly in fresh cold water and, using your hands, squeeze out the excess moisture. Pat dry before using.

Use an assertively flavored mushroom, such as porcini or portobello, in this recipe to ensure it stands up to the buckwheat.

Nutrient Tip

All the cholesterol comes from the egg and unless you are sensitive to dietary cholesterol (about 25% of the population) it should not have any effect on your blood cholesterol levels. In fact, eggs are considered to be a nutrient-dense food and a healthy choice.

1 cup	water	250 mL
½ cup	kasha or toasted buckwheat groats (see Tips, left)	125 mL
½ cup	bulgur	125 mL
¾ cup	ice water	175 mL
2 tbsp	olive oil (approx.), divided	25 mL
1	small eggplant (1 lb/500 g), peeled, finely chopped and sweated (see Tips, left)	1
½	onion, finely chopped	½
2	cloves garlic, minced	2
2	drained oil-packed sun-dried tomatoes, finely chopped (about 2 tbsp/25 mL)	2
2	eggs, beaten	2
	Salt and freshly ground black pepper	

TOMATO-MUSHROOM GRAVY

1 tbsp	crumbled dried mushrooms, such as portobello (see Tips, left)	15 mL
¼ cup	hot water	50 mL
1 tbsp	olive oil	15 mL
2 tbsp	finely chopped onion	25 mL
1	can (14 oz/398 mL) no-salt-added diced tomatoes with juice	1
	Salt and freshly ground black pepper	
2 tbsp	finely chopped parsley	25 mL

1. In a saucepan over medium-high heat, bring water to a boil. Gradually add kasha, stirring constantly to prevent clumping. Reduce heat to low. Cover and simmer until all the liquid is absorbed and kasha is tender, about 10 minutes. Remove from heat. Fluff up with a fork. Meanwhile, in a bowl, combine bulgur and ice water. Stir well and set aside until liquid is absorbed, about 10 minutes. Add to kasha and mix well. Set aside.

2. In a skillet, heat 1 tbsp (15 mL) of the oil over medium heat. Add eggplant, onion and garlic and cook, stirring, until eggplant begins to brown, about 8 minutes. Transfer to a large bowl and let cool. Stir in sun-dried tomatoes, eggs and reserved kasha and bulgur. Season to taste with salt and pepper, being aware that the eggplant will have retained some residual salt from its blanching. Shape into 8 patties.

3. In a skillet, heat remaining 1 tbsp (15 mL) of oil over medium heat. Add burgers, in batches, and cook until well browned and heated through, flipping once and adding more oil, if necessary, about 5 minutes per side.

4. *Tomato-Mushroom Gravy:* Meanwhile, in a bowl, combine dried mushrooms and hot water. Set aside for 20 minutes. Strain through a fine sieve, reserving mushrooms and liquid separately.

5. In a skillet, heat oil over medium heat for 30 seconds. Add onion and cook, stirring, until softened, about 3 minutes. Add reconstituted mushrooms and toss well. Add tomatoes with juice and reserved mushroom soaking liquid and bring to a boil. Cook, stirring, until mixture reduces by about one quarter, about 5 minutes. Season to taste with salt and pepper. Stir in parsley.

6. *To serve:* Place burgers on a plate and top with Mushroom-Tomato Gravy.

Variation

Instead of the Tomato-Mushroom Gravy, you can also top with your favorite chutney or chili sauce.

Nutrients per serving	
Calories	352
Protein	11.1 g
Carbohydrates	50.8 g
Fat (Total)	14.4 g
Saturated Fat	2.4 g
Monounsaturated Fat	9.1 g
Polyunsaturated Fat	1.9 g
Dietary Fiber	9.4 g
Sodium	331 mg
Cholesterol	93 mg

EXCELLENT SOURCE OF magnesium, manganese, copper and selenium.

GOOD SOURCE OF vitamin E (alpha-tocopherol), niacin, thiamine, riboflavin, folate, pantothenic acid, phosphorus, iron and zinc.

SOURCE OF vitamins A and C and calcium.

CONTAINS a very high amount of dietary fiber.

Buckwheat-Stuffed Onions

Although this is a bit of work, if you're trying to eat more buckwheat this is a delicious way to up your intake of this extremely nutritious grain. I prefer the milder flavor of groats that I toast myself and love the look and taste of a liberal garnishing of dill. An apple corer makes easy work of hollowing out the onions.

Makes 4 servings

TIPS

You'll need about ⅓ oz (10 g) dried mushrooms for this recipe.

If you prefer a milder buckwheat flavor, toast your own groats. Otherwise, use groats sold as kasha, which have been pretoasted. To toast groats, place them in a dry skillet over medium heat and toast, stirring constantly, until fragrant and lightly browned, about 4 minutes.

Nutrient Tip

If you're concerned about your sodium intake, reduce the quantity of added salt to ½ tsp (2 mL).

- **Preheat oven to 350°F (180°C)**
- **Deep baking dish, lightly greased**

4	large Spanish onions	4
4	dried shiitake mushrooms (see Tips, left)	4
2 cups	hot water	500 mL
1 tbsp	butter or olive oil	15 mL
12 oz	cremini mushrooms, stems removed, caps thinly sliced	375 g
2 tbsp	reduced-sodium soy sauce	25 mL
1 tbsp	olive oil	15 mL
4	cloves garlic, minced	4
1 tsp	dried thyme leaves	5 mL
1 tsp	paprika	5 mL
1 tsp	salt	5 mL
	Freshly ground black pepper	
1 cup	toasted buckwheat groats (see Tips, left)	250 mL
¼ cup	ketchup	50 mL
	Finely chopped fresh dill	

1. Bring a large pot of water to a boil. Meanwhile, slice about ½ inch (1 cm) off tops of onions, peel and scoop out the centers, leaving 3 to 4 rings. Discard tough core, finely chop remainder and set aside. (Use 1 cup/250 mL in this recipe and save the remainder for another use.) Drop onion shells into boiling water and cook until slightly tender, about 15 minutes. Drain on paper towels.

2. In a heatproof bowl, combine dried mushrooms and hot water. Stir well and let stand for 30 minutes. Strain through a fine sieve, reserving mushrooms and liquid separately. Remove stems, pat mushrooms dry, chop finely and set aside. Add water to soaking liquid to make 2 cups (500 mL). Set both aside.

3. Meanwhile, in a skillet, melt butter or heat olive oil over medium-high heat. Add cremini mushrooms and cook, stirring, until liquid evaporates, about 8 minutes. Season with soy sauce and transfer to a bowl.

4. Reduce heat to medium and heat oil for 30 seconds. Add reserved chopped onions and cook, stirring, until softened, about 3 minutes. Add garlic, thyme, paprika, salt, pepper to taste and reserved reconstituted mushrooms and cook, stirring, for 1 minute. Add toasted groats and toss until well coated with mixture. Add reserved cremini mushrooms, mushroom soaking liquid and ketchup and bring to a boil. Reduce heat to low. Cover and simmer until liquid is absorbed, about 10 minutes.

5. Place blanched onions in prepared baking dish and fill centers with buckwheat mixture, allowing the excess to spill over into the dish. Cover and bake in preheated oven until hot and bubbly, for 30 minutes. Garnish with dill.

Nutrients per serving

Calories	388
Protein	12.1 g
Carbohydrates	74.6 g
Fat (Total)	8.1 g
Saturated Fat	2.6 g
Monounsaturated Fat	3.6 g
Polyunsaturated Fat	1.1 g
Dietary Fiber	11.8 g
Sodium	1083 mg
Cholesterol	8 mg

EXCELLENT SOURCE OF riboflavin, folate, niacin, pantothenic acid, phosphorus, magnesium, manganese, copper and selenium.

GOOD SOURCE OF vitamin C, thiamine, iron and zinc.

SOURCE OF vitamins A and E (alpha-tocopherol) and calcium.

CONTAINS a very high amount of dietary fiber.

Sides, Sundries and Basics

Red Beans and Red Rice

Red Beans and Red Rice

Here's a fresh twist on the classic Southern dish of red beans and rice. Bulked up with muscular red rice, this is very hearty — with the addition of salad, it's a meal in itself. The green peas add a burst of color, making this a visually attractive dish that looks good on a buffet. It is particularly tasty as an accompaniment to roast chicken or pork, or pork chops or a platter of roasted vegetables.

Makes 8 servings

TIPS

If you're using chicken stock rather than water to cook the rice, you may not need the added salt.

I like to use red rice, but brown rice or mixture of brown rice and wild rice would work well, too. The cooking time is the same.

You can cook your own beans or use 1 can (14 to 19 oz/398 to 540 mL) no-salt-added red kidney or small red beans, drained and rinsed.

1 tbsp	olive oil	15 mL
1	onion, finely chopped	1
1	green bell pepper, seeded and diced	1
4	stalks celery, diced	4
4	cloves garlic, minced	4
1 tsp	dried thyme leaves	5 mL
½ tsp	salt (see Tips, left)	2 mL
½ tsp	cracked black peppercorns	2 mL
¼ tsp	cayenne pepper	1 mL
1 cup	Wehani or Camargue red rice, rinsed and drained (see Tips, left)	250 mL
2 cups	water or reduced-sodium chicken stock	500 mL
2 cups	drained, rinsed cooked or canned red beans (see Tips, left)	500 mL
2 cups	cooked green peas	500 mL

1. In a Dutch oven, heat oil over medium heat for 30 seconds. Add onion, bell pepper, celery and garlic and cook, stirring, until pepper is softened, about 5 minutes. Add thyme, salt, peppercorns and cayenne and cook, stirring, for 1 minute.

2. Add rice and toss to coat. Add water and bring to a boil. Reduce heat to low. Cover and simmer until rice is tender and most of the water is absorbed, about 1 hour. Stir in beans and peas and cook, covered, until heated through, about 10 minutes.

Variation

Red Rice, Sausage and Beans: To turn this into a heartier dish, perfect for a pot luck or buffet, add 4 oz (125 g) diced kielbasa along with the peas.

Nutrients per serving

Calories	203
Protein	7.9 g
Carbohydrates	38.6 g
Fat (Total)	2.6 g
Saturated Fat	0.3 g
Monounsaturated Fat	1.3 g
Polyunsaturated Fat	0.4 g
Dietary Fiber	6.9 g
Sodium	191 mg
Cholesterol	0 mg

EXCELLENT SOURCE OF folate.

GOOD SOURCE OF thiamine, iron and manganese.

SOURCE OF vitamins A and C, riboflavin, niacin, phosphorus, magnesium, zinc and copper.

CONTAINS a very high amount of dietary fiber.

Brown Rice Risotto

Short-grain brown rice is glutinous, which means you can use it to make a terrific risotto without the stirring. This dish is so easy to make that I often serve it as a side for weekday dinners. It's a great accompaniment to roasted or grilled meat, fish or a meatless main and is much more nutritious than versions made with white rice.

Makes 6 servings

TIPS

I have found that when making this recipe, soaking the rice speeds up the cooking and produces a creamier result. But if you don't have time, add about 10 minutes to the cooking time with the lid on.

The addition of white wine adds a pleasantly acidic note to risotto, but if you prefer, use an additional ½ cup (125 mL) of stock.

Nutrient Tip

I used homemade vegetable stock to make this risotto because it is so low in sodium.

1 cup	short-grain brown rice (see Tips, left)	250 mL
1 cup	warm water	250 mL
1 tbsp	olive oil	15 mL
1	onion, finely chopped	1
2 cups	Homemade Vegetable Stock (see recipe, page 75) or reduced-sodium chicken stock	500 mL
½ cup	dry white wine (see Tips, left)	125 mL
	Freshly ground black pepper	
1 tbsp	butter, optional	15 mL
2 tbsp	finely chopped parsley, optional	25 mL
2 tbsp	freshly grated Parmesan cheese, optional	25 mL

1. In a bowl, combine rice and water. Stir well and set aside for at least 3 hours or overnight. When ready to cook, drain, reserving soaking liquid.

2. In a heavy saucepan with a tight-fitting lid, heat oil over medium heat for 30 seconds. Add onion and cook, stirring, until softened, about 3 minutes. Add stock, wine and reserved soaking liquid and bring to a boil. Add drained rice and pepper to taste. Stir well and bring to a boil. Reduce heat to low. Cover and simmer for 35 minutes, placing a heat diffuser on the element, if necessary, to keep the mixture at a true simmer. Remove lid, stir well and simmer, uncovered, stirring occasionally, until liquid is absorbed and rice is tender, about 15 minutes.

3. Stir in butter, parsley and cheese, if using.

Variation

Substitute up to 2 tbsp (25 mL) of the short-grain brown rice with a more colorful robust rice, such as Colusari red rice or Wehani, to add texture and visual detail.

Nutrients per serving

Calories	147
Protein	2.6 g
Carbohydrates	26.3 g
Fat (Total)	3.1 g
Saturated Fat	0.5 g
Monounsaturated Fat	2.0 g
Polyunsaturated Fat	0.5 g
Dietary Fiber	2.1 g
Sodium	3 mg
Cholesterol	0 mg

EXCELLENT SOURCE OF manganese.

GOOD SOURCE OF magnesium.

SOURCE OF thiamin, niacin, pantothenic acid, phosphorus, iron, zinc and copper.

CONTAINS a moderate amount of dietary fiber.

Italian-Style Green Rice

Here's a deliciously different rice that makes a perfect companion for grilled meats and fish. Your guests will be very impressed, as the short-grain rice is quite glutinous and the results mimic risotto. You can fib and say you spent endless time stirring to produce such a stunning effect.

Makes 6 servings

TIP

If your spinach has not been prewashed, be sure to rinse it thoroughly in a basin of lukewarm water. Swish it around to remove all traces of grit, then rinse it again in a colander under cold running water.

1 cup	short-grain brown rice	250 mL
1¼ cups	water, divided	300 mL
2 cups	reduced-sodium chicken or vegetable stock	500 mL
1 lb	fresh spinach leaves, stems removed (see Tip, left)	500 g
2	green onions, white part only, finely chopped	2
	Salt and freshly ground black pepper	
2 tbsp	extra virgin olive oil	25 mL
¼ cup	freshly grated Parmesan cheese	50 mL

1. In a bowl, combine rice and 1 cup (250 mL) of the water. Stir well. Cover and set aside for at least 3 hours or overnight. Drain, reserving liquid.

2. In a heavy saucepan with a tight-fitting lid, combine stock and reserved soaking water. Bring to a boil. Stir in rice and return to a boil. Reduce heat to low. Cover and simmer for 35 minutes. Remove lid, stir well and simmer, uncovered, stirring occasionally, until liquid is absorbed and rice is tender, about 15 minutes.

3. When rice is almost cooked, in another saucepan over low heat, combine spinach and ¼ cup (50 mL) of water. Cover and cook until wilted, about 5 minutes. Using a slotted spoon, transfer to a cutting board and chop finely. Transfer to a bowl. Season to taste with salt and pepper. Stir in green onions. Set aside.

4. *To serve:* Spread cooked rice evenly over a deep platter. Arrange spinach evenly over the center, leaving some rice exposed around the edge. Drizzle olive oil over the spinach and sprinkle with Parmesan. Serve immediately.

Nutrients per serving

Calories	195
Protein	7.0 g
Carbohydrates	27.5 g
Fat (Total)	6.8 g
Saturated Fat	1.5 g
Monounsaturated Fat	4.0 g
Polyunsaturated Fat	0.9 g
Dietary Fiber	3.6 g
Sodium	314 mg
Cholesterol	4 mg

EXCELLENT SOURCE OF vitamin A, folate, magnesium and manganese.

GOOD SOURCE OF vitamin E (alpha-tocopherol) and iron.

SOURCE OF vitamin C, thiamine, riboflavin, niacin, pantothenic acid, zinc, calcium, phosphorus and copper.

CONTAINS a moderate amount of dietary fiber.

Saffron-Scented Millet Pilaf with Toasted Almonds

This tasty pilaf is very easy to make so long as you have saffron in the house. Its mildly exotic flavors will give your taste buds a lift. It makes a delicious accompaniment to roast chicken or a platter of roasted vegetables.

Makes 6 servings

TIP

To toast almonds, place on a rimmed baking sheet in the center of 350°F (180°C) preheated oven and toast, stirring occasionally, until lightly browned, 5 to 10 minutes.

Nutrient Tip

I like to make this with homemade vegetable stock because it is so low in sodium.

1 cup	millet	250 mL
1 tbsp	olive oil	15 mL
1	onion, finely chopped	1
2½ cups	Homemade Vegetable Stock (see recipe, page 75) or reduced-sodium vegetable or chicken stock or water	625 mL
¼ tsp	crumbled saffron threads, dissolved in 2 tbsp (25 mL) boiling water	1 mL
	Freshly ground black pepper	
2 tbsp	toasted sliced almonds (see Tip, left)	25 mL
2 tbsp	finely chopped parsley	25 mL

1. In a saucepan over medium heat, toast millet, stirring, until it crackles and releases its aroma, about 5 minutes. Transfer to a bowl.

2. In same saucepan, heat oil over medium heat for 30 seconds. Add onion and cook, stirring, until softened, about 3 minutes. Add stock and saffron liquid and bring to a boil. Gradually stir in reserved millet and return to a boil. Season to taste with pepper.

3. Reduce heat to low. Cover, placing a heat diffuser under the pot if necessary, and simmer until liquid is absorbed, about 25 minutes. Remove from heat and let stand for 5 minutes. Fluff with a fork. Stir in toasted almonds and parsley.

Variation

Saffron-Scented Millet Pilaf with Toasted Pine Nuts: Substitute an equal quantity of toasted pine nuts for the almonds.

Nutrients per serving

Calories	166
Protein	4.4 g
Carbohydrates	27.5 g
Fat (Total)	4.3 g
Saturated Fat	0.6 g
Monounsaturated Fat	2.5 g
Polyunsaturated Fat	1.0 g
Dietary Fiber	3.6 g
Sodium	4 mg
Cholesterol	0 mg

GOOD SOURCE OF magnesium and manganese.

SOURCE OF vitamin E (alpha-tocopherol), thiamine, riboflavin, niacin, folate, phosphorus, iron, zinc and copper.

CONTAINS a moderate amount of dietary fiber.

Roasted Red Pepper Risotto

This is a great way to dress up a simple dinner or to handle unexpected guests. Pick up a rotisserie chicken or two or a vegetable stir-fry, and a precooked vegetable, such as asparagus vinaigrette. Make this risotto, open a bottle of wine and everyone will think you're amazing.

Makes 6 servings

TIP
You can make this recipe without presoaking the rice, but you'll need to cook it for an extra 15 minutes and even then the result will be quite *al dente* and not as creamy. If you're not presoaking the rice, don't forget to add 1 cup (250 mL) water along with the stock.

1 cup	short-grain brown rice	250 mL
1 cup	water	250 mL
1 tbsp	olive oil	15 mL
1	onion, finely chopped	1
2 tbsp	diced pancetta, optional	25 mL
½ tsp	sweet or hot paprika	2 mL
¼ tsp	freshly ground black pepper	1 mL
½ cup	dry white wine or additional stock	125 mL
1½ cups	reduced-sodium chicken or vegetable stock	375 mL
¾ cup	diced roasted red peppers (about 2)	175 mL
2 tbsp	freshly grated Parmesan cheese	50 mL

1. In a bowl, combine rice and water. Stir well. Cover and set aside for at least 3 hours or overnight. Drain, reserving liquid (see Tip, left).

2. In a heavy saucepan with a tight-fitting lid, heat oil over medium heat for 30 seconds. Add onion and pancetta, if using, and cook, stirring, until onion softens, about 3 minutes. Add paprika and black pepper and cook, stirring, for 1 minute. Add wine and cook, stirring, until liquid evaporates, about 5 minutes. Add stock and reserved soaking liquid and bring to a boil. Stir in rice and return to a boil. Reduce heat to low. Cover and simmer for 35 minutes.

3. Stir in red pepper. Simmer, uncovered, stirring occasionally, until liquid is absorbed and rice is tender, about 15 minutes. Remove from heat and stir in Parmesan. Serve immediately.

Variations

Risotto with Cabbage: Substitute 2 cups (500 mL) thinly shredded cabbage (preferably Savoy) for the roasted red peppers and ½ tsp (2 mL) dried thyme leaves for the paprika.

Smoked Cheese Risotto: Omit pancetta, paprika and roasted red peppers. Add 2 cloves minced garlic, along with the onion. After the rice is tender (Step 3), stir in 1 cup (250 mL) shredded smoked Gouda or mozzarella until melted, then add Parmesan.

Nutrients per serving

Calories	167
Protein	4.3 g
Carbohydrates	28.2 g
Fat (Total)	3.8 g
Saturated Fat	0.8 g
Monounsaturated Fat	2.2 g
Polyunsaturated Fat	0.6 g
Dietary Fiber	2.6 g
Sodium	241 mg
Cholesterol	2 mg

EXCELLENT SOURCE OF vitamin C and manganese.

GOOD SOURCE OF magnesium.

SOURCE OF vitamins A and E (alpha-tocopherol), thiamine, niacin, folate, pantothenic acid, phosphorus, iron, zinc and copper.

CONTAINS a moderate amount of dietary fiber.

Chile Rice

This robust rice makes a great accompaniment to grilled fish or meat or a platter of roasted vegetables and is superb with Saffron-Scented Shrimp (see recipe, page 149). Use two chiles if you're a heat seeker and one if you prefer a tamer result. Either way, this is a winner.

Makes 6 servings

TIP

Unless you have a stove with a true simmer, after reducing the heat to low I recommend placing a heat diffuser under the pot to prevent the mixture from boiling. This device also helps to ensure the rice will cook evenly and prevents hot spots, which might cause scorching, from forming. Heat diffusers are available at kitchen supply and hardware stores and are made to work on gas or electric stoves.

1 tbsp	olive oil	15 mL
1	onion, thinly sliced on the vertical	1
2	cloves garlic, minced	2
1 tbsp	minced gingerroot	15 mL
1 to 2	long red or green chile peppers, seeded and minced	1 to 2
2	bay leaves	2
1 tsp	ground cumin	5 mL
	Salt and freshly ground black pepper	
1 cup	brown basmati or brown long-grain rice, rinsed and drained	250 mL
1	can (28 oz/796 mL) no-salt-added diced tomatoes with juice	1
1 cup	water	250 mL
½ cup	finely chopped parsley	125 mL

1. In a large saucepan with a tight-fitting lid, heat oil over medium–high heat for 30 seconds. Add onion and cook, stirring, until well browned, about 10 minutes. Add garlic, ginger, chile pepper, bay leaves, cumin and salt and black pepper to taste and cook, stirring, for 1 minute.

2. Add rice and toss until coated. Stir in tomatoes with juice and water. Bring to a boil. Reduce heat to low. Cover and simmer until rice is tender, about 1 hour. Remove from heat and let stand for 5 minutes. Fluff with a fork and garnish with parsley.

Variation

For variety, try adding some red rice to the brown rice when cooking it. Two tablespoons (25 mL) of Colusari or Camargue red rice or Wehani, per cup (250 mL) adds a visual and textural spark to the dish.

Nutrients per serving

Calories	194
Protein	5.1 g
Carbohydrates	37.3 g
Fat (Total)	3.7 g
Saturated Fat	0.4 g
Monounsaturated Fat	1.8 g
Polyunsaturated Fat	1.2 g
Dietary Fiber	5.0 g
Sodium	46 mg
Cholesterol	0 mg

EXCELLENT SOURCE OF magnesium and manganese.

GOOD SOURCE OF vitamins A and C, thiamine, niacin, iron and copper.

SOURCE OF vitamin E (alpha-tocopherol), riboflavin, folate, pantothenic acid, calcium, phosphorus and zinc.

CONTAINS a high amount of dietary fiber.

Fragrant Coconut Rice

This is a deliciously rich rice — perhaps a bit too much for every day, but a wonderful treat now and again. I like to serve it as an accompaniment to a spicy curry because its robustness nicely complements the creamy sweetness of the rice.

Makes 4 servings

Nutrient Tip

This dish is high in saturated fat, but the source is coconut, which appears to have many healthy properties. Although the research into coconut oil is in the preliminary stages, it contains a number of fatty acids that have anti-inflammatory properties and may help your body fight infections.

1½ cups	coconut milk	375 mL
1 cup	water	250 mL
1	stick cinnamon, about 2 inches (5 cm) long	1
1 cup	brown basmati or brown long-grain rice, rinsed and drained	250 mL

1. In a saucepan over medium-high heat, bring coconut milk, water and cinnamon stick to a rapid boil. Stir in rice and return to a boil. Reduce heat to low. Cover and simmer until rice is tender and liquid is absorbed, about 50 minutes.

Nutrients per serving

Calories	339
Protein	5.3 g
Carbohydrates	38.6 g
Fat (Total)	19.3 g
Saturated Fat	16.2 g
Monounsaturated Fat	1.2 g
Polyunsaturated Fat	0.7 g
Dietary Fiber	3.6 g
Sodium	13 mg
Cholesterol	0 mg

EXCELLENT SOURCE OF iron, magnesium and manganese.

GOOD SOURCE OF niacin, phosphorus, zinc and copper.

SOURCE OF thiamine, folate, pantothenic acid and selenium.

CONTAINS a moderate amount of dietary fiber.

Baked Rice with Rosemary-Roasted Tomatoes

This is a great dish for entertaining — it's delicious, impressive and different enough to inspire your guests. Although it's a bit time-consuming, I like to make it on weekdays, too, especially when fresh tomatoes are in season. It's a wonderful accompaniment to grilled fish and meat and a perfect way to finish simple roast chicken. If you're cooking for a crowd, double the quantity. You may even want to serve this as a light main course accompanied by a tossed green salad.

Makes 6 servings

Nutrient Tip
This recipe contains a very high amount of dietary fiber, which comes from three basic sources. The whole wheat bread crumbs and the brown rice each provide 2.3 grams, while the tomatoes provide 1.8 grams.

Nutrients per serving

Calories	326
Protein	6.9 g
Carbohydrates	51.2 g
Fat (Total)	10.7 g
Saturated Fat	3.6 g
Monounsaturated Fat	5.0 g
Polyunsaturated Fat	1.6 g
Dietary Fiber	6.6 g
Sodium	577 mg
Cholesterol	10 mg

EXCELLENT SOURCE OF thiamine, magnesium and manganese.
GOOD SOURCE OF vitamins A and C, niacin, folate, phosphorus and iron.
SOURCE OF vitamin E (alpha-tocopherol), riboflavin, pantothenic acid, zinc, calcium, copper and selenium.
CONTAINS a very high amount of dietary fiber.

- **Preheat oven to 425°F (220°C)**
- **Shallow 8-cup (2 L) baking dish, lightly greased**
- **6-cup (1.5 L) baking dish**

2½ cups	reduced-sodium vegetable or chicken stock or water	625 mL
1¼ cups	short-grain brown rice, rinsed and drained	300 mL
2 tbsp	melted butter, divided	25 mL
5	large tomatoes, cored and thinly sliced	5
2 tbsp	extra virgin olive oil, divided	25 mL
4	cloves garlic, minced	4
1 tbsp	finely chopped fresh rosemary leaves	15 mL
	Salt and freshly ground black pepper	
1 cup	dry whole wheat bread crumbs	250 mL
2 tbsp	finely chopped parsley or chives	25 mL

1. In a large saucepan with a tight-fitting lid over medium–high heat, bring stock to a boil. Add rice and return to a boil. Reduce heat to low. Cover and simmer until rice is tender, about 50 minutes. Spread in prepared 8–cup (2 L) baking dish and brush with 1 tbsp (15 mL) of the melted butter.

2. Meanwhile, place tomatoes in 6-cup (1.5 L) baking dish, overlapping as necessary, and sprinkle with garlic and rosemary. Drizzle with 1 tbsp (15 mL) of the olive oil and season with salt and pepper to taste. Roast in preheated oven for 15 minutes. Turn tomatoes over and drizzle with a bit more oil (about 1½ tsp/7 mL). Roast for 10 minutes more. Remove from oven.

3. In a bowl, combine bread crumbs with remaining 1 tbsp (25 mL) of melted butter and parsley. Set aside.

4. *To assemble:* Preheat broiler. Broil rice until lightly browned and crusty, about 2 minutes. Spread roasted tomatoes evenly over rice. Sprinkle bread crumb mixture evenly over tomatoes. Drizzle with remaining olive oil. Broil until crumbs are lightly browned, about 2 minutes.

Variation
If you prefer, substitute 4 cups (1 L) halved cherry tomatoes for the regular ones.

Currant-Studded Couscous

This version of couscous, enhanced with currants and toasted almonds, is very easy to make. If you're serving a plain main course, such as grilled fish or vegetables, and feel it needs a boost, this will do the trick.

Makes 6 servings

TIPS

The saffron adds a pleasantly bitter note to the couscous, which is particularly nice with poultry or fish.

Add the chile pepper if you like a bit of heat.

To toast almonds, preheat oven to 350°F (180°C). Place sliced nuts on a rimmed baking sheet and bake, stirring occasionally, until golden, about 8 minutes.

1½ cups	Homemade Vegetable Stock with no-salt-added (see recipe, page 75) or reduced-sodium chicken stock	375 mL
¼ tsp	crumbled saffron threads, optional (see Tips, left)	1 mL
1	stick cinnamon, about 2 inches (5 cm) long	1
1	dried red chile pepper, optional (see Tips, left)	1
½ tsp	freshly ground black pepper	2 mL
1 cup	whole wheat, spelt or barley couscous	250 mL
2 tsp	extra virgin olive oil	10 mL
1 tsp	freshly squeezed lemon juice	5 mL
½ cup	currants	125 mL
¼ cup	toasted sliced almonds (see Tips, left)	50 mL

1. In a saucepan over medium heat, bring vegetable stock to a boil. Add saffron, if using, and stir until infused. Add cinnamon stick, chile pepper, if using, and black pepper and return to a boil. Add couscous in a steady stream, stirring constantly. Cover, remove from heat and let stand for 15 minutes. Fluff with a fork and use your hands to break up any clumps.

2. In a small bowl, mix together olive oil and lemon juice. Add to couscous along with currants and almonds. Stir well and serve.

Nutrients per serving

Calories	187
Protein	5.8 g
Carbohydrates	34.9 g
Fat (Total)	4.0 g
Saturated Fat	0.4 g
Monounsaturated Fat	2.3 g
Polyunsaturated Fat	0.6 g
Dietary Fiber	5.2 g
Sodium	1 mg
Cholesterol	0 mg

SOURCE OF vitamin E (alpha-tocopherol), iron, magnesium, manganese and copper.

CONTAINS a high amount of dietary fiber.

Old English Celery and Barley Bake

This dish, which I've adapted from a traditional English recipe, is a great accompaniment to just about anything — from roast poultry and meat to a rich luscious vegetable stew. I make it often because it's a great way to use up the less tender outer stalks of celery, which often linger in the crisper long after the tender heart has been used.

Makes 6 servings

TIP

This recipe was tested using a variety of whole barley that takes about 1 hour to cook on the stovetop. If you're using hull-less barley, which takes 1½ hours or longer to cook, I recommend that you bring the stock plus ½ cup (125 mL) water or additional stock to a boil on top of the stove, add the barley and cook, covered, for about 45 minutes before adding it to the baking dish.

- **Preheat oven to 325°F (160°C)**
- **Shallow 6-cup (1.5 L) baking dish, lightly greased**

1 cup	whole (hulled) barley, rinsed and drained	250 mL
1	bay leaf	1
4	large stalks celery, diced	4
2½ cups	reduced-sodium vegetable or chicken stock or water	625 mL

1. Spread barley evenly over bottom of prepared baking dish. Place bay leaf in the center and arrange celery evenly over top. Add stock and bake in preheated oven until liquid is absorbed and barley is tender, about 1½ hours.

Nutrients per serving

Calories	116
Protein	4.2 g
Carbohydrates	24.2 g
Fat (Total)	0.8 g
Saturated Fat	0.2 g
Monounsaturated Fat	0.1 g
Polyunsaturated Fat	0.4 g
Dietary Fiber	5.9 g
Sodium	39 mg
Cholesterol	0 mg

EXCELLENT SOURCE OF manganese.

GOOD SOURCE OF thiamine and selenium.

SOURCE OF riboflavin, niacin, folate, phosphorus, iron, zinc and copper.

CONTAINS a high amount of dietary fiber.

Wild Rice Stuffing with Cranberries

This stuffing is different enough to satisfy any needs for something exotic, yet traditionally North American in terms of its ingredients. There's enough here to stuff six game hens or an 8- to 10-lb (4 to 5 kg) turkey. Vegans can use it to stuff baked squash or bell peppers.

**Makes about
6 cups (1.5 L)**

TIPS

To toast pecans, preheat oven to 350°F (180°C). Place chopped nuts on a baking sheet and bake, stirring occasionally, until fragrant, about 10 minutes.

If you prefer, rather than using this to stuff poultry, bake it in a greased covered baking dish at 350°F (180°C) for 1 hour.

2 cups	cooked wild rice (see cooking instructions, page 36), cooled	500 mL
1 cup	dry whole wheat bread crumbs	250 mL
6	green onions, white part only, finely chopped	6
2	stalks celery, diced	2
½ cup	dried cranberries	125 mL
½ cup	toasted chopped pecans (see Tips, left)	125 mL
1	jalapeño pepper, seeded and minced, optional	1
1 tbsp	fresh thyme leaves or 1 tsp (5 mL) dried thyme	15 mL
1 tbsp	freshly grated orange zest	15 mL
½ cup	freshly squeezed orange juice	125 mL
2 tbsp	melted butter or extra virgin olive oil	25 mL
	Salt and freshly ground black pepper	

1. In a bowl, combine wild rice, bread crumbs, green onions, celery, cranberries, pecans, jalapeño pepper, if using, thyme and orange zest. Mix well. Add orange juice and melted butter or olive oil and stir well. Season to taste with salt and black pepper.

Nutrients per serving

Calories	136
Protein	3.0 g
Carbohydrates	19.1 g
Fat (Total)	5.9 g
Saturated Fat	1.7 g
Monounsaturated Fat	2.5 g
Polyunsaturated Fat	1.3 g
Dietary Fiber	2.8 g
Sodium	87 mg
Cholesterol	5 mg

GOOD SOURCE OF manganese.

SOURCE OF vitamin C, thiamine, riboflavin, niacin, folate, phosphorus, iron, magnesium, zinc, copper and selenium.

CONTAINS a moderate amount of dietary fiber.

Moroccan-Style Couscous Stuffing

This deliciously different stuffing is wonderful with roast chicken or even whole boned fish. I like to use it to stuff a large capon, which I roast and serve as a splendid Sunday dinner. Vegans can use it as a stuffing for roasted bell peppers or eggplant.

Makes about 4 cups (1 L)

TIPS

If you don't have saffron, substitute 1 tsp (5 mL) turmeric. Add along with the cinnamon.

To toast almonds, preheat oven to 350°F (180°C). Place chopped nuts on a rimmed baking sheet and cook, stirring occasionally, until golden, about 8 minutes.

If you prefer, rather than using the stuffing to stuff a bird, bake at 350°F (180°C) in a greased covered baking dish for 1 hour.

1 cup	reduced-sodium vegetable or chicken stock	250 mL
Pinch	saffron threads, crumbled (see Tips, left)	Pinch
¾ cup	whole wheat couscous	175 mL
⅔ cup	toasted coarsely chopped blanched almonds (see Tips, left)	150 mL
⅔ cup	chopped pitted dates	150 mL
½ cup	dried cherries	125 mL
1 tbsp	freshly grated orange zest, optional	15 mL
1 tsp	ground cinnamon	5 mL
½ tsp	salt	2 mL
½ tsp	freshly ground black pepper	2 mL

1. In a saucepan over medium–high heat, bring stock to a boil. Add saffron and stir until infused. Add couscous in a steady stream, stirring constantly. Cover, remove from heat and let stand for 15 minutes. Fluff with a fork and use your hands to break up any clumps.

2. In a food processor fitted with a metal blade, combine almonds, dates, cherries, orange zest, cinnamon, salt and pepper. Pulse until chopped and integrated. Add to couscous and stir well.

Variations

If you're serving a holiday turkey, double the quantity. If you don't want to entirely break with tradition, substitute dried cranberries for the cherries.

Substitute an equal quantity of spelt or barley couscous for the whole wheat.

Nutrients per serving

Calories	191
Protein	5.2 g
Carbohydrates	34.5 g
Fat (Total)	5.1 g
Saturated Fat	0.4 g
Monounsaturated Fat	3.1 g
Polyunsaturated Fat	1.1 g
Dietary Fiber	5.2 g
Sodium	149 mg
Cholesterol	0 mg

GOOD SOURCE OF vitamin E (alpha-tocopherol) and manganese.

SOURCE OF niacin, calcium, phosphorus, iron, magnesium and copper.

CONTAINS a high amount of dietary fiber.

Basic Polenta and Grits

Polenta, the Italian version of cornmeal mush, is a magnificent way to add whole grains to your diet. When properly cooked, it is a soothing comfort food that functions like a bowl of steaming mashed potatoes, the yummy basis upon which more elaborate dishes can strut their stuff. Many people — and for a long time, I was one of them — aren't keen to make polenta because they think it takes hours of stirring over a hot stove. In fact, even on the stove, you can make great polenta in less than 40 minutes and if, like me, you're inclined to be lazy, you can produce excellent results in a slow cooker or the oven, with virtually no stirring at all. Grits, which are more coarsely ground than cornmeal, are even more delicious if you can find artisanal versions being produced in the southern U.S. They are prepared just like stone-ground cornmeal, but take longer to cook.

Makes about 5 cups (1.25 L) or 6 servings

TIPS

If you prefer, substitute vegetable or chicken stock for the water.

If you're using the oven method, use an ovenproof saucepan to ease cleanup.

4½ cups	water (see Tip, left)	1.125 L
¼ tsp	salt	1 mL
1 cup	coarse stone-ground cornmeal or coarse stone-ground grits	250 mL

1. In a saucepan over medium heat, bring water and salt to a boil. Gradually stir in cornmeal in a steady stream. Cook, stirring constantly, until smooth and blended and mixture bubbles like lava, about 5 minutes.

Stovetop Method

Complete Step 1, above.

2. Reduce heat to low (placing a heat diffuser under the pot if your stove doesn't have a true simmer). Continue cooking, stirring frequently, while the mixture bubbles and thickens, until the grains are tender and creamy, about 30 minutes for polenta; about 1 hour for grits. Serve immediately.

Oven Method

• **Preheat oven to 350°F (180°C)**
• **8-cup (2 L) ovenproof saucepan or baking dish, lightly greased**

Complete Step 1, above.

2. Transfer pot to preheated oven or if you don't have an ovenproof saucepan, transfer mixture to lightly greased baking dish. Bake, covered, until cornmeal is tender and creamy, about 40 minutes for cornmeal and 1 hour for grits.

Variations

Creamy Polenta: Substitute 2½ cups (625 mL) milk or cream and 2 cups (500 mL) water or stock for the liquid, left. If you prefer, stir in 2 tbsp (25 mL) freshly grated Parmesan cheese after the cornmeal has been added to the liquid.

Polenta Squares: To make polenta squares, transfer the hot cooked polenta into a greased baking pan or dish (depending upon the thickness you want), using the back of a spoon to even the top. Set aside to cool (it will solidify during the process) and cut into squares.

Cheesy Baked Grits: Complete Step 1. Remove from heat and stir in 2 cups (500 mL) shredded Cheddar or Jack cheese and 2 beaten eggs. You can also add a finely chopped roasted red pepper or half of a chipotle pepper in adobo sauce, if you prefer. Stir well and transfer to a greased 6-cup (1.5 L) baking dish. Bake at 350°F (180°C) until grits are tender and pudding is set, about 1 hour.

Slow Cooker Methods

There are two ways to make polenta or grits in the slow cooker. You can cook it directly in the slow cooker stoneware, in which case I recommend using a small (maximum 3½ quart) slow cooker, lightly greased. This method produces a soft creamy polenta, which is how my husband likes it. It takes a bit longer to firm up than polenta cooked on the stove or in the oven. If you have a large oval slow cooker, I recommend using a baking dish (see below).

Direct Method

Complete Step 1, left.

2. Transfer mixture to prepared slow cooker stoneware. Cover and cook polenta on Low for 1½ hours. Cover and cook grits on Low for 3 hours, until set.

Baking Dish Method

Complete Step 1, left.

2. Transfer mixture to a lightly greased 6-cup (1.5 L) baking dish. Cover with foil and secure with a string. Place dish in slow cooker stoneware and pour in enough boiling water to come 1 inch (2.5 cm) up the sides of the dish. Cover and cook polenta on Low for 1½ hours. Cover and cook grits on Low for 3 hours.

Grits Tip

Grits are very sticky. Greasing the saucepan or using one with a nonstick finish helps with cleanup.

Nutrients per serving	
Calories	73
Protein	1.4 g
Carbohydrates	15.6 g
Fat (Total)	0.8 g
Saturated Fat	0.1 g
Monounsaturated Fat	0.2 g
Polyunsaturated Fat	0.4 g
Dietary Fiber	2.7 g
Sodium	100 mg
Cholesterol	0 mg

SOURCE OF phosphorus, magnesium and manganese.

CONTAINS a moderate amount of dietary fiber.

Bulgur Pilaf

Bulgur makes a particularly nice pilaf. It has a pleasantly mild flavor that complements just about anything.

Makes 6 servings

TIP
When making this pilaf, use water or a stock that complements the main dish it will accompany.

1 tbsp	olive oil	15 mL
1	onion, finely chopped	1
2	cloves garlic, minced	2
	Salt and freshly ground black pepper	
1 cup	coarse bulgur	250 mL
1 tbsp	tomato paste, optional	15 mL
1½ cups	water or reduced-sodium vegetable, chicken or beef stock (see Tip, left)	375 mL

1. In a saucepan with a tight-fitting lid, heat oil over medium heat for 30 seconds. Add onion and cook, stirring, until softened, about 3 minutes. Add garlic and salt and pepper to taste and cook, stirring, for 1 minute.

2. Add bulgur, tomato paste, if using, and water. Stir well and bring to a boil. Reduce heat to low. Cover and simmer for 10 minutes. Remove from heat. Stir well, cover and let stand until all the liquid is absorbed, about 10 minutes.

Variations

Bulgur Chickpea Pilaf: Stir in 1 cup (250 mL) drained, rinsed cooked or canned chickpeas along with the bulgur.

Beef and Bulgur Pilaf: This can be a light main course. Cook 8 oz (250 g) extra lean ground beef along with onions, until meat is no longer pink, about 5 minutes. Use beef stock for the liquid.

Cabbage and Bulgur Pilaf: This is a great way to use up extra cabbage. Add 1 tsp (5 mL) sweet paprika and 2 cups (500 mL) finely shredded cabbage along with garlic. Cook, stirring, for 1 minute. Then add 1 can (14 oz/398 mL) diced tomatoes with juice. Bring to a boil. Cover and cook for 5 minutes. Continue with Step 2, omitting tomato paste and using only 1 cup (250 mL) of liquid.

Nutrients per serving

Calories	109
Protein	3.1 g
Carbohydrates	19.9 g
Fat (Total)	2.6 g
Saturated Fat	0.4 g
Monounsaturated Fat	1.7 g
Polyunsaturated Fat	0.4 g
Dietary Fiber	2.8 g
Sodium	6 mg
Cholesterol	0 mg

EXCELLENT SOURCE OF manganese.
GOOD SOURCE OF magnesium.
SOURCE OF niacin, phosphorus, iron, zinc and copper.
CONTAINS a moderate amount of dietary fiber.

Whole Wheat Pie Crust

This is a very tender and tasty crust that I enjoy as much as any conventional crust. This quantity makes enough for a single-crust pie. For a two-crust pie, double the quantity.

	Makes 1 single 9- to 10-inch (23 to 25 cm) crust	

TIP

For best results, place the cubed butter in the freezer for a few minutes before using. The crust mixture will be very crumbly. Kneading brings it together.

Nutrient Tip

The nutrient analysis was done using salted butter. I actually prefer to use unsalted butter, which would reduce the sodium content of 1 serving significantly to 149 mg.

1 cup	whole wheat pastry flour	250 mL
½ cup	all-purpose flour	125 mL
½ tsp	salt	2 mL
½ cup	cold butter, cut into 1-inch (2.5 cm) cubes (see Tip, left)	125 mL
¼ cup	whipping (35%) cream	50 mL
1 tsp	cider vinegar	5 mL

1. In a food processor fitted with a metal blade, combine whole wheat and all-purpose flours and salt. Pulse to blend. Add butter and process until mixture resembles rolled oats, about 10 seconds.

2. In a measuring cup, combine whipping cream and vinegar. Add to work bowl and pulse until mixture is barely combined, about 6 times. Transfer to a floured board and knead until smooth and pliable. Roll out and place in pie plate. Refrigerate until you're ready to fill.

Nutrients per serving (1 slice out of 8)

Calories	205
Protein	3.1 g
Carbohydrates	17.1 g
Fat (Total)	14.5 g
Saturated Fat	9.0 g
Monounsaturated Fat	3.8 g
Polyunsaturated Fat	0.7 g
Dietary Fiber	2.1 g
Sodium	229 mg
Cholesterol	40 mg

EXCELLENT SOURCE OF manganese.

GOOD SOURCE OF selenium.

SOURCE OF vitamins A and E (alpha-tocopherol), thiamine, riboflavin, niacin, folate, phosphorus, iron, magnesium and zinc.

CONTAINS a moderate amount of dietary fiber.

Whole-Grain Pizza Dough

Equally tender and even more tasty than pizza crust made with refined flour, this dough is a real winner.

Makes one 10-inch (25 cm) pizza or four 5-inch (12.5 cm) small pizzas

TIP

The amount called for here is about half a package of active dry yeast.

• **Preheat oven and pizza stone, if using, to 400°F (200°C)**

1 tsp	active dry yeast (see Tip, left)	5 mL
½ cup	warm water (105° to 115°F/40° to 46°C)	125 mL
1 cup	whole wheat flour (approx.)	250 mL
½ cup	whole barley flour (approx.)	125 mL
½ tsp	granulated sugar	2 mL
½ tsp	salt	2 mL
1 tbsp	olive oil (approx.)	15 mL

1. In a glass measure, sprinkle yeast over water. Set aside.
2. In a large bowl, combine whole wheat and barley flours, sugar and salt. Make a well in the center and add olive oil and reserved yeast mixture. Mix until a stiff dough forms. (If dough is too sticky, add more barley flour, 1 tbsp/15 mL at a time, until stiff.) Turn out onto a floured work surface and knead until smooth and elastic, about 8 minutes. Shape into a smooth ball. Lightly coat the inside of a bowl with olive oil, place the dough in the bowl and roll until lightly coated with oil. Cover with plastic wrap and let rise in a warm spot until doubled in size, 1 to 1½ hours.
3. Punch down the dough, form into a ball and place on a lightly floured surface. Roll out to form a 10-inch (25 cm) circle and use your fingers to make a rim. Transfer to a baking sheet or pizza stone. Pierce all over with a fork. Add toppings of your choice and bake in preheated oven until crust is brown (and toppings are to your taste), about 20 minutes.

Nutrients per serving (1 of 6 slices)

Calories	138
Protein	4.4 g
Carbohydrates	25.3 g
Fat (Total)	2.9 g
Saturated Fat	0.4 g
Monounsaturated Fat	1.7 g
Polyunsaturated Fat	0.5 g
Dietary Fiber	3.9 g
Sodium	193 mg
Cholesterol	0 mg

EXCELLENT SOURCE OF manganese and selenium.

GOOD SOURCE OF magnesium.

SOURCE OF vitamin E (alpha-tocopherol), thiamine, riboflavin, niacin, folate, phosphorus, iron, zinc and copper.

CONTAINS a moderate amount of dietary fiber.

Gluten-Free Pizza Crust

Thanks to Donna Washburn and Heather Butt for allowing me to use this recipe from the Complete Gluten-Free Cookbook. Add your favorite toppings and enjoy.

Makes 6 pieces, each 5 inches (12.5 cm) square

TIPS

Partially baked pizza dough can be wrapped airtight and frozen for up to 4 weeks. Thaw in the refrigerator overnight before using to make pizza.

Xanthan gum, which is made from corn syrup and used as a thickener, is available in natural foods stores.

Nutrients per serving (1 of 6 slices)

Calories	157
Protein	3.1 g
Carbohydrates	29.0 g
Fat (Total)	3.2 g
Saturated Fat	0.4 g
Monounsaturated Fat	1.9 g
Polyunsaturated Fat	0.5 g
Dietary Fiber	2.2 g
Sodium	304 mg
Cholesterol	0 mg

GOOD SOURCE OF folate.

SOURCE OF thiamine, riboflavin, niacin, pantothenic acid, phosphorus, iron, magnesium, manganese, zinc and copper.

CONTAINS a moderate amount of dietary fiber.

- **Preheat oven to 400°F (200°C)**
- **15-by 10-inch (40 by 25 cm) jelly-roll pan, lightly greased**

⅔ cup	sorghum flour	150 mL
½ cup	quinoa flour	125 mL
⅓ cup	potato starch	75 mL
¼ cup	tapioca starch	50 mL
1 tsp	granulated sugar	5 mL
1 tsp	xanthan gum	5 mL
1 tbsp	quick-rising (instant) yeast	15 mL
¾ tsp	salt	4 mL
1¼ cups	water	300 mL
1 tbsp	olive oil	15 mL
1 tsp	cider vinegar	5 mL

1. In a large bowl, combine sorghum and quinoa flours, potato starch, tapioca starch, sugar, xanthan gum, yeast and salt. Mix well and set aside.

2. In a separate bowl, using a heavy-duty electric mixer with paddle attachment, combine water, olive oil and vinegar until well blended. With mixer on lowest speed, slowly add dry ingredients until combined. Stop machine and scrape bottom and sides of bowl with a rubber spatula. With mixer on medium speed, beat for 4 minutes.

3. Gently transfer the dough to prepared pan and spread evenly to the edges. Do not smooth top. Bake in preheated oven until bottom is golden and crust is partially baked, for 12 minutes. Add your favorite toppings and continue baking until golden, about 25 minutes.

Variations

Add 1 to 2 tsp (5 to 10 mL) dried or 1 to 2 tbsp (15 to 25 mL) chopped fresh rosemary, oregano, basil or thyme to the dry ingredients.

To make individual pizzas, divide dough into 4 equal portions and pat into 6-inch (15 cm) diameter circles. Bake on greased baking sheets for 10 to 12 minutes before adding toppings. After adding toppings, bake for an additional 10 to 12 minutes.

Whole-Grain Olive Oil Crust

This recipe makes a crust that is surprisingly tender. Use it as you would a regular crust.

Makes two 8- to 9-inch (20 to 23 cm) crusts

TIP

If you're watching your intake of saturated fat, making a pie crust with olive oil is a great option.

1 cup	whole barley flour	250 mL
1 cup	whole wheat flour	250 mL
1 tsp	salt	5 mL
½ cup	olive oil	125 mL
⅓ cup	cold water	75 mL

1. In a bowl, combine barley and whole wheat flours and salt. Stir to combine and make a well in the center. In a measuring cup, combine olive oil and water. Pour into well and, using a fork, mix rapidly until a ragged dough forms.

2. Divide dough into 2 balls and, using your hand, flatten slightly. Place one portion between 2 sheets of waxed paper and place on a lightly moistened surface. (This prevents the paper from slipping.) Roll out to a uniform thickness, place in pie plate and refrigerate until you're ready to fill. Repeat for top crust.

Nutrients per serving (1 of 8 servings)

Calories	234
Protein	4.0 g
Carbohydrates	24.7 g
Fat (Total)	14.1 g
Saturated Fat	1.9 g
Monounsaturated Fat	10.0 g
Polyunsaturated Fat	1.6 g
Dietary Fiber	3.7 g
Sodium	289 mg
Cholesterol	0 mg

EXCELLENT SOURCE OF manganese and selenium.

GOOD SOURCE OF vitamin E (alpha-tocopherol) and magnesium.

SOURCE OF thiamine, niacin, phosphorus, iron, zinc and copper.

CONTAINS a moderate amount of dietary fiber.

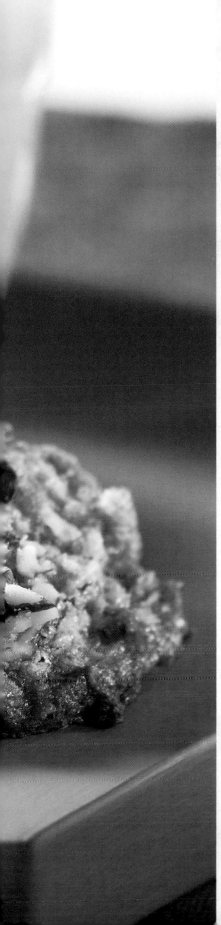

Desserts

Chewy Oatmeal Coconut Cookies with Cranberries and Pecans

Chewy Oatmeal Coconut Cookies with Cranberries and Pecans

The luscious cookies are appealingly chewy with just a hint of honey flavor. Once you've had one, it's hard to resist another.

Makes about 48 cookies

TIP
These cookies are a bit soft when they come out of the oven, but they firm up while cooling. Just make sure they are just golden while baking — they continue to cook on the sheet after removal from the oven.

- **Preheat oven to 350°F (180°C)**
- **Baking sheets, lightly greased or lined with parchment**

¾ cup	whole wheat pastry flour	175 mL
¾ cup	whole barley flour	175 mL
1 tsp	baking powder	5 mL
½ tsp	salt	2 mL
1 cup	butter, softened	250 mL
1 cup	packed Demerara or other raw cane sugar	250 mL
1	egg	1
1 tsp	vanilla extract	5 mL
½ cup	liquid honey	125 mL
2 cups	old-fashioned (large flake) rolled oats	500 mL
1 cup	sweetened flaked coconut	250 mL
½ cup	dried cranberries	125 mL
½ cup	chopped pecans	125 mL

1. In a bowl, combine whole wheat and barley flours, baking powder and salt.

2. In a separate bowl, beat butter and sugar until light and creamy. Add egg, vanilla and honey, beating and scraping down the sides of the bowl until blended. Gradually add flour mixture, beating until smooth. Stir in oats, coconut, cranberries and pecans.

3. Drop dough by tablespoonfuls (15 mL), about 2 inches (5 cm) apart, on prepared baking sheet. Bake in preheated oven until golden, about 12 minutes. Let cool for 5 minutes on sheets, then transfer to a wire rack and let cool completely.

Variations

If you don't like nuts, eliminate the pecans and double the quantity of cranberries. Similarly, if you don't like cranberries, leave them out and double the amount of pecans.

Nutrients per serving (1 cookie)

Calories	112
Protein	1.4 g
Carbohydrates	15.1 g
Fat (Total)	5.6 g
Saturated Fat	3.1 g
Monounsaturated Fat	1.6 g
Polyunsaturated Fat	0.6 g
Dietary Fiber	1.1 g
Sodium	65 mg
Cholesterol	14 mg

GOOD SOURCE OF manganese.
SOURCE OF magnesium and selenium.

Pretty Traditional Rice Pudding

This is a classic rice pudding, made with more-nutritious brown rice instead of white. If you want to deviate a bit more from tradition, try soaking the raisins in a bit of rum, or substituting them with dried cherries or cranberries (see Variations, below). Whenever I make this, I'm usually in the mood for indulging and finish the dish with a bit of pouring cream.

Makes 6 servings

TIP

If you don't have a shallow dish, you can make this in a deep baking dish or a soufflé dish of the same volume. It will take longer to cook, about 1 hour and 10 minutes, depending upon the dimensions of your dish.

- **Preheat oven to 325°F (160°C)**
- **Shallow 6-cup (1.5 L) baking dish, greased (see Tip, left)**

2 cups	cooked brown rice, cooled (see cooking instructions, page 29)	500 mL
3 cups	2% milk	750 mL
½ cup	granulated sugar	125 mL
3	eggs	3
2 tsp	finely grated lemon zest	10 mL
2 tsp	vanilla extract	10 mL
½ cup	raisins	125 mL

CINNAMON-SUGAR TOPPING

1 tbsp + 2 tsp	granulated sugar	25 mL
1 tsp	ground cinnamon	5 mL
	Table (18%) cream, optional	

1. In a large bowl, whisk together milk, sugar, eggs, lemon zest and vanilla. Add rice and raisins and mix well. Transfer to prepared baking dish.

2. *Cinnamon-Sugar Topping:* In a small bowl, combine sugar and cinnamon and mix well. Sprinkle evenly over rice mixture.

3. Bake, uncovered, in preheated oven just until set, about 35 minutes. Serve warm or chill thoroughly. Accompany with cream, if desired.

Variations

Soak raisins in 2 tbsp (25 mL) dark rum for 10 minutes.

Substitute an equal quantity of dried cherries or cranberries for the raisins. If using cranberries, substitute an equal quantity of orange zest for the lemon.

Nutrients per serving

Calories	286
Protein	9.2 g
Carbohydrates	51.1 g
Fat (Total)	5.5 g
Saturated Fat	2.3 g
Monounsaturated Fat	1.9 g
Polyunsaturated Fat	0.7 g
Dietary Fiber	1.7 g
Sodium	85 mg
Cholesterol	103 mg

EXCELLENT SOURCE OF manganese and selenium.

GOOD SOURCE OF phosphorus, calcium, magnesium and riboflavin.

SOURCE OF vitamins A and E (alpha-tocopherol), thiamine, niacin, folate, pantothenic acid, iron, zinc and copper.

Oatmeal Shortbread Squares

These crisp cookies make a great accompaniment to fresh berries or, with a glass of cold milk, a refreshing snack. They are rich and delicious. One will certainly be enough.

Makes 25 cookies

TIP

Store shortbread at room temperature in an airtight container, between layers of waxed paper, for up to 1 week.

- **Preheat oven to 350°F (180°C)**
- **9-inch (2.5 L) square cake pan, ungreased**

2 cups	old-fashioned (large flake) rolled oats	500 mL
½ cup	all-purpose flour	125 mL
½ cup	whole wheat flour	125 mL
¾ cup	packed Demerara or other raw cane sugar	175 mL
½ tsp	baking soda	2 mL
½ tsp	salt	2 mL
1 cup	cold butter, cubed	250 mL
1 tsp	vanilla extract	5 mL

1. In a food processor, combine oats, all-purpose and whole wheat flours, sugar, baking soda and salt. Process for 30 seconds to blend and grind sugar. Add butter and process until mixture resembles coarse crumbs. Sprinkle vanilla over top and pulse until blended. Using your hands, knead to form a smooth dough.

2. Press dough evenly into pan and bake in preheated oven until edges begin to brown, about 25 minutes. Place pan on a wire rack. Using a serrated knife, score the top to form 25 squares. Let cool completely in pan on rack. Recut and remove squares from pan.

Nutrients per serving (1 cookie)

Calories	136
Protein	1.8 g
Carbohydrates	15.2 g
Fat (Total)	7.9 g
Saturated Fat	4.8 g
Monounsaturated Fat	2.1 g
Polyunsaturated Fat	0.5 g
Dietary Fiber	1.0 g
Sodium	127 mg
Cholesterol	20 mg

GOOD SOURCE OF manganese.
SOURCE OF vitamin A, thiamine, phosphorus, iron, magnesium and selenium.

Gingery Shortbread

I love the gingery flavor and crumbly texture of this shortbread. It's delicious with a cup of tea, as a complement to fresh berries, or anytime a cookie will do.

Makes about 24 cookies

TIP

Store shortbread at room temperature in an airtight container, between layers of waxed paper, for up to 1 week.

- **Preheat oven to 325°F (160°C)**
- **Baking sheets, ungreased**

1 cup	brown rice flour	250 mL
½ cup	whole barley flour	125 mL
½ cup	all-purpose flour	125 mL
½ cup	packed Demerara or other raw cane sugar	125 mL
1 tsp	ground ginger	5 mL
¼ tsp	baking powder	1 mL
¼ tsp	salt	1 mL
1 cup	cold butter, cubed	250 mL
⅓ cup	chopped crystallized ginger	75 mL
1 tsp	vanilla extract	5 mL

1. In a food processor, combine brown rice flour, barley and all-purpose flours, sugar, ground ginger, baking powder and salt. Process for 30 seconds to blend and grind sugar.

2. Add butter and process until integrated. Add crystallized ginger and vanilla and process until crumbly. Roll into 2 logs, each about 6 inches (15 cm) long. Wrap in plastic wrap and refrigerate until firm enough to slice, about 30 minutes.

3. Slice into cookies about ¼ inch (0.5 cm) thick and place on baking sheets. Bake in preheated oven until edges are golden, about 20 minutes. Let cool on sheet on a wire rack, then transfer to rack to cool completely.

Nutrients per serving (1 cookie)

Calories	139
Protein	1.2 g
Carbohydrates	16.4 g
Fat (Total)	7.9 g
Saturated Fat	4.9 g
Monounsaturated Fat	2.1 g
Polyunsaturated Fat	0.4 g
Dietary Fiber	0.7 g
Sodium	86 mg
Cholesterol	20 mg

GOOD SOURCE OF manganese.
SOURCE OF vitamin A, thiamine, niacin, iron and magnesium.

Barley Pudding with Cherries and Almonds

Chilled leftovers of this soothing dessert are rapidly becoming my favorite afternoon snack. It's equally good warm — the mild taste, pleasing combination of flavors and tiny bit of nutty crunch ensure it is destined to become a comfort food classic.

Makes 8 servings

TIP

I like to use whole unblanched almonds in this recipe, which I chop in a food processor, but some specialty stores sell chopped unblanched almonds. To toast chopped almonds, spread them on a rimmed baking sheet and place in a preheated 350°F (180°C) oven and toast, stirring often, until they begin to brown, about 6 minutes.

Nutrients per serving

Calories	234
Protein	6.8 g
Carbohydrates	35.9 g
Fat (Total)	7.9 g
Saturated Fat	2.6 g
Monounsaturated Fat	3.5 g
Polyunsaturated Fat	1.2 g
Dietary Fiber	3.9 g
Sodium	50 mg
Cholesterol	58 mg

EXCELLENT SOURCE OF manganese.

GOOD SOURCE OF vitamin E (alpha-tocopherol), zinc and selenium.

SOURCE OF vitamin A, thiamine, riboflavin, niacin, folate, pantothenic acid, calcium, phosphorus, iron, magnesium and copper.

CONTAINS a moderate amount of dietary fiber.

- **Preheat oven to 350°F (180°C)**
- **Shallow 6-cup (1.5 L) baking dish, greased**

2 cups	cooked whole barley, cooled (see cooking instructions, page 16)	500 mL
½ cup	finely chopped almonds, toasted, divided (see Tip, left)	125 mL
1½ cups	1% milk	375 mL
½ cup	pure maple syrup	125 mL
2 tsp	almond extract	10 mL
Pinch	salt	Pinch
2	eggs, beaten	2
½ cup	dried cherries	125 mL
¼ cup	whipping (35%) cream	50 mL

CINNAMON-BROWN SUGAR TOPPING, OPTIONAL

2 tbsp	packed Demerara sugar or other raw cane sugar	25 mL
1 tsp	ground cinnamon	5 mL

1. Sprinkle bottom and sides of prepared baking dish with half the almonds. (The finer ones will stick to the sides, the others will collect on the bottom, which is okay.) Set aside.

2. In a bowl, combine milk, maple syrup, almond extract, salt and eggs. Mix well. Stir in barley and cherries. Turn into prepared pan. Drizzle whipping cream evenly over top.

3. *Cinnamon-Brown Sugar Topping:* In a small bowl, combine sugar and cinnamon and mix well. Sprinkle pudding with remaining almonds and cinnamon–brown sugar, if using. Bake in preheated oven until set, about 35 minutes. Serve warm or chilled.

Variation

Wheat Berry Pudding with Apricots and Almonds: Substitute an equal quantity of cooked wheat berries (see cooking instructions, page 34) for the barley and an equal quantity of chopped dried apricots for the cherries.

Amaretto-Spiked Quinoa Pudding with Cherries

This pudding is so deliciously decadent it's almost impossible to believe it is loaded with whole-grain goodness. Enjoy every succulent mouthful.

Makes 8 servings

TIPS

If you prefer, substitute an equal quantity of plain almond milk for the regular milk.

If you don't have almond liqueur, substitute an additional ½ tsp (2 mL) almond extract plus 2 tbsp (25 mL) water.

Nutrients per serving

Calories	327
Protein	9.9 g
Carbohydrates	55.7 g
Fat (Total)	7.7 g
Saturated Fat	3.4 g
Monounsaturated Fat	2.5 g
Polyunsaturated Fat	1.0 g
Dietary Fiber	2.5 g
Sodium	97 mg
Cholesterol	87 mg

EXCELLENT SOURCE OF manganese.

GOOD SOURCE OF riboflavin, magnesium, selenium, calcium, phosphorus and iron.

SOURCE OF vitamins A and C, thiamine, niacin, folate, pantothenic acid, copper and zinc.

CONTAINS a moderate amount of dietary fiber.

- **Preheat oven to 350°F (180°C)**
- **6-cup (1.5 L) baking dish, greased**

1½ cups	water	375 mL
1 tbsp	finely grated orange zest	15 mL
½ cup	freshly squeezed orange juice	125 mL
1 cup	quinoa, rinsed and drained	250 mL
1	can (14 oz/396 g OR 300 mL) sweetened condensed milk	1
¾ cup	dried cherries	175 mL
½ cup	milk or half-and-half (10%) cream (see Tips, left)	125 mL
2 tbsp	almond-flavored liqueur, such as Amaretto (see Tips, left)	25 mL
1 tsp	almond extract	5 mL
½ tsp	ground cinnamon	2 mL
3	eggs, beaten	3

1. In a saucepan over medium-high heat, bring water, orange zest and juice to a boil. Add quinoa in a steady stream, stirring to prevent lumps from forming, and return to a boil. Reduce heat to low. Cover and simmer until tender and liquid is absorbed, about 15 minutes. Remove from heat and let stand for 5 minutes. Fluff with a fork and let cool slightly.

2. Add condensed milk, cherries, milk, almond liqueur, almond extract, cinnamon and eggs and mix well. Transfer to prepared dish. Bake in preheated oven until set, about 45 minutes. Serve warm.

Black Sticky Rice Pudding

Years ago, when my husband, daughter and I traveled in Thailand, we became addicted to mangoes and sticky rice, a truly delicious sweet. After our return, we tried but could never duplicate the superb taste and texture of the authentic version. Although this black sticky rice pudding is a different dish, it reminds me of that delightful concoction. In fact, it's so good you don't even need the fruit. Although it's high in saturated fat, it comes from the coconut milk, which may have healthful benefits.

Makes 6 servings

TIPS

Thai black sticky rice is available in Asian markets. To cook black sticky rice, see page 93.

I like to make this pudding using piloncillo, unrefined Mexican sugar, which is sold in cones in Latin markets. Use a 4-oz (125 g) cone in this recipe.

2 cups	cooked Thai black sticky rice (see Tips, left)	500 mL
1	can (14 oz/400 mL) coconut milk	1
½ cup	packed Demerara or other raw cane sugar (see Tips, left)	125 mL
½ tsp	salt	2 mL
1 cup	sliced strawberries or kiwifruit or chopped peaches or mango	250 mL
¼ cup	toasted shredded sweetened coconut Finely chopped mint, optional	50 mL

1. In a saucepan, combine coconut milk, brown sugar and salt. Bring to a boil over medium heat and cook, stirring, until sugar dissolves. Stir in rice and cook, stirring, until thickened, about 10 minutes. Transfer to a serving bowl and chill, if desired.

2. When you're ready to serve, top with fruit and garnish with coconut and mint, if using.

Nutrients per serving

Calories	305
Protein	3.3 g
Carbohydrates	41.4 g
Fat (Total)	15.4 g
Saturated Fat	13.2 g
Monounsaturated Fat	0.6 g
Polyunsaturated Fat	0.2 g
Dietary Fiber	1.0 g
Sodium	221 mg
Cholesterol	0 mg

EXCELLENT SOURCE OF manganese.

GOOD SOURCE OF iron and magnesium.

SOURCE OF vitamin C, thiamine, niacin, folate, phosphorus, zinc, copper and selenium.

Deep-Dish Apple Pie with Streusel Topping

Here's a luscious fruit pie, bursting with old-fashioned goodness. Make this in the autumn, when apples are plentiful and in season. Although it's relatively high in fat, it also contains a high amount of fiber. Treat it as an occasional indulgence.

Makes 8 servings

TIPS

When buying Demerara sugar, check the label to make sure you are getting pure raw cane sugar. Some brands are just refined sugar in disguise.

I like as much fruit as possible in pies. When raw, this quantity of apples will extend beyond the height of the pie plate. Don't worry. They will reduce on baking.

Nutrients per serving

Calories	474
Protein	5.3 g
Carbohydrates	65.7 g
Fat (Total)	23.3 g
Saturated Fat	13 g
Monounsaturated Fat	6.8 g
Polyunsaturated Fat	1.9 g
Dietary Fiber	5.0 g
Sodium	282 mg
Cholesterol	55 mg

EXCELLENT SOURCE OF manganese and selenium.
GOOD SOURCE OF vitamin A, thiamine, iron and magnesium.
SOURCE OF vitamins C and E (alpha-tocopherol), calcium, phosphorus, riboflavin, niacin, folate, pantothenic acid, zinc and copper.
CONTAINS a high amount of dietary fiber.

- **Preheat oven to 425°F (220°C)**
- **10-inch (25 cm) deep-dish pie plate**

1	recipe Whole Wheat Pie Crust (see page 245)	1
STREUSEL TOPPING		
½ cup	old-fashioned (large flake) rolled oats	125 mL
½ cup	packed Demerara or other raw cane sugar (see Tips, left)	125 mL
2 tbsp	whole wheat flour	25 mL
Pinch	salt	Pinch
¼ cup	butter, softened	50 mL
¼ cup	chopped pecans	50 mL
FILLING		
8 cups	sliced peeled apples (about 10 medium)	2 L
1 tsp	finely grated lemon zest	5 mL
2 tbsp	freshly squeezed lemon juice	25 mL
½ cup	packed Demerara sugar or other raw cane sugar	125 mL
2 tbsp	whole wheat flour	25 mL
1 tsp	ground cinnamon	5 mL
Pinch	salt	Pinch

1. *Streusel Topping:* In a bowl, combine oats, sugar, flour and salt. Mix well. Using a pastry blender or your fingers, work in butter until mixture resembles coarse crumbs. Stir in pecans. Set aside.

2. *Filling:* In a bowl, combine apples, lemon zest and juice, sugar, flour, cinnamon and salt. Toss until combined. Place in chilled pie shell and bake in preheated oven for 10 minutes. (Place filled pie on a baking sheet to capture any spillage.) Sprinkle Streusel Topping evenly over apples. Reduce heat to 350°F (180°C) and bake until apples are tender and bubbling and pastry is slightly browned, about 1 hour. (Check the pie about halfway through baking and every 10 minutes or so after that. If the crust and top are becoming too brown, cover loosely with foil.)

Brown Bread Ice Cream

Thanks to my dear friend, Marilyn Linton, for allowing me to use this mouthwatering recipe, which appeared in her terrific book, 125 Best Ice Cream Recipes. I view this as a splurge — something to treat yourself to now and again. However, I did increase the quantity of whole wheat bread crumbs so you don't have to feel too guilty about licking the bowl (which I'm certain you'll do).

Makes 8 servings

TIP

You can use 2% milk in this recipe knowing that it tastes just as good as the full-fat version.

* **Ice cream maker**

4	egg yolks	4
⅓ cup	granulated sugar	75 mL
1½ cups	2% milk (see Tip, left)	375 mL
1 cup	whipping (35%) cream	250 mL
1 tsp	finely grated lemon zest	5 mL
1 tsp	vanilla extract	5 mL
3 tbsp	unsalted butter	45 mL
2½ cups	fresh whole wheat bread crumbs (see Tips, page 206)	625 mL
½ cup	packed Demerara or other raw cane sugar	125 mL

1. In a bowl, whisk egg yolks with granulated sugar until thickened and pale yellow. Set aside.

2. In a saucepan over medium-low heat, bring milk and cream to a simmer. Gradually whisk into egg mixture.

3. Return entire mixture to the saucepan. Cook over low heat, stirring constantly, until mixture is thick enough to coat the back of a wooden spoon. Be careful not to let it boil. Strain into a clean large bowl. Let cool to room temperature.

4. Stir in lemon zest and vanilla. Cover and refrigerate until completely cold or overnight.

5. Meanwhile, in another saucepan over medium heat, melt butter. Add bread crumbs and Demerara sugar. Cook, stirring, until golden brown and bread crumbs are evenly coated, 4 to 5 minutes. Set aside.

6. Transfer chilled cream mixture to an ice cream maker and freeze according to manufacturer's instructions. Add bread crumb mixture during the last 5 minutes of freezing and let machine stir it in. Transfer to a freezerproof container and store in the main part of your freezer, not on the door.

Nutrients per serving

Calories	308
Protein	5.0 g
Carbohydrates	31.2 g
Fat (Total)	18.9 g
Saturated Fat	10.7 g
Monounsaturated Fat	5.8 g
Polyunsaturated Fat	1.1 g
Dietary Fiber	0.9 g
Sodium	112 mg
Cholesterol	155 mg

GOOD SOURCE OF vitamin A, manganese and selenium.

SOURCE OF vitamin E (alpha-tocopherol), thiamine, riboflavin, niacin, folate, pantothenic acid, calcium, phosphorus, iron, magnesium, zinc and copper.

Blueberry and Wild Rice Pudding

This delicious pudding exemplifies the theory that foods that grow together taste good in combination. Although blueberries grow on land and wild rice is the seed of an aquatic grass, are found in the same geographic regions. Remarkably light, slightly sweet and a little bit crunchy, this pudding is comfort food for the new millennia.

Makes 8 servings

Nutrient Tip

Dried blueberries are available in natural food stores. They add concentrated blueberry flavor to dishes and offer the same nutritious profile as their fresh counterparts. Blueberries are particularly high in antioxidants, signaled by their deep dark color. In one laboratory test, USDA researchers found that blueberry consumption improved the learning ability of mice and slowed age-related memory loss.

- **Preheat oven to 325°F (160°C)**
- **Shallow 6-cup (1.5 L) baking dish, greased**

2 cups	cooked wild rice, cooled (see cooking instructions, page 36)	500 mL
½ cup	dried blueberries	125 mL
3 cups	2% milk	750 mL
½ cup	packed Demerara or other raw cane sugar	125 mL
3	eggs	3
1 tbsp	finely grated lemon zest	15 mL
1 tsp	vanilla extract	5 mL
½ tsp	freshly grated nutmeg	2 mL
	Maple syrup, optional	

1. In prepared baking dish, combine wild rice and blueberries.
2. In a saucepan over medium heat, heat milk and sugar, just until bubbles appear around the edges, stirring occasionally to dissolve the sugar. Remove from heat.
3. In a bowl, beat together eggs, lemon zest, vanilla and nutmeg. Add a bit of the milk mixture and stir well. Add to saucepan and mix well. Pour over rice mixture and carefully stir to blend. Bake in preheated oven until top is set and edges just begin to brown, about 1 hour. Serve warm with a drizzle of maple syrup, if using.

Variation

Cranberry and Wild Rice Pudding: Substitute an equal quantity of dried cranberries for the dried blueberries and 1 tbsp (15 mL) grated orange zest for the lemon.

Nutrients per serving

Calories	186
Protein	7.1 g
Carbohydrates	31.9 g
Fat (Total)	3.9 g
Saturated Fat	1.7 g
Monounsaturated Fat	1.3 g
Polyunsaturated Fat	0.5 g
Dietary Fiber	1.7 g
Sodium	68 mg
Cholesterol	77 mg

GOOD SOURCE OF riboflavin and selenium.

SOURCE OF vitamin A, niacin, folate, pantothenic acid, calcium, phosphorus, iron, magnesium, manganese, zinc and copper.

Middle Eastern Bulgur Pudding with Almonds and Dates

Depending upon the source, this pudding is Jewish, Egyptian or Syrian. Two things for sure — its origins are Mediterranean and it's a light and delicious dessert. It is also surprisingly easy to make.

Makes 8 servings

TIP

When buying nuts be sure to source them from a purveyor with high turnover. Because nuts are very high in unsaturated fats, they tend to become rancid very quickly. This is especially true of walnuts. In my experience, the vast percentage of walnuts sold in supermarkets have already passed their peak. Taste before you buy.

1 cup	bulgur	250 mL
1¼ cups	ice water	300 mL
1 cup	2% milk or almond or soy milk	250 mL
½ cup	liquid honey	125 mL
2 tsp	finely grated lemon zest	10 mL
1 tsp	ground cinnamon	5 mL
Pinch	salt	Pinch
1 cup	toasted chopped almonds or walnuts (see Tip, left and page 256)	250 mL
1 cup	chopped Medjool dates	250 mL
	Pomegranate seeds, optional	

1. In a bowl, combine bulgur and cold water. Stir well and set aside until liquid is absorbed, about 10 minutes.

2. Meanwhile, in a saucepan, combine milk, honey, lemon zest, cinnamon and salt. Heat over medium heat until honey is dissolved and bubbles form around the edge of the mixture. Add to bulgur and stir well. Stir in almonds and dates. Serve warm or chilled sprinkled with pomegranate seeds, if using.

Nutrients per serving

Calories	280
Protein	6.5 g
Carbohydrates	51.8 g
Fat (Total)	7.7 g
Saturated Fat	0.9 g
Monounsaturated Fat	4.5 g
Polyunsaturated Fat	1.8 g
Dietary Fiber	5.2 g
Sodium	18 mg
Cholesterol	2 mg

EXCELLENT SOURCE OF magnesium and manganese.

GOOD SOURCE OF vitamin E (alpha-tocopherol), phosphorus and copper.

SOURCE OF thiamine, riboflavin, niacin, folate, pantothenic acid, calcium, iron and zinc.

CONTAINS a high amount of dietary fiber.

Tunisian Couscous Cake

This "cake," which I adapted from a recipe in Claudia Roden's The Book of Jewish Food, is a pleasing combination of texture and flavors that is oddly addictive. Once I start eating it, I have trouble putting down my spoon. For dessert, I serve it with pouring cream. I thoroughly enjoy leftovers for breakfast, chilled, and with milk.

Makes 8 servings

TIP

If you use a large saucepan, it will be cool enough after standing to act as a mixing bowl. Add the remaining ingredients to the pot and, using your hands, mix them into the couscous, being sure to scrape up the bits that will be stuck to the bottom.

- **Preheat oven to 350°F (180°C)**
- **8-inch (2 L) square cake pan, lightly greased**

1½ cups	water	375 mL
½ cup	packed Demerara or other raw cane sugar	125 mL
2 tsp	finely grated orange zest	10 mL
¼ cup	freshly squeezed orange juice	50 mL
½ tsp	ground cinnamon	2 mL
1½ cups	whole wheat couscous	375 mL
½ cup	chopped pitted Medjool dates	125 mL
½ cup	chopped pitted dried apricots	125 mL
½ cup	dried cherries	125 mL
½ cup	toasted chopped walnuts	125 mL
½ cup	toasted sliced almonds (see Tips, page 237)	125 mL
	Confectioner's (icing) sugar, optional	
	Table (18%) cream or non-dairy alternative	

1. In a large saucepan with a tight-fitting lid, bring water, sugar, orange zest and juice and cinnamon to a boil. Gradually add couscous, stirring well. Remove from heat, cover and let stand for at least 15 minutes. Fluff up with a fork, and break up, using your fingers.

2. Add dates, apricots, cherries, walnuts and almonds and, using your hands, mix well. Transfer to prepared cake pan and press down with your fingers. Cover tightly with foil and bake in preheated oven until heated through, about 20 minutes. Turn out onto a serving plate and dust with confectioner's sugar, if using. Serve warm or chilled. Pass the cream at the table.

Nutrients per serving

Calories	352
Protein	8.3 g
Carbohydrates	65.8 g
Fat (Total)	8.6 g
Saturated Fat	0.7 g
Monounsaturated Fat	2.7 g
Polyunsaturated Fat	4.2 g
Dietary Fiber	7.6 g
Sodium	12 mg
Cholesterol	0 mg

EXCELLENT SOURCE OF manganese.

GOOD SOURCE OF vitamin E (alpha-tocopherol), iron, magnesium and copper.

SOURCE OF vitamins A and C, niacin, folate, calcium phosphorus and zinc.

CONTAINS a very high amount of dietary fiber.

Coconut Pecan Blondies

Made with whole-grain flours and raw cane sugar, this updated classic is every bit as good as the original and even provides a moderate amount of dietary fiber. Serve warm for dessert, with a dollop of ice cream if you feel like a splurge, and keep any leftovers on hand for delicious snacks or afternoon tea.

Makes 16 squares

TIP
Sweetened shredded coconut is more readily available, but unsweetened coconut works just as well in this and other recipes.

- **Preheat oven to 350°F (180°C)**
- **8-inch (2 L) square cake pan, greased**

¾ cup	whole wheat flour	175 mL
¾ cup	whole barley flour	175 mL
1 tsp	baking powder	5 mL
½ tsp	salt	2 mL
1 cup	packed Demerara or other raw cane sugar	250 mL
½ cup	butter, softened	125 mL
2	eggs	2
1 tsp	vanilla extract	5 mL
¾ cup	chopped pecans	175 mL
¾ cup	sweetened shredded coconut (see Tip, left)	175 mL

1. In a bowl, combine whole wheat and barley flours and baking powder and salt.

2. In another bowl, beat sugar and butter until smooth and creamy. Add eggs, one at a time, beating after each addition. Beat in vanilla. Add flour mixture and mix until blended. Stir in pecans and coconut.

3. Spread evenly in prepared pan. Bake in preheated oven just until the edges begin to pull away from the pan, about 30 minutes. Remove from oven, run a knife around the edge and let cool completely in pan on a wire rack. Cut into squares.

Nutrients per serving (1 cookie)

Calories	212
Protein	2.9 g
Carbohydrates	25.6 g
Fat (Total)	11.8 g
Saturated Fat	5.6 g
Monounsaturated Fat	3.9 g
Polyunsaturated Fat	1.5 g
Dietary Fiber	2.1 g
Sodium	156 mg
Cholesterol	39 mg

EXCELLENT SOURCE OF manganese.

GOOD SOURCE OF selenium

SOURCE OF vitamins A and E (alpha-tocopherol), thiamine, niacin, phosphorus, iron, magnesium, zinc and copper.

CONTAINS a moderate amount of dietary fiber.

Wine-Soaked Cornmeal Cake with Balsamic Berries

The best sweet cornmeal cakes are usually Italian, but the addition of white wine is a French touch. This makes a great dessert when fresh berries are in season — in my opinion as delicious as shortcake and more nutritious, containing a wide range of nutrients and a very high amount of dietary fiber, almost half of which comes from the whole grains.

Makes 8 servings

TIP

If you have leftover cake, use it to make trifle.

Nutrients per serving

Calories	342
Protein	5.1 g
Carbohydrates	47.7 g
Fat (Total)	15.4 g
Saturated Fat	7.9 g
Monounsaturated Fat	4.7 g
Polyunsaturated Fat	1.6 g
Dietary Fiber	7.4 g
Sodium	328 mg
Cholesterol	77 mg

EXCELLENT SOURCE OF manganese.

GOOD SOURCE OF vitamin E (alpha-tocopherol), magnesium and selenium.

SOURCE OF vitamins A and C, thiamine, riboflavin, niacin, folate, pantothenic acid, calcium, phosphorus, iron, zinc and copper.

CONTAINS a very high amount of dietary fiber.

- **Preheat oven to 350°F (180°C)**
- **8-inch (2 L) square cake pan, lined with parchment**

1 cup	stone-ground yellow cornmeal	250 mL
½ cup	whole barley flour	125 mL
¼ cup	ground almonds	50 mL
2 tsp	baking powder	10 mL
½ tsp	salt	2 mL
½ cup	cold butter, cut into 1-inch (2.5 cm) cubes	125 mL
¾ cup	packed Demerara or other raw cane sugar	175 mL
2	eggs	2
2 tsp	finely grated lemon zest	10 mL
¾ cup	dry white wine	175 mL
¼ cup	water	50 mL

FRUIT TOPPING

4 cups	fresh raspberries	1 L
1 tbsp	balsamic vinegar	15 mL
	Granulated sugar	
	Whipped cream, optional	

1. In a food processor, combine cornmeal, barley flour, almonds, baking powder and salt. Pulse until cornmeal is quite fine. Add butter and sugar and pulse until mixture is crumbly. Add eggs, lemon zest, wine and water and pulse until blended. Pour into prepared pan, smoothing top. Bake in preheated oven until center springs back when lightly pressed, about 50 minutes. Let cool completely in pan on rack.

2. *Fruit Topping:* In a bowl, combine raspberries, balsamic vinegar and sugar to taste. Cut cake into serving size pieces and top with berry mixture, and a dollop of whipped cream, if using.

Variations

Substitute an equal quantity of sliced hulled strawberries for the raspberries, or use blueberries and substitute freshly squeezed lemon juice for the balsamic vinegar.

Diabetes Food Values

The diabetes food values for all the recipes were prepared by Info Access (1988) Inc.

Info Access is a Canadian firm of registered dietitians and computer experts specializing in computer-assisted nutrient analysis, assessing more than 4,000 recipes annually for a broad range of international clients. The Nutritional Accounting System component of the CBORD Menu Management System is used, as well as the Canadian Nutrient File, augmented as necessary with data from other reliable sources.

Info Access has also been involved with the assignment of food choice values in Canada, acting as the consulting firm assigning values for the Canadian Diabetes Association. The U.S. determinations were based on Exchange List Guidelines for Recipe/Food Label Calculations, Page 174, Diabetes Medical Nutrition Therapy, The American Dietetic Association/American Diabetes Association, 1997.

While the U.S. and Canadian diabetes assignment methodologies are similar, there are some variations in the approaches taken and the base values used that account for the observed differences. In the U.S. System, dietary fiber is generally not deducted from total carbohydrate (except for high fiber cereals); thus carbohydrate choices may be higher with the U.S. assignments. Vegetables (up to 5 g carbohydrate) are considered "free" in Canada, whereas vegetable assignments are made in the U.S. In the U.S., the Starch Exchange assumes 1 g fat per choice; in Canada the same assignment assumes no fat. Consequently fat assignments may be higher in Canada. In the U.S., half meat and fat exchanges are not allowed; in Canada, half values may be assigned for these choices. Thus, there may be some rounding changes introduced.

Recipes	Page No.	Canadian Diabetes Association Values	American Diabetes Association Values
Amaranth (½ cup)	14	½ Carbohydrate	1 Starch
Buckwheat Groats (½ cup)	17	1½ Carbohydrates	1½ Starch
Long-Grain Brown Rice (½ cup)	27	1½ Carbohydrates	1½ Starch
Millet Seeds (½ cup)	22	1 Carbohydrate	1½ Starch
Quinoa (½ cup)	25	1 Carbohydrate	1 Starch
Rolled Oats (½ cup)	23	½ Carbohydrate	½ Starch
Rye Berries (½ cup)	30	1 Carbohydrate	1½ Starch
Sorghum (½ cup)	31	2 Carbohydrates	2 Starch
Stone Ground Yellow Cornmeal (½ cup)	19	1 Carbohydrate	1 Starch
Wheat Berries (½ cup)	33	1½ Carbohydrates	1½ Starch
Whole (Hulled) Barley (½ cup)	15	1 Carbohydrate	1 Starch
Wild Rice (½ cup)	35	1 Carbohydrate	1 Starch

Note: Based on instructions for cooking grains provided in *The Complete Whole Grains Cookbook,* pages 14 through 37.

Recipes	Page No.	Canadian Diabetes Association Values	American Diabetes Association Values
Almond-Flavored Millet with Cherries (1/6 of recipe)	59	2½ Carbohydrates, ½ Fat	2 Starch, 1 Fruit
Amaranth Banana Walnut Bread (1/16 of recipe)	44	1½ Carbohydrates, 1 Fat	1 Starch, ½ Other, 1 Fat
Amaretto-Spiked Quinoa Pudding with Cherries (1/8 of recipe)	257	3½ Carbohydrates, 1 Fat	1 Starch, 1 Fruit, 1½ Other, 1 Low-Fat Meat, 1 Fat
Arroz con Pollo (1/6 of recipe)	110	1½ Carbohydrates, 4 Meat, 1 Fat	1½ Starch, 2 Vegetables, 4 Medium-Fat Meat
Asian-Spiced Beef with Soba Noodles (1/6 of recipe)	175	2½ Carbohydrates, 3 Meat, 1 Fat	3 Starch, 1 Vegetable, 4 Low-Fat Meat
Asian-Style Beef and Wheat Berry Salad with Arugula (1/4 of recipe)	86	1 Carbohydrate, 2 Meat, 2 Fat	1½ Starch, 1 Vegetable, 2 Medium-Fat Meat, 1 Fat
Asian-Style Quinoa Salad with Chili-Orange Dressing (1/6 of recipe)	94	1½ Carbohydrates, ½ Fat	1½ Starch, 1 Vegetable
Baked Beans 'n' Barley (1/8 of recipe)	187	3 Carbohydrates, ½ Meat	2 Starch, 1 Vegetable, 1½ Other
Baked Rice with Rosemary-Roasted Tomatoes (1/6 of recipe)	236	2½ Carbohydrates, 2 Fat	3 Starch, 1 Vegetable, 1½ Fat
Barley Jambalaya (1/6 of recipe)	124	1½ Carbohydrates, 3 Meat	2 Starch, 1 Vegetable, 3 Low-Fat Meat
Barley Pudding with Cherries and Almonds (1/8 of recipe)	256	2 Carbohydrates, 1½ Fat	1½ Starch, 1 Other, 1½ Fat
Barley Salad with Confetti of Carrot and Dill (1/10 of recipe)	96	1 Carbohydrate, 1½ Fat	1 Starch, 1 Vegetable, 1½ Fat
Barley-Stuffed Peppers with Crispy Bread Crumbs (1/6 of recipe)	160	1 Carbohydrate, 2 Meat, 1 Fat	1½ Starch, 2 Vegetables, 2 Medium-Fat Meat, 1 Fat
Basic Grits (1/6 of recipe)	242	1 Carbohydrate	1½ Starch
Basic Polenta (1/6 of recipe)	242	1 Carbohydrate	1 Starch
Beef Biriyani (1/10 of recipe)	180	2 Carbohydrates, 2½ Meat	2 Starch, 1 Vegetable, 3 Low-Fat Meat
Beef Stew with Rye Berries, Sauerkraut and Dill (1/8 of serving)	174	1 Carbohydrate, 3 Meat	1 Starch, 2 Vegetables, 3 Low-Fat Meat
Best Ever Buckwheat Burgers with Bulgur in Tomato-Mushroom Gravy (1/4 of recipe)	222	2½ Carbohydrates, ½ Meat, 2½ Fat	3 Starch, 1 Vegetable, 2½ Fat
Black Sticky Rice Pudding (1/6 of recipe)	258	2½ Carbohydrates, 3 Fat	1 Starch, 1½ Other, 3 Fat
Black Sticky Rice Salad (1/8 of recipe)	93	1 Carbohydrate, 1 Fat	1 Starch, ½ Fat

Recipes	Page No.	Canadian Diabetes Association Values	American Diabetes Association Values
Blueberry and Wild Rice Pudding ($\frac{1}{8}$ of recipe)	262	2 Carbohydrates, $\frac{1}{2}$ Fat	1 Starch, 1 Other, 1 Low-Fat Meat
Blueberry Lemon Muffins ($\frac{1}{12}$ of recipe)	48	2 Carbohydrates, 1 Fat	$1\frac{1}{2}$ Starch, 1 Other, 1 Fat
Blueberry Wild Rice Pancakes ($\frac{1}{4}$ of recipe)	43	3 Carbohydrates, $\frac{1}{2}$ Fat	$2\frac{1}{2}$ Starch, 1 Other
Breakfast Rice ($\frac{1}{6}$ of recipe)	54	3 Carbohydrates	$\frac{1}{2}$ Starch, 1 Fruit
Brown Bread Ice Cream ($\frac{1}{8}$ of recipe)	261	2 Carbohydrates, $3\frac{1}{2}$ Fat	1 Starch, 1 Other, $3\frac{1}{2}$ Fat
Brown Rice Risotto ($\frac{1}{6}$ of recipe)	229	$1\frac{1}{2}$ Carbohydrates, $\frac{1}{2}$ Fat	$1\frac{1}{2}$ Starch, $\frac{1}{2}$ Fat
Buckwheat Pilaf with Paprika-Seasoned Chicken ($\frac{1}{4}$ of recipe)	141	2 Carbohydrates, 3 Meat	2 Starch, 1 Vegetable, 3 Low-Fat Meat
Buckwheat-Stuffed Onions ($\frac{1}{4}$ of recipe)	224	4 Carbohydrates, $1\frac{1}{2}$ Fat	4 Starch, 2 Vegetables, 1 Fat
Bulgur Pilaf ($\frac{1}{6}$ of recipe)	244	1 Carbohydrate, $\frac{1}{2}$ Fat	1 Starch, $\frac{1}{2}$ Fat
Buttermilk Buckwheat Pancakes ($\frac{1}{14}$ of recipe)	42	1 Carbohydrate, $\frac{1}{2}$ Fat	1 Starch
Chapati ($\frac{1}{8}$ of recipe)	51	1 Carbohydrate, 1 Fat	1 Starch, 1 Fat
Cheesy Jalapeño Cornbread ($\frac{1}{8}$ of recipe)	41	$1\frac{1}{2}$ Carbohydrates, $\frac{1}{2}$ Meat, 2 Fat	$1\frac{1}{2}$ Starch, 1 Medium-Fat Meat, 1 Fat
Chewy Oatmeal Coconut Cookies with Cranberries and Pecans ($\frac{1}{48}$ of recipe)	252	1 Carbohydrate, 1 Fat	1 Other, 1 Fat
Chicken and Barley Bake ($\frac{1}{6}$ of recipe)	118	$1\frac{1}{2}$ Carbohydrates, $3\frac{1}{2}$ Meat	$1\frac{1}{2}$ Starch, 2 Vegetables, 3 Medium-Fat Meat
Chicken and Wheat Berry Salad with Avocado ($\frac{1}{6}$ of recipe)	87	1 Carbohydrate, 2 Meat, 3 Fat	1 Starch, 1 Vegetable, 2 Medium-Fat Meat, 2 Fat
Chicken Chili Pie with Millet Crust ($\frac{1}{6}$ of recipe)	128	2 Carbohydrates, 3 Meat	2 Starch, 1 Vegetable, 3 Low-Fat Meat, $\frac{1}{2}$ Fat
Chicken Paprikash with Wheat Berry Gravy ($\frac{1}{8}$ of recipe)	133	1 Carbohydrate, $3\frac{1}{2}$ Meat	$1\frac{1}{2}$ Starch, 2 Vegetables, 3 Low-Fat Meat
Chicken with Bulgur and Walnuts ($\frac{1}{4}$ of recipe)	135	$1\frac{1}{2}$ Carbohydrates, 3 Meat, 1 Fat	2 Starch, 1 Vegetable, 3 Low-Fat Meat, 1 Fat
Chile Spiked Quinoa Pudding with Corn ($\frac{1}{6}$ of recipe)	221	$1\frac{1}{2}$ Carbohydrates, $\frac{1}{2}$ Meat, 1 Fat	2 Starch, 1 Vegetable, 1 Fat
Chili Con Wheat Berries ($\frac{1}{8}$ of recipe)	161	$1\frac{1}{2}$ Carbohydrates, 2 Meat	$1\frac{1}{2}$ Starch, 2 Vegetables, 2 Low-Fat Meat

Recipes	Page No.	Canadian Diabetes Association Values	American Diabetes Association Values
Chili Rice (1/6 of recipe)	234	2 Carbohydrates, 1/2 Fat	2 Starch, 1 Vegetable, 1/2 Fat
Chinese-Style Chicken Fried Rice (1/4 of recipe)	117	2 Carbohydrates, 2 Meat, 1 Fat	2 1/2 Starch, 1 Vegetable, 2 Medium-Fat Meat
Chinese-Style Pork Fried Rice (1/6 of recipe)	190	1 Carbohydrate, 3 Meat	1 Starch, 1 Vegetable, 3 Medium-Fat Meat
Citrus Lamb with Spinach and Couscous (1/6 of recipe)	201	1 1/2 Carbohydrates, 3 Meat, 1 Fat	2 Starch, 1 Vegetable, 3 Low-Fat Meat, 1/2 Fat
Coconut Chicken With Quinoa (1/4 of recipe)	116	1 1/2 Carbohydrates, 4 Meat, 1 Fat	1 1/2 Starch, 2 Vegetables, 4 Low-Fat Meat, 2 Fat
Coconut Pecan Blondies (1/16 of recipe)	265	1 1/2 Carbohydrates, 2 1/2 Fat	1/2 Starch, 1 Other, 2 1/2 Fat
Coconut-Spiked Pork with Quinoa and Peanuts (1/6 of recipe)	196	1 1/2 Carbohydrates, 2 Meat, 1 Fat	1 1/2 Starch, 2 Vegetables, 2 Medium-Fat Meat
Cold Soba Noodles (1/6 of recipe)	92	2 Carbohydrates, 2 Fat	2 Starch, 1 1/2 Fat
Congee with Chinese Greens and Barbecued Pork (1/6 of recipe)	83	1 Carbohydrate, 1 Meat	1 1/2 Starch, 1 Low-Fat Meat
Cranberry Pecan Couscous Salad (1/8 of recipe)	101	1 1/2 Carbohydrates, 2 1/2 Fat	2 Starch, 2 Fat
Cranberry Quinoa Porridge (1/6 of recipe)	57	1 1/2 Carbohydrates, 1/2 Fat	1 Starch, 1 Fruit
Cranberry-Orange Pecan Muffins (1/12 of recipe)	46	2 Carbohydrates, 2 1/2 Fat	1 Starch, 1 Other, 2 Fat
Creamy Cabbage Borscht with Bulgur and Dill (1/6 of recipe)	70	1 Carbohydrate, 2 Meat, 1 Fat	1 Starch, 2 Vegetables, 1 Medium-Fat Meat, 2 Fat
Creole Chicken with Red Rice (1/6 of recipe)	122	2 Carbohydrates, 3 1/2 Meat, 1 Fat	2 Starch, 2 Vegetables, 3 Medium-Fat Meat
Cuban-Style Hash with Fried Plantains (1/6 of recipe)	170	3 1/2 Carbohydrates, 1 1/2 Meat, 1 Fat	1 Starch, 2 1/2 Fruit, 2 Vegetables, 1 Medium-Fat Meat, 1 1/2 Fat
Currant-Studded Couscous (1/6 of recipe)	237	2 Carbohydrates, 1 Fat	2 Starch, 1/2 Fat
Curried Sweet Potato and Millet Soup (1/6 of recipe)	76	2 1/2 Carbohydrates, 1/2 Fat	2 Starch, 1 Vegetable, 1 Other, 1/2 Fat
Deep-Dish Apple Pie with Streusel Topping (1/8 of recipe)	260	4 Carbohydrates, 4 1/2 Fat	1 1/2 Starch, 1 Fruit, 2 Other, 4 Fat
Everyday Tuna and Warm Red Rice Salad (1/4 of recipe)	104	1 1/2 Carbohydrates, 1 Meat, 2 Fat	2 Starch, 1 Low-Fat Meat, 2 Fat
Fennel-Scented Tomato and Wild Rice Soup (1/8 of recipe)	71	1 Carbohydrate, 1/2 Fat	1 Starch, 2 Vegetables, 1/2 Fat

Recipes	Page No.	Canadian Diabetes Association Values	American Diabetes Association Values
Fragrant Beef and Barley Soup with Chinese Mushrooms ($\frac{1}{6}$ of recipe)	72	1 Carbohydrate, $1\frac{1}{2}$ Meat	1 Starch, 2 Vegetables, 1 Medium-Fat Meat
Fragrant Coconut Rice ($\frac{1}{4}$ of recipe)	235	2 Carbohydrates, 4 Fat	$2\frac{1}{2}$ Starch, $3\frac{1}{2}$ Fat
Fragrant Lamb Curry with Barley ($\frac{1}{6}$ of recipe)	188	$1\frac{1}{2}$ Carbohydrates, 2 Meat	$1\frac{1}{2}$ Starch, 1 Vegetable, 3 Low-Fat Meat
French-Style Red Rice with Chicken ($\frac{1}{6}$ of recipe)	121	$2\frac{1}{2}$ Carbohydrates, $3\frac{1}{2}$ Meat	3 Starch, 2 Vegetables, 3 Low-Fat Meat, 0.5 Fat
Gingery Chicken and Wild Rice Soup ($\frac{1}{6}$ of recipe)	68	$1\frac{1}{2}$ Carbohydrates, $2\frac{1}{2}$ Meat	$1\frac{1}{2}$ Starch, 1 Vegetable, 2 Low-Fat Meat
Gingery Shortbread ($\frac{1}{24}$ of recipe)	255	1 Carbohydrate, $1\frac{1}{2}$ Fat	1 Starch, $1\frac{1}{2}$ Fat
Gluten-Free Pizza Crust ($\frac{1}{6}$ of recipe)	248	2 Carbohydrates, $\frac{1}{2}$ Fat	2 Starch
Home-Style Skillet Rice with Tomato Crust ($\frac{1}{6}$ of recipe)	198	2 Carbohydrates, 1 Meat, 2 Fat	2 Starch, 2 Vegetables, 2.5 Fat
Hot Millet Amaranth Cereal ($\frac{1}{6}$ of recipe)	52	1 Carbohydrate $\frac{1}{2}$ Fat	$1\frac{1}{2}$ Starch
Indian-Spiced Chicken with Barley ($\frac{1}{6}$ of recipe)	134	2 Carbohydrates, $2\frac{1}{2}$ Meat	$2\frac{1}{2}$ Starch, 3 Low-Fat Meat
Indonesian-Style Shrimp Fried Rice ($\frac{1}{4}$ of recipe)	148	$2\frac{1}{2}$ Carbohydrates, $3\frac{1}{2}$ Meat, 1 Fat	$2\frac{1}{2}$ Starch, 3 Medium-Fat Meat
Irish Oatmeal ($\frac{1}{6}$ of recipe)	55	$\frac{1}{2}$ Carbohydrates	$\frac{1}{2}$ Starch
Italian-Style Chicken and Rice ($\frac{1}{6}$ of recipe)	112	2 Carbohydrates, $3\frac{1}{2}$ Meat, 1 Fat	$2\frac{1}{2}$ Starch, 2 Vegetables, 3 Medium-Fat Meat, 1 Fat
Italian-Style Chicken in White Wine with Olives and Polenta ($\frac{1}{8}$ of recipe)	130	1 Carbohydrate, $3\frac{1}{2}$ Meat	1 Starch, 1 Vegetable, 4 Low-Fat Meat, 1 Fat
Italian-Style Green Rice ($\frac{1}{6}$ of recipe)	230	$1\frac{1}{2}$ Carbohydrates, $1\frac{1}{2}$ Fat	$1\frac{1}{2}$ Starch, 1 Vegetable, 1 Fat
Kasha and Beet Salad with Celery and Feta ($\frac{1}{8}$ of recipe)	90	1 Carbohydrate, $1\frac{1}{2}$ Fat	1 Starch, 1 Vegetable, $1\frac{1}{2}$ Fat
Khitchuri with Tomatoes and Green Peppers ($\frac{1}{6}$ of recipe)	215	$2\frac{1}{2}$ Carbohydrates, $\frac{1}{2}$ Meat 1 Fat	3 Starch, 2 Vegetables, $\frac{1}{2}$ Fat
Korean-Style Rice Bowl ($\frac{1}{4}$ of recipe)	210	$2\frac{1}{2}$ Carbohydrates, $2\frac{1}{2}$ Fat	$2\frac{1}{2}$ Starch, 2 Vegetables, 2 Fat
Lemon Lovers' Tabbouleh ($\frac{1}{10}$ of recipe)	100	1 Carbohydrate, $1\frac{1}{2}$ Fat	1 Starch, 1 Vegetable, $1\frac{1}{2}$ Fat
Lemon Poppy Seed Blueberry Scones ($\frac{1}{18}$ of recipe)	50	1 Carbohydrate, 1 Fat	1 Starch, 1 Fat

Recipes	Page No.	Canadian Diabetes Association Values	American Diabetes Association Values
Luscious Avgolemono Soup with Wheat Berries ($\frac{1}{6}$ of recipe)	67	1 Carbohydrate, 1 Meat, $\frac{1}{2}$ Fat	1$\frac{1}{2}$ Starch, 1 Vegetable, 1 Fat
Meatballs with Couscous in Spinach Sauce ($\frac{1}{8}$ of recipe)	172	1$\frac{1}{2}$ Carbohydrates, 2 Meat, 2 Fat	2 Starch, 2 Medium-Fat Meat, 2 Fat
Mexican-Style Millet and Shrimp ($\frac{1}{6}$ of recipe)	155	1$\frac{1}{2}$ Carbohydrates, 2 Meat, 1 Fat	2 Starch, 1 Vegetable, 2 Medium-Fat Meat
Mexican-Style Seafood Stew with Hominy ($\frac{1}{6}$ of recipe)	154	$\frac{1}{2}$ Carbohydrates, 3 Meat	$\frac{1}{2}$ Starch, 2 Vegetables, 3 Low-Fat Meat
Middle Eastern Bulgur Pudding with Almonds and Dates ($\frac{1}{8}$ of recipe)	263	3 Carbohydrates, 1$\frac{1}{2}$ Fat	1 Starch, 1 Fruit, 1 Other, 1$\frac{1}{2}$ Fat
Millet Salad with Lemony Chickpeas and Tomatoes ($\frac{1}{10}$ of recipe)	102	1$\frac{1}{2}$ Carbohydrates, 2 Fat	1$\frac{1}{2}$ Starch, 1 Vegetable, 1$\frac{1}{2}$ Fat
Millet-Crusted Tamale Pie ($\frac{1}{6}$ of recipe)	191	2$\frac{1}{2}$ Carbohydrates, 2 Meat, 2 Fat	3 Starch, 2 Medium-Fat Meat, 1 Fat
Minestrone Genovese ($\frac{1}{6}$ of recipe)	81	2 Carbohydrates, 1$\frac{1}{2}$ Fat	2$\frac{1}{2}$ Starch, 1 Vegetable, 1 Fat
Miso-Spiked Vegetable Soup with Barley ($\frac{1}{6}$ of recipe)	80	1$\frac{1}{2}$ Carbohydrates, 1 Fat	1$\frac{1}{2}$ Starch, 2 Vegetables, $\frac{1}{2}$ Fat
Moroccan Chicken with Couscous and Cinnamon-Spiked Prunes ($\frac{1}{6}$ of recipe)	126	2$\frac{1}{2}$ Carbohydrates, 3$\frac{1}{2}$ Meat	2 Starch, 1 Fruit, 1 Vegetable, 3 Low-Fat Meat, $\frac{1}{2}$ Fat
Moroccan-Style Chicken Stew with Chickpeas and Rice ($\frac{1}{4}$ of recipe)	140	2 Carbohydrates, 3 Meat	2 Starch, 2 Vegetables, 3 Low-Fat Meat
Moroccan-Style Couscous Stuffing ($\frac{1}{8}$ of recipe)	240	2 Carbohydrates, 1 Fat	1 Starch, 1 Fruit, 1 Fat
Multigrain Cereal with Fruit ($\frac{1}{8}$ of recipe)	56	2 Carbohydrates	$\frac{1}{2}$ Starch, 1 Fruit
Mushroom and Barley Ragoût ($\frac{1}{8}$ of recipe)	218	2 Carbohydrates, $\frac{1}{2}$ Meat, $\frac{1}{2}$ Fat	2$\frac{1}{2}$ Starch, 2 Vegetables
Mushroom Varnishkes ($\frac{1}{6}$ of recipe)	220	2 Carbohydrates, 2 Fat	2 Starch, 1 Vegetable, 1$\frac{1}{2}$ Fat
Mushroom, Sausage and Wild Rice Stir-Fry ($\frac{1}{6}$ of recipe)	199	1 Carbohydrate, 1 Meat, 2 Fat	1$\frac{1}{2}$ Starch, 1 Vegetable, 1 Medium-Fat Meat, 1.5 Fat
Mushroom-Scented Quinoa Congee With Zucchini ($\frac{1}{6}$ of recipe)	66	1 Carbohydrate, $\frac{1}{2}$ Fat	1 Starch, 2 Vegetables, $\frac{1}{2}$ Fat
Mussels in Spicy Lemongrass Broth with Chinese Black Rice ($\frac{1}{4}$ of recipe)	153	2 Carbohydrates, 1 Meat	2 Starch, 1 Vegetable, 1 Low-Fat Meat
Oatmeal Shortbread Squares ($\frac{1}{25}$ of recipe)	254	1 Carbohydrate, 1$\frac{1}{2}$ Fat	1 Starch, 1$\frac{1}{2}$ Fat
Old English Celery and Barley Bake ($\frac{1}{6}$ of recipe)	238	1 Carbohydrate	1$\frac{1}{2}$ Starch

Recipes	Page No.	Canadian Diabetes Association Values	American Diabetes Association Values
Old-Fashioned Cornbread (1/8 of recipe)	40	2 Carbohydrates, 1 Fat	2 Starch, 1 Fat
Old-Fashioned Scotch Broth (1/8 of recipe)	65	1 1/2 Carbohydrates, 2 Meat	2 Starch, 1 Vegetable, 2 Low-Fat Meat
Orange-Flavored Breakfast Barley with Cranberries and Pecans (1/4 of recipe)	58	1 1/2 Carbohydrates, 1 Fat	1 Starch, 1 Fruit, 1 Fat
Peppery Chicken Quinoa (1/4 of recipe)	114	2 Carbohydrates, 3 Meat, 1 Fat	2 Starch, 1 Vegetable, 4 Low-Fat Meat
Peppery Coconut Chicken with Wheat Berries (1/6 of recipe)	120	1 1/2 Carbohydrates, 3 Meat, 3 Fat	1 1/2 Starch, 2 Vegetables, 2 Medium-Fat Meat, 3 Fat
Peppery Meat Loaf with Couscous (1/8 of recipe)	176	1 Carbohydrate, 2 1/2 Meat	1 Starch, 2 Vegetables, 2 Medium-Fat Meat
Peppery Polenta Bake with Mushrooms and Sausages (1/8 of recipe)	200	1 Carbohydrate, 2 Meat, 1 Fat	1 Starch, 1 Vegetable, 1 Medium-Fat Meat, 2 Fat
Peppery Quinoa Stew with Corn and Crispy Snapper (1/6 of recipe)	152	2 Carbohydrates, 3 Meat	2 Starch, 2 Vegetables, 3 Low-Fat Meat
Peppery Shrimp with Couscous (1/4 of recipe)	150	2 Carbohydrates, 3 Meat	2 Starch, 3 Vegetables, 2 Medium-Fat Meat
Pork Posole (1/8 of recipe)	184	1/2 Carbohydrate, 3 Meat	1/2 Starch, 2 Vegetables, 3 Low-Fat Meat
Pot Roast with Wheat Berries and Cumin-Spiked Gravy (1/10 of recipe)	168	1 Carbohydrate, 3 Meat	1 1/2 Starch, 1 Vegetable, 3 Low-Fat Meat, 1 Fat
Pretty Traditional Rice Pudding (1/6 of recipe)	253	3 Carbohydrates, 1/2 Fat	2 1/2 Starch, 1 Other, 1/2 Fat
Quinoa and Radish Salad with Avocado Dressing (1/6 of recipe)	95	1 Carbohydrate, 2 1/2 Fat	1 1/2 Starch, 1 Vegetable, 2 1/2 Fat
Quinoa Chili (1/6 of recipe)	213	2 1/2 Carbohydrates, 1 Fat	3 Starch, 2 Vegetables, 1/2 Fat
Quinoa-Stuffed Tomatoes (1/6 of serving)	205	1 Carbohydrate, 1 Meat 2 Fat	1 Starch, 1 Vegetable, 1 Medium-Fat Meat, 2 Fat
Red Beans and Red Rice (1/8 of recipe)	228	2 Carbohydrates, 1/2 Fat	2 Starch, 2 Vegetables
Rhubarb Orange Muffins (1/12 of recipe)	49	1 1/2 Carbohydrates, 1 1/2 Fat	1 1/2 Starch, 1 Fat
Rice Salad Niçoise (1/4 of recipe)	89	1 Carbohydrate, 1 Meat, 3 1/2 Fat	1 1/2 Starch, 1 Vegetable, 1 Medium-Fat Meat, 3 Fat
Rice-Stuffed Eggplant (1/6 of recipe)	214	2 Carbohydrates, 1/2 Meat, 1 1/2 Fat	2 Starch, 2 Vegetables, 1 1/2 Fat
Roast Chicken with Fruit-Studded Wheat Berries (1/4 of service)	108	3 1/2 Carbohydrates, 3 Meat, 1 Fat	1 Starch, 2 Vegetables, 2 1/2 Other, 3 Low-Fat Meat, 2 Fat

Recipes	Page No.	Canadian Diabetes Association Values	American Diabetes Association Values
Roast Pork With Red Rice and Beans (1/10 of recipe)	192	2 1/2 Carbohydrates, 4 Meat	3 Starch, 1 Vegetable, 4 Very Low-Fat Meat, 1/2 Fat
Roasted Mushrooms with Millet and Goat Cheese (1/4 of recipe)	209	1 Carbohydrate, 1 Meat, 3 Fat	1 Starch, 2 Vegetables, 1 Medium-Fat Meat, 2 Fat
Roasted Red Pepper Risotto (1/6 of recipe)	232	1 1/2 Carbohydrates, 1 Fat	1 1/2 Starch, 1 Vegetable, 1/2 Fat
Ropa Vieja With Wheat Berries (1/6 of recipe)	164	1 1/2 Carbohydrates, 3 Meat	1 1/2 Starch, 2 Vegetables, 3 Medium-Fat Meat
Saffron-Scented Chicken and Barley Stew with Easy Rouille (1/8 of recipe)	136	1 Carbohydrate, 3 1/2 Meat, 1 Fat	1 1/2 Starch, 1 Vegetable, 4 Medium-Fat Meat
Saffron-Scented Millet Pilaf with Toasted Almonds (1/6 of recipe)	231	1 1/2 Carbohydrates, 1 Fat	2 Starch, 1/2 Fat
Saffron-Scented Shrimp With Chile Rice (1/6 of recipe)	149	2 Carbohydrates, 2 Meat, 2 Fat	2 Starch, 2 Vegetables, 2 Low-Fat Meat, 1 1/2 Fat
Salmon and Wild Rice Cakes with Avocado Chili Topping (1/4 of recipe)	147	1 Carbohydrate, 2 Meat, 2 Fat	1 1/2 Starch, 2 Medium-Fat Meat, 1 Fat
Salmon Stew with Corn and Quinoa (1/8 of recipe)	146)	1 1/2 Carbohydrates, 2 1/2 Meat, 2 Fat	1 1/2 Starch, 1 Vegetable, 2 Medium-Fat Meat, 1 1/2 Fat
Sausage and Wheat Berry Salad with Shredded Hearts of Romaine (1/8 of recipe)	97	1 Carbohydrate, 1 1/2 Meat, 1 1/2 Fat	1 Starch, 1 Vegetable, 1 Low-Fat Meat, 2 Fat
Sausage-Spiked Peas 'n' Rice (1/6 of recipe)	186	2 Carbohydrates, 2 Meat, 2 Fat	2 1/2 Starch, 1 Vegetable, 1 Medium-Fat Meat
Savory Lamb Shanks with Eggplant and Barley (1/8 of recipe)	194	1 Carbohydrate, 4 Meat	1 Starch, 3 Vegetables, 4 Medium-Fat Meat
Sloppy Joes Zucchini (1/6 of recipe)	166	1 1/2 Carbohydrates, 2 Meat, 1 Fat	1 1/2 Starch, 3 Vegetables, 1 Medium-Fat Meat, 1 Fat
Soba Noodles with Broccoli Sauce (1/4 of serving)	204	4 1/2 Carbohydrates, 1 Fat	3 Starch, 1 Vegetable, 1 1/2 Other, 1/2 Fat
Southwestern Bean and Barley Salad with Roasted Peppers (1/8 of recipe)	98	1 1/2 Carbohydrates, 3 Fat	2 Starch, 1 Vegetable, 2 1/2 Fat
Southwestern Turkey Chowder (1/8 of recipe)	78	2 Carbohydrates, 2 Meat	2 1/2 Starch, 2 Vegetables, 1 Low-Fat Meat
Southwestern Turkey Stew with Cornmeal Dumplings (1/6 of recipe)	138	1 1/2 Carbohydrates, 2 Meat 1/2 Fat	2 Starch, 2 Vegetables, 2 Low-Fat Meat
Southwestern-Style Chile Chicken with Wehani Rice (1/8 of recipe)	132	1 1/2 Carbohydrates, 3 1/2 Meat	1 1/2 Starch, 1 Vegetable, 4 Low-Fat Meat, 1 Fat
Southwestern-Style Rice-Stuffed Peppers (1/4 of recipe)	167	3 1/2 Carbohydrates, 1 Meat, 2 Fat	4 Starch, 2 Vegetables, 1 Medium-Fat Meat, 1 Fat
Steak and Mushroom Pie with Barley and Whole Wheat Crust (1/8 of recipe)	178	1/2 Carbohydrates, 3 Meat	1/2 Starch, 1 Vegetable, 3 Low-Fat Meat

Recipes	Page No.	Canadian Diabetes Association Values	American Diabetes Association Values
Tailgaters' Favorite Stew (1/8 of recipe)	162	1½ Carbohydrates, 3½ Meat, 1 Fat	2 Starch, 2 Vegetables, 3 Low-Fat Meat, ½ Fat
Thai-Inspired Peanut and Wild Rice Soup (1/6 of recipe)	82	1½ Carbohydrates, 1½ Meat, 3 Fat	1½ Starch, 1 Vegetable, 1 Medium-Fat Meat, 3 Fat
Traditional Cockaleekie Soup (1/8 of recipe)	64	1½ Carbohydrates, 3 Meat	1½ Starch, 2 Vegetables, 3 Low-Fat Meat
Tunisian Couscous Cake (1/8 of recipe)	264	4 Carbohydrates, 1½ Fat	2 Starch, 1½ Fruit, 1 Other, 1½ Fat
Turkey Cutlets in Gingery Lemon Gravy with Cranberry Rice (1/4 of recipe)	142	2½ Carbohydrates, 2½ Meat, 1 Fat	2 Starch, 1 Fruit, 3 Low-Fat Meat
Turkish-Style Wheat Berry Soup (1/6 of recipe)	74	1 Carbohydrate, 1 Fat	1½ Starch, 1 Vegetable, 1 Fat
Wheat Berries with Cauliflower and Crispy Bread Crumbs (1/6 of serving)	208	1½ Carbohydrates, ½ Meat, 2 Fat	2 Starch, 1 Vegetable, 2 Fat
Wheat Berry Minestrone with Leafy Greens (1/6 of recipe)	62	2½ Carbohydrates, 1 Meat	3 Starch, 1 Vegetable
Whole Wheat Mac and Cheese (1/8 of serving)	206	2 Carbohydrates, 2 Meat, 2 Fat	2 Starch, 2 Medium-Fat Meat, 1.5 Fat
Whole Wheat Pie Crust (1/8 of recipe)	245	1 Carbohydrate, 3 Fat	1 Starch, 3 Fat
Whole-Grain Olive Oil Crust (1/8 of recipe)	249	1½ Carbohydrates, 3 Fat	1½ Starch, 2½ Fat
Whole-Grain Pizza Dough (1/6 of recipe)	246	1½ Carbohydrates, ½ Fat	1½ Starch, ½ Fat
Whole-Grain Spaghetti with Bulgur-Laced Meatballs (1/8 of recipe)	158	4 Carbohydrates, 2 Meat, 1 Fat	3½ Starch, 3 Vegetables, 2 Low-Fat Meat, 1 Fat
Wild Rice and Smoked Turkey Salad with Dried Cherries (1/6 of recipe)	88	1½ Carbohydrates, ½ Meat, 2 Fat	1 Starch, 1 Fruit, 1 Medium-Fat Meat, 1 Fat
Wild Rice Cakes (1/4 of recipe)	212	2 Carbohydrates, 2 Meat, 1 Fat	2½ Starch, 1 Vegetable, 2 Low-Fat Meat, 1 Fat
Wild Rice Stuffing with Cranberries (1/12 of recipe)	239	1 Carbohydrate, 1 Fat	1 Starch, 1 Fat
Wine-Soaked Cornmeal Cake with Balsamic Berries (1/8 of recipe)	266	2½ Carbohydrates, 3 Fat	1½ Starch, 1½ Other, 3 Fat
Zucchini Lemon Loaf with Cranberries (1/18 of recipe)	45	1½ Carbohydrates, 1 Fat	1 Starch, ½ Other, 1 Fat
Zuni Stew (1/8 of recipe)	216	2½ Carbohydrates, 1 Meat, 1 Fat	3 Starch, 2 Vegetables, 1 Medium-Fat Meat

Library and Archives Canada Cataloguing in Publication

Finlayson, Judith
 The complete whole grains cookbook / Judith Finlayson.

Includes index.
ISBN 978-0-7788-0178-8

1. Cookery (Cereals) 2. Grain. I. Title.

TX808.F55 2008   641.6'31   C2007-905734-9

Index